The Place Where We Dwell:

Reading and Writing about New York City

Third Edition

Juanita But

Mark Noonan

Sean Scanlan

New York City College of Technology
City University of New York

Kendall Hunt
publishing company

Cover image from *José Parlá: Walls, Diaries, and Paintings* by José Parlá. Copyright 2011
José Parlá. All Rights Reserved. Member of ARSNY & DACS U.K.

Kendall Hunt
publishing company

www.kendallhunt.com
Send all inquiries to:
4050 Westmark Drive
Dubuque, IA 52004-1840

Copyright © 2005, 2007, 2012 by Juanita But, Mark Noonan and Sean Scanlan
Revised Printing: 2014.
ISBN 978-1-4652-2831-4

Printed in the United States of America
10 9 8 7 6 5 4 3

CONTENTS

SECTION II: Literary New York   **275**

Fiction

Poetry

ALTERNATE THEMATIC SEQUENCES

Class
DeWitt Clinton, Free Schools
Stephen Crane, A Dark-Brown Dog
Lewis Wickes Hine, Sweat Shop, New York City
Ha Jin, A Good Fall
Emma Lazarus, The New Colossus
Alfred Lubrano, Bricklayer's Boy
Margaret Morton, The Homeless
James Parrott, As Income Gap Widens, New York Grows Apart
Colin Powell, My American Journey
Brian Paul, Affordable Housing Policies May Spur Gentrification, Segregation

Community
Mark Berkey-Gerard, Youth Gangs
Edwidge Danticat, New York Was Our City on the Hill
Ian Frazier, Take the F
GangStarr, The Place Where We Dwell
O. Henry, The Making of a New Yorker
Nelson George, Fort Greene Dreams
Mark Naison, From Doo Wop to Hip Hop: The Bittersweet Odyssey of African Americans in the South Bronx
Jessica Guerra, The Williamsburg Renaissance

Cultural Identity
Frances Chung, Yo Vivo En El Barrio Chino
Junot Díaz, The Money
Monique Ferrell, Tu Sabes: A Story in Three Parts
Suki Kim, Facing Poverty with a Rich Girl's Habits
Claude McKay, The Tropics in New York
Mark Naison, From Doo Wop to Hip Hop: The Bittersweet Odyssey of African Americans in the South Bronx
Willie Perdomo, Where I'm From
Edwidge Danticat, New York Day Women

Ethics
Joseph Anastasio, My Life in Graffiti
Ralph Ellison, Prologue to "Invisible Man"
Langston Hughes, Good Morning
Ha Jin, A Good Fall
Emma Lazarus, The New Colossus
Lewis Wickes Hine, Sweat Shop, New York City
Courtney Gross, Despite Setbacks, Bloomberg Plan Has Made New York Greener
Margaret Morton, The Homeless
James Parrott, As Income Gap Widens, New York Grows Apart
Brian Paul, Affordable Housing Policies May Spur Gentrification, Segregation
Aarti Shahani, Legalization and De-legalization

Family
Stephen Crane, A Dark-Brown Dog
Edwidge Danticat, New York Was Our City on the Hill
Junot Díaz, The Money
Alfred Lubrano, Bricklayer's Boy
Taiyo Na, Lovely to Me (Immigrant Mother)
Dinanda H. Nooney, Home of Gerald Basquiat, Joe Roifer and Friend
Colin Powell, My American Journey
Edwidge Danticat, New York Day Women

Globalization
Kiran Desai, The Inheritance of Loss
Howard Gardner, Five Minds for the Future
Ha Jin, A Good Fall
Ben Shepard, Fighting Police Brutality in Global Brooklyn
Claudia Wallace and Sonja Steptoe, How to Bring Our Schools Into the 21st Century

History

Mark Berkey-Gerard, Youth Gangs
Dewitt Clinton, Free Schools
Gloria Deák, The People, Parks, and Ambience of Brooklyn
Jennifer Egan, Reading Lucy
Rem Koolhaas, Prediction
Phillip Lopate, The Brooklyn Bridge
Ernest Poole, The Harbor
Donald Reynolds, The Making of an Icon
Russell Shorto, Henry Hudson, The Pollinator
Walt Whitman, Mannahatta

Gender

Jennifer Egan, Reading Lucy
Lewis Wickes Hine, Sweat Shop, New York City
Suki Kim, Facing Poverty with a Rich Girl's Habits
Anna Quindlen, Pregnant in New York
Katie Roiphe, A Coney Island of the Mind
Edith Wharton, Mrs. Manstey's View
Anzia Yezierska, America and I

Language

Frances Chung, Riding the Subway Is an Adventure
Suki Kim, Facing Poverty with a Rich Girl's Habits
Willie Perdomo, Where I'm From
Esmeralda Santiago, When I Was Puerto Rican
Anzia Yezierska, America and I

Transportation

Frances Chung, Riding the Subway is an Adventure
Ralph Ellison, New York, 1936
Ian Frazier, Take the F
Langston Hughes, Subway Rush Hour
Amy Lowell, The Taxi
Hilda Morely, New York Subway
John Dos Passos, Ferryslip
Ezra Pound, In a Station of the Metro
Anna Quindlen, Pregnant in New York
Walt Whitman, Crossing Brooklyn Ferry

Work

Kiran Desai, The Inheritance of Loss
Jennifer Egan, Reading Lucy
Ha Jin, A Good Fall
Alfred Lubrano, Bricklayer's Boy
Herman Melville, Bartleby, the Scrivener
José Parlá, Research and Memory
Ernest Poole, The Harbor
Donald Reynolds, The Making of an Icon
Edwidge Danticat, New York Day Women

9/11

Meena Alexander, Central Park, Carousel
Edwidge Danticat, New York Was Our City on the Hill
George Guida, Life in the New World
Suki Kim, Facing Poverty with a Rich Girl's Habits
Toni Morrison, The Dead of 9/11
Colson Whitehead, The Colossus of New York

PREFACE

When the writer F. Scott Fitzgerald was getting ready to leave New York City in 1932, he had a moment of illumination, an epiphany, while at the top of the Empire State Building. From this perspective, Fitzgerald realized:

> that the city was not the endless succession of canyons that he had supposed but that it had limits—from the tallest structure he saw for the first time that it faded out into the country on all sides, into an expanse of green and blue that alone was limitless. And with the awful realization that New York was a city after all and not a universe, the whole shining edifice that he had reared in his imagination came crashing to the ground. ("My Lost City," *The Crack Up,* 1932)

Fast-forward eighty years. Many outsiders might still view the city as inscrutable, a place too vast and complex to understand—never mind to live in. But residents of New York know the city as a place that has both limits *and* great possibilities. This new edition allows students to explore their city in all of its complexity.

Students taking their first or second composition class might approach writing and critical thinking as overwhelming, much like New York City to the newcomer. The aim of the third edition of *The Place Where We Dwell* is to try to contextualize critical reading, writing, and thinking, while exploring this place we call home.

The intention of this third edition of *The Place Where We Dwell* is to inspire animated discussion and to sustain conversations through several defined themes. In Section One, the thematic organization of each chapter allows students to make connections among reading selections and examine specific topics such as city life, immigration, urban education, art and design, current issues, and the waterfront.

The first chapter, "New Yorkers and Their Neighborhoods," consists mainly of narrative and descriptive works. Aside from being rich and engaging reading, these essays exemplify the use of details and critical reflection that students could incorporate into their own writing. The elaborate sentences, careful language use, and richly developed paragraphs of writers such as Colson Whitehead, Katie Roiphe, and Ian Frazier make this chapter an ideal place to begin improving college reading and writing skills.

Chapter Two, "Immigrants and the American Dream," can be effectively used to work on the rhetorical strategy of comparison and contrast. For example, writers such as Edwidge Danticat and Anzia Yezierska critically reflect on the transformations that occur upon leaving their native land and adopting New York as their new home. The writing assignments at the end of the chapter allow students to compare and contrast two or more instances of immigrant crossings in connection to their own experiences.

Chapter Three, "Urban Education," allows students to work with arguments about school systems, methods of pedagogy, globalization, and technology in the classroom. Written from multiple perspectives, these essays serve as exemplary models of exposition, analysis, and argumentation and offer a broad context for student response.

Chapter Four, "Urban Art and Design," introduces urban aesthetics from both older and also very recent perspectives. Graffiti, photography, architecture and design, and music play a role not only in daily city life, but in the issues and arguments in the political and social realm. This chapter helps students read the city in written texts as well as in images, sounds, and designs.

Chapter Five, "Current Issues," allows students to develop their critical thinking and writing skills by engaging in recent debates on urban issues. The thought-provoking essays in this section are designed to serve as catalysts for further student research.

Chapter Six, "Exploring the Waterfront," focuses on the history and development of New York's waterfront. This chapter will help students realize the significance of the city's proximity to water—its port, rivers, and access to the Atlantic, which helped make New York a global metropolis and Brooklyn America's first suburb and industrial center. Besides the historical aims of this chapter, it also serves to help students launch their own research on waterfront issues.

Even as we insist that students be involved in understanding and critically inquiring into topics concerning their home city, we also recognize that they need to be introduced to the treasures of New York's literary world. Accordingly, Section Two, entitled "Literary New York," offers a sampling of imaginative writing that both expands upon many of the themes found throughout the reader and offers readers imaginative visions of the urban experience.

Editorial Apparatus

- A range of *interesting topics and texts* about New York City for students to choose from to develop and apply their critical reading, writing, and thinking skills.
- Every chapter begins with an *introduction* that provides a larger context for each reading selection to help students understand, enjoy, and connect the selections.
- Author's *biography* precedes each selection.
- *Pre-reading* questions prepare students to read and think critically about the topic presented in the selection that follows.
- *Discussion questions* are designed to promote thinking about the meaning and implications of the text and to ask students to relate some aspects of the text to a value, practice, or belief in their personal experience or other readings.

- *Writing tasks* are related to the topic of the reading selection. These assignments encourage students to continue to articulate and develop their own perspectives on the topic by using the text to situate their discussion.
- *Connecting ideas* questions at the end of each chapter ask students to compare the texts they are reading either with other texts included in the chapter or with the students' own experiences.
- A *Researching New York* section provides additional resources such as Web sites, books, articles, and films for students' research assignments.
- *Alternate thematic sequences* offer more options and greater flexibility for lesson plans.
- A companion website: http://openlab.citytech.cuny.edu/

Juanita But
Mark Noonan
Sean Scanlan

New York City College of Technology
City University of New York

ACKNOWLEDGEMENTS

We would like to thank the following friends and colleagues, whose comments, advice, and support helped us to make this a better and more useful anthology: Nina Bannett, Aaron Barlow, Jane Feder, Monique Ferrell, George Guida, Victor Ha, Richard Hanley, Caroline Hellman, Lily Lam, Sean McGlade, Suzanne Miller, Robert Ostrom, Jennifer Sears, and Benjamin Shepard. Special thanks also to *The Gotham Gazette*, Taiyo Na, and José and Rey Parlá.

SECTION I:
Here Is New York

"Woolworth Tower in Clouds," New York © CORBIS.

The city is like poetry; it compresses all life, all races and breeds, into a small island and adds music and the accompaniment of internal engines. The island of Manhattan is without any doubt the greatest human concentrate on earth, the poem whose magic is comprehensible to millions of permanent residents but whose full meaning will always remain elusive.

E. B. White, From *Here is New York* (1949)

A hundred times have I thought New York is a catastrophe, and fifty times: It is a beautiful catastrophe.

Le Corbusier, Architect

CHAPTER 1

New Yorkers and Their Neighborhoods

© SeanPavonePhoto, 2012. Used under license from Shutterstock, Inc.

I'm crazy about this City.

Daylight slants like a razor cutting the buildings in half. In the top half I see looking faces and it's not easy to tell which are people, which the work of stonemasons. Below is shadow where any blasé thing takes place: clarinets and lovemaking, fists and the voices of sorrowful women. A city like this one makes me dream tall and feel in on things. Hep. It's the bright steel rocking above the shade below that does it. When I look over strips of green grass lining the river, at church steeples and into the cream-and-copper halls of apartment buildings, I'm strong. Alone, yes, but top-notch and indestructible—like the City in 1926 when all the wars are over and there will never be another one. The people down there in the shadow are happy about that. At last, at last, everything's ahead. The smart ones say so and people listening to them and reading what they write down agree: Here comes the new. Look out. There goes the sad stuff. The bad stuff. The things-nobody-could-help stuff. The way everybody was then and there. Forget that. History is over, you all, and everything's ahead at last.

Toni Morrison, From *Jazz* (1992)

I'd rather be a lampost in New York than the Mayor of Chicago.

Mayor James J. Walker

New Yorkers and Their Neighborhoods

This chapter shows how New York City is as much the capital of the world—the ultimate metropolis—as it is the home where we live. The voices collected here are from the eternally loyal, those who can honestly say, as Toni Morrison's narrator in *Jazz* puts it, "I'm crazy about this City." The readings remind us of the fact that New York is more than just a place that inspires awe, imagination, or even envy. Admit it or not, we do take this city personally.

In "The Colossus of New York," Colson Whitehead suggests that the moment we record our first memory of New York, we become a New Yorker. For him, "Our streets are calendars containing who we were and who we will be next." It is a city in which we both lose ourselves and find ourselves, always growing in the process. Similarly, Katie Roiphe in "A Coney Island of the Mind" looks back at a defining New York moment that directed the trajectory of her life. In her reminiscence of a first date on the Coney Island Cyclone, she too comes to understand the powerful role the city plays in influencing life decisions.

In New York, even a subway ride can be transformative. Newly arrived from the South, Ralph Ellison considers his first subway experience in "New York, 1936" as both daunting and liberating. He realizes that in New York's crowded subway cars there are no racial and personal boundaries. For both Anna Quindlen and Ian Frazier, the subway is a place of happenings as well, where one observes or partakes in unanticipated encounters and mini-spectacles. From an insider's perspective, Quindlen's "Pregnant in New York" explores the character of the city in terms of gender difference and etiquette. With a good sense of humor, she illustrates what it means to be "disabled" in New York. Frazier's "Take the F," in turn, presents dynamic and diverse images of F train passengers and his neighbors in Park Slope.

To outsiders, New York may be a nice place to visit, but only those who live here can speak to life on the inside. Using bold and provocative language, Willie Perdomo and Nelson George capture the uniqueness of their neighborhoods. Though both pieces are very different, each reveals how place shapes identity.

E.B. White's "Here is New York" serves as the anchor to this chapter. It is a monumental piece that breathes the spirit of the city. This essay is at the same time an inward expression, an outward description, as well as a thorough assessment of New York. White's essay checks the pulses of the city and offers an insightful prognosis of urban life.

The Colossus of New York

Colson Whitehead

Colson Whitehead was born in 1969, and was raised in Manhattan. After graduating from Harvard University, he started working at *The Village Voice*, where he wrote reviews of television, books, and music. He is the author of *The Intuitionist* (2000), *John Henry Days* (2001), *The Colossus of New York* (2003), *Apex Hides the Hurt* (2006), *Sag Harbor* (2009), and *Zone One* (2011). He lives in Brooklyn.

Pre-Reading

What was your first memory of New York City?

I'm here because I was born here and thus ruined for anywhere else, but I   1
don't know about you. Maybe you're from here, too, and sooner or later it will come out that we used to live a block away from each other and didn't even know it. Or maybe you moved here a couple years ago for a job. Maybe you came here for school. Maybe you saw the brochure. The city has spent a considerable amount of time and money putting the brochure together, what with all the movies, TV shows and songs—the whole If You Can Make It There business. The city also puts a lot of effort into making your hometown look really drab and tiny, just in case you were wondering why it's such a drag to go back sometimes.

No matter how long you have been here, you are a New Yorker the first time you say, That used to be Munsey's, or That used to be the Tic Toc Lounge. That before the internet café plugged itself in, you got your shoes resoled in the mom-and-pop operation that used to be there. You are a New Yorker when what was there before is more real and solid than what is here now.

You start building your private New York the first time you lay eyes on it. Maybe you were in a cab leaving the airport when the skyline first roused itself into view. All your worldly possessions were in the trunk, and in your hand you held an address on a piece of paper. Look: there's the Empire State Building, over there are the Twin Towers. Somewhere in that fantastic, glorious mess was the address on the piece of paper, your first home here. Maybe your parents dragged you here for a vacation when you were a kid and towed you up and down the gigantic avenues to shop for Christmas gifts. The only skyscrapers visible from your stroller were the legs of adults, but you got to know the ground pretty well and started to wonder why some sidewalks sparkle at certain angles, and others don't. Maybe you came to visit your old buddy, the one who moved here last summer, and there was some mix-up as to where you were supposed to meet. You stepped out of Penn Station into the dizzying hustle of Eighth Avenue and fainted. Freeze it there: that instant is the first brick in your city.

I started building my New York on the uptown No. 1 train. My first city memory is of looking out a subway window as the train erupted from the tunnel on the way to 125th Street and palsied up onto the elevated tracks. It's the early seventies, so everything is filthy. Which means everything is still filthy, because that is my city and I'm sticking to it. I still call it the Pan Am Building, not out of affectation, but because that's what it is. For that new transplant from Des Moines, who is starting her first week of work at a Park Avenue South insurance firm, that titan squatting over Grand Central is the Met Life Building, and for her it always will be. She is wrong, of course—when I look up there, I clearly see the gigantic letters spelling out Pan Am, don't I? And of course I am wrong, in the eyes of the old-timers who maintain the myth that there was a time before Pan Am.

History books and public television documentaries are always trying   5
to tell you all sorts of "facts" about New York. That Canal Street used to be a canal. That Bryant Park used to be a reservoir. It's all hokum. I've been to Canal Street, and the only time I ever saw a river flow through it was during the last water-main explosion. Never listen to what people tell you about old New York, because if you didn't witness it, it is not a part of your New York and might as well be Jersey. Except for that bit about the Dutch buying Manhattan for twenty-four bucks—there are and always will be braggarts who "got in at the right time."

There are eight million naked cities in this naked city—they dispute and disagree. The New York City you live in is not my New York City; how could it be? This place multiplies when you're not looking. We move over here, we move over there. Over a lifetime, that adds up to a lot of neighborhoods, the motley construction material of your jerry-built metropolis. Your favorite newsstands, restaurants, movie theaters, subway stations and barbershops are replaced by your next neighborhood's favorites. It gets to be quite a sum. Before you know it, you have your own personal skyline.

Go back to your old haunts in your old neighborhoods and what do you find: they remain and have disappeared. The greasy spoon, the deli, the dry cleaner you scouted out when you first arrived and tried to make those new streets yours: they are gone. But look past the windows of the travel agency that replaced your pizza parlor. Beyond the desks and computers and promo posters for tropical adventures, you can still see Neapolitan slices cooling, the pizza cutter lying next to half a pie, the map of Sicily on the wall. It is all still there, I assure you. The man who just paid for a trip to Jamaica sees none of that, sees his romantic getaway, his family vacation, what this little shop on this little street has granted him. The disappeared pizza parlor is still here because you are here, and when the beauty parlor replaces the travel agency, the gentleman will still have his vacation. And that lady will have her manicure.

You swallow hard when you discover that the old coffee shop is now a chain pharmacy, that the place where you first kissed So-and-so is now a discount electronics retailer, that where you bought this very jacket is now rubble behind a blue plywood fence and a future office building. Damage has been done to your city. You say, It happened overnight. But of course it didn't. Your pizza parlor, his shoeshine stand, her hat store: when they were here, we neglected them. For all you know, the place closed down moments after the last time you walked out the door. (Ten months ago? Six years? Fifteen? You can't remember, can you?) And there have been five stores in that spot before the travel agency. Five different neighborhoods coming and going between then and now, other people's other cities. Or fifteen, twenty-five, a hundred neighborhoods. Thousands of people pass that storefront every day, each one haunting the streets of his or her own New York, not one of them seeing the same thing.

We can never make proper good-byes. It was your last ride in a Checker cab and you had no warning. It was the last time you were going to have Lake Tung Ting shrimp in that kinda shady Chinese restaurant and you had no idea. If you had known, perhaps you would have stepped behind the counter and shaken everyone's hand, pulled out the camera and issued posing instructions. But you had no idea. There are unheralded tipping points, a certain number of times that we will unlock the front door of an apartment. At some point you were closer to the last time than you were to the first time, and you didn't even know it. You didn't know that each time you passed the threshold you were saying good-bye.

I never got a chance to say good-bye to some of my old buildings. Some   10
I lived in, others were part of a skyline I thought would always be there. And they never got a chance to say good-bye to me. I think they would have liked to—I refuse to believe in their indifference. You say you know these streets pretty well? The city knows you better than any living person because it has seen you when you are alone. It saw you steeling yourself for the job interview, slowly walking home after the late date, tripping over nonexistent impediments on the sidewalk. It saw you wince when the single frigid drop fell from the air conditioner twelve stories up and zapped you. It saw the bewilderment on your face as you stepped out of the stolen

matinee, incredulous that there was still daylight after such a long movie. It saw you half-running up the street after you got the keys to your first apartment. The city saw all that. Remembers, too.

Consider what all your old apartments would say if they got together to swap stories. They could piece together the starts and finishes of your relationships, complain about your wardrobe and musical tastes, gossip about who you are after midnight. 7J says, So that's what happened to Lucy—I knew it would never work out. You picked up yoga, you put down yoga, you tried various cures. You tried on selves and got rid of them, and this makes your old rooms wistful: why must things change? 3R goes, Saxophone, you say—I knew him when he played guitar. Cherish your old apartments and pause for a moment when you pass them. Pay tribute, for they are the caretakers of your reinventions.

Our streets are calendars containing who we were and who we will be next. We see ourselves in this city every day when we walk down the sidewalk and catch our reflections in store windows, seek ourselves in this city each time we reminisce about what was there fifteen, ten, forty years ago, because all our old places are proof that we were here. One day the city we built will be gone, and when it goes, we go. When the buildings fall, we topple, too.

Maybe we become New Yorkers the day we realize that New York will go on without us. To put off the inevitable, we try to fix the city in place, remember it as it was, doing to the city what we would never allow to be done to ourselves. The kid on the uptown No. 1 train, the new arrival stepping out of Grand Central, the jerk at the intersection who doesn't know east from west: those people don't exist anymore, ceased to be a couple of apartments ago, and we wouldn't have it any other way. New York City does not hold our former selves against us. Perhaps we can extend the same courtesy.

Our old buildings still stand because we saw them, moved in and out of their long shadows, were lucky enough to know them for a time. They are a part of the city we carry around. It is hard to imagine that something will take their place, but at this very moment the people with the right credentials are considering how to fill the craters. The cement trucks will roll up and spin their bellies, the jackhammers will rattle, and after a while the postcards of the new skyline will be available for purchase. Naturally we will cast a wary eye toward those new kids on the block, but let's be patient and not judge too quickly. We were new here, too, once.

What follows is my city. Making this a guidebook, with handy color-coded maps and minuscule fine print you should read very closely so you won't be surprised. It contains your neighborhoods. Or doesn't. We overlap. Or don't. Maybe you've walked these avenues, maybe it's all Jersey to

15

you. I'm not sure what to say. Except that probably we're neighbors. That we walk past each other every day, and never knew it until now.

Discussion Questions

1. Colson Whitehead writes that everyone's New York is different. What is his "private" New York like? What was the "first brick" in his city?
2. According to Whitehead, when does someone become a New Yorker?
3. What is the significance of the title?
4. According to the author, why are there no "proper good-byes" in New York?
5. How does the author establish the tone of the essay?
6. In paragraph 3 what are skyscrapers compared to? Can you find any other metaphors in the essay?
7. Whitehead uses many expressive verbs such as "roused" (para. 3), "erupted," and "palsied" (para. 4). What are the effects of these words?
8. In paragraph 10 the author writes, "The city knows you better than any living person because it has seen you when you are alone." Find other examples of personification in the essay and comment on them.
9. In the original version of this essay—which was a response to 9–11—Whitehead began paragraph 14 in a different way. Instead of "Our old buildings still stand . . .," he originally wrote "Our towers still stand . . ." What is the effect of this change?

Writing Tasks

- Recount your first memory of being in New York. Focus on a particular image, sensation, event, or encounter.
- What changes have you noticed in your neighborhood? How do you feel about them?
- In New York, many neighborhoods have been undergoing economic development in which run-down buildings and vacant lots have been turned into upscale residential apartments and chain stores (such as Starbucks). What do you feel are the advantages and disadvantages of this change—known as gentrification?

A Coney Island of the Mind

Katie Roiphe

Katie Roiphe grew up in New York City. She attended Harvard University and received a Ph.D. in English literature from Princeton University. She is best known as the author of *The Morning After: Fear, Sex, and Feminism* (1994). She is also the author of *Last Night in Paradise: Sex and Morals at the Century's End* (1997), *Still She Haunts Me* (2001), and *Uncommon Arrangements* (2007).

Pre-Reading

Have you ever wished to alter a decision or an action that has brought about negative consequences? What would you have done instead?

MY FATHER LEFT Flatbush sixty-five years ago with no intention of ever   1
returning, and one brilliant fall day I find myself going back to deepest Brooklyn, to Coney Island, to the last stop on the F train.

My date stops in front of the Cyclone that curls ominously above us. I am astonished that he wants to ride it. I feel twinges of panic on elevators and airplanes, but it somehow seems too early in our acquaintance for him to know that I am too fragile for roller coasters. My date does not give the impression of being afraid of anything. So we end up at the ticket counter. The ticket seller catches a crazy glint in my eyes and says, "Nothing's happened to anyone in the seven years that I've worked here," and we hear the whoops and shouts and rattle of the cars above us, and I look up at my date and wonder how well I know him.

As we climb into the car it feels rickety. The wooden track rising against the sky reminds me of the dinosaur bones in the American Museum of Natural History, which is not a reassuring image. The other passengers are teenagers from the neighborhood who look as if they do things every day that make the Cyclone about as exciting as a crosstown bus.

Once the ride starts, it does not feel safe. It shakes and moans. This is not the sleek modern sound of speed. This is speed from another era. It's the roller-coaster equivalent of reading by gas lamps or sending telegrams. The Cyclone was built in 1927. "Don't worry," my date tells me.

How does he know I am worrying? Am I not doing a good job of hiding my worry? "There's a guy who checks every inch of the track every day." But this is hardly reassuring. This seems to me like a fallibly human system. Why should we trust a man checking a track, a man whose mind could be wandering to his girlfriend's erratic behavior the night before, or what he might be having for lunch?

We are pulled into the sky. I feel as if I am nothing but stomach, air, and fear. As we hurtle to the top, I grasp my bag, my date's legs against mine, and I see the rotating water and sky and sand, the crowd milling below us, and it's the greatest view in the whole city, thrill and terror blending into clarity, panic focusing the mind. I feel like I have never seen the ocean before.

5

Down below us is the boardwalk where my father used to come with his friends in the early thirties to swim and buy Nathan's Famous hot dogs for a nickel. He rode the Cyclone in the brighter, grander, better painted days of its youth. He grew up only a few miles from here, on East Twenty-second Street between Avenue T and Avenue U, in a house that I have never really seen. He drove us there once, on my mother's insistence, but when we got to his block he suddenly put his foot on the gas, and we perceived his childhood house, the house he was evicted from during the Depression, as a blur of color. (Years later, after he dies, I will wish I had gotten him to give me the number of the house; I will wish I had gotten him to talk about the movie theaters where he learned English from Ingrid Bergman, about his parent's marriage, about the Battle of the Somme.) But for now I am a tourist in my father's childhood. I am sailing over the past he wouldn't talk about. I am almost reaching it.

The track dips and the car zips down. My date and I are in our late twenties—he at least seems, ostensibly, to be an adult, but the years are stripped away by wind and fear and we are children again, clutching each other's hands.

It seems as if there is only a small chance that the metal bar will actually hold us in. At any moment we are going to fly out—little dots against the horizon. I imagine us falling through the air, like astronauts in a movie, our hair streaming out in the wind, frozen in a black-and-white photograph the next day in the tabloids.

As we turn the curve, even the teenagers shriek, but I am too scared to scream. It seems as if all of my energy has to be focused on staying alive. In 1911, the Cyclone's predecessor, the Giant Racer, flew off its tracks, killing two women. Picture the tracks bending through the air, the pretty cars careening through the danger they are built to simulate. Think how long it will take the observers to realize that the screams are real.

It feels as if the earth is falling out from under us and I have to close my　10
eyes, no matter what my date will think. We swoop and swerve and finally
clatter to a halt. It has been one hundred seconds.

I wonder woozily why I feel so good. I feel sort of bruised and banged
up but that feeling is part of the beauty of the Cyclone. It's about terror and
the release from terror, about how close dreams are to nightmares, and how
easy it is to escape from your life. A journalist from the turn of the century
wrote, "Coney Island has a code of conduct all her own," and for the first
time I know exactly what he means. The Cyclone gives you the feeling that
nothing matters but the second you are in, a feeling worth much more than
the four dollars of the ticket. In fact it may be the platonic ideal of dates—a
whole journey of risk and reassurance condensed into a minute and a half.

By this point, I am beginning to understand why the city has always
had a romantic fixation on this place. Lawrence Ferlinghetti wrote his
famous poem "A Coney Island of the Mind" about this too: "There's always complications like maybe she has no eyes for him or him no eyes
for her . . . or something or other stands in the way like his mother or her
father or someone like that but they go right on trying to get it all the
time like in Shakespeare or Proust remembering his Things Past or wherever and there they all are struggling toward each other or after each
other like those marble maidens on that Grecian Urn or any market street
or merry-go-round around and around they go all hunting love and half
the hungry time not even knowing just what is really eating them . . ."
It's not a happy poem, really, it's not a poem that bodes well, but who
remembers anything but the title?

As I step onto what seems like solid ground, I feel lightheaded and
shaky and my date puts his arm around me. We pass a freak show and a
dance contest. We walk on the boardwalk in the warm air. My date is tall
and quieter than any other man I have ever met. He does not narrate and
analyze his inner life in the same compulsive way as everyone else I know.
I look back at the Cyclone, arched against the sky. The brightly painted
food stands and arcades bear more of a resemblance to the old peep shows
in Times Square than to the glamorous architecture of Coney Island's past.
But you can still feel the seediness and greatness of the place, the vague
feeling of menace, of leisure and unemployment mixing, along with the
elation of a day at the beach.

Four years later, I will marry my date in something of the same spirit as
that Cyclone ride. I will be taking a risk that I feel as a risk, and yet it will
feel inevitable, as I have bought my ticket and am pulled skyward. Later,
when he has moved out, I will go back over time. I will review with some
puzzlement what I could have been thinking: Where was that man who

checks every inch of the track? What was that man dreaming about when he should have been checking the track?

In Delmore Schwartz's haunting short story "In Dreams Begin Responsibilities," a grown man watches a movie of his parents' courtship. His father wears a tie. His mother wears a hat with feathers. They are trying to impress each other. They ride a streetcar to Coney Island. They ride a merry-go-round, reaching for the brass rings. Then they stand on this same boardwalk, looking out at this same ocean, when his father asks his mother to marry him. Just at that moment the narrator stands up and shouts at this movie screen: "Don't do it. It's not too late to change your minds, both of you. Nothing good will come of it." This is the feeling I have looking at this moment now. Stop the movie, there on the boardwalk. I feel like shouting at myself through the years. But this is what you can't do. *Don't do it. It's not too late to change your mind.*

For now, though, my date buys a large bag of Nathan's French fries, and I wonder how on earth he can eat after what we have just been through, and the crowd is enveloping us with stuffed dogs, and blown-up alligators tucked under their arms, and the sun glistens in the sand, and the sky is as blue as the cotton candy sold by vendors and for now, I am enchanted by the unknown territories of another person, and of the city itself.

Discussion Questions

1. Why did the author decide to take a ride on the Cyclone despite being hesitant?
2. What was the author's initial impression about her date?
3. What analogies are used to describe her ride on the Cyclone?
4. What is her response to her date's remarks on the safety check of the roller coaster? What does it disclose?
5. How does the author feel during and after the ride?
6. What does Roiphe mean when she says, "Coney Island has a code of conduct all her own"?
7. How does the author compare her marriage with the Cyclone ride?

Writing Tasks

- Write an essay about a memorable or transforming experience you had in the city. Like the approach Roiphe uses in her essay, you should present a unique perspective that combines memories and vivid descriptions.
- Look up Lawrence Ferlinghetti's poem "Coney Island of the Mind," and write an essay in which you compare it to Roiphe's piece.

Subway Rush Hour

Langston Hughes

James Langston Hughes was born February 1, 1902, in Joplin, Missouri. His parents divorced when he was a small child, and his father moved to Mexico. He graduated from Central High School in Cleveland and then went on to New York where he studied, for one year, at Columbia University. He lived in Harlem for much of his life. Hughes's first book of poetry, *The Weary Blues,* was published in 1926. In addition to leaving us a large body of poetic work, Hughes wrote eleven plays and many works of prose, including the well-known "Simple" books such as *Simple Speaks His Mind.* Hughes died on May 22, 1967, in New York. In his memory, his residence at 20 East 127th Street in Harlem, New York City, has been given landmark status by the New York City Preservation Commission, and East 127th Street has been renamed "Langston Hughes Place."

Pre-Reading

What makes subway riding so enjoyable or, at times, so miserable?

Subway Rush Hour

Mingled   1
breath and smell
so close
mingled
black and white   5
so near
no room for fear.

Discussion Questions

1. Hughes is legendary for being able to say so much in very few lines. How does he accomplish this?

Writing Task

*   Write a paper in which you discuss all of Hughes' poems found in this anthology.

New York, 1936

Ralph Ellison

Born in Oklahoma in 1914 and educated at the Tuskegee Institute in Alabama, Ralph Ellison established his literary reputation with his first and only novel, *Invisible Man,* first published in 1947 and reprinted numerous times since. His collections of essays include *Shadow and Act* (1964) and *Going to the Territory* (1986). This essay is excerpted from his memoir entitled *An Extravagance of Laughter* (1986). Ellison died in 1994.

Pre-Reading

How does New York compare to other places you know?

In 1936, a few weeks after my arrival in New York City, I was lucky enough   1
to be invited by an old hero and newfound friend, Langston Hughes, to be his guest at what would be my introduction to Broadway theater. I was so delighted and grateful for the invitation that I failed to ask my host the title of the play, and it was not until we arrived at the theater that I learned that it would be Jack Kirkland's dramatization of Erskine Caldwell's famous novel *Tobacco Road.* . . . I failed to note the irony of circumstance that would have as my introduction to New York theater a play with a southern setting and characters that were based upon a type and class of whites whom I had spent the last three years trying to avoid. Had I been more alert, it might have occurred to me that somehow a group of white Alabama farm folk had learned of my presence in New York, thrown together a theatrical troupe, and flown north to haunt me. . . . And yet that irony arose precisely from the mixture of motives—practical, educational, and romantic—that had brought me to the North in the first place.

Among these was my desire to enjoy a summer free of the South and its problems while meeting the challenge of being on my own for the first time in a great northern city. Fresh out of Alabama, with my junior year at Tuskegee Institute behind me, I was also in New York seeking funds with which to complete my final year as a music major—a goal at which I was having less success than I had hoped. However, there had been compensations. For between working in the Harlem YMCA cafeteria as a substitute for vacationing waiters and countermen and searching for a more profitable job, I had used my free time exploring the city, making new acquaintances, and enjoying the many forms of social freedom that were unavailable to me in Alabama. The very idea of being in New York was dreamlike, for like many young Negroes of the time, I thought of it as the freest of American cities and considered Harlem as the site and symbol of Afro-American progress and hope. Indeed, I was both young and bookish enough to think of Manhattan as my substitute for Paris and of Harlem as a place of Left Bank excitement.

And yet I soon discovered, much to my chagrin, that while I was physically out of the South, I was restrained—sometimes consciously, sometimes not—by certain internalized thou-shalt-nots that had structured my public conduct in Alabama. It was as though I had come to the Eden of American culture and found myself indecisive as to which of its fruits were free for my picking. Beyond the borders of Harlem's briar patch—which seemed familiar because of my racial and cultural identification with the majority of its people and the lingering spell that had been cast nationwide by the music, dance, and literature of the so-called Harlem Renaissance—I viewed New Yorkers through the overlay of my Alabama experience. Contrasting the whites I encountered with those I had observed in the South, I weighed class against class and compared southern styles with their northern counterparts. I listened to diction and noted dress, and searched for attitudes in inflections, carriage, and manners. And in pursuing this aspect of my extracurricular education, I explored the landscape.

I crossed Manhattan back and forth from river to river and up, down, and around again, from Spuyten Duyvil Creek to the Battery, looking and listening and gadding about; rode streetcar and el, subway and bus; took a hint from Edna Millay* and spent an evening riding back and forth on the Staten Island Ferry. From the elevated trains I saw my first penthouses with green trees growing atop tall buildings, caught remote glimpses of homes, businesses, and factories while moving above the teeming streets, and felt a sense of quiet tranquillity despite the bang and clatter. Yes, but the subways were something else again.

In fact, the subways were utterly confusing to my southern-bred idea 5 of good manners, and especially the absence of a certain gallantry that men were expected to extend toward women. Subway cars appeared to be underground arenas where northern social equality took the form of an endless shoving match in which the usual rules of etiquette were turned upside down—or so I concluded after watching a 5:00 footrace in a crowded car.

---

*Edna St. Vincent Millay was a Greenwich Village poet famous for her poem "Recuerdo," which appears in the Literary New York section.

The contest was between a huge white woman who carried an armful of bundles, and a small Negro man who lugged a large suitcase. At the time I was standing against the track-side door, and when the train stopped at a downtown station I saw the two come charging through the opening doors like racehorses leaving the starting gate at Belmont. And as they spied and dashed for the single empty seat, the outcome appeared up for grabs, but it was the woman, thanks to a bustling, more ruthless stride (and more subway know-how) who won—though but by a hip and a hair. For just as they reached the seat she swung a well-padded hip and knocked the man off stride, thus causing him to lose his balance as she turned, slipped beneath his reeling body, and plopped into the seat. It was a maneuver that produced a startling effect—at least on me.

For as she banged into the seat it caused the man to spin and land smack-dab in her lap—in which massive and heaving center of gravity he froze, stared into her face nose-tip to nose, and then performed a spring like leap to his feet as from a red-hot stove. It was but the briefest conjunction, and then, as he reached down and fumbled for his suitcase, the woman began adjusting her bundles, and with an elegant toss of her head she then looked up into his face with the most ladylike and triumphant of smiles.

I had no idea of what to expect next, but to her sign of good sportswomanship the man let out with an exasperated "Hell, you can have it, I don't want it!" A response that evoked a phrase from an old forgotten ditty to which my startled mind added the unstated line—"Sleeping in the bed with your hand right on it"—and shook me with visions of the train screeching to a stop and a race riot beginning. . . .

But not at all. For while the defeated man pushed his way to another   10 part of the car, the crowd of passengers simply looked on and laughed.

Still, for all their noise and tension, it was not the subways that most intrigued me, but the buses. In the South you occupied the back of the bus, and nowhere *but* the back, or so help you God. Being in the North and encouraged by my anonymity, I experimented by riding all *over* New York buses, excluding only the driver's seat—front end, back end, right side, left side, sitting or standing as the route and flow of passengers demanded. *And,* since those were the glorious days of double-deckers, both enclosed and open, I even rode *top*side.

Thus having convinced myself that no questions of racial status would be raised by where I chose to ride, I asked myself whether a seat at the back of the bus wasn't actually more desirable than one at the front. For not only did it provide more legroom, it offered a more inclusive perspective on both the interior and exterior scenes. I found the answer obvious and quite amusing. But now that I was no longer forced by law and compelled

by custom to ride at the back, what was more desirable—the possibility of exercising what was routinely accepted in the North as an abstract, highly symbolic (even trivial) form of democratic freedom, or the creature comfort that was to be had by occupying a spot from which more of the passing scene could be observed? And in my own personal terms, what was more important—my individual comfort, or the exercise of the democratic right to be squeezed and jostled by strangers? Such questions were akin to that of whether you lived in a Negro neighborhood because you were forced to do so, or because you preferred living among those of your own background. Having experienced life in mixed neighborhoods as a child, I preferred to live where people spoke my own version of the American language, and where misreading of tone or gesture was less likely to ignite lethal conflict.

Discussion Questions

1. Why does Ellison come to New York in 1936? What do you think was his most urgent reason?
2. How does Ellison utilize his free time?
3. How do his experiences help explain the appeal of New York for African-Americans during the 1930s?
4. Why does the author call Harlem "the site and symbol of Afro-American progress and hope"? Does this still hold true?
5. Why doesn't Ellison feel entirely "out of the South" while in New York?
6. Describe the humor in Ellison's subway story. What does he learn from this incident about New York and himself?
7. Why is Ellison so intrigued with buses in New York?

Writing Tasks

- Write an essay in which you compare New York to another part of the country.
- Write an essay which analyzes the many ways New York offers its inhabitants exceptional freedom. Try to include ways in which the city also limits people.
- Describe something about New York that you particularly enjoy.

Pregnant in New York

Anna Quindlen

Anna Quindlen (b. 1952) is the best-selling author of six novels and nine nonfiction books. Her *New York Times* column, "Public and Private," won the Pulitzer Prize in 1992.

Pre-Reading

Have you ever given up your seat to someone in the subway? Under what circumstances?

I have two enduring memories of the hours just before I gave birth to my   1
first child. One is of finding a legal parking space on Seventy-eighth Street between Lexington and Park, which made my husband and me believe that we were going inside the hospital to have a child who would always lead a charmed life. The other is of walking down Lexington Avenue, stopping every couple of steps to find myself a visual focal point—a stop sign, a red light, a pair of $200 shoes in a store window—and doing what the Lamaze[1] books call first-stage breathing. It was 3:00 A.M. and coming toward me through a magenta haze of what the Lamaze books call discomfort were a couple in evening clothes whose eyes were popping out of their perfect faces. "Wow," said the man when I was at least two steps past them. "She looks like she's ready to burst."

I love New York, but it's a tough place to be pregnant. It's a great place for half sour pickles, chopped liver, millionaires, actors, dancers, akita dogs, nice leather goods, fur coats, and baseball, but it is a difficult place to have any kind of disability and, as anyone who has filled out the forms for a maternity leave lately will tell you, pregnancy is considered a disability. There's no privacy in New York; everyone is right up against everyone else and they all feel compelled to say what they think. When you look like a hot-air balloon with insufficient ballast, that's not good.

New York has no pity: it's every man for himself, and since you are yourself-and-a-half, you fall behind. There's a rumor afoot that if you are

[1]Lamaze *adj.* Relating to or being a method of childbirth in which the expectant mother is prepared psychologically and physically to give birth without the use of drugs.

pregnant you can get a seat on the A train at rush hour, but it's totally false. There are, in fact, parts of the world in which pregnancy can get you a seat on public transportation, but none of them are within the boundaries of the city—with the possible exception of some unreconstructed parts of Staten Island.

What you get instead are rude comments, unwarranted intrusions and deli countermen. It is a little-known fact that New York deli countermen can predict the sex of an unborn child. (This is providing that you order, of course. For a counterman to provide this service requires a minimum order of seventy-five cents.) This is how it works: You walk into a deli and say, "Large fruit salad, turkey on rye with Russian, a large Perrier and a tea with lemon." The deli counterman says, "Who you buying for, the Rangers?" and all the other deli countermen laugh.

This is where many pregnant women make their mistake. If it is win-   5
tertime and you are wearing a loose coat, the preferred answer to this question is, "I'm buying for all the women in my office." If it is summer and you are visibly pregnant, you are sunk. The deli counterman will lean over the counter and say, studying your contours, "It's a boy." He will then tell a tedious story about sex determination, his Aunt Olga, and a clove of garlic, while behind you people waiting on line shift and sigh and begin to make Zero Population Growth and fat people comments. (I once dealt with an East Side counterman who argued with me about the tea because he said it was bad for the baby, but he was an actor waiting for his big break, not a professional.) Deli countermen do not believe in amnio-centesis. Friends who have had amniocentesis tell me that once or twice they tried to argue: "I already know it's a girl." "You are wrong." They gave up: "Don't forget the napkins."

There are also cabdrivers. One promptly pulled over in the middle of Central Park when I told him I had that queasy feeling. When I turned to get back into the cab, it was gone. The driver had taken the $1.80 on the meter as a loss. Luckily, I never had this problem again, because as I grew larger, nine out of ten cabdrivers refused to pick me up. They had read the tabloids. They knew about all those babies christened Checker (actually, I suppose now most of them are Plymouths) because they're born in the back seat in the Midtown Tunnel. The only way I could get a cabdriver to pick me up after the sixth month was to hide my stomach by having a friend walk in front of me. The exception was a really tiresome young cabdriver whose wife's due date was a week after mine and who wanted to practice panting with me for that evening's childbirth class. Most of the time I wound up taking public transportation.

And so it came down to the subways: men looking at their feet, reading their newspapers, working hard to keep from noticing me. One day on the IRT I was sitting down—it was a spot left unoccupied because the rainwater had spilled in the window from an elevated station—when I noticed a woman standing who was or should have been on her way to the hospital.

"When are you due?" I asked her. "Thursday," she gasped. "I'm September," I said. "Take my seat." She slumped down and said, with feeling, "You are the first person to give me a seat on the subway since I've been pregnant." Being New Yorkers, with no sense of personal privacy, we began to exchange subway, taxi, and deli counterman stories. When a man sitting nearby got up to leave, he snarled, "You wanted women's lib, now you got it."

Well, I'm here to say that I did get women's lib, and it is my only fond memory of being pregnant in New York. (Actually, I did find pregnancy useful on opening day at Yankee Stadium, when great swarms of people parted at the sight of me as though I were Charlton Heston in *The Ten Commandments.* But it had a pariah quality that was not totally soothing.)

One evening rush hour during my eighth month I was waiting for a   10
train at Columbus Circle. The loudspeaker was crackling unintelligibly and ominously and there were as many people on the platform as currently live in Santa Barbara, Calif. Suddenly I had the dreadful feeling that I was being surrounded. "To get mugged at a time like this," I thought ruefully. "And this being New York, they'll probably try to take the baby, too." But as I looked around I saw that the people surrounding me were four women, some armed with shoulder bags. "You need protection," one said, and being New Yorkers, they ignored the fact that they did not know one another and joined forces to form a kind of phalanx around me, not unlike those that offensive linemen build around a quarterback.

When the train arrived and the doors opened, they moved forward, with purpose, and I was swept inside, not the least bit bruised. "Looks like a boy," said one with a grin, and as the train began to move, we all grabbed the silver overhead handles and turned away from one another.

Discussion Questions

1. Why is it difficult to be pregnant or "have any kind of disability" in New York?
2. What two enduring memories does Quindlen include in the opening paragraph? How do these details frame the rest of the essay?
3. Quindlen writes that "There's no privacy in New York" and "New York has no pity." How does she demonstrate this? Do you agree with her general assessment?
4. How do New York cabdrivers react to pregnant passengers?

5. What metaphor does the author use to describe the helpful women on the platform? How does this scene illustrate the general attitude towards privacy amongst New Yorkers?

Writing Tasks

- Narrate a subway moment of your own that you consider to be typically New York.
- Write a short essay in which you discuss at least three qualities that make a New Yorker. Be sure to provide examples.

Take the F

Ian Frazier

Ian Frazier (b. 1951) grew up in Ohio and lived for years in Brooklyn. He is a regular contributor to *The New Yorker* and *The Atlantic Monthly*. His recent books include *On the Rez* (2000) and *Gone to New York: Adventures in the City* (2005).

Pre-Reading

Do you recall any vivid moments on the subway? What made those moments memorable?

Brooklyn, New York, has the undefined, hard-to-remember shape of a stain. 1 I never know what to tell people when they ask me where in it I live. It sits at the western tip of Long Island at a diagonal that does not conform neatly to the points of the compass. People in Brooklyn do not describe where they live in terms of north or west or south. They refer instead to their neighborhoods, and to the nearest subway lines. I live on the edge of Park Slope, a neighborhood by the crest of a low ridge that runs through the borough. Prospect Park is across the street. Airplanes in the landing pattern for LaGuardia Airport sometimes fly right over my building; every few minutes, on certain sunny days, perfectly detailed airplane shadows slide down my building and up the building opposite in a blink. You can see my building from the plane—it's on the left-hand side of Prospect Park, the longer patch of green you cross after the expanse of Green-Wood Cemetery.

We moved to a co-op apartment in a four-story building a week before our daughter was born. She is now six. I grew up in the country and would not have expected ever to live in Brooklyn. My daughter is a city kid, with less sympathy for certain other parts of the country. When we visited Montana, she was disappointed by the scarcity of pizza places. I overheard her explaining—she was three or four then—to a Montana kid about Brooklyn. She said, "In Brooklyn, there is a lot of broken glass, so you have to wear shoes. And, there is good pizza." She is stern in her judgment of pizza. At the very low end of the pizza-ranking scale is some pizza she once had in New Hampshire, a category now called New Hampshire pizza. In the middle is some O.K. pizza she once had at the Bronx Zoo, which she calls zoo pizza. At the very top is the pizza at the pizza place where the big kids go, about two blocks from our house.

Our subway is the F train. It runs under our building and shakes the floor. The F is generally a reliable train, but one spring as I walked in the park I saw emergency vehicles gathered by a concrete-sheathed hole in the lawn. Firemen lifted a metal lid from the hole and descended into it. After a while, they reappeared, followed by a few people, then dozens of people, then a whole lot of people—passengers from the disabled F train, climbing one at a time out an exit shaft. On the F, I sometimes see large women in straw hats reading a newspaper called the *Caribbean Sunrise,* and Orthodox Jews bent over Talmudic texts in which the footnotes have footnotes, and groups of teenagers wearing identical red bandannas with identical red plastic baby pacifiers in the corners of their mouths, and female couples in porkpie hats, and young men with the silhouettes of the Manhattan skyline razored into their short side hair from one temple around to the other, and Russian-speaking men with thick wrists and big wristwatches, and a hefty, tall woman with long, straight blond hair who hums and closes her eyes and absently practices cello fingerings on the metal subway pole. As I watched the F-train passengers emerge among the grass and trees of Prospect Park, the faces were as varied as usual, but the expressions of indignant surprise were all about the same.

Just past my stop, Seventh Avenue, Manhattan-bound F trains rise from underground to cross the Gowanus Canal. The train sounds different— lighter, quieter—in the open air. From the elevated tracks, you can see the roofs of many houses stretching back up the hill to Park Slope, and a bumper crop of rooftop graffiti, and neon signs for Eagle Clothes and Kentile Floors, and flat expanses of factory roofs where seagulls stand on one leg around puddles in the sagging spots. There are fuel-storage tanks surrounded by earthen barriers, and slag piles, and conveyor belts leading down to the oil-slicked waters of the canal. On certain days, the sludge at the bottom of the canal causes it to bubble. Two men fleeing the police jumped in the canal a while ago; one made it across, the other quickly died. When the subway doors open at the Smith-Ninth Street stop, you can see the bay, and sometimes smell the ocean breeze. This stretch of elevated is the highest point of the New York subway system. To the south you can see the Verrazano-Narrows Bridge, to the north the World Trade towers. For just a few moments, the Statue of Liberty appears between passing buildings. Pieces of a neighborhood—laundry on clotheslines, a standup swimming pool, a plaster saint, a satellite dish, a rectangle of lawn—slide by like quickly dealt cards. Then the train descends again; growing over the wall just before the tunnel is a wisteria bush, which blooms pale blue every May.

I have spent days, weeks on the F train. The trip from Seventh Avenue   5
to midtown Manhattan is long enough so that every ride can produce
its own minisociety of riders, its own forty-minute Ship of Fools. Once a
woman an arm's length from me on a crowded train pulled a knife on a
man who threatened her. I remember the argument and the principals, but
mostly I remember the knife—its flat, curved wood-grain handle inlaid
with brass fittings at each end, its long, tapered blade. Once a man sang
the words of the Lord's Prayer to a mournful, syncopated tune, and he
fitted the mood of the morning so exactly that when he asked for money
at the end the riders reached for their wallets and purses as if he'd pulled
a gun. Once a big white kid with some friends was teasing a small old
Hispanic lady, and when he got off the train I looked at him through the
window and he slugged it hard next to my face. Once a thin woman and
a fat woman sitting side by side had a long and loud conversation about
someone they intended to slap silly: "Her butt be in the *hospital!*" Bring out
the ar-*tillery!*" The terminus of the F in Brooklyn is at Coney Island, not far
from the beach. At an off hour, I boarded the train and found two or three
passengers and, walking around on the floor, a crab. The passengers were
looking at the crab. Its legs clicked on the floor like varnished fingernails.
It moved in this direction, then that, trying to get comfortable. It backed
itself under a seat, against the wall. Then it scooted out just after some new
passengers had sat down there, and they really screamed. Passengers at
the next stop saw it and laughed. When a boy lifted his foot as if to stomp
it, everybody cried, "Noooh!" By the time we reached Jay Street-Borough
Hall, there were maybe a dozen of us in the car, all absorbed in watching
the crab. The car doors opened and a heavyset woman with good posture
entered. She looked at the crab; then, sternly, at all of us. She let a moment
pass. Then she demanded, *"Whose is that?"* A few stops later, a short man
with a mustache took a manila envelope, bent down, scooped the crab into
it, closed it, and put it in his coat pocket.

The smells in Brooklyn: coffee, fingernail polish, eucalyptus, the breath
from laundry rooms, pot roast, Tater Tots. A woman I know who grew
up here says she moved away because she could not stand the smell of
cooking food in the hallway of her parents' building. I feel just the opposite. I used to live in a converted factory above an Army-Navy store, and
I like being in a place that smells like people live there. In the mornings, I
sometimes wake to the smell of toast, and I still don't know exactly whose
toast it is. And I prefer living in a borough of two and a half million inhabitants, the most of any borough in the city. I think of all the rural places,
the pine-timbered canyons and within-commuting-distance farmland,
that we are preserving by not living there. I like the immensities of the
borough, the unrolling miles of Eastern Parkway and Ocean Parkway and

Linden Boulevard, and the dishevelled outlying parks strewn with tree limbs and with shards of glass held together by liquor-bottle labels, and the tough bridges—the Williamsburg and the Manhattan—and the gentle Brooklyn Bridge. And I like the way the people talk; some really do have Brooklyn accents, really do say "dese" and "dose." A week or two ago, a group of neighbors stood on a street corner watching a peregrine falcon on a building cornice contentedly eating a pigeon it had caught, and the sunlight came through its tail feathers, and a woman said to a man, "Look at the tail," "it's so ah-range," and the man replied, "Yeah, I soar it." Like many Americans, I fear living in a nowhere, in a place that is no-place; in Brooklyn, that doesn't trouble me at all.

Everybody, it seems, is here. At Grand Army Plaza, I have seen traffic tieups caused by Haitians and others rallying in support of President Aristide, and by St. Patrick's Day parades, and by Jews of the Lubavitcher sect celebrating the birthday of their Grand Rebbe with a slow procession of ninety-three motor homes—one for each year of his life. Local taxis have bumper stickers that say "Allah Is Great": one of the men who made the bomb that blew up the World Trade Center used an apartment just a few blocks from me. When an election is held in Russia, crowds line up to cast ballots at a Russian polling place in Brighton Beach. A while ago, I volunteer-taught reading at a public elementary school across the park. One of my students, a girl, was part Puerto Rican, part Greek, and part Welsh. Her looks were a lively combination, set off by sea-green eyes. I went to a map store in Manhattan and bought maps of Puerto Rico, Greece, and Wales to read with her, but they didn't interest her. A teacher at the school was directing a group of students to set up chairs for a program in the auditorium, and she said to me, "We have a problem here—each of these kids speaks a different language." She asked the kids to tell me where they were from. One was from Korea, one from Brazil, one from Poland, one from Guyana, one from Taiwan. In the program that followed, a chorus of fourth and fifth graders sang "God Bless America," "You're a Grand Old Flag," and "I'm a Yankee-Doodle Dandy."

Discussion Questions

1. How do people in Brooklyn describe where they are from? Do you yourself find this to be true?
2. What does the comment of Frazier's daughter, "In Brooklyn, there is a lot of broken glass," imply about urban life? Can you think of other features that also represent the city?
3. Focus on Frazier's use of topic sentences. How do they work to organize the essay?

4. What is the effect of Frazier's close attention to details throughout his essay? Focus on specific examples.
5. How does the final scene connect with the overall theme of the essay?

Writing Tasks

- Write about what you miss the most when you are away from New York.
- Take a subway ride and get off at a stop you are not familiar with. With pen in hand, explore and observe the environment. Compare and contrast this neighborhood with your own.

Where I'm From

Willie Perdomo

Willie Perdomo is the author of *Where a Nickel Costs a Dime* and *Smoking Lovely*, which received a PEN Open Book Award. He has also been published in *The New York Times Magazine*, *Bomb*, *Poems of New York*, and *The Harlem Reader.* He is a three-time Poetry and Fiction Fellow at the New York Foundation for the Arts and currently teaches at Fordham University.

Pre-Reading

When asked to describe where you are from, how do you usually respond?

Where I'm From

Because she liked the "kind of music" that I listened to and she liked the   1
way I walked as well as the way I talked, she always wanted to know where I was from.

If I said that I was from 110th Street and Lexington Avenue, right in the heart of a transported Puerto Rican town, where the hodedores live and night turns to day without sleep, do you think then she might know where I was from?

Where I'm from, Puerto Rico stays on our minds when the fresh breeze of *café con leche y pan con mantequilla* comes through our half-open windows and under our doors while the sun starts to rise.

Where I'm from, babies fall asleep to the bark of a German shepherd named Tarzan. We hear his wandering footsteps under a midnight sun. Tarzan has learned quickly to ignore the woman who begs her man to stop slapping her with his fist. "Please, baby! Por favor! I swear it wasn't me. I swear to my mother. Mameeee!!" (Her dead mother told her that this would happen one day.)

Where I'm from, Independence Day is celebrated every day. The final   5
gunshot from last night's murder is followed by the officious knock of a warrant squad coming to take your bread, coffee and freedom away.

Where I'm from, the police come into your house without knocking. They throw us off rooftops and say we slipped. They shoot my father and say he was crazy. They put a bullet in my head and say they found me that way.

Where I'm from, you run to the hospital emergency room because some little boy spit a razor out of his mouth and carved a crescent into your face. But you have to understand, where I'm from even the dead have to wait until their number is called.

Where I'm from, you can listen to Big Daddy retelling stories on his corner. He passes a pint of light Bacardi, pouring the dead's tributary swig onto the street. "I'm God when I put a gun to your head. I'm the judge and you in my courtroom."

Where I'm from, it's the late night scratch of rats' feet that explains what my mother means when she says slowly, *"Bueno, mijo, eso es la vida del pobre."* (Well, son, that is the life of the poor.)

Where I'm from, it's sweet like my grandmother reciting a quick prayer   10
over a pot of hot rice and beans. Where I'm from, it's pretty like my niece stopping me in the middle of the street and telling me to notice all the stars in the sky.

Discussion Questions

1. Why is the speaker's friend so interested in him at first?
2. What elements of his neighborhood does the speaker emphasize?
3. Describe the relationship between the residents and the police.
4. What is the effect of beginning the second stanza with the conditional word "if"? Do you think that the speaker's friend will ever get the whole story of his culture and background?
5. Many of the descriptive scenes throughout this poem are harsh, but the final stanza is radically different. Discuss this shift in tone.
6. What is the effect of using so much Spanish in this poem? Refer to specific instances.

Writing Task

- Write your own "Where I'm From" poem. To do this, begin five stanzas with the dependant clause "Where I'm From, ..." Complete each dependant clause with a descriptive passage that describes either your neighborhood or literally the place where you are from (if not New York).

Fort Greene Dreams

Nelson George

Nelson George (b. 1957) is a music and culture critic, journalist, and filmmaker. After attending St. John's University, he served as a music editor for *Billboard* magazine from 1982 to 1989. In 1986, he helped to finance director Spike Lee's debut feature *She's Gotta Have It*. He is also the author of *Where Did Our Love Go: The Rise and Fall of the Motown Sound*, *The Death of Rhythm & Blues*, and, most recently, a memoir called *City Kid*, from which the following essay is excerpted.

Pre-Reading

What do you like or dislike most about your neighborhood?

In spring 1985 I was awakened in my Jamaica, Queens, apartment by a phone call from a young filmmaker I'd recently befriended. His high-pitched voice filled my ear.   1

"Nelson, this is Spike! Loved your piece on Russell Simmons in the *Voice!*"

He was referring to my profile of Russ that had run in April of that year. I thanked him, and we chatted. I told him I was moving to Brooklyn, to an area called Fort Greene.

"That's where I live!" he told me excitedly. Turned out I was moving right around the corner from him. I didn't know it at the time, but the publication of the Simmons profile, and moving from Queens to Fort Greene, was the end and beginning of two eras for me.

Moving from my Queens apartment with Rocky took me out of daily   5
contact with the business of hip-hop and, happily, ended my long-ass E and F train rides into the city. I was back in Brooklyn, but to a very different 'hood than the one I'd grown up in. All I knew was that Fort Greene was just east of downtown Brooklyn, where I had spent my whole childhood going shopping with my mother. When I did my internship at the *Phoenix* I actually worked just blocks from Fort Greene. Yet streets such as DeKalb, St. Felix, and Carlton were as foreign to me as avenues in Staten

Island. I knew that the Fort Greene projects had produced the basketball greats Bernard and Albert King. The area was also always regarded as a hotbed for gang activity—first in the seventies, with the Tomahawks, and in the eighties, with the Decepticons.

Fort Greene, and my new place at 19 Willoughby Avenue, were easy to love. In contrast to where I'd grown up in Brownsville and lived in Queens, Fort Greene was very close to Manhattan. On almost every major subway line, Fort Greene was no more than two or three stops into Brooklyn, so going out, especially anywhere below Fourteenth Street, was made very convenient. The streets were lined with tall, thick trees fronting magnificent brownstones. There was a picturesque park with rolling hills and tennis courts, and in the fall it filled with hard, brown, fallen acorns that I used to collect and on occasion toss at friends. Fort Greene was close enough to Manhattan that I could leave my apartment at 7:30 P.M. and catch an 8:15 P.M. show at the Bottom Line in Greenwich Village, which made my life infinitely easier.

Plus, the apartment itself was a marvel. It was a duplex with wood floors, two bedrooms, twenty-foot-high ceilings, a large kitchen, exposed-brick walls, and a large backyard. I vowed when my family moved out of the projects that I would never live in a large apartment building again. However, I never imagined that I could live in a place this spacious.

I was able to afford this place because my quickie bio of Michael Jackson had been a bestseller. For the first time in my life I had disposable income, much of which I would squander on wine, women, and vinyl. But whatever I wasted in riches came back to me threefold in experience.

My first month in 19 Willoughby I actually slept upstairs in the long living room, in awe of all the space as I thought back to the bedroom and cramped closet I'd shared with my sister. I calculated that you could have fit our entire public housing apartment in my upstairs. I would live in 19 Willoughby from 1985 to 1992, the most important years of my life in terms of my immersion in music, film, writing, and sex. In 19 Willoughby I wrote five books, including my breakthough work, *The Death of Rhythm and Blues*. I invested in *She's Gotta Have It*, and a couple of other movies, and wrote and produced screenplays. Alone in this large apartment my ambition grew, as if I had to think bigger to fill the space I was now living in. Sometimes it ate at me at night, forcing me out of bed, back to my legal pad to grind out one more record review, and to jot down ideas for books I was sure would change the world. It's likely I was overstimulated by all the vitality of that period's black culture. It was absolutely true that the talent around me was inspiring.

Going out to pick up take-out soul food at a basement spot on DeKalb, walking to the tasty Italian restaurant Cino's or to Junior's on Flatbush   10

Avenue for thick chocolate cake, I'd stroll past the apartments of Spike Lee, writer Thulani Davis, a slew of jazz musicians (Lester Bowie, Wynton and Branford Marsalis, Cecil Taylor, Betty Carter), and other not as well known but vital writers, designers, musicians, and actors. The crackle of creative energy animated the air, as black folk made art all around me. It was a tactile, tangible feeling, and I adored it. With my take-out food in a bag I'd hurry back to 19 Willoughby to wolf down my meal and get back to work, anxious not to be left behind.

It's not that Fort Greene circa mid-eighties was paradise. One reason all these great brownstone apartments were affordable by young artists was crime. Just a long block from my apartment were several public housing projects, which bordered the park on the Myrtle Avenue side. They weren't quite as grim as the Tilden projects I'd grown up in, but they were plenty tough. When crack began running amok in Brooklyn's streets, these projects were a center of trafficking, spawning a wave of dealers and addicts that had you keeping your eyes open at night.

My first week in 19 Willoughby I'd set up my office in the back bedroom, which had big gated windows looking into the backyard. I was sitting in front of my first laptop seeking inspiration when a man appeared in my backyard with a TV in his arms. He'd somehow hopped my neighbor's fence with it, and was preparing to do the same to mine to escape onto the street. I was about to call the cops when, over the fence abutting the street, two policemen hopped over and snagged the thief. I felt like I was watching a live theatrical version of the reality show *Cops*. Welcome to Fort Greene, I guess.

In all my years in Brooklyn I've never been mugged. There's only been one robbery at one of my places in Fort Greene, and it was my fault. As I was leaving one morning a FedEx package arrived. I got distracted as I was signing, and left my door open. When I got home my VCR was gone. Much worse, my satin *Soul Train* jacket, with my name embossed on the lapel, was stolen too. Somewhere out there is my personalized *Soul Train* jacket, a loss I mourn to this day.

After *She's Gotta Have It* (which I'll get to in a bit) was released in 1986, Fort G became internationally known as home base to my generation of artists. What Spike's film did was expand that early community, and attract other artsy black folk. Chris Rock, Rosie Perez, rapper Daddy-O of Stetsasonic, Living Colour's Vernon Reid, actress Alva Rogers of *Daughters of the Dust*, saxophonist/bandleader Steve Coleman, and Def Jam executive Bill Stephney were among the wave that moved to Fort Greene post-Spike. *The New York Times* was among the many publications that profiled the area, making Fort Greene synonymous with a "Brooklyn boheme" vibe. Spike was very much the mayor of that moment, being the most celebrated artist, the biggest employer of local talent, and a buyer of real estate. At one point he owned five buildings in Fort Greene.

This mix of youth, creativity, and proximity meant parties were a regular staple of Fort Greene. I'd roll into the house of actor Wesley Snipes or cartoonist Barbara Brandon for food, drinks, and dancing. There are folks I saw at those parties who married each other, had kids and, in a few cases, are now divorced. There was lots of sex to be had, and lots of cheating too. 15

One tangible document of the creative ferment in Fort Greene, and the overall New York black community, was a photo taken by Anthony Barboza for an unpublished *The New York Times Magazine* piece on the "new black aesthetic" by Trey Ellis in 1989. It was taken at the then new offices of Spike's 40 Acres and a Mule Filmworks on DeKalb Avenue across from Brooklyn Technical High School. Most in the photo were residents of brownstone Brooklyn—Spike; the writer Lisa Jones; her sister, the art historian Keli; visual artist Lorna Simpson; guitarist Vernon Reid; Bill Stephney; Chris Rock; and myself. In addition, there were fellow travelers from Harlem, Warrington and Reggie Hudlin, and downtown Manhattan icons like theater director George C. Wolf, Fab Five Freddie, and Russell Simmons.

While living at 19 Willoughby I learned what kind of writer, what kind of lover, and even what kind of son I was. But the most surprising revelation was that I was a mentor and, like my mother, a kind of teacher. Not only did I write about artists and hang with them, but I found myself being a kind of one-man support network for people—mostly aspiring artists—I believed in. During the mid-eighties they tended to be my peers, gifted folks who needed some contacts or an introduction to someone to move forward. This dynamic was at work with Russell, as well as with Andre Harrell, a so-so MC who'd go on to form the signature rap label Uptown, and the indie filmmaking brothers Warrington and Reggie Hudlin in the years before they broke through with the hit comedy *House Party*.

Over time I grew more settled in the role, and I became a more hands-on mentor, either collaborating with younger artists or critiquing screenplays, essays, or recordings with tough love. My attorney used to tell me I was a natural producer, but at first I wasn't sure if that was a good thing. Producers in film and television seemed more businessmen than artists, and I always saw myself as a creator.

Yet, as I came to understand the place where mentoring, criticism, and producing overlapped, I moved into that sphere more gracefully than I'd ever imagined. Somewhere in my makeup—perhaps from my mother—I had a nurturing gene that first manifested itself at 19 Willoughby, and that would blossom in the years ahead, and would, in fact, define my life, and self-image, as much as writing.

A few of the people I helped became household names, but, like the 20 majority of ambitious folks who use the city as a springboard, most either went on to humble careers or didn't make it at all. Sometimes they were too insecure to survive the disappointments and rejection. Others allowed their egos to blind them to their limitations, and sometimes, despite immense talent, never learned to play well with others. Whether these artists won or lost, I found being close to their struggles exciting and drew lessons from them that I applied to myself.

The most important lesson was to measure myself not by sudden success or rapid failure but by my body of work. My dream was to write a bookshelf of volumes, so many that one day I might drown in them, paper and ink suffocating me in an ocean of my own thoughts. More practically, I wanted to have a full, active life, and being productive seemed the way to ensure that.

Many writers aspire to be Ralph Ellison, to write a starburst of a book that would light the literary sky forever. I was more interested in emulating Richard Wright, Langston Hughes, or Gordon Parks, all of whom had long, varied careers that produced many works and embraced many disciplines. This philosophy gave me patience and a perspective on success (or lack of it). So many folks I met burned out on early success and early failure. If you were in it for the long haul, rolling with the highs and lows was easier, knowing it was all part of a larger whole. Jimi Hendrix may be a deeply romantic figure in our culture, but I'd rather have the body of work of Prince and Stevie Wonder (not to mention the life span). Achieving sustained excellence is what I preached to others and sought for myself.

Discussion Questions

1. Who is the "Spike" that calls the author at the start of the essay? What do you know of this Brooklyn filmmaker's work?
2. Explain what you think Nelson George means when he says, "I was back in Brooklyn, but to a very different 'hood than the one I'd grown up in." Was Fort Greene entirely different from the Tilden projects where he grew up?
3. What are the advantages to living in Fort Greene especially for a music critic such as Nelson?
4. Why do you think Fort Greene was such a creative area in the 1980s? What reputation does it have currently?
5. What significant self-realization does Nelson George have while living at 19 Willoughby?
6. What lessons about writing and fame does the author learn?
7. Nelson claims that the influence of Fort Greene on black pop culture came close to rivaling that of the Harlem Renaissance of the 1920s. Where do you

think the next new wave of artists and writers will come from? What will their subject matter be?

Writing Tasks

- Write an essay in which you describe the effects your living space and/or neighborhood have on your life.
- Write an essay in which you explore the work of a famous Fort Greene resident such as novelist Richard Wright, filmmaker Spike Lee, poets Walt Whitman or Marianne Moore, or basketball player Bernard King. Alternately, research and write about a famous New Yorker who hails from your neighborhood.
- Research the early history of Fort Greene. Was it once an actual fort? Who advocated for Fort Greene park? Who were its earliest residents?

Here Is New York

E. B. White

E. B. White was born in 1899 in Mount Vernon, New York and graduated from Cornell University. He joined *The New Yorker* magazine in 1925 and wrote columns in "Talk of the Town." It was while living in Brooklyn that he wrote two famous children's books: *Stuart Little* (1945) and *Charlotte's Web* (1952). White died in 1985.

Pre-Reading

What do you believe makes New York unlike any other city?

On any person who desires such queer prizes, New York will bestow the gift of loneliness and the gift of privacy. It is this largess that accounts for the presence within the city's walls of a considerable section of the population; for the residents of Manhattan are to a large extent strangers who have pulled up stakes somewhere and come to town, seeking sanctuary or fulfillment or some greater or lesser grail. The capacity to make such dubious gifts is a mysterious quality of New York. It can destroy an individual, or it can fulfill him, depending a good deal on luck. No one should come to New York to live unless he is willing to be lucky.

New York is the concentrate of art and commerce and sport and religion and entertainment and finance, bringing to a single compact arena the gladiator, the evangelist, the promoter, the actor, the trader and the merchant. It carries on its lapel the unexpungeable odor of the long past, so that no matter where you sit in New York you feel the vibrations of great times and tall deeds, of queer people and events and undertakings. I am sitting at the moment in a stifling hotel room in 90-degree heat, halfway down an air shaft, in midtown. No air moves in or out of the room, yet I am curiously affected by emanations from the immediate surroundings. I am twenty-two blocks from where Rudolph Valentino lay in state, eight blocks from where Nathan Hale was executed, five blocks from the publisher's office where Ernest Hemingway hit Max Eastman on the nose, four miles from where Walt Whitman sat sweating out editorials for the Brooklyn Eagle, thirty-four blocks from the street Willa Cather lived in when she came to New York to write books about Nebraska. . . . (I could continue

1

this list indefinitely); and for that matter I am probably occupying the very room that any number of exalted and some wise memorable characters sat in, some of them on hot, breathless afternoons, lonely and private and full of their own sense of emanations from without.

New York blends the gift of privacy with the excitement of participation; and better than most dense communities it succeeds in insulating the individual (if he wants it, and almost everybody wants or needs it) against all enormous and violent and wonderful events that are taking place every minute. Since I have been sitting in this miasmic air shaft, a good many rather splashy events have occurred in town. A man shot and killed his wife in a fit of jealousy. It caused no stir outside his block and got only small mention in the papers. I did not attend. Since my arrival, the greatest air show ever staged in all the world took place in town. I didn't attend and neither did most of the eight million other inhabitants, although they say there was quite a crowd. I didn't even hear any planes except a couple of westbound commercial airliners that habitually use this air shaft to fly over. . . .

I mention these merely to show that New York is peculiarly constructed to absorb almost anything that comes along (whether a thousand-foot liner out of the East or a twenty-thousand-man convention out of the West) without inflicting the event on its inhabitants; so that every event is, in a sense, optional, and the inhabitant is in the happy position of being able to choose his spectacle and so conserve his soul. In most metropolises, small and large, the choice is often not with the individual at all. . . .

The quality in New York that insulates its inhabitants from life may   5
simply weaken them as individuals. Perhaps it is healthier to live in a community where, when a cornice falls, you feel the blow; where, when the governor passes, you see at any rate his hat.

I am not defending New York in this regard. Many of its settlers are probably here merely to escape, not face, reality. But whatever it means, it is a rather rare gift, and I believe it has a positive effect on the creative capacities of New Yorkers—for creation is in part merely the business of forgoing the great and small distractions.

Although New York often imparts a feeling of great forlornness or forsakeness, it seldom seems dead or unresourceful; and you always feel that either by shifting your location ten blocks or by reducing your fortune by five dollars you can experience rejuvenation. Many people who have no real independence of spirit depend on the city's tremendous variety and sources of excitement for spiritual sustenance and maintenance of morale. In the country there are a few chances of sudden rejuvenation—a shift in weather, perhaps, or something arriving in the mail. But in New York the chances are endless. I think that although many persons are here from some excess of spirit (which caused them to break away from their small town), some, too, are here from a deficiency of spirit, who find in New York a protection, or an easy substitution.

There are roughly three New Yorks. There is, first, the New York of the man or woman who was born here, who takes the city for granted and accepts its size and its turbulence as natural and inevitable. Second, there is the New York of the commuter—the city that is devoured by locusts each day and spat out each night. Third, there is the New York of the person who was born somewhere else and came to New York in quest of something. Of these three trembling cities the greatest is the last—the city of final destination, the city that is a goal. It is this third city that accounts for New York's high-strung disposition, its poetical deportment, its dedication to the arts, and its incomparable achievements. Commuters give the city its tidal restlessness; natives give it solidity and continuity; but the settlers give it passion. And whether it is a farmer arriving from Italy to set up a small grocery store in a slum, or a young girl arriving from a small town in Mississippi to escape the indignity of being observed by her neighbors, or a boy arriving from the Corn Belt with a manuscript in his suitcase and a pain in his heart, it makes no difference: each embraces New York with the intense excitement of first love, each absorbs New York with the fresh eyes of an adventurer, each generates heat and light to dwarf the Consolidated Edison Company. . . .

A poem compresses much in a small space and adds music, thus heightening its meaning. The city is like poetry: it compresses all life, all races and breeds, into a small island and adds music and the accompaniment of internal engines. The island of Manhattan is without any doubt the greatest human concentrate on earth, the poem whose magic is comprehensible to millions of permanent residents but whose full meaning will always remain illusive. At the feet of the tallest and plushiest offices lie the crummiest slums. The genteel mysteries housed in the Riverside Church are only a few blocks from the voodoo charms of Harlem. The merchant princes, riding to Wall Street in their limousines down the East River Drive, pass within a few hundred yards of the gypsy kings; but the princes do not know they are passing kings, and the kings are not up yet anyway—they live a more leisurely life than the princes and get drunk more consistently.

New York is nothing like Paris; it is nothing like London; and it is not   10
Spokane multiplied by sixty, or Detroit multiplied by four. It is by all odds the loftiest of cities. It even managed to reach the highest point in the sky at the lowest moment of the depression. The Empire State Building shot twelve hundred and fifty feet into the air when it was madness to put out as much as six inches of new growth. (The building has a mooring mast

that no dirigible has ever tied to; it employs a man to flush toilets in slack times; it has been hit by an airplane in a fog, struck countless times by lightning, and been jumped off of by so many unhappy people that pedestrians instinctively quicken step when passing Fifth Avenue and 34th Street.)

Manhattan has been compelled to expand skyward because of the absence of any other direction in which to grow. This, more than any other thing, is responsible for its physical majesty. It is to the nation what the white church spire is to the village—the visible symbol of aspiration and faith, the white plume saying that the way is up. . . .

It is a miracle that New York works at all. The whole thing is implausible. Every time the residents brush their teeth, millions of gallons of water must be drawn from the Catskills and the hills of Westchester. When a young man in Manhattan writes a letter to his girl in Brooklyn, the love message gets blown to her through a pneumatic tube—pfft—just like that. The subterranean system of telephone cables, power lines, steam pipes, gas mains and sewer pipes is reason enough to abandon the island to the gods and the weevils. Every time an incision is made in the pavement, the noisy surgeons expose ganglia that are tangled beyond belief. By rights New York should have destroyed itself long ago, from panic or fire or rioting or failure of some vital supply line in its circulatory system or from some deep labyrinthine short circuit. Long ago the city should have experienced an insoluble traffic snarl at some impossible bottleneck. It should have perished of hunger when food lines failed for a few days. It should have been wiped out by a plague starting in its slums or carried in by ships' rats. It should have been overwhelmed by the sea that licks at it on every side. The workers in its myriad cells should have succumbed to nerves, from the fearful pall of smoke-fog that drifts over every few days from Jersey, blotting out all light at noon and leaving the high offices suspended, men groping and depressed, and the sense of world's end. It should have been touched in the head by the August heat and gone off its rocker.

Mass hysteria is a terrible force, yet New Yorkers seem always to escape it by some tiny margin: they sit in stalled subways without claustrophobia, they extricate themselves from panic situations by some lucky wisecrack, they meet confusion and congestion with patience and grit—a sort of perpetual muddling through. Every facility is inadequate—the hospitals and schools and playgrounds are overcrowded, the express highways are feverish, the unimproved highways and bridges are bottlenecks; there is not enough air and not enough light, and there is usually either too much heat or too little. But the city makes up for its hazards and its deficiencies by supplying its citizens with massive doses of a supplementary vitamin—the sense of belonging to something unique, cosmopolitan, mighty and unparalleled. . . .

The oft-quoted thumbnail sketch of New York is, of course: "It's a wonderful place, but I'd hate to live there." I have an idea that people from villages and small towns, people accustomed to the convenience and the friendliness of neighborhood over-the-fence living, are unaware that life in New York follows the neighborhood pattern. The city is literally a composite of tens of thousands of tiny neighborhood units. There are, of course, the big districts and big units: Chelsea and Murray Hill and Gramercy (which are residential units), Harlem (a racial unit), Greenwich Village (a unit dedicated to the arts and other matters), and there is Radio City (a commercial development), Peter Cooper Village (a housing unit), the Medical Center (a sickness unit) and many other sections each of which has some distinguishing characteristic. But the curious thing about New York is that each large geographical unit is composed of countless small neighborhoods. Each neighborhood is virtually self-sufficient. Usually it is no more than two or three blocks long and a couple of blocks wide. Each area is a city within a city within a city. Thus, no matter where you live in New York, you will find within a block or two a grocery store, a barbershop, a newsstand and shoeshine shack, an ice-coal-and-wood cellar (where you write your order on a pad outside as you walk by), a dry cleaner, a laundry, a delicatessen (beer and sandwiches delivered at any hour to your door), a flower shop, an undertaker's parlor, a movie house, a radio-repair shop, a stationer, a haberdasher, a tailor, a drugstore, a garage, a tearoom, a saloon, a hardware store, a liquor store, a shoe-repair shop. Every block or two, in most residential sections of New York, is a little main street. A man starts for work in the morning and before he has gone two hundred yards he has completed half a dozen missions: bought a paper, left a pair of shoes to be soled, picked up a pack of cigarettes, ordered a bottle of whiskey to be dispatched in the opposite direction against his home-coming, written a message to the unseen forces of the wood cellar, and notified the dry cleaner that a pair of trousers awaits call. Homeward bound eight hours later, he buys a bunch of pussy willows, a Mazda bulb, a drink, a shine—all between the corner where he steps off the bus and his apartment. So complete is each neighborhood, and so strong the sense of neighborhood, that many a New Yorker spends a lifetime within the confines of an area smaller than a country village. Let him walk two blocks from his corner and he is in a strange land and will feel uneasy till he gets back.

Storekeepers are particularly conscious of neighborhood boundary 15 lines. A woman friend of mine moved recently from one apartment to another, a distance of three blocks. When she turned up, the day after the move, at the same grocer's that she had patronized for years, the proprietor was in ecstasy—almost in tears—at seeing her. "I was afraid," he said, "now that you've moved away I wouldn't be seeing you any more." To him, *away* was three blocks, or about seven hundred and fifty feet. . . .

I've been remembering what it felt like as a young man to live in the same town with giants. When I first arrived in New York my personal giants were a dozen or so columnists and critics and poets whose names appeared regularly in the papers. . . .The city is always full of young worshipful beginners—young actors, young aspiring poets, ballerinas, painters, reporters, singers—each depending on his own brand of tonic to stay alive, each with his own stable of giants.

New York provides not only a continuing excitation but also a spectacle that is continuing. I wander around, re-examining this spectacle, hoping that I can put it on paper. It is Saturday, toward the end of the afternoon. I turn through West 48th Street. From the open windows of the drum and saxophone parlors come the listless sounds of musical instruction, monstrous insect noises in the brooding field of summer. The Cort Theater is disgorging its matinee audience. Suddenly the whole block is filled with the mighty voice of a street singer. He approaches, looking for an audience, a large, cheerful Negro with grand-opera contours, strolling with head thrown back, filling the canyon with uninhibited song. He carries a long cane as his sole prop, and is tidily but casually dressed—slacks, seersucker jacket, a book showing in his pocket. . . .

In the café of the Lafayette, the regulars sit and talk. It is busy yet peaceful. Nursing a drink, I stare through the west windows at the Manufacturers Trust Company and at the red brick fronts on the north side of Ninth Street, watching the red turning slowly to purple as the light dwindles. Brick buildings have a way of turning color at the end of the day, the way a red rose turns bluish as it wilts. The café is a sanctuary. The waiters are ageless and they change not. Nothing has been modernized. Notre Dame stands guard in its travel poster. The coffee is strong and full of chicory, and good.

Walk the Bowery under the El at night and all you feel is a sort of cold guilt. Touched for a dime, you try to drop the coin and not touch the hand, because the hand is dirty; you try to avoid the glance, because the glance accuses. This is not so much personal menace as universal—the cold menace of unresolved human suffering and poverty and the advanced stages of the disease alcoholism. On a summer night the drunks sleep in the open. The sidewalk is a free bed, and there are no lice. Pedestrians step along and over and around the still forms as though walking on a battlefield among the dead. In doorways, on the steps of the savings bank, the bums lie sleeping it off. Standing sentinel at each sleeper's head is the empty bottle from which he drained his release. Wedged in the crook of his arm is the paper bag containing his things. The glib barker on the sight-seeing bus tells his passengers that this is the "street of lost souls," but the Bowery does not think of itself as lost; it meets its peculiar problem in its own way—plenty of gin mills, plenty of flop-houses, plenty of indifference, and always, at the end of the line, Bellevue. . . .

The Consolidated Edison Company says there are eight million people in the five boroughs of New York, and the company is in a position to know. Of these eight million, two million are Jews—or one person in every four. Among this two million who are Jewish are, of course, a great many nationalities—Russian, German, Polish, Rumanian, Austrian, a long list. The Urban League of Greater New York estimates that the number of Negroes in New York is about 700,000. Of these, about 500,000 live in Harlem, a district that extends northward from 110th Street. The Negro population has increased rapidly in the last few years. There are half again as many Negroes in New York today as there were in 1940. There are about 230,000 Puerto Ricans living in New York. There are half a million Irish, half a million Germans. There are 900,000 Russians, 150,000 English, 400,000 Poles, and there are quantities of Finns and Czechs and Swedes and Danes and Norwegians and Latvians and Belgians and Welsh and Greeks, and even Dutch, who have been here from away back. It is very hard to say how many Chinese there are. Officially there are 12,000, but there are many Chinese who are in New York illegally and who don't like census takers.

The collision and the intermingling of these millions of foreign-born people representing so many races and creeds make New York a permanent exhibit of the phenomenon of one world. The citizens of New York are tolerant not only from disposition but from necessity. The city has to be tolerant, otherwise it would explode in a radioactive cloud of hate and rancor and bigotry. If the people were to depart even briefly from the peace of cosmopolitan intercourse, the town would blow up higher than a kite. . . .

To a New Yorker the city is both changeless and changing. In many respects it neither looks nor feels the way it did twenty-five years ago. . . . The slums are gradually giving way to the lofty housing projects—high in stature, high in purpose, low in rent. There are a couple of dozens of these new developments scattered around; each is a city in itself (one of them in the Bronx accommodates twelve thousand families), sky acreage hitherto untilled, lifting people far above the street, standardizing their sanitary life, giving them some place to sit other than an orange crate. Federal money, state money, city money and private money have flowed into these projects. Banks and insurance companies are in back of some of them. Architects have turned the buildings slightly on their bases, to catch more light. In some of them, rents are as low as eight dollars a room. Thousands of new units are still needed and will eventually be built, but New York never quite catches up with itself, is never in equilibrium. In flush times the population mushrooms and the new dwellings sprout from the rock. Come bad times and the population scatters and the lofts are abandoned and the landlord withers and dies.

New York has changed in tempo and in temper during the years I have known it. There is greater tension, increased irritability. You encounter it in many places, in many faces. The normal frustrations of modern life are here multiplied and amplified—a single run of a crosstown bus contains, for the driver, enough frustration and annoyance to carry him over the edge of sanity: the light that changes always an instant too soon, the passenger that bangs on the shut door, the truck that blocks the only opening, the coin that slips to the floor, the question asked at the wrong moment. There is greater tension and there is greater speed. Taxis roll faster than they rolled ten years ago—and they were rolling fast then. Hackmen used to drive with verve; now they sometimes seem to drive with desperation, toward the ultimate tip. On the West Side Highway, approaching the city, the motorist is swept along in a trance—a sort of fever of inescapable motion, goaded from behind, hemmed in on either side, a mere chip in a millrace. . . .

The subtlest change in New York is something people don't speak much about but that is in everyone's mind. The city, for the first time in its long history, is destructible. A single flight of planes no bigger than a wedge of geese can quickly end this island fantasy, burn the towers, crumble the bridges, turn the underground passages into lethal chambers, cremate the millions. The intimation of mortality is part of New York now: in the sound of jets overhead, in the black headlines of the latest edition.

All dwellers in cities must live with the stubborn fact of annihilation; in New York the fact is somewhat more concentrated because of the concentration of the city itself, and because, of all targets, New York has a certain clear priority. In the mind of whatever perverted dreamer might loose the lightning, New York must hold a steady, irresistible charm. . . .

A block or two west of the new City of Man in Turtle Bay there is an old willow tree that presides over an interior garden. It is a battered tree, long suffering and much climbed, held together by strands of wire but beloved of those who know it. In a way it symbolizes the city: life under difficulties, growth against odds, sap-rise in the midst of concrete, and the steady reaching for the sun. Whenever I look at it nowadays, and feel the cold shadow of the planes, I think: "This must be saved, this particular thing, this very tree." If it were to go, all would go—this city, this mischievous and marvelous monument which not to look upon would be like death.

25

Discussion Questions

1. What are the two "dubious gifts" New York presents its citizens? What can they do to an individual?
2. According to White, what are the three types of New Yorkers? What conclusion does he draw from his divisions?
3. What does the author mean when he says that in New York "every event is, in a sense, optional"?
4. Why does White say: "It is a miracle that New York works at all"?
5. How does White define the city in relation to its neighborhoods?
6. What thoughts cross White's mind when he walks past a homeless person? Discuss his ambivalence.
7. What function does the metaphor of an old willow tree in the concluding paragraph serve? Can you think of another metaphor to describe New York?
8. This essay was written in 1948. How have things changed? In what ways are they the same?

Writing Tasks

- Choose your favorite passage. Summarize and respond to it according to your personal experience.
- Write an essay that encapsulates the characteristics of "your" New York.
- Look up a few of White's many references to people, places, and things. Share with your classmates what you discover.

Making Connections

1. Write an essay on the traits that make a New Yorker that incorporates and elaborates on the reflections made in two or more of the readings in this section.
2. Write an essay that discusses the elements that define your neighborhood (or your favorite place in the city). Consider the following possibilities, utilized by the writers you have read, for developing your essay. You may discuss a personal memory, describe the people and the highlights of the neighborhood (bridges, buildings, parks, restaurants, etc.), and/or document its sights and sounds. Consider also themes such as privacy, community, tensions, neighborhood transformations, and/or your relationship to the place where you dwell.

CHAPTER 2

Immigrants and the American Dream

Shop in Chinatown © Bob Krist/CORBIS.

How far my little grass-roofed, hill-wrapped village from this gigantic rebellion which was New York! And New York's rebellion called to me excitedly, this savagery which piled great concrete block on concrete block, topping at the last moment as in an afterthought, with crowns as delicate as pinnacled ice; this lavishness which, without a prayer, pillaged coal mines and waterfalls for light, festooning the great nature-severed city with diamonds of frozen electrical phenomena—it fascinated me . . . .

Younghill Kang From *East Meets West* (1937)

Immigrants and the American Dream

"Give me your tired, your poor,/Your huddled masses yearning to breathe free . . ." Ever since these words were inscribed at the foot of the Statue of Liberty over a century ago, many have responded and made their passage to New York, their land of promise. This chapter presents a historical and cultural cross section of these numerous crossings, each of which depicts a unique experience and an extravagant vision that contribute to the greatness of New York. These nine readings chronicle the dreams and sacrifices, struggles and fulfillment of individuals in their process of becoming New Yorkers.

"The New Colossus," by Emma Lazarus, is a welcoming invitation that echoes the promise of the American Dream. Her poem speaks of hope and a power that transforms and delivers new lives. Anzia Yezierska, a Jewish immigrant from Russia, is one of them. "America and I" is an intimate account of her personal journey from a sweatshop worker on the Lower East Side to a notable writer. The invaluable lesson she learns from the first Pilgrims inspires and empowers her to create her own America.

Langston Hughes' poem "Good Morning" voices the discontents of those who have had to struggle to make New York their home. Hughes communicates a skepticism that exposes the true features of the American Dream, which is merely an unattainable fable for those who have been victims of racism and discrimination. Along with Hughes, Claude McKay, who is another Harlem Renaissance poet, reaches out to the past. His "The Tropics in New York" expresses a deep longing and nostalgia for his homeland triggered by looking at a New York storefront.

Frances Chung presents two different scenarios in her poems, "Yo Vivo En El Barrio Chino" and "Riding the Subway Is an Adventure." The former depicts the speaker's ambivalence towards her neighborhood in Chinatown, and the latter describes an unsettling subway trip taken by a newly arrived immigrant who faces a language barrier.

In "The Money," Junot Díaz learns important lessons in his humorous and ironic story about being part of the Dominican diaspora. One lesson involves family trust and the other reveals the duplicity of his "best" friends. Articulating a different experience of the American Dream is Edwidge Danticat's "New York Was My City on the Hill." In her essay, Danticat traces the footsteps of her parents from Haiti to New York and recounts their labor and sacrifices that have inspired her own intellectual pilgrimage in what used to be her "city on the hill." Suki Kim's "Facing Poverty with a Rich Girl's Habits" explores another set of challenges that young immigrants face today. She expresses her dilemma relating to cultural identity, class difference, and generational prejudice growing up as a young Korean in New York.

The New Colossus

Emma Lazarus

Emma Lazarus (1849–1887) was of German-Jewish descent. In 1883 a committee was formed to raise funds for a pedestal for "Liberty Enlightening the People," a gift from the French to be installed on Ellis Island. "The New Colossus" was written as part of this fund-raising effort.

Pre-Reading

What does the Statue of Liberty mean to you?

The New Colossus

Not like the brazen giant of Greek fame,   1
With conquering limbs astride from land to land;
Here at our sea-washed, sunset gates shall stand
A mighty woman with a torch, whose flame
Is the imprisoned lightning, and her name   5
Mother of Exiles. From her beacon-hand
Glows world-wide welcome; her mild eyes command
The air-bridged harbor that twin cities frame.
"Keep, ancient lands, your storied pomp!" cries she
With silent lips. "Give me your tired, your poor,   10
Your huddled masses yearning to breathe free,
The wretched refuse of your teeming shore.
Send these, the homeless, tempest-tost to me,
I lift my lamp beside the golden door!"

Emma Lazarus, *The Poems of Emma Lazarus*, Vol. 1, 1889.

Discussion Questions

1. What is the significance of the title?
2. What distinguishes Lady Liberty from her Greek predecessor?
3. Can you determine what the phrase "twin cities" refers to? What bridge is referred to in the poem?
4. What do you think Lazarus and the committee who commissioned her work wanted to communicate? Do you think her promise still holds true?

Writing Tasks

- Write a response that compares the message of the poem to your own experiences or observations.
- Write an explication of this poem that fully analyzes the meaning of each line.

Welcome to the Land of Freedom Illustation © Stefano Bianchetti/Corbis.

Good Morning

Langston Hughes

Pre-Reading

Can you think of any significant lessons you have learned from your parents about your heritage?

Good Morning

Good morning daddy!	1
I was born here, he said,	
watched Harlem grow	
until colored folks spread	
from river to river	5
across the middle of Manhattan	
out of Penn Station	
dark tenth of a nation,	
planes from Puerto Rico,	
and holds of boats, chico,	10
up from Cuba Haiti Jamaica,	
in buses marked New York	
from Georgia Florida Louisiana	
to Harlem Brooklyn the Bronx	
but most of all to Harlem	15
dusky sash across Manhattan	
I've seen them come dark	
wondering	
wide-eyed	
dreaming	20
out of Penn Station—	
but the trains are late.	

The gates open—
Yet there're bars
at each gate.   25
What happens
to a dream deferred?
Daddy, ain't you heard?

Discussion Questions

1. In the time when the poem was written, what ethnic groups comprised the population in Harlem?
2. Why do you think Hughes titled the poem "Good Morning"?
3. What is the main idea of the poem?
4. What does Hughes imply in lines 20–25. "out of Penn Station—/ but the trains are late./ The gates open—/ Yet there are bars/ at each gate"?
5. What do you think the phrase "a dream deferred" in line 26 means?

Writing Tasks

- Analyze the literary elements of this poem that help convey its theme and power. Consider, for example, the author's use of rhythm, tone, imagery, and/ or irony.
- The key to understanding poetry is in listening to the spoken and unspoken words and reading for details. Try to transform this poem into a short story, focusing on probable dialogue, descriptions, and actions that are beneath the surface of the poem.

America and I

Anzia Yezierska

Anzia Yezierska (1881–1970) was born in the Russian-Polish ghetto of Plotsk, and emigrated to New York City with her family in 1890. She worked as a servant, a laundress, and a button sewer in sweatshops on the Lower East Side. She also attended night school and in 1904 graduated from Columbia Teachers College. She is the author of five novels and two volumes of short stories, *Hungry Hearts* (1920) and *Children of Loneliness* (1923).

Pre-Reading

What is required for success in America?

As one of the dumb, voiceless ones I speak. One of the millions of immigrants beating, beating out their hearts at your gates for a breath of understanding. [1]

Ach! America! From the other end of the earth from where I came, America was a land of living hope, woven of dreams, aflame with longing and desire.

Choked for ages in the airless oppression of Russia, the Promised Land rose up—wings for my stifled spirit—sunlight burning through my darkness—freedom singing to me in my prison—deathless songs tuning prison-bars into strings of a beautiful violin.

I arrived in America. My young, strong body, my heart and soul pregnant with the unlived lives of generations clamoring for expression.

What my mother and father and their mother and father never had a chance to give out in Russia, I would give out in America. The hidden sap of centuries would find release; colors that never saw light—songs that died unvoiced—romance that never had a chance to blossom in the black life of the Old World. [5]

In the golden land of flowing opportunity I was to find my work that was denied me in the sterile village of my forefathers. Here I was to be free from the dead drudgery for bread that held me down in Russia. For the first time in America, I'd cease to be a slave of the belly. I'd be a creator, a giver, a human being! My work would be the living job of fullest self-expression.

Originally appeared in *CHILDREN OF LONELINESS*, 1923.

But from my high visions, my golden hopes, I had to put my feet down on earth. I had to have food and shelter. I had to have the money to pay for it.

I was in America, among the Americans, but not *of* them. No speech, no common language, no way to win a smile of understanding from them, only my young, strong body and my untried faith. Only my eager, empty hands, and my full heart shining from my eyes!

God from the world! Here I was with so much richness in me, but my mind was not wanted without the language. And my body, unskilled, untrained, was not even wanted in the factory. Only one of two chances was left open to me: the kitchen, or minding babies.

My first job was as a servant in an Americanized family. Once, long ago,   10
they came from the same village from where I came. But they were so well-dressed, so well-fed, so successful in America, that they were ashamed to remember their mother tongue.

"What were to be my wages?" I ventured timidly, as I looked up to the well-fed, well-dressed "American" man and woman.

They looked at me with a sudden coldness. What have I said to draw away from me their warmth? Was it so low from me to talk of wages? I shrank back into myself like a low-down bargainer. Maybe they're so high up in well-being they can't any more understand my low thoughts for money.

From his rich height the man preached down to me that I must not be so grabbing for wages. Only just landed from the ship and already thinking about money when I should be thankful to associate with "Americans."

The woman, out of her smooth, smiling fatness assured me that this was my chance for a summer vacation in the country with her two lovely children. My great chance to learn to be a civilized being, to become an American by living with them.

So, made to feel that I was in the hands of American friends, invited   15
to share with them their home, their plenty, their happiness, I pushed out from my head the worry for wages. Here was my first chance to begin my life in the sunshine, after my long darkness. My laugh was all over my face as I said to them: "I'll trust myself to you. What I'm worth you'll give me." And I entered their house like a child by the hand.

The best of me I gave them. Their house cares were my house cares. I got up early. I worked till late. All that my soul hungered to give I put into the passion with which I scrubbed floors, scoured pots, and washed clothes. I was so grateful to mingle with the American people, to hear the music of the American language, that I never knew tiredness.

There was such a freshness in my brains and such a willingness in my heart that I could go on and on—not only with the work of the house, but work with my head—learning new words from the children, the grocer, the butcher, the iceman. I was not even afraid to ask for words from the policeman on the street. And every new word made me see new American things with American eyes. I felt like a Columbus, finding new worlds through every new word.

But words alone were only for the inside of me. The outside of me still branded me for a steerage immigrant. I had to have clothes to forget myself that I'm a stranger yet. And so I had to have money to buy these clothes.

The month was up. I was so happy! Now I'd have money. *My own, earned* money. Money to buy a new shirt on my back—shoes on my feet. Maybe yet an American dress and hat!

Ach! How high rose my dreams! How plainly I saw all that I would do   20
with my visionary wages shining like a light over my head!

In my imagination I already walked in my new American clothes. How beautiful I looked as I saw myself like a picture before my eyes! I saw how I would throw away my immigrant rags tied up in my immigrant shawl. With money to buy—free money in my hands—I'd show them that I could look like an American in a day.

Like a prisoner in his last night in prison, counting the seconds that will free him from his chains, I trembled breathlessly for the minute I'd get the wages in my hand.

Before dawn I rose.

I shined up the house like a jewel-box.

I prepared breakfast and waited with my heart in my mouth for my   25
lady and gentleman to rise. At last I heard them stirring. My eyes were jumping out of my head to them when I saw them coming in and seating themselves by the table.

Like a hungry cat rubbing up to its boss for meat, so I edged and simpered around them as I passed them the food. Without my will, like a beggar, my hand reached out to them.

The breakfast was over. And no word yet from my wages.

"Gottuniu!" I thought to myself. "Maybe they're so busy with their own things they forgot it's the day for my wages. Could they who have everything know what I was to do with my first American dollars? How could they, soaking in plenty, how could they feel the longing and the fierce hunger in me, pressing up through each visionary dollar? How could they know the gnawing ache of my avid fingers for the feel of my own, earned dollars? My dollars that I could spend like a free person. *My* dollars that would make me feel with everybody alike!"

Lunch came. Lunch past.

Oi-i weh! Not a word yet about my money.   30

It was near dinner. And not a word yet about my wages.

I began to set the table. But my head—it swam away from me. I broke a glass. The silver dropped from my nervous fingers. I couldn't stand it any longer. I dropped everything and rushed over to my American lady and gentleman.

"Oi weh! The money—my money—my wages!" I cried breathlessly.

Four cold eyes turned on me.

"Wages? Money?" The four eyes turned into hard stone as they looked me up and down. "Haven't you a comfortable bed to sleep, and three good meals a day? You're only a month here. Just came to America. And you already think about money. Wait till you're worth any money. What use are you without knowing English? You should be glad we keep you here. It's like a vacation for you. Other girls pay money yet to be in the country."

It went black for my eyes. I was so chocked no words came to my lips. Even the tears went dry in my throat.

I left. Not a dollar for all my work.

For a long, long time my heart ached and ached like a sore wound. If murderers would have robbed me and killed me it wouldn't have hurt me so much. I couldn't think through my pain. The minute I'd see before me how they looked at me, the words they said to me—then everything began to bleed in me. And I was helpless.

For a long, long time the thought of ever working in an "American" family made me tremble with fear, like the fear of wild wolves. No—never again would I trust myself to an "American" family, no matter how fine their language and how sweet their smile.

It was blotted out in me all trust in friendship from "Americans." But the life in me still burned to live. The hope in me still craved to hope. In darkness, in dirt, in hunger and want, but only to live on!

There had been no end to my day—working for the "American" family.

Now rejecting false friendships from higher-ups in America, I turned back to the Ghetto. I worked on a hard bench with my own kind on either side of me. I knew before I began what my wages were to be. I knew what my hours were to be. And I knew the feeling of the end of the day.

From the outside my second job seemed worse than the first. It was in a sweat-shop of a Delancey Street basement, kept up by an old, wrinkled woman that looked like a black witch of greed. My work was sewing on buttons. While the morning was still dark I walked into a dark basement. And darkness met me when I turned out of the basement.

Day after day, week after week, all the contact I got with America was handling dead buttons. The money I earned was hardly enough to pay for bread and rent. I didn't have a room to myself. I didn't even have a bed. I slept on a mattress on the floor in a rat-hole of a room occupied by a dozen other immigrants. I was always hungry—oh, so hungry! The scant meals

35

40

I could afford only sharpened my appetite for real food. But I felt myself better off than working in the "American" family, where I had three good meals a day and a bed to myself. With all the hunger and darkness of the sweat-shop, I had at least the evening to myself. And all night was mine. When all were asleep, I used to creep up on the roof of the tenement and talk out my heart in silence to the stars in the sky.

Interior of Tenement House © CORBIS.

"Who am I? What am I? What do I want with my life? Where is America? Is there an America? What is this wilderness in which I'm lost?"   45

I'd hurl my questions and then think and think. And I could not tear it out of me, the feeling that America must be somewhere, somehow—only I couldn't find it—*My America,* where I would work for love and not for a living. I was like a thing following blindly after something far off in the dark!

"Oi weh!" I'd stretch out my hand up in the air. "My head is so lost in America! What's the use of all my working if I'm not in it? Dead buttons is not me."

Then the busy season started in the shop. The mounds of buttons grew and grew. The long day stretched out longer. I had to begin with the buttons earlier and stay with them till later in the night. The old witch turned into a huge greedy maw for wanting more and more buttons.

For a glass of tea, for a slice of herring over black bread, she would buy us up to stay another and another hour, till there seemed no end to her demands.

One day, the light of self-assertion broke into my cellar darkness. 50

"I don't want the tea. I don't want your herring," I said with terrible boldness. "I only want to go home. I only want the evening to myself!"

"You fresh mouth, you!" cried the old witch. "You learned already too much in America. I want no clock-watchers in my shop. Out you go!"

I was driven out to cold and hunger. I could no longer pay for my mattress on the floor. I no longer could buy the bite in my mouth. I walked the streets. I knew what it is to be alone in a strange city, among strangers.

But I laughed through my tears. So I learned too much already in America because I wanted the whole evening to myself? Well America has yet to teach me still more: how to get not only the whole evening to myself, but a whole day a week like the American workers.

That sweat-shop was a bitter memory but a good school. It fitted me for 55 a regular factory. I could walk in boldly and say I could work at something, even if it was only sewing on buttons.

Gradually, I became a trained worker. I worked in a light, airy factory, only eight hours a day. My boss was no longer a sweater and a blood-squeezer. The first freshness of the morning was mine. And the whole evening was mine. All day Sunday was mine.

Now I had better food to eat. I slept on a better bed. Now, I even looked dressed up like the American-born. But inside of me I knew that I was not yet an American. I choked with longing when I met an American-born, and I could say nothing.

Something cried dumb in me. I couldn't help it. I didn't know what it was I wanted. I only knew I wanted. I wanted. Like the hunger in the heart that never gets food.

An English class for foreigners started in our factory. The teacher had such a good, friendly face, her eyes looked so understanding, as if she could see right into my heart. So I went to her one day for advice:

"I don't know what is with me the matter," I began. "I have no rest in 60 me. I never get done what I want."

"What is it you want to do, child?" she asked me.

"I want to do something with my head, my feelings. All day long, only with my hands I work."

"First you must learn English." She patted me as if I was not yet grown up. "Put your mind on that, and then we'll see."

So for a time I learned the language. I could almost begin to think with English words in my head. But in my heart the emptiness still hurt. I burned to give, to give something, to do something, to be something. The dead work with my hands was killing me. My work left only hard stones on my heart.

Again I went to our factory teacher and cried out to her: "I know   65
already to read and write the English language, but I can't put it into words
what I want. What is it in me so different that can't come out?"

She smiled at me down from her calmness as if I were a little bit out of
my head. "What *do you want* to do?"

"I feel. I see. I hear. And I want to think it out. But I'm like dumb in me.
I only feel I'm different—different from everybody."

She looked at me close and said nothing for a minute. "You ought to
join one of the social clubs of the Women's Association," she advised.

"What's the Women's Association?" I implored greedily.

"A group of American women who are trying to help the working-girl   70
find herself. They have a special department for immigrant girls like you."

I joined the Women's Association. On my first evening there they announced a lecture: "The Happy Worker and His Work," by the Welfare
director of the United Mills Corporation.

"Is there such a thing as a happy worker at his work?" I wondered.
Happiness is only by working at what you love. And what poor girl can
ever find it to work at what she loves? My old dreams about my America
rushed through my mind. Once I thought that in America everybody works
for love. Nobody has to worry for a living. Maybe this welfare man came to
show me the *real* America that till now I sought in vain.

With a lot of polite words the head lady of the Women's Association introduced a higher-up that looked like the king of kings of business. Never before
in my life did I ever see a man with such a sureness in his step, such power
in his face, such friendly positiveness in his eye as when he smiled upon us.

"Efficiency is the new religion of business," he began. "In big business
houses, even in up-to-date factories, they no longer take the first comer and
give him any job that happens to stand empty. Efficiency begins at the employment office. Experts are hired for the one purpose, to find out how best
to fit the worker to his work. It's economy for the boss to make the worker
happy." And then he talked a lot more on efficiency in educated language
that was over my head.

I didn't know exactly what it meant—efficiency—but if it was to make   75
the worker happy at his work, then that's what I had been looking for since
I came to America. I only felt from watching him that he was happy by his
job. And as I looked on this clean, well-dressed, successful one, who wasn't
ashamed to say he rose from an office-boy, it made me feel that I, too, could
lift myself up for a person.

He finished his lecture, telling us about the Vocational-Guidance Center that the Women's Association started.

The very next evening I was at the Vocational-Guidance Center.
There I found a young, college-looking woman. Smartness and health

shining from her eyes! She, too, looked as if she knew her way in America. I could tell at the first glance: here is a person that is happy by what she does.

"I feel you'll understand me," I said right away.

She leaned over with pleasure in her face: "I hope I can."

"I want to work by what's in me. Only, I don't know what's in me. I only feel I'm different." 80

She gave me a quick, puzzled look from the corner of her eyes. "What are you doing now?"

"I'm the quickest shirtwaist hand on the floor. But my heart wastes away by such work. I think and think, and my thoughts can't come out."

"Why don't you think out your thoughts in shirtwaists? You could learn to be a designer. Earn more money."

"I don't want to look on waists. If my hands are sick from waists, how could my head learn to put beauty into them?"

"But you must earn your living at what you know, and rise slowly from job to job." 85

I looked at her office sign: "Vocational Guidance." "What's your vocational guidance?" I asked, "How to rise from job to job—how to earn more money?"

The smile went out from her eyes. But she tried to be kind yet. "What *do* you want?" she asked, with a sigh of last patience.

"I want America to want me."

She fell back in her chair, thunderstruck with my boldness. But yet, in a low voice of educated self-control, she tried to reason with me:

"You have to *show* that you have something special for America before America has need of you." 90

"But I never had a chance to find out what's in me, because I always had to work for a living. Only, I feel it's efficiency for America to find out what's in me so different, so I could give it out by my work."

Her eyes half closed as they bored through me. Her mouth opened to speak, but no words came from her lips. So I flamed up with all that was choking in me like a house on fire:

"America gives free bread and rent to criminals in prison. They got grand houses with sunshine, fresh air, doctors and teachers, even for the crazy ones. Why don't they have free boarding-schools for immigrants— strong people—willing people? Here you see us burning up with something different, and America turns her head away from us."

Her brows lifted and dropped down. She shrugged her shoulders away from me with the look of pity we give to cripples and hopeless lunatics.

"America is no Utopia. First you must become efficient in earning a living before you can indulge in your poetic dreams." 95

I went away from the vocational-guidance office with all the air out of my lungs. All the light out of my eyes. My feet dragged after me like dead wood.

Till now there had always lingered a rosy veil of hope over my emptiness, a hope that a miracle would happen. I would open up my eyes some day and suddenly find the America of my dreams. As a young girl hungry for love sees always before her eyes the picture of lover's arms around her, so I saw always in my heart the vision of Utopian America.

But now I felt that the America of my dreams never was and never could be. Reality had hit me on the head as with a club. I felt that the America that I sought was nothing but a shadow—an echo—a chimera of lunatics and crazy immigrants.

Stripped of all illusion, I looked about me. The long desert of wasting days of drudgery stared me in the face. The drudgery that I had lived through, and the endless drudgery still ahead of me rose over me like a withering wilderness of sand. In vain were all my cryings, in vain were all frantic efforts of my spirit to find the living waters of understanding for my perishing lips. Sand, sand was everywhere. With every seeking, every reaching out I only lost myself deeper and deeper in a vast sea of sand.

I knew now the American language. And I knew now, if I talked to the   100 Americans from morning till night, they could not understand what the Russian soul of me wanted. They could not understand *me* any more than if I talked to them in Chinese. Between my soul and the American soul were worlds of difference that no words could bridge over. What was that difference? What made the Americans so far apart from me?

I began to read the American history. I found from the first pages that America started with a band of Courageous Pilgrims. They had left their native country as I had left mine. They had crossed an unknown ocean and landed in an unknown country, as I.

But the great difference between the first Pilgrims and me was that they expected to make America, build America, create their own world of liberty. I wanted to find it ready made.

I read on. I delved deeper down into the American history. I saw how the Pilgrim Fathers came to a rocky desert country, surrounded by Indian savages on all sides. But undaunted, they pressed on—through danger— through famine, pestilence, and want—they pressed on. They did not ask the Indians for sympathy, for understanding. They made no demands on anybody, but on their own indomitable spirit of persistence.

And I—I was forever begging a crumb of sympathy, a gleam of understanding from strangers who could not understand.

I, when I encountered a few savage Indian scalpers, like the old witch of   105 the sweat-shop, like my "Americanized" countryman, who cheated me of my wages—I, when I found myself on the lonely, untrodden path through which all seekers of the new world must pass, I lost heart and said: "There is no America!"

Then came a light—a great revelation! I saw America—a big idea—a deathless hope—a world still in the making. I saw that it was the glory of America that it was not yet finished. And I, the last comer, had her share to give, small or great, to the making of America, like those Pilgrims who came in the *Mayflower.*

Fired up by this revealing light, I began to build a bridge of understanding between the American-born and myself. Since their life was shut out from such as me, I began to open up my life and the lives of my people to them. And life draws life. In only writing about the Ghetto I found America.

Great chances have come to me. But in my heart is always a deep sadness. I feel like a man who is sitting down to a secret table of plenty, while his near ones and dear ones are perishing before his eyes. My very joy in doing the work I love hurts me like secret guilt, because all about me I see so many with my longings, my burning eagerness, to do and to be, wasting their days in drudgery they hate, merely to buy bread and pay rent. And America is losing all that richness of the soul.

The Americans of tomorrow, the America that is every day nearer coming to be, will be too wise, too open-hearted, too friendly-handed, to let the least lastcomer at their gates knock in vain with his gifts unwanted.

Discussion Questions

1. What is Yezierska's initial impression of America? How does she compare it to her life in Russia?
2. What does she aspire to do when she first arrives in America? What must she do first?
3. Do you think her "Americanized family" treats her fairly? Why or why not?
4. What was the best part of her second job on Delancey Street? Why did she end up losing it?
5. What kind of work does Anzia prefer to do? What is stopping her?
6. Do you agree with the author's argument that immigrants should receive free room and board? Why or why not?
7. What lessons did she learn from the Pilgrims? How did this knowledge transform her idea of what it takes to succeed in America? Do you agree with her assessment?
8. How does the author utilize the concepts of "hunger" and "appetite" to bring out her thesis?

Writing Tasks

- Write an essay arguing whether immigrants should have the right to receive preferential treatments. Give examples from Yezierska's essay and your own experience to support your argument.
- Write an essay explaining your dreams and expectations of living in New York. What obstacles do you foresee in your pursuit of the American Dream?
- Write an essay in which you explain how living in New York has transformed you. Provide examples of specific learning experiences.

The Money

Junot Díaz

Junot Díaz was born in Santo Domingo, Dominican Republic and is the author of *Drown* and *The Brief Wondrous Life of Oscar Wao*, which won the 2008 Pulitzer Prize. His fiction has appeared in *The New Yorker, African Voices*, and *Best American Short Stories*. He is currently a professor of creative writing at the Massachusetts Institute of Technology (MIT).

Pre-Reading

What is the most courageous thing that you have ever done?

All the Dominicans I knew in those days sent money home. My mother   1
didn't have a regular job besides caring for us five kids, so she scrimped the loot together from whatever came her way. My father was always losing his forklift jobs, so it wasn't like she ever had a steady flow. But my grandparents were alone in Santo Domingo, and those remittances, beyond material support, were a way, I suspect, for Mami to negotiate the absence, the distance, caused by our diaspora. She chipped dollars off the cash Papi gave her for our daily expenses, forced our already broke family to live even broker. That was how she built the nut—two, maybe three hundred dollars—that she sent home every six months or so.

We kids knew where the money was hidden, but we also knew that to touch it would have meant a violent punishment approaching death. I, who could take the change out of my mother's purse without thinking, couldn't have brought myself even to look at that forbidden stash.

So what happened? Exactly what you'd think. The summer I was twelve, my family went away on a "vacation"—one of my father's half-baked get-to-know-our-country-better-by-sleeping-in-the-van extravaganzas—and when we returned to Jersey, exhausted, battered, we found our front door unlocked. My parents' room, which was where the thieves had concentrated their search, looked as if it had been tornado-tossed. The thieves had kept it simple; they'd snatched a portable radio, some of my Dungeons & Dragons hardcovers, and, of course, Mami's remittances.

It's not as if the robbery came as a huge surprise. In our neighborhood, cars and apartments were always getting jacked, and the kid stupid enough

First published in *The New Yorker* and reprinted by permission of Junot Díaz and Aragi Inc.

to leave a bike unattended for more than a tenth of a second was the kid who was never going to see that bike again. Everybody got hit; no matter who you were, eventually it would be your turn.

And that summer it was ours.   5

Still, we took the burglary pretty hard. When you're a recent immigrant, it's easy to feel targeted. Like it wasn't just a couple of assholes that had it in for you but the whole neighborhood—hell, maybe the whole country.

No one took the robbery as hard as my mom, though. She cursed the neighborhood, she cursed the country, she cursed my father, and of course she cursed us kids, swore that we had run our gums to our idiot friends and they had done it.

And this is where the tale should end, right? Wasn't as if there was going to be any "C.S.I."-style investigation or anything. Except that a couple of days later I was moaning about the robbery to these guys I was hanging with at that time and they were cursing sympathetically, and out of nowhere it struck me. You know when you get one of those moments of mental clarity? When the nictitating membrane obscuring the world suddenly lifts? That's what happened. I realized that these two dopes I called my friends had done it. They were shaking their heads, mouthing all the right words, but I could see the way they looked at each other, the Raskolnikov glances.* I *knew.*

Now, it wasn't like I could publicly denounce these dolts or go to the police. That would have been about as useless as crying. Here's what I did: I asked the main dope to let me use his bathroom (we were in front of his apartment) and while I pretended to piss I unlatched the window. Then we all headed to the park as usual, but I pretended that I'd forgotten something back home. Ran to the dope's apartment, slid open the bathroom window, and in broad daylight wriggled my skinny ass in.

Where the hell did I get these ideas? I have not a clue. I guess I was   10
reading way too much Encyclopedia Brown and the Three Investigators in those days. And if mine had been a normal neighborhood this is when the cops would have been called and my ass would have been caught *burglarizing.*

The dolt and his family had been in the U.S. all their lives and they had a ton of stuff, a TV in every room, but I didn't have to do much searching. I popped up the dolt's mattress and underneath I found my D. & D. books and most of my mother's money. He had thoughtfully kept it in the same envelope.

---

*Raskolnikov is the name of the main character in the novel *Crime and Punishment* (1866) by Fyodor Dostoyevsky. In the novel, Raskolnikov commits murder but ultimately is overwhelmed by guilt over his act.

And that was how I solved the Case of the Stupid Morons. My one and only case.

The next day at the park, the dolt announced that someone had broken into *his* apartment and stolen all his savings. This place is full of thieves, he complained bitterly, and I was, like, No kidding.

It took me two days to return the money to my mother. The truth was I was seriously considering keeping it. But in the end the guilt got to me. I guess I was expecting my mother to run around with joy, to crown me her favorite son, to cook me my favorite meal. Nada. I'd wanted a party or at least to see her happy, but there was nothing. Just two hundred and some dollars and fifteen hundred or so miles—that's all there was.

Discussion Questions

1. How does the author's mother come up with enough money to send to her parents?
2. How would you describe the parent-children relationship in Díaz's family?
3. In your opinion, what elements in the story appear to be typical in immigrant families?
4. How does Díaz find out about the stolen money? Do you think he did the right thing in retrieving the money? If not, what could he have done instead?
5. How does Díaz's mother react when he returns the money? Why do you think she does not give her son some sort of reward? What do the concluding lines of the story imply?
6. Identify some of the comic moments in the story. What exactly makes those moments amusing?

Writing Task

- The transaction of money, whether legitimate or not, remains at the center of Díaz's story. Write an essay that discusses how money affects the behavior of the different characters.

The Tropics in New York

Claude McKay

Claude McKay (1890–1948) grew up in Jamaica, and his poems often express nostalgia for life there. After leaving Jamaica in 1912, he studied at Tuskegee Institute and then came to New York, where he established himself as a poet, novelist, and radical spokesman. He is the author of the poetry collection *Harlem Shadows* and the novel *Home to Harlem.*

Pre-Reading

Can you recall a time when something or someone you saw brought back past memories.

The Tropics in New York

Bananas ripe and green, and ginger-root,	1
Cocoa in pods and alligator pears,	
And tangerines and mangoes and grape fruit,	
Fit for the highest prize at parish fairs,	
Set in the window, bringing memories	5
Of fruit-trees laden by low-singing rills,	
And dewy dawns, and mystical blue skies	
In benediction over nun-like hills.	
My eyes grew dim, and I could no more gaze;	
A wave of longing through my body swept,	10
And, hungry for the old, familiar ways,	
I turned aside and bowed my head and wept.	

From *Harlem Shadows: The Poems of Claude McKay,* Harcourt Brace, 1922.

Discussion Questions

1. What does the title of the poem imply?
2. Read the visual imagery in the poem carefully and explain how the author's emotions shift from one stanza to another.
3. What foods, events, or sights evoke memories for you?

Writing Tasks

- Write an essay that focuses on the ethnic characteristics of a neighborhood in New York. Make sure you include as many sensory details as you can.
- Write an essay that discusses the unique challenges that immigrants face coming to a new land and culture.

Riding the Subway Is an Adventure

Frances Chung

Frances Chung (1950–1990) published her poetry in several anthologies and journals, including *The Portable Lower East Side* and *IKON*. Chung's poetry perceptively depicts New York's Chinatown and the Lower East Side. She incorporates Spanish and Chinese into her English to evoke feelings about the fantasies, commerce, and hardships of these neighborhoods. Her work is published in *Crazy Melon and Chinese Apple* (2000).

Pre-Reading

Have you ever been in a foreign country where you couldn't understand the language? How did you get around?

Riding The Subway Is An Adventure

Riding the subway is an adventure	
especially if you cannot read the signs.	1
One gets lost. One becomes anxious and	
does not know whether to get off when	
the other Chinese person in your car	5
does. (Your crazy logic tells you that	
the both of you must be headed for the	
same stop.) One woman has discovered the	
secret of one-to-one correspondence.	
She keeps the right amount of pennies	10
in one pocket and upon arriving in each	
new station along the way she shifts one	
penny to her other pocket. When all the	
pennies in the first pocket have disappeared,	
she knows that she is home.	15

Discussion Questions

1. Why does the woman in the poem have such difficulties in the subway? What other challenges do you anticipate she faces when she ventures out into the city?
2. What is the tone of the poem?
3. What do you think the poet wants to show us in lines 3–5?

Writing Tasks

- Write an essay that captures an adventure you have recently experienced on the subway.
- Write an essay in which you suggest ways in which the MTA can improve travel in the subway system for all New Yorkers.

Yo Vivo En El Barrio Chino

Frances Chung

Pre-Reading

What is your impression of the Chinatown in New York?

YO VIVO En El Barrio Chino

Yo vivo en el barrio chino	1
de Neuva York . . . I live in	
New York's Chinatown. Some	
call it a ghetto, some call it	
a slum, some call it home.	5
Little Italy or Northern	
Chinatown, to my mind, the	
boundaries have become fluid.	
I have two Chinatown moods.	
Time when Chinatown is a	10
terrible place to live in.	
Time when Chinatown is	
the *only* place to live . . .	

Discussion Questions

1. Why does the author write in two languages in this poem?
2. What does the author hope to convey about places some people refer to as slums?
3. Elaborate on the two Chinatown moods the author feels in the poem.

Writing Task

- Take a walk through Chinatown or another ethnic enclave and record your experiences.

New York Was Our City on the Hill

Edwidge Danticat

Edwidge Danticat was born in Port-au-Prince Haiti in 1969. Her father immigrated to the United States in 1971. Her mother followed him in 1973. Danticat remained in Haiti eight more years, raised by her aunt. At age twelve she reunited with her parents in a predominantly Haitian-American neighborhood in Brooklyn, New York. Two short years later, Danticat published an article that inspired her first novel, *Breath, Eyes, Memory.* She has also published *Krik? Krak!* (1996), *The Farming of Bones* (1998), *The Dew Breaker* (2004), *Brother, I'm Dying* (2007), and a collection of essays *Create Dangerously: Immigrant Writers at work* (2010).

Pre-Reading

Have you ever been disillusioned by a place before?

If you are an immigrant in New York, there are some things you inevitably   1
share. For one, if you're a new immigrant, you probably left behind someone you love in the country of your birth. In my case, I was the person left in Haiti when my mother and father escaped the brutal regimes of François and Jean-Claude Duvalier in the early 1970's and fled the extreme poverty caused by the Duvaliers' mismanagement and excesses.

The plan was for my parents to send for me and my younger brother, André, who were 4 and 2 years old at the time of their departure, when they found jobs and got settled in New York. But because of United States immigration red tape, our family separation lasted eight years. The near decade we were apart was filled with long letters, lengthy voice messages on cassette tapes and tearful phone calls, all brimming with the promise that one day my brother and I would be united not only with our parents but with our two Brooklyn-born brothers whom we didn't know at all.

Still André and I were constantly reminded by our Aunt Denise and Uncle Joseph, who were caring for us in an impoverished and politically volatile neighborhood in the Haitian capital, Port-au-Prince, that we were lucky our parents were in New York. If we dared to disagree with that idea, the Faustian bargain our parents had faced would be clearly laid out for us. They could have stayed behind with us and we could have all gone without a great many necessary things, or they could have gone to New York to work so that we could have not only clothes and food and school fees but also a future.

As my Uncle Joseph liked to say, for people like us, the *malere*, the poor, the future was not a given. It was something to be clawed from the edge of despair with sweat and blood. At least in New York, our parents would be rewarded for their efforts.

If living in one of the richest cities in the world did not guarantee a   5
struggle-free life, my brother and I didn't realize it. New York was our city on the hill, the imaginary haven of our lives. When we fantasized, we saw ourselves walking the penny-gilded streets and buying all the candies we could stuff into ourselves. Eventually we grew to embrace the idea that New York was where we were meant to be, as soon as the all-powerful gatekeepers saw fit to let us in, and if we could help it, we would never leave once we were again at our parents' side.

Our parents might have had utopian fantasies of their own when they sold most of their belongings to pay for passports, visas and plane fares to New York. I can't imagine making the choices they made without being forced, mapping out a whole life in a place that they'd seen only in one picture, a snow-covered street taken by my mother's brother, who lived there.

Later my parents would tell me that what kept them trudging through that snow to their factory jobs was their visions of their two New York–born children playing with the children they'd left in Haiti and the future that we might all forge as individuals and as a family.

When I finally joined my parents in Brooklyn, in 1981, at age 12, I became acutely aware of something else that New York immigrants shared. If they were poor, they were likely to be working more hours than anyone else, for less money, and with few if any benefits.

For years my father had worked two minimum-wage jobs to support two households in two countries. One job was in a textile factory, where my mother also worked, and another in a night car wash. Tired of intermittent layoffs and humiliating immigration raids, my father finally quit both jobs when André and I arrived so he could accompany my brothers and me to and from school.

That same year, our family car also became a gypsy cab, a term that,   10
when I first heard and researched it, led me to think that we were part of a small clan of nomads whose leader, my father, chauffeured other people around when he was not driving us.

Though my brothers and I weren't aware of it at the time, our financial situation was precarious at best. Once my parents paid the rent and utility bills and bought a week's worth of groceries, there was little left for much else. My father never knew from day to day or week to week how much he would collect in fares.

Winter mornings were more profitable than summer afternoons. But in the winter, our needs were greater: coats and boots for four growing children, and regular hospital trips for my youngest brother, Karl, who was prone to ear infections and, as one doctor pointed out to us, might have suffered through 25 different colds one long winter.

We had no health insurance, of course, and each of Karl's visits to the doctor, or those for my brother Kelly—the only child I knew who got migraines, which we later discovered were a result of some kind of pressure on his optic nerve—were negotiated down at Cumberland Hospital's payment services department when my father took in my parents' joint tax return.

I remember going to the same hospital's women's clinic with my mother for one of her regular checkups when I was 16. She had a headache, her blood pressure was high, and the doctor told her that she'd have to be hospitalized that day if she wanted to avoid a stroke.

"Doctor, I have children at home and work tomorrow," my mother said, 15 before signing papers declaring that she'd been advised of the treatment for her condition but had refused it. On the bus home, I watched her carefully, fearful that she would keel over and die for our sake, but she made it home, and despite the persistent headache, she went to work the next day.

I don't know what a catastrophic illness might have cost our family financially. But it was something my parents always had in mind. My father tried to pay all his bills religiously so that if we ever needed a bank loan for a sudden emergency, we would have no trouble getting it.

What we would eventually need a loan for was our house, which my parents purchased 18 years ago in East Flatbush. The day we moved in was one of the scariest and most exhilarating of our lives. My parents invited groups of church friends over to celebrate and bless our new home, but at the same time, they warned my brothers and me that the biggest battle they'd face from then on would be to try to keep it. The mortgage was nearly double the amount they'd paid in rent, and some months my father drove his cab both at night and during the day to make the payment, which he then took to the bank, in person, during the final hours of the grace period.

It is the burden of each generation to embrace or reject the dreams set out by those who came before.

In my family it was no different. My parents wanted me to be a doctor, and when I wasn't accepted by a Brooklyn high school specializing in the health professions, my father met with the principal and persuaded him to reverse the decision.

When I decided, after a brief school-sponsored internship at Kings   20
County Hospital Center, that medicine was not for me, my parents were
disappointed, but accepted my decision. My brother André has never forgotten the day he turned 14 and my father took him to the post office to
buy a money order for the application fee for his first summer job. And
over time we have all nearly wept when tallying small loans and advances
from Mom and Dad on salaries spent way before they were collected.

Over the years, I have also come to understand my parents' intense
desire to see my brothers and me financially stable. They had sacrificed so
much that to watch us struggle as they had would have been, to quote a
Creole expression, like *lave men siye atè*—washing one's hands only to dry
them in the dirt.

These days, if you're an immigrant in New York, you might not consider yourself an immigrant at all, but a transnational, someone with vot-
ing privileges and living quarters not just in one country but in two. This
was my parents' dream until they reached middle age and realized that
with their decade-long friendships and community ties in Brooklyn, they
didn't want to live anywhere else.

Last year, when my father became ill with pulmonary fibrosis—a result, some doctors say, of environmental pollution, to which he was especially vulnerable from working such long hours in his cab—he began
to have long talks with my brothers and me, fearing that as the disease
progressed, it might become harder and harder for him to speak. While I
was writing this, we talked a little about how New York had changed from
the time he arrived.

The most striking difference, he observed, is that these days, like most
New Yorkers, he has to worry about terrorism, both becoming a victim
and being blamed for it. He also worries about the high cost of everything
from food to housing, about doors closing behind him, and thousands of
families never having the kind of opportunities that we've enjoyed. When
he first got to New York, all he did was work nonstop and pray to see his
children and grandchildren grow up. Looking back, it feels like a simpler
time, but maybe it wasn't. Then and now, he whispered wistfully, one can
only hope that the journey was worthwhile.

On Nov. 3, after this essay was submitted, my Uncle Joseph died at age   25
81. More formally known as the Rev. Joseph N. Danticat, he died in Miami
after fleeing gang violence and death threats in Haiti. He was detained by
Department of Homeland Security officials after requesting asylum in the
United States and died in their custody. The department said the cause was
pancreatitis.

Discussion Questions

1. Why was life so hard in America for Danticat's parents at first?
2. Explain the "Faustian bargain" offered to the children. Do you think it was a fair offer?
3. How did Uncle Joseph and the children differ in their views of America? What contributes to their respective points of view?
4. What is the first lesson that Danticat learns about life in New York? Do you think this lesson is commonly shared by immigrants? Is it fair?
5. Discuss the quote: "it is the burden of each generation to embrace or reject the dreams set out by those who came before." What do children owe their parents when many sacrifices have been made?
6. What is the difference between an immigrant and a "transnational"? What are the advantages and disadvantages of each? Which label do Danticat's parents ultimately choose? Why?
7. How does Danticat's father's American experience worsen after 9/11? Why do you think this treatment of him occurred?
8. What is the connection of Uncle Joseph's death to the beginning of the essay?
9. Why do you think the past tense is used in the title of the essay?

Writing Task

- Write an essay in which you discuss the many challenges someone you know has gone through to achieve a particular goal. What lessons did they learn along the way?

Facing Poverty with a Rich Girl's Habits

Suki Kim

Kim was born in Seoul, South Korea. She emigrated to the United States with her family when she was 13. Kim graduated from Barnard College in 1992, with a BA in English and a minor in East Asian Literature. Her novel *The Interpreter* (2003) won the PEN Beyond Margins Award and the Gustavus Myers Outstanding Book Award. It was translated into Dutch, French, Korean, and Japanese. Kim currently lives in New York City.

Pre-Reading

When did you first become conscious of your ethnicity or class?

Queens in the early 80's struck me as the Wild West. Our first home there was   1
the upstairs of a two-family brownstone in Woodside. It was a crammed, ugly place, I thought, because in South Korea I had been raised in a hilltop mansion with an orchard and a pond and peacocks until I entered the seventh grade, when my millionaire father lost everything overnight. Gone in an instant was my small world, made possible by my father's shipping company, mining business and hotels. Because bankruptcy was punishable by a jail term, we fled, penniless, to America.

The ugly house was owned by a Korean family that ran a dry cleaner in Harlem. Their sons, Andy and Billy, became my first playmates in America, though playmate was a loose term, largely because they spoke English and I didn't. The first English word I learned at the junior high near Queens Boulevard was F.O.B., short for "fresh off the boat." It was a mystery why some kids called me that when I'd actually flown Korean Air to Kennedy Airport.

At 13, I took public transportation to school for the first time instead of being driven by a chauffeur. I had never done homework without a governess helping me. I also noticed that things became seriously messy if no maids were around. Each week, I found it humiliating to wheel our dirty clothes to a bleak place called Laundromat.

One new fact that took more time to absorb was that I was now Asian, a term that I had heard mentioned only in a social studies class. In Korea, yellow was the color of the forsythia that bloomed every spring along the fence that separated our estate from the houses down the hill. I certainly never thought of my skin as being the same shade.

Unlike students in Korean schools, who were taught to bow to teachers at every turn, no one batted an eye when a teacher entered a classroom. Once I saw a teacher struggle to pronounce foreign-sounding names from the attendance list while a boy in the front row French-kissed a girl wearing skintight turquoise Jordache jeans. In Korea, we wore slippers to keep the school floor clean, but here the walls were covered with graffiti, and some mornings, policemen guarded the gate and checked bags.

My consolation was the English as a Second Language class where I could speak Korean with others like me. Yet it did not take me long to realize that the other students and I had little in common. The wealthier Korean immigrants had settled in Westchester or Manhattan, where their children attended private schools. In Queens, most of my E.S.L. classmates came from poor families who had escaped Korea's rigid class hierarchy, one dictated by education level, family background and financial status.

Immigration is meant to be the great equalizer, yet it is not easy to eradicate the class divisions of the old country. What I recall, at 13, is an acute awareness of the distance between me and my fellow F.O.B.'s, and another, more palpable one between those of us in E.S.L. and the occasional English-speaking Korean-American kids, who avoided us as though we brought them certain undefined shame.

It was not until years later that I learned that we were, in fact, separated from them by generations.

We who sat huddled in that E.S.L. class grew up to represent the so-called 1.5 generation. Many of us came to America in our teens, already rooted in Korean ways and language. We often clashed with the first generation, whose minimal command of English traps them in a time-warped immigrant ghetto, but we identified even less with the second generation, who, with their Asian-American angst and anchorman English, struck us as even more foreign than the rest of America.

Even today, we, the 1.5 generation, can just about maneuver our anchor. We hip-hop to Usher with as much enthusiasm as we have for belting out Korean pop songs at a karaoke. We celebrate the lunar Korean thanksgiving as well as the American one, although our choice of food would most likely be the moon-shaped rice cake instead of turkey. We appreciate eggs Benedict for brunch, but on hung-over mornings, we cannot do without a bowl of thick ox-bone soup and a plate of fresh kimchi. We are 100 percent American on paper but not quite in our soul.

In Queens of the early 80's, I did not yet understand the layers of division that existed within an immigrant group. I preferred my Hello Kitty backpack to the ones with pictures of the Menudo boys, and I cried for weeks because my parents would not let me get my ears pierced. I watched reruns of "Three's Company" in an attempt to learn English, thinking the whole time that John Ritter was running a firm called Three's. I stayed up until dawn to make sense of *Great Expectations*, flipping through the dictionary for the definition of words like "Pip."

More brutal than learning English was facing poverty with a rich girl's habits and memory. In my neighborhood, a girl who grew up with a governess and a chauffeur belonged to a fairy tale. This was no Paris Hilton's "Simple Life," but the beginning of my sobering, often-terrifying, never simple American journey. I soon discovered that I had no choice but to adjust. I had watched my glamorous mother, not long ago a society lady who lunched, taking on a job as a fish filleter at a market.

Before the year was over, my parents moved us out of the neighborhood in search of better jobs, housing and education. As for the family who owned the house in Woodside, I did not see any of them again until the fall of 2001, when Billy walked into the Family Assistance Center at Pier 94, where I was volunteering as an interpreter. He was looking for his brother, Andy, who had been working on the 93rd floor when the first plane crashed into the north tower.

Discussion Questions

1. Why did the author and her family immigrate to America?
2. What was Kim's initial experience as a new immigrant in New York like? Do you think her experience is common among most new immigrants?
3. What does the term "F.O.B." imply?
4. How does the author react to the racial prescriptions imposed on her?
5. Why do you think the English-speaking Korean-American kids avoided their newly immigrated Korean classmates? Do you think this division is typical also in other immigrant communities?
6. How are the schools in New York different from those in Korea?
7. What defines the "1.5 generation" immigrants? What are the challenges they face?
8. What does the author want us to reflect on in the final paragraph?

Writing Task

- Write an essay exploring the causes of division between different generations of immigrants (or different ethnic groups).

Making Connections

1. Several pieces in this chapter deal, more or less directly, with the different aspects of cultivating and living the American Dream. Discuss what America has meant to one or more of these authors and the disparity with what they experienced here. Connect these episodes to your own aspirations and experiences.

2. Review the works in this chapter and discuss with classmates the broad issues they raise (longing, struggle, family, freedom, work, language, education, disillusionment, generational conflict, etc.). Choose one or more of these themes and examine how they are presented in two of the selections. Write a paper in which you compare, contrast, and evaluate the pieces and how you feel about the issues they raise. Feel free to bring in your personal experience and/or observations.

3. Do you think immigrants are treated fairly in America? Write an essay that draws from the readings in this section, other sources, and/or your own experiences.

Urban Education

"An early American urban public school"
Museum of the City of New York, The Jacob A. Riis Collection.

The basic purpose of a liberal arts education is to liberate the human being to exercise his or her potential to the fullest.

Barbara M. White

The mind is a mansion, but most of the time we are content to live in the lobby.

William Michaels

Urban Education

This chapter addresses issues of urban education at the historical, sociological, personal, and global level. The selected readings offer widely divergent perspectives, questions, and possible answers to the central aims of public education. Our main focus in this chapter is to raise both old and new issues so that students can then explore them further on their own. These readings can help students question their own experiences and beliefs about education, and guide them to research and critically evaluate the world around them as they navigate their own educational paths.

According to DeWitt Clinton, a former governor of New York, the government can best help the state by helping citizens gain knowledge. To achieve this aim, Clinton believes that education should be free and accessible to all children, a radical idea 200 years ago. His essay "Free Schools" asserts that free education promotes equality and is essential for a stable and peaceful civil society. Colin Powell's essay "My American Journey" reinforces the idea that public education is important, especially for those citizens not able to afford expensive private institutions. In his balanced essay, Powell says he will continue to be "a champion of public secondary and higher education," as long as he has "the good sense to remember where [he] came from."

The next three essays by Bilal Ramani, Esmeralda Santiago, and Alfred Lubrano are personal narratives written from widely different perspectives. Bilal Ramani, a second-semester biology student at New York City College of Technology, describes his initially skeptical attitude toward education. He then reflects on a moment of illumination in his English class that many students might have experienced, or might soon experience. Esmeralda Santiago's essay "When I Was Puerto Rican" is taken from her memoir of the same title. In it, she remembers the day when she first entered the eighth grade as a confident immigrant who disagreed with the school's principal about her language abilities and her educational goals. In Alfred Lubrano's essay "Bricklayer's Boy," we read about the ways that differences in education levels within one family can cause disagreements.

Our last two essays in this chapter highlight the ways that globalization, ethics, and technology will influence education today and tomorrow. Howard Gardner's "Five Minds for the Future" makes an argument for thinking about education in terms of softer skills like adaptation, creativity, and communication that will push students to engage with the wider world if they wish to succeed. We end this chapter with an overview of future directions in learning. In "How to Bring Our Schools into the 21st Century," Claudia Wallis and Sonja Steptoe believe that students must achieve the right balance between subject knowledge and "portable skills," such as critical thinking. Both of these essays describe changing classroom environments, but they also emphasize the need to develop online skills and global literacy—where students learn about and respect other cultures. The reason is that if there is one thing that the global economy does well and does often, it is to bring many different people into close contact.

Free Schools

DeWitt Clinton

DeWitt Clinton (1769–1828) was the mayor of New York between 1803 and 1815, during which time he spearheaded the founding of the New York Historical Society, the Literary and Philosophical Society, the American Bible Society, the African Free School, the New York Institution for the Deaf and Dumb, and the Orphan Asylum. Clinton's view of the government's role was founded on a belief in education for the entire population. This essay was first published in 1809, with the title of "Address on Monitorial Education," while Clinton was the Governor of New York.

Pre-Reading

What do you think are the goals of public education?

In casting a view over the civilized world, we find universal agreement   1
on the benefits of education; unfortunately, this opinion has not been put into practice. While magnificent Colleges and Universities are erected, we behold few liberal appropriations for diffusing the blessings of knowledge among all descriptions of people. The fundamental error of Europe has been to confine the light of knowledge to the wealthy, while the humble and the depressed have been excluded from its participation . . . The consequence of this has been that ignorance, the prolific parent of every crime and vice, has predominated over the great body of the people, and a corresponding moral debasement has prevailed. "Man differs more from man, than man from beast," says Montaigne, a once celebrated writer. This remark, however generally false, will certainly apply with great force to a man in a state of high mental cultivation, and man in a state of extreme ignorance.

Ignorance is the cause as well as the effect of bad governments, and without the cultivation of our rational powers, we can entertain no just ideas of the obligations of morality or the excellencies of religion. Although England is justly renowned for its cultivation of the arts and sciences, yet there is no Protestant country where the education of the poor has been so grossly and infamously neglected. If a fair sum had been applied to the education of the poor, the blessings of order, knowledge, and innocence would have been diffused among them, and a total revolution would have

From *The Life and Writing of DeWitt Clinton*, by DeWitt Clinton, 1849.

taken place in the habits and lives of the people, favorable to the cause of industry, good morals, good order, and rational religion.

More just and rational views have been entertained on this subject in the United States. Here, no privileged orders—no distinctions in society—no hereditary nobility—exist, to interpose barriers between the people, and to create distinct classifications in society. All men being considered as enjoying an equality of rights, the propriety and necessity of dispensing, without distinction, the blessings of education, followed of course. In New England the greatest attention has been invariably given to this important object. In Connecticut, particularly, the schools are supported at least three-fourths of the year by the interest of a very large fund created for that purpose, and a small tax on the people. The result of this beneficial arrangement is obvious and striking. Our Eastern brethren are a well-informed and moral people. In those States it is as uncommon to find a poor man who cannot read and write, as it is rare to see one in Europe who can.

New York has proceeded in the same career, but on a different, and perhaps more eligible plan. For a few years back, a fund has been accumulating appropriated to the support of common schools. This fund consists at present of near four hundred thousand dollars in bank stock, mortgages, and bonds. The capital will be increased by the accumulating interest and the sale of three hundred and thirty-six thousand acres of land. It is highly probable that the whole fund will, in a few years, amount to one million two hundred and fifty thousand dollars, a sum more than sufficient to accommodate all our poor with a gratuitous education.

We have every reason to believe, that this great fund, established for sinking vice and ignorance, will never be diverted or destroyed, but that it will remain unimpaired across the years, as an illustrious establishment, erected by the benevolence of the State for the propagation of knowledge, and the diffusion of virtue among the people. 5

A number of benevolent persons had seen, with concern, the increasing vices of this city, arising in a great degree from the neglected education of the poor. Great cities are at all times the nurseries and hot-beds of crime. Bad men from all quarters repair to them, in order to obtain the benefit of concealment, and to enjoy in a superior degree the advantages of rapine and fraud. And the dreadful examples of vice, which are presented to youth, and the alluring forms in which it is arrayed, cannot fail to increase the mass of moral depravity. "In London," it is reported, "above twenty thousand individuals rise every morning, without knowing how, or by what means they are to be supported through the passing day, and in many instances even where they are to lodge on the ensuing night." There can be no doubt that hundreds are in the same situation in this city, prowling about our streets for prey, the victims of intemperance [alcohol abuse], the slaves of idleness, and ready to fall into any vice, rather than to cultivate industry and good order.

After a full view of the case, those persons of whom I have spoken agreed that the evil must be corrected at its source, and that education was the sovereign prescription.

Discussion Questions

1. According to Clinton, what was Europe's fundamental error in terms of knowledge? How could this error be corrected?
2. What point does Clinton want to make by using this quote from Montaigne: "Man differs more from man, than man from beast"?
3. What is the author's view of New England's educational system?
4. What was the cause for the increased crime rate of New York City during Clinton's time? Do you think Clinton's view still holds true today?
5. Discuss the impact of Clinton's educational reform ideas. Do you think that he would be happy with today's public education? Why or why not?

Writing Task

- DeWitt Clinton believed that free education for the entire population would create equality among people from different classes. Do you agree with him? Write an essay in support of or arguing against the point of view that free education guarantees equal opportunities.

My American Journey

Colin Powell

Colin Powell (b. 1937) was the 65th United States Secretary of State, serving from 2001 to 2005 under President George W. Bush. When appointed, Powell became the highest ranking African American government official in the history of the United States. As a general in the United States Army, Powell also served as National Security Advisor (1987–89) and Chairman of the Joint Chiefs of Staff (1989–93). After retiring from office, Powell joined the Board of Directors on the Council of Foreign Relations.

Pre-Reading

Do you believe that private education is better than public education?

Following my sister's example and Mom and Pop's wishes, I applied to   1
two colleges, the City College of New York and New York University. I must have been better than I thought, since I was accepted at both. Choosing between the two was a matter of simple arithmetic; tuition at NYU, a private school, was $750 a year; at CCNY, a public school, it was $10. I chose CCNY. My mother turned out to be my guidance counselor. She had consulted with the family. My two Jamaican cousins, Vernon and Roy, were studying engineering. "That's where the money is," Mom advised. And she was not far wrong. In the boom years of the fifties, demand for consumer goods and for engineers to design the refrigerators, automobiles, and hi-fi sets was strong. And so I was to be an engineering major, despite my allergy to science and math.

The Bronx can be a cold, harsh place in February, and it was frigid the day I set out for college. After two bus rides, I was finally deposited, shivering, at the corner of 156th Street and Convent Avenue in Harlem. I got out and craned my neck like a bumpkin in from the sticks, gazing at handsome brownstones and apartment houses. This was the best of Harlem, where blacks with educations and good jobs lived, the Gold Coast.

I stopped at the corner of Convent and 141st and looked into the campus of the City College of New York. I was about to enter a college established in the previous century "to provide higher education for the children of the working class." Ever since then, New York's poorest and brightest have seized that opportunity. Those who preceded me at CCNY include the polio vaccine discoverer, Dr. Jonas Salk, Supreme Court Justice Felix Frankfurter, the muckraker novelist Upton Sinclair, the actor Edward G. Robinson, the playwright Paddy Chayefsky, the *New York Times* editor Abe Rosenthal, the novelist Bernard Malamud, the labor leader A. Philip Randolph, New York City mayors Abraham Beam and Edward Koch, U.S. Senator Robert Wagner, and eight Nobel Prize winners. As I took in the grand Gothic structures, a C-average student out of middling Morris High School, I felt overwhelmed. And then I heard a friendly voice: "Hey, kid, you new?"

He was a short, red-faced, weather-beaten man with gnarled hands, and he stood behind a steaming cart of those giant pretzels that New Yorkers are addicted to. I had met a CCNY fixture called, for some unaccountable reason, "Raymond the Bagel Man," though he sold pretzels. I bought a warm, salty pretzel from Raymond, and we shot the breeze for a few minutes. That broke the ice for me. CCNY was somehow less intimidating. I was to become a regular of Raymond's over the next four and a half years. And it either speaks well of his character or poorly of my scholarship that while my memory of most of my professors has faded, the memory of Raymond the Bagel Man remains undimmed.

As I headed toward the main building, Sheppard Hall, towering like a   5
prop out of a horror movie, I passed by an undistinguished old building. I do not remember paying any attention to it at the time. It was, however, to become the focus of my life for the next four years, the ROTC drill hall.

My first semester as an engineering major went surprisingly well, mainly because I had not yet taken any engineering courses. I decided to prepare myself that summer with a course in mechanical drawing. One hot afternoon, the instructor asked us to draw "a cone intersecting a plane in space." The other students went at it; I just sat there. After a while, the instructor came to my desk and looked over my shoulder at a blank page. For the life of me, I could not visualize a cone intersecting a plane in space. If this was engineering, the game was over.

My parents were disappointed when I told them that I was changing my major. There goes Colin again, nice boy, but no direction. When I announced my new major, a hurried family council was held. Phone calls flew between aunts and uncles. Had anybody ever heard of anyone studying geology? What did you do with geology? Where did you go with it? Prospecting for oil? A novel pursuit for a black kid from the South Bronx. And, most critical to these security-haunted people, could geology lead to a pension? That was the magic word in our world. I remember coming home after I had been in the Army for five years and visiting my well-meaning, occasionally meddling Aunt Laurice. What kind of career was this Army? she asked, like a cross-examiner. What was I doing with my life? Snatching at the nearest defense, I mentioned that after twenty years I would get a half-pay pension. And I would only be forty-one. Her eyes widened. A pension? At forty-one? The discussion was over. I had made it.

During my first semester at CCNY, something had caught my eye—young guys on campus in uniform. CCNY was a hotbed of liberalism, radicalism, even some leftover communism from the thirties; it was not a place where you would expect much of a military presence. When I returned to school in the fall of 1954, I inquired about the Reserve Officers Training Corps, and I enrolled in ROTC. I am not sure why. Maybe it was growing up in World War II and coming of age during the Korean conflict: the little banners in windows with a blue star, meaning someone from the family was in the service, or a gold star, meaning someone was not coming back. *Back to Bataan, Thirty Seconds over Tokyo, Guadalcanal Diary,* Colin Kelly, Audie Murphy, the five Sullivan brothers who went down with the cruiser U.S.S. *Juneau, Pork Chop Hill,* and *The Bridges at Toko-Ri.* All these images were burned into my consciousness during my most impressionable years. Or maybe it was the common refrain of that era—you are going to be drafted anyway, you might as well go in as an officer. I was not alone. CCNY might not have been West Point, but during the fifties it had the largest voluntary ROTC contingent in America, fifteen hundred cadets at the height of the Korean War.

There came a day when I stood in line in the drill hall to be issued olive-drab pants and jacket, brown shirt, brown tie, brown shoes, a belt with a brass buckle, and an overseas cap. As soon as I got home, I put the uniform on and looked in the mirror. I liked what I saw. At this point, not a single Kelly Street friend of mine was going to college. I was seventeen. I felt cut off and lonely. The uniform gave me a sense of belonging, and something I had never experienced all the while I was growing up; I felt distinctive.

In class, I stumbled through math, fumbled through physics, and did 10 reasonably well in, and even enjoyed, geology. All I ever looked forward to was ROTC. Colonel Harold C. Brookhart, Professor of Military Science and Tactics, was our commanding officer. The colonel was a West Pointer and regular Army to his fingertips. He was about fifty years old, with thinning hair, of only medium height, yet he seemed imposing because of his bearing, impeccable dress, and no-nonsense manner. His assignment could not have been a coveted one for a career officer. I am sure he would have preferred commanding a regiment to teaching ROTC to a bunch of smart-aleck city kids on a liberal New York campus. But the Korean War had ended the year before. The Army was overloaded with officers, and Brookhart was probably grateful to land anywhere. Whatever he felt, he never let us sense that what we were doing was anything less than deadly serious.

That fall, I experienced the novel pleasure of being courted by the three military societies on campus, the Webb Patrol, Scabbard and Blade, and the Pershing Rifles, ROTC counterparts of fraternities. Rushing consisted mostly of inviting potential pledges to smokers where we drank beer and watched pornographic movies. The movies, in the sexually repressed fifties, were supposed to be a draw. I hooted and hollered with the rest of the college boys through these grainy 8-millimeter films, in which the male star usually wore socks. But they were not what drew me to the Pershing Rifles. I pledged the PRs because they were the elite of the three groups.

The pledge period involved typical ritualistic bowing and scraping before upperclassmen, and some hazing that aped West Point traditions. A junior would stand you at attention and demand the definition of certain words. To this day I can parrot the response for milk: "She walks, she talks, she's made of chalk, the lactile fluid extracted from the female of the bovine species..." and on and on. I can spout half a dozen similar daffy definitions. When we finished the pledge period, we were allowed crests on our uniforms. I found that I was much attracted by forms and symbols.

One Pershing Rifles member impressed me from the start. Ronald Brooks was a young black man, tall, trim, handsome, the son of a Harlem Baptist preacher and possessed of a maturity beyond most college students. Ronnie was only two years older than I, but something in him commanded deference. And unlike me, Ronnie, a chemistry major, was a brilliant student. He was a cadet leader in the ROTC and an officer in the Pershing Rifles. He could drill men so that they moved like parts of a watch. Ronnie was sharp, quick, disciplined, organized, qualities then invisible in Colin Powell. I had found a model and a mentor. I set out to remake myself in the Ronnie Brooks mold.

My experience in high school, on basketball and track teams, and briefly in Boy Scouting had never produced a sense of belonging or many permanent friends. The Pershing Rifles did. For the first time in my life I was a member of a brotherhood. The PRs were in the CCNY tradition only in that we were ethnically diverse and so many of us were the sons of immigrants. Otherwise, we were out of sync with both the student radicals and the conservative engineering majors, the latter easy to spot by the slide rules hanging from their belts. PRs drilled together. We partied together. We cut classes together. We chased girls together. We had a fraternity office on campus from which we occasionally sortied out to class or, just as often, to the student lounge, where we tried to master the mambo. I served as an unlikely academic advisor, steering other Pershing Rifles into geology as an easy yet respectable route to a degree.

The discipline, the structure, the camaraderie, the sense of belonging were what I craved. I became a leader almost immediately. I found a   15 selflessness within our ranks that reminded me of the caring atmosphere within my family. Race, color, background, income meant nothing. The PRs would go the limit for each other and for the group. If this was what soldiering was all about, then maybe I wanted to be a soldier.

***

I returned to college in the fall of 1955, commuting from Kelly Street. I did not have to be an urbanologist to see that the old neighborhood was deteriorating. The decline was just the latest chapter in the oldest story in New York, people moving up and out as their fortunes improved, and poorer people moving in to take their places. The Jewish families who had escaped Lower East Side tenements for the South Bronx were now moving to the suburbs. Poor Puerto Ricans were moving into their old apartments. Hunts Point had never been verandas and wisteria. And now it was getting worse, from gang fights to gang wars, from jackknives to switchblades, from zip guns to real guns, from marijuana to heroin. One day, I came home from CCNY to find that a kid I knew had been found in a hallway, dead of a heroin overdose. He would not be the last. I had managed to steer clear of the drug scene. I never smoked marijuana, never got high, in fact never experimented with any drugs. And for a simple reason: my folks would have killed me.

As better-off families continued to flee, properties began to decay, even to be abandoned. Landlords cut their losses short and walked away from their buildings. In years to come, my own 952 Kelly Street would be abandoned, then burned out and finally demolished. But that was all in the future. For now, conversation among my relatives typically began, "When you getting out?" Aunt Laurice moved to the northern edge of the Bronx. So did Godmother Brash. Aunt Dot was already in Queens. When were Luther and Arie going to leave?

The secret dream of these tenement dwellers had always been to own their own home. And so the Powell family began heading for the upper Bronx or Queens, Sunday after Sunday, house hunting in desirable black neighborhoods. But the prices were outrageous—$15,000, $20,000, with my parents' combined income totaling about $100 a week. Weekends often ended with the real estate agent sick to death of us and my sister embarrassed to tears.

My father also dreamed about numbers. He bought numbers books at the newsstands to work out winning combinations. And he still went in every day with Aunt Beryl. They usually played quarters. Then, one Saturday night, my father dreamed a number, and the next morning at St. Margaret's the *same* number appeared on the hymn board. This, surely, was God taking Luther Powell by the hand and leading him to the Promised

Land. Somehow, Pop and Aunt Beryl managed to scrape up $25 to put on the number. And they hit it, straight.

I still remember the atmosphere of joy, disbelief, and anxiety when   20
the numbers runner delivered the brown paper bags to our house. Pop took them to his room and dumped the money on his bed, $10,000 in tens and twenties, more than three years' pay. He let me help him count it. The money was not going into any bank. This strike was nobody's business. The bills were stashed all over the house, with my mother terrified that the tax man or thieves would be coming through the door any minute.

And that was how the Powells managed to buy 183–68 Elmira Avenue, in the community of Hollis in the borough of Queens—for $17,500. The house was a three-bedroom bungalow in a neighborhood in transition; the whites were moving out and the blacks moving in. My folks bought from a Jewish family named Wiener, one of the few white families left. The neighborhood looked beautiful to us, and the Hollis address carried a certain cachet, a cut above Jamaica, Queens, and just below St. Albans, then another gold coast for middle-class blacks. Our new home was ivy-covered, well kept, and comfortable, and had a family room and a bar in the finished basement. Pop was now a property holder, eager to mow his postage-stamp lawn and prune his fruit trees. Luther Powell had joined the gentry....

I now began commuting from Queens to CCNY via the subway, which led to my first serious romance, with a CCNY student. We began riding the A train from the campus downtown, where we would transfer, I out to Queens and the girl out to Brooklyn. I took her to meet my parents. They were perfectly polite to her, but reserved.

My main college interest remained ROTC and the Pershing Rifles. Geology continued to be secondary, though I did enjoy the field trips. We went upstate and clambered over formations of synclines and anticlines. We had to diagram them and figure out their mirror images. If you had an anticline here, you should be able to predict a complementing syncline bulging out somewhere else. Very satisfying when I got it right. Geology allowed me to display my brilliance to my noncollege friends. "You know, the Hudson really isn't a river." "What are you talking about? College kid. Schmuck. Everybody knows the Hudson River's a river." I would then explain that the Hudson was a "drowned" river, up to about Poughkeepsie. The Ice Age had depressed the riverbed to a depth that allowed the Atlantic Ocean to flood inland. Consequently, the lower Hudson was really a saltwater estuary. I proudly pinpointed the farthest advance of the Ice Age. It stopped at Hillside Avenue running through Queens. You can see the ground sloping down along that line into St. Albans and Jamaica. I was startled to earn an A in one of my geology courses and wound up with three A's in my major by graduation.

On June 9, 1958, at 8:00 P.M., I entered CCNY's Aronowitz Auditorium. A few weeks before, my father had come into my room, sat on the edge of the bed, and, with a twinkling eye, handed me an envelope. He had cleaned out a savings account that he and my mother had been keeping for me since I was a child. Six hundred dollars. I was rich! The first thing I did was to head downtown to Morry Luxenberg's, regarded as the best military haberdasher in New York, to be outfitted.

The First Army band was playing and I was wearing Morry's uniform   25 when I strode past my parents onto the Aronowitz Auditorium stage. "I, Colin Luther Powell, do solemnly swear that I will support and defend the Constitution of the United States against all enemies foreign and domestic," I repeated with my classmates, "and that I will well and faithfully discharge the duties of the office upon which I am about to enter, so help me God." We live in a more cynical age today. We are embarrassed by expressions of patriotism. But when I said those words almost four decades ago, they sent a shiver down my spine. They still do.

Because I was a "Distinguished Military Graduate," I was offered a regular rather than a reserve commission, which meant that I would have to serve three rather than two years on active duty. I eagerly accepted.

For me, graduation from college the next day was anticlimactic. The night before, after our commissioning, I had gone out celebrating with the boys. We had resumed the revelry the following noon at a college hangout called the Emerald Bar. My mother, knowing where to find me, had to send a cousin to haul me over to my graduation, which in her mind had been the whole point of the previous four and a half years. I tended to look on my B.S. in geology as an incidental dividend.

For much of our growing up, Marilyn and I had been "latchkey kids," left by ourselves or with neighbors and relatives after school. This situation is supposed to be a prescription for trouble. But that day, Luther and Arie Powell, Jamaican immigrants, garment-district workers, were the parents of two college graduates, with their son now an Army officer as well. Small achievements as the world measures success, but mountain-tops in their lives. Thirty-five years later, I was asked by *Parade* magazine to talk about those two people. "My parents," I said, "did not recognize their own strengths." It was nothing they ever said that taught us, I recalled. "It was the way they lived their lives," I said. "If the values seem correct or relevant, the children will follow the values." I had been shaped not by preaching, but by example, by moral osmosis. Banana Kelly, the embracing warmth of an extended family, St. Margaret's Church, and let's weave in the Jamaican roots and a little calypso—all provided an enviable send-off on life's journey.

I also owe an unpayable debt to the New York City public education system. I typified the students that CCNY was created to serve, the sons and daughters of the inner city, the poor, the immigrant. Many of my college classmates had the brainpower to attend Harvard, Yale, or Princeton. What they lacked was money and influential connections. Yet they have gone on to compete with and often surpass alumni of the most prestigious private campuses in this country.

I have made clear that I was no great shakes as a scholar. I have joked   30 over the years that the CCNY faculty handed me a diploma, uttering a sigh of relief, and were happy to pass me along to the military. Yet, even this C-average student emerged from CCNY prepared to write, think, and communicate effectively and equipped to compete against students from colleges that I could never have dreamed of attending. If the Statue of Liberty opened the gateway to this country, public education opened the door to attainment here. Schools like my sister's Buffalo State Teachers College and CCNY have served as the Harvards and Princetons of the poor. And they served us well. I am, consequently, a champion of public secondary and higher education. I will speak out for them and support them for as long as I have the good sense to remember where I came from.

Discussion Questions

1. Why does Powell ultimately decide to go to CUNY? Do you think he made the wise decision?
2. How does Powell feel upon his arrival at City College? What causes him to feel this way?
3. Why does Powell spend so much time discussing the involvement of his parents and extended family in *his* American journey? Cite specific examples in the text to make your point.
4. According to the author, what specific skills did CUNY provide him that allowed him to compete with anybody from anywhere later in life? Do you agree with his assessment?

Writing Tasks

- Discuss your extracurricular activities and how they help you with the demands of college.
- Research the life of a well-known New Yorker, then write an essay discussing the factors that led to his or her success.
- Write an essay that focuses on the educational process of someone in your family, or someone who has been instrumental to your education.

Chronicles of a Once-Pessimistic College Freshman

Bilal Rahmani

Bilal Rahmani is a student at New York City College of Technology and plans to graduate in 2014. He is passionate about his writing, computer programming, and philosophy. He is pursuing his BS in Biology, with an English minor. He hopes to one day become a surgeon.

Pre-Reading

Can you think of a moment when you had a breakthrough that changed the way you regard education?

I'm in, and then I'm out. I don't feel like I belong here. Why *am* I here—in this school? I've been pushed around the crucible of the New York City public education system for so long now. Rejected from my middle school of choice and shoved into The High School for Health Professions and Human Services on the Lower East Side, that no one has heard of. I'm one of the smart kids. I always performed well in school: I did all my assignments, was friendly to my teachers, and got an impressive score on my SAT's—the ideal student. Sure I slacked off sometimes. Maybe I cut class a little, maybe I shouldn't have spent so much time with my girlfriend, or with my best friends, but should I really have been punished for the mistakes I made as a naïve teenager? I mean, looking back on it, high school was horrible in the way it sifted and sorted kids so arbitrarily. There was never a rational grading system. I've worked endless hours on certain assignments only to fail, and alternately, I've skipped entire semesters of classes and ended up with an "A." A part of me says "stop making excuses Bilal, get out the golden cage of your fragile ego." The other part refuses to listen, preferring to wallow over what could have been.

In the middle of June 2010, I could no longer push back the need to register for classes at City Tech, so one evening I set off on a two-hour journey on the wonderfully-organized and ever-so-punctual New York City Public Transportation System. After another long wait, I met with a guidance counselor who was supposed to help me select my classes, but who simply dictated to me that I would be taking English, math, biology, and psychology for my first semester. I wasn't given much of a choice about class selection, but, to tell you the truth, none of the classes really interested me.

My first month of college passed in this depressed state. I was completely indifferent to anything and everything. I didn't join any clubs; I didn't make any friends; I didn't go to any rallies or shows or games. I didn't care. I believed that everyone here was in a general state of apathy. No efforts were made on either side. You went to class, spoke to no one; you left class, spoke to no one; and you went home to do your homework, alone. From my dreary perspective at the time, my lackluster professors seemed to give little effort towards inspiring their students, and the students made no effort to better their classes in any way. I sat through these classes with no ambition, while my instructors taught out of books I had no interest in buying. To me, no one seemed to really *attend* this college; everyone seemed to be in a state of leaving, ears pinned to an invisible evacuation siren.

The following semester in the spring of 2011, English class rolled in once again. Here I was with my classmates discussing the short story, "Cat in the Rain," by Ernest Hemingway. Hemingway! What an amazing author. But, I thought to myself, these simple students will never be able to understand the enigmatic allegories he presents in his writing, so I guess I'll have to answer all the questions. I raised my hand to offer an interpretation that the cat represents a woman trapped in a man's world, when the dumb girl next to me raised her hand. She got called on first and explained that Hemingway was being misogynistic; to her, the author believed all women just wanted to be dominated and to have long hair and children. This was utterly ridiculous; I mean it's Hemingway! How could one ever interpret him in that sort of way? As if the great Hemingway could possibly possess such an immature trait. This was what I thought, before the teacher explained that Hemingway was, in fact, very sexist. Just a minor slip up; I was still sure my interpretation was smarter and more creative than hers anyway. I settled down and listened to the class discuss the piece. Suddenly, they were shooting out ideas that all made so much sense. My prejudices crashed in on me. The classroom became ink, penetrating the water, which was my mind, adding new colors, creating something completely new, something I alone could never hope to create. The discussion dragged me in, and I too began to share my ideas, adding to the excitement of the classroom. To my surprise, my wall of egotism vanished, and a new air of life breathed in me. At that moment, I began to see this class—no, this college—for what it truly was.

When I first entered this college, I had no ambition to pursue anything. 5 I walked through its doors only to find myself counting the hours until I could leave. I expected nothing from this school, but I'm now inculcated with the ideas and flashing wisdom of hundreds of peers and instructors. I had completely overlooked the potential greatness that this institution could bring to each student, to each class, and, in particular, to me. Now, my mind has opened to this college and has been flooded with the thoughts of hundreds of students as eager and ambitious to learn as I am. This public institution of learning, so often looked down upon, has come to shape the person I've always wanted to become.

Today, as a functioning member of this vibrant community, I find myself engaged in my classes in a way that I never had before. I take courses which grab my attention, with professors who are just as eager to share their wisdom with me as I am to receive it. With every debate over the meaning of a painting in my Art History course, every question about our country's business laws in Microeconomics, or every question about the thoughts of Sartre, Kierkegaard, or Descartes in my philosophy course, I grow stronger. I, in turn, offer my skills to the community by tutoring my peers. I also participate in literary contests, and I join the many City Tech clubs, giving all I can, and receiving much more in return. My experiences, knowledge, and ambitions have joined together to create who I am: a no-longer-pessimistic student at New York City College of Technology.

Discussion Questions

1. Bilal Rahmani describes an uneven grading system in high school. Discuss your own experiences in high school. Can you think of a time when you felt that you deserved a better grade, or conversely, that you received a high grade that you didn't entirely deserve?
2. What is the source of classroom boredom? Does it come from the subject matter, the way subjects are taught, or from the student?
3. What happened during the discussion of Ernest Hemingway's short story "Cat in the Rain"? What did Rahmani learn?
4. Discuss how Rahmani uses humor and irony in his essay.

Writing Tasks

- Rahmani yearns to dive into the college experience, but approaches school, initially, with a "dreary perspective." Write an essay in which you consider ways that would bring more students together and help them overcome their indifference toward college life.
- Write an essay in which you compare and contrast your own experience with Rahmani's.

When I Was Puerto Rican

Esmeralda Santiago

Esmeralda Santiago (b. 1948) was born in San Juan, Puerto Rico, and she came to the United States when she was thirteen. Santiago attended New York City's Performing Arts High School, where she majored in drama and dance. After eight years of part-time study at community colleges, she transferred to Harvard University with a full scholarship. She graduated magna cum laude in 1976. Since then, Santiago has written for many national publications including *The New York Times*, *The Boston Globe* and *Sports Illustrated*. She has published novels, screenplays, and three acclaimed memoirs: *When I was Puerto Rican* (1994), *Almost a Woman* (1999), and *The Turkish Lover* (2004).

Pre-Reading

Think of a time when you took a great risk as a student?

The first day of school Mami walked me to a stone building that loomed   1
over Graham Avenue, its concrete yard enclosed by an iron fence with spikes at the top. The front steps were wide but shallow and led up to a set of heavy double doors that slammed shut behind us as we walked down the shiny corridor. I clutched my eighth-grade report card filled with A's and B's, and Mami had my birth certificate. At the front office we were met by Mr. Grant, a droopy gentleman with thick glasses and a kind smile who spoke no Spanish. He gave Mami a form to fill out. I knew most of the words in the squares we were to fill in: NAME, ADDRESS (CITY, STATE), and OCCUPATION. We gave it to Mr. Grant, who reviewed it, looked at my birth certificate, studied my report card, then wrote on the top of the form "7–18."

Don Julio had told me that if students didn't speak English, the schools in Brooklyn would keep them back one grade until they learned it.

"Seven gray?" I asked Mr. Grant, pointing at his big numbers, and he nodded.

"Ino guan seven gray. I eight gray. I teeneyer."

"You don't speak English," he said. "You have to go to the seventh   5
grade while you're learning."

"I have A's in school Puerto Rico. I learn good. I no seven gray girl."

Mami stared at me, not understanding but knowing I was being rude to an adult.

"What's going on?" she asked me in Spanish. I told her they wanted to send me back one grade and I would not have it. This was probably the first rebellious act she had seen from me outside my usual mouthiness within the family.

"Negi, leave it alone. Those are the rules," she said, a warning in her voice.

"I don't care what their rules say," I answered. "I'm not going back to   10
seventh grade. I can do the work. I'm not stupid."

Mami looked at Mr. Grant, who stared at her as if expecting her to do something about me. She smiled and shrugged her shoulders.

"Meester Grant," I said, seizing the moment, "I go eight gray six mons. Eef I no learn inglish, I go seven gray. Okay?"

"That's not the way we do things here," he said hesitating.

"I good studen. I learn queek. You see notes." I pointed to the A's on my report card. "I pass seven gray."

So we made a deal.   15

"You have until Christmas," he said. "I'll be checking on your prog-ress." He scratched out "7–18" and wrote in "8–23." He wrote something on a piece of paper, sealed it inside an envelope, and gave it to me. "Your teacher is Miss Brown. Take this note upstairs to her. Your mother can go," he said and disappeared into his office.

"Wow!" Mami said, "You can speak English!"

I was so proud of myself, I almost burst. In Puerto Rico, if I'd been that pushy, I would have been called *mal educada* by the Mr. Grant equivalent and sent home with a note to my mother. But here it was my teacher who was getting the note, I got what I wanted and my mother was sent home.

"I can find my way after school," I said to Mami. "You don't have to come get me."

"Are you sure?"   20

"Don't worry," I said. "I'll be all right."

I walked down the black-tiled hallway, past many doors that were half glass, each one labeled with a room number in neat black lettering. Other students stared at me, tried to get my attention, or pointedly ignored me. I kept walking as if I knew where I was going, heading for the sign that said STAIRS with an arrow pointing up. When I reached the end of the hall and looked back, Mami was still standing at the front door watching me, a worried expression on her face. I waved and she waved back. I started up the stairs, my stomach churning into tight knots. All of a sudden, I was afraid that I was about to make a fool of myself and end up in seventh grade in the middle of the school year. Having to fall back would be worse than just accepting my fate now and hopping forward if I proved to be as good a student as I had convinced Mr. Grant I was. "What have I done?" I kicked myself with the back of my right shoe, much to the surprise of the fellow walking behind me, who laughed uproariously, as if I had meant it as a joke.

Miss Brown's was the learning disabled class, where the administration sent kids with all sort of problems, none of which, from what I could see, had anything to do with their ability to learn but more with their willingness to do so. They were an unruly group. Those who came to class, anyway. Half of them never showed up, or, when they did, they slept through the lesson or nodded off in the middle of Miss Brown's carefully parsed sentences.

We were outcasts in a school where the smartest eighth graders were in the 8–1 homeroom, each subsequent drop in number indicating one notch less smart. If your class was in the low double digits (8–10 for instance), you were smart, but not a pinhead. Once you got into the teens, your intelligence was in question, especially as the numbers rose to the high teens. And then there were the twenties. I was in 8–23, where the dumbest most undesirable people were placed. My class was, in some ways, the equivalent of seventh grade, perhaps even sixth or fifth.

Miss Brown, the homeroom teacher, who also taught English composition, was a young black woman who wore sweat pads under her arms. The strings holding them in place sometimes slipped outside the short sleeves of her well-pressed white shirts, and she had to turn her back to us in order to adjust them. She was very pretty, with almond eyes and a hairdo that was flat and straight at the top of her head then dipped into tight curls at the ends. Her fingers were well manicured, the nails painted pale pink with white tips. She taught English composition as if everyone cared about it, which I found appealing.

After the first week she moved me from the back of the room to the front seat by her desk, and after that, it felt as if she were teaching me alone. We never spoke except when I went up to the blackboard.

"Esmeralda," she called in a musical voice, "would you please come up and mark the prepositional phrase?"

In her class, I learned to recognize the structure of the English language, and to draft the parts of a sentence by the position of words relative to pronouns and prepositions without knowing exactly what the whole thing meant.

Every day after school I went to the library and took out as many children's books as I was allowed. I figured that if American children learned English through books, so could I, even if I was starting later. I studied the bright illustrations and learned the words for the unfamiliar objects of our new life in the United States: A for Apple, B for Bear, C for Cabbage. As my vocabulary grew, I moved to large-print chapter books. Mami bought me an English-English dictionary because that way, when I looked up a word I would be learning others.

By my fourth month in Brooklyn, I could read and write English much   30
better than I could speak it, and at midterms I stunned the teachers by scoring high in English, History, and Social Studies. During the January assembly, Mr. Grant announced the names of the kids who had received high marks in each class. My name was called out three times. I became a different person to the other eighth graders. I was still in 8–23, but they knew, and I knew, that I didn't belong there.

Discussion Questions

1. What criteria does Mr. Grant use before he places Esmeralda Santiago in 7–18? Do you think that this decision is reasonable?
2. What is Santiago's reaction to her initial placement? Would you do the same if you were in her situation?
3. Why was her mother worried about her daughter's outspokenness?
4. How could Mr. Grant have handled Santiago's placement differently? Or, what other criteria could Mr. Grant have used?
5. Santiago describes 8–23 as a class of outcasts. What does outcast mean in this context? How does her own status change by the end of the essay?
6. What lesson does Santiago learn when she persuades the principal to put her in the eighth grade?
7. Do you think that Santiago would have done as well if she were placed in, say, 8–1? Why or why not?

Writing Tasks

- Write an essay in which you describe how you overcame somebody's misperception of your ability.
- Write an essay that either defends or criticizes the way schools categorize students on the basis of academic and/or language skills.

Bricklayer's Boy

Alfred Lubrano

New York City native Alfred Lubrano is a reporter for *The Philadelphia Inquirer*. He is a frequent contributor to national publications, and he was a commentator for *National Public Radio* for sixteen years. He contributes to *Gentlemen's Quarterly*, where this essay originally appeared. His book *Limbo: Blue-Collar Roots, White-Collar Dreams*, was published in 2005.

Pre-Reading

Do you and your parents share the same educational values?

My father and I were college buddies back in the mid 1970s. While I was in   1
class at Columbia, struggling with the *esotérica du jour,* he was on a bricklayer's scaffold not far up the street, working on a campus building.

Sometimes we'd hook up on the subway going home, he with his tools, I with my books. We didn't chat much about what went on during the day. My father wasn't interested in Dante, I wasn't up on arches. We'd share a *New York Post* and talk about the Mets.

My dad has built lots of places in New York City he can't get into: colleges, condos, office towers. He makes his living on the outside. Once the walls are up, a place takes on a different feel for him, as if he's not welcome anymore. It doesn't bother him, though. For my father, earning the dough that paid for my entrée into a fancy, bricked-in institution was satisfaction enough, a vicarious access.

We didn't know it then, but those days were the start of a branching off, a redefining of what it means to be a workingman in our family. Related by blood, we're separated by class, my father and I. Being the white-collar son of a blue-collar man means being the hinge on the door between two ways of life.

It's not so smooth jumping from Italian old-world style to U.S. yup-   5
pie in a single generation. Despite the myth of mobility in America, the true rule, experts say, is rags to rags, riches to riches. According to Bucknell University economist and author Charles Sackrey, maybe 10 percent climb from the working to the professional class. My father has had a

tough time accepting my decision to become a mere newspaper reporter, a field that pays just a little more than construction does. He wonders why I haven't cashed in on that multi-brick education and taken on some lawyer-lucrative job. After bricklaying for thirty years, my father promised himself I'd never pile bricks and blocks into walls for a living. He figured an education—genielike and benevolent—would somehow rocket me into the consecrated trajectory of the upwardly mobile, and load some serious loot into my pockets. What he didn't count on was his eldest son breaking blue-collar rule No. 1: Make as much money as you can, to pay for as good a life as you can get.

He'd tell me about it when I was nineteen, my collar already fading to white. I was the college boy who handed him the wrong wrench on help-around-the-house Saturdays. "You better make a lot of money," my blue-collar handy dad wryly warned me as we huddled in front of a disassembled dishwasher I had neither the inclination nor the aptitude to fix. "You're gonna need to hire someone to hammer a nail into a wall for you."

In 1980, after college and graduate school, I was offered my first job, on a now-dead daily paper in Columbus, Ohio. I broke the news in the kitchen, where all the family business is discussed. My mother wept as if it were Vietnam. My father had a few questions: "Ohio? Where the hell is Ohio?"

I said it's somewhere west of New York City, that it was like Pennsylvania, only more so. I told him I wanted to write, and these were the only people who'd take me.

"Why can't you get a good job that pays something, like in advertising in the city, and write on the side?"

"Advertising is lying," I said, smug and sanctimonious, ever the unc-   10 tuous undergraduate. "I wanna tell the truth."

"The truth?" the old man exploded, his face reddening as it does when he's up twenty stories in high wind. "What's truth?" I said it's real life, and writing about it would make me happy. "You're happy with your family," my father said, spilling blue-collar rule No. 2. "That's what makes you happy. After that, it all comes down to dollars and cents. What gives you comfort besides your family? Money, only money."

During the two weeks before I moved, he reminded me that newspaper journalism is a dying field, and I could do better. Then he pressed advertising again, though neither of us knew anything about it, except that you could work in Manhattan, the borough with the water-beading high gloss, the island polished clean by money. I couldn't explain myself, so I packed, unpopular and confused. No longer was I the good son who studied hard and fumbled endearingly with tools. I was hacking people off.

One night, though, my father brought home some heavy tape and that clear, plastic bubble stuff you pack your mother's second-string dishes in.

"You probably couldn't do this right," my father said to me before he sealed the boxes and helped me take them to UPS. "This is what he wants," my father told my mother the day I left for Columbus in my grandfather's eleven-year-old gray Cadillac. "What are you gonna do?" After I said my good-byes, my father took me aside and pressed five $100 bills into my hands. "It's okay," he said over my weak protests. "Don't tell your mother."

When I broke the news about what the paper was paying me, my father suggested I get a part-time job to augment the income. "Maybe you could drive a cab." Once, after I was chewed out by the city editor for something trivial, I made the mistake of telling my father during a visit home. "They pay you nothin', and they push you around too much in that business," he told me, the rage building. "Next time, you gotta grab the guy by the throat and tell him he's a big jerk."

"Dad, I can't talk to the boss like that."   15

"Tell him. You get results that way. Never take any shit." A few years before, a guy didn't like the retaining wall my father and his partner had built. They tore it down and did it again, but the guy still bitched. My father's partner shoved the guy into the freshly laid bricks. "Pay me off," my father said, and he and his partner took the money and walked. Blue-collar guys have no patience for office politics and corporate bile-swallowing. Just pay me off and I'm gone. Eventually, I moved on to a job in Cleveland, on a paper my father has heard of. I think he looks on it as a sign of progress, because he hasn't mentioned advertising for a while.

When he was my age, my father was already dug in with a trade, a wife, two sons and a house in a neighborhood in Brooklyn not far from where he was born. His workaday, family-centered life has been very much in step with his immigrant father's. I sublet what the real-estate people call a junior one-bedroom in a dormlike condo in a Cleveland suburb. Unmarried and unconnected in an insouciant, perpetual student kind of way, I rent movies during the week and feed single women in restaurants on Saturday nights. My dad asks me about my dates, but he goes crazy over the word "woman." "A girl," he corrects. "You went out with a girl. Don't say 'woman.' It sounds like you're takin' out your grandmother."

I've often believed blue-collaring is the more genuine of lives, in greater proximity to primordial manhood. My father is provider and protector, concerned only with the basics: food and home, love and progeny. He's also a generation closer to the heritage, a warmer spot nearer the fire that forged and defined us. Does heat dissipate and light fade further from the source? I live for my career, and frequently feel lost and codeless, devoid of the blue-collar rules my father grew up with. With no baby-boomer groomer to show me the way, I've been choreographing my own tentative shuffle across the wax-shined dance floor on the edge of the Great Middle Class, a different rhythm in a whole new ballroom.

I'm sure it's tough on my father, too, because I don't know much about bricklaying, either, except that it's hell on the body, a daily sacrifice. I idealized my dad as a kind of dawn-rising priest of labor, engaged in holy ritual. Up at five every day, my father has made a religion of responsibility. My younger brother, a Wall Street white-collar guy with the sense to make a decent salary, says he always felt safe when he heard Dad stir before him, as if Pop were taming the day for us. My father, fifty-five years old, but expected to put out as if he were three decades stronger, slips on machine-washable vestments of khaki cotton without waking my mother. He goes into the kitchen and turns on the radio to catch the temperature. Bricklayers have an occupational need to know the weather. And because I am my father's son, I can recite the five-day forecast at any given moment.

My father isn't crazy about this life. He wanted to be a singer and actor   20
when he was young, but that was frivolous doodling to his Italian family, who expected money to be coming in, stoking the stove that kept hearth fires ablaze. Dreams simply were not energy-efficient. My dad learned a trade, as he was supposed to, and settled into a life of pre-scripted routing. He says he can't find the black-and-white publicity glossies he once had made.

Although I see my dad infrequently, my brother, who lives at home, is with the old man every day. Chris has a lot more blue-collar in him than I do, despite his management-level career; for a short time, he wanted to be a construction worker, but my parents persuaded him to go to Columbia. Once in a while he'll bag a lunch and, in a nice wool suit, meet my father at a construction site and share sandwiches of egg salad on semolina bread.

It was Chris who helped my dad most when my father tried to change his life several months ago. My dad wanted a civil-service bricklayer foreman's job that wouldn't be so physically demanding. There was a written test that included essay questions about construction work. My father hadn't done anything like it in forty years. Why the hell they needed bricklayers to write essays I have no idea, but my father sweated it out. Every morning before sunrise, Chris would be ironing a shirt, bleary-eyed, and my father would sit at the kitchen table and read aloud his practice essays on how to wash down a wall, or how to build a tricky corner. Chris would suggest words and approaches.

It was so hard for my dad. He had to take a Stanley Kaplan-like prep course in a junior high school three nights a week after work for six weeks. At class time, the outside men would come in, twenty-five construction workers squeezing themselves into little desks. Tough blue-collar guys armed with No. 2 pencils leaning over and scratching out their practice essays, cement in their hair, tar on their pants, their work boots too big and clumsy to fit under the desks.

"Is this what finals felt like?" my father would ask me on the phone when I pitched in to help long-distance. "Were you always this nervous?" I told him yes. I told him writing's always difficult. He thanked Chris and me for the coaching, for putting him through school this time. My father thinks he did okay, but he's still awaiting the test results. In the meantime, he takes life the blue-collar way, one brick at a time.

When we see each other these days, my father still asks how the money is. Sometimes he reads my stories; usually he likes them, although he recently criticized one piece as being a bit sentimental: "Too schmaltzy," he said. Some psychologists say that the blue-white-collar gap between fathers and sons leads to alienation, but I tend to agree with Dr. Al Baraff, a clinical psychologist and director of the Men-Center in Washington, D.C. "The core of the relationship is based on emotional and hereditary traits," Baraff says. "Class [distinctions] just get added on. If it's a healthful relationship from when you're a kid, there's a respect back and forth that'll continue." 25

Nice of the doctor to explain, but I suppose I already knew that. Whatever is between my father and me, whatever keeps us talking and keeps us close, has nothing to do with work and economic class.

During one of my visits to Brooklyn not long ago, he and I were in the car, on our way to buy toiletries, one of my father's weekly routines. "You know, you're not as successful as you could be," he began, blue-collar blunt as usual. "You paid your dues in school. You deserve better restaurants, better clothes." Here we go, I thought, the same old stuff. I'm sure every family has five or six similar big issues that are replayed like well-worn videotapes. I wanted to fast-forward this thing when we stopped at a red light.

Just then my father turned to me, solemn and intense. His knees were aching and his back muscles were throbbing in dockable intervals that registered in his eyes. It was the end of a week of lifting fifty-pound blocks. "I envy you," he said quietly. "For a man to do something he likes and get paid for it—that's fantastic." He smiled at me before the light changed, and we drove on. To thank him for the understanding, I sprang for the deodorant and shampoo. For once, my father let me pay.

Discussion Questions

1. According to what you have read, describe the author's relationship with his father.

2. What are the blue-collar rules mentioned in the story? What do they imply? Do you think they represent the values of only one particular class?
3. What does the writer's father mean when he says that his son's collar is "fading into white"? What typifies a white-collar lifestyle?
4. What differences can you see between the writer's and his father's values? How do they resolve the differences?
5. What insight did the writer's father gain when he was preparing for his test? How does it affect his relationship with his sons?
6. What is the significance of the essay's conclusion in which Lubrano's father lets him pay for the first time?
7. Lubrano is not a bricklayer, but he does labor over words. Discuss the writing strategies he uses to build his essay.

Writing Tasks

- Write an essay in which you discuss the differences and similarities between your values and beliefs and those of your parents'.
- What is the most important factor to you when choosing a career: money, satisfaction, helping others, prestige, or something else? Write an essay explaining your answer.

Five Minds for the Future

Howard Gardner

Howard Gardner is currently the John H. and Elisabeth A. Hobbs Professor of Cognition and Education at the Harvard Graduate School of Education. He is the author of twenty-four books including *Frames of Mind: The Theory of Multiple Intelligences* (1983) and *The Development and Education of the Mind* (2005). In 1981, Gardner was awarded the prestigious MacArthur Prize Fellowship. His work continues to focus on the theory of multiple intelligences and on the idea of social responsibility at work and at play.

Pre-Reading

What kind of intelligence do you think is most relevant for your area of study?

FOR SEVERAL DECADES, as a researcher in psychology, I have been pondering the human mind. I've studied how the mind develops, how it is organized, what it's like in its fullest expanse. I've studied how people learn, how they create, how they lead, how they change the minds of other persons or their own minds. For the most part, I've been content to describe the typical operations of the mind—a daunting task in itself. But on occasion, I've also offered views about how we *should* use our minds.

In *Five Minds for the Future* I venture further. While making no claims to have a crystal ball, I concern myself here with the kinds of minds that people will need if they—if *we*—are to thrive in the world during the eras to come. The larger part of my enterprise remains descriptive—I specify the operations of the minds that we will need. But I cannot hide the fact that I am engaged as well in a "values enterprise": the minds that I describe are also the ones that I believe we *should* develop in the future.

Why the shift from description to prescription? In the interconnected world in which the vast majority of human beings now live, it is not enough to state what each individual or group needs to survive on its own turf. In the long run, it is not possible for parts of the world to thrive while others remain desperately poor and deeply frustrated. Recalling the words of Benjamin Franklin, "We must indeed all hang together, or, most assuredly, we shall all hang separately." Further, the world of the future—with its ubiquitous search engines, robots, and other computational devices—will

1

demand capacities that until now have been mere options. To meet this new world on its own terms, we should begin to cultivate these capacities now.

As your guide, I will be wearing a number of hats. As a trained psychologist, with a background in cognitive science and neuroscience, I will draw repeatedly on what we know from a scientific perspective about the operation of the human mind and the human brain. But humans differ from other species in that we possess history as well as prehistory, hundreds and hundreds of diverse cultures and subcultures, and the possibility of informed, conscious choice; and so I will be drawing equally on history, anthropology, and other humanistic disciplines. Because I am speculating about the directions in which our society and our planet are headed, political and economic considerations loom large. And, to repeat, I balance these scholarly perspectives with a constant reminder that a description of minds cannot escape a consideration of human values.

Enough throat clearing. Time to bring onstage the five *dramatis personae*   5
of this literary presentation. Each has been important historically; each figures to be even more crucial in the future. With these "minds," as I refer to them, a person will be well equipped to deal with what is expected, as well as what cannot be anticipated; without these minds, a person will be at the mercy of forces that he or she can't understand, let alone control.

The disciplined mind has mastered at least one way of thinking—a distinctive mode of cognition that characterizes a specific scholarly discipline, craft, or profession. Much research confirms that it takes up to ten years to master a discipline. The disciplined mind also knows how to work steadily over time to improve skill and understanding—in the vernacular, it is highly disciplined. Without at least one discipline under his belt, the individual is destined to march to someone else's tune.

The synthesizing mind takes information from disparate sources, understands and evaluates that information objectively, and puts it together in ways that make sense to the synthesizer and also to other persons. Valuable in the past, the capacity to synthesize becomes ever more crucial as information continues to mount at dizzying rates.

Building on discipline and synthesis, *the creating mind* breaks new ground. It puts forth new ideas, poses unfamiliar questions, conjures up fresh ways of thinking, arrives at unexpected answers. Ultimately, these creations must find acceptance among knowledgeable consumers. By virtue of its anchoring in territory that is not yet rule-governed, the creating mind seeks to remain at least one step ahead of even the most sophisticated computers and robots.

Recognizing that nowadays one can no longer remain within one's shell or on one's home territory, *the respectful mind* notes and welcomes differences between human individuals and between human groups, tries to understand these "others," and seeks to work effectively with them. In a world where we are all interlinked, intolerance or disrespect is no longer a viable option.

Proceeding on a level more abstract than the respectful mind, *the ethical mind* ponders the nature of one's work and the needs and desires of the society in which one lives. This mind conceptualizes how workers can serve purposes beyond self-interest and how citizens can work unselfishly to improve the lot of all. The ethical mind then acts on the basis of these analyses.

10

Disciplined

Even as a young child, I loved putting words on paper, and I have continued to do so throughout my life. As a result, I have honed skills of planning, executing, critiquing, and teaching writing. I also work steadily to improve my writing, thus embodying the second meaning of the word *discipline:* training to perfect a skill.

My formal discipline is psychology, and it took me a decade to think like a psychologist. When I encounter a controversy about the human mind or human behavior, I think immediately about how to study the issue empirically, what control groups to marshal, how to analyze the data and revise my hypotheses when necessary.

Turning to management, I have many years of experience supervising teams of research assistants of various sizes, scopes, and missions—and I have the lessons and battle scars to show for it. My understanding has been enriched by observing successful and not-so-successful presidents, deans, and department chairs around the university; addressing and consulting with corporations; and studying leadership and ethics across the professions over the past fifteen years. Beyond question, both management and leadership are disciplines—though they can be informed by scientific studies, they are better thought of as crafts. By the same token, any professional—whether she's a lawyer, an architect, an engineer—has to master the bodies of knowledge and the key procedures that entitle her to membership in the relevant guild. And all of us—scholars, corporate leaders, professionals—must continually hone our skills.

Synthesizing

As a student I enjoyed reading disparate texts and learning from distinguished and distinctive lecturers, I then attempted to make sense of these sources of information, putting them together in ways that were generative, at least for me. In writing papers and preparing for tests that would be evaluated by others, I drew on this increasingly well-honed skill of synthesizing. When I began to write articles and books, the initial ones were chiefly works of synthesis: textbooks in social psychology and developmental psychology, and, perhaps more innovatively, the first booklength examination of cognitive science.

Whether one is working at a university, a law firm, or a corporation,   15 the job of the manager calls for synthesis. The manager must consider the job to be done, the various workers on hand, their current assignments and skills, and how best to execute the current priority and move on to the next one. A good manager also looks back over what has been done in the past months and tries to anticipate how best to carry out future missions. As she begins to develop new visions, communicate them to associates, and contemplate how to realize these innovations, she invades the realms of strategic leadership and creativity within the business or profession. And of course, synthesizing the current state of knowledge, incorporating new findings, and delineating new dilemmas is part and parcel of the work of any professional who wishes to remain current with her craft.

Creating

In my scholarly career, a turning point was my publication in 1983 of *Frames of Mind: The Theory of Multiple Intelligences*. At the time, I thought of this work as a synthesis of cognition from many disciplinary perspectives. In retrospect, I have come to understand that *Frames of Mind* differed from my earlier books. I was directly challenging the consensual view of intelligence and putting forth my own iconoclastic notions, which were ripe, in turn, for vigorous critiques. Since then, my scholarly work is better described as a series of attempts to break new ground—efforts at forging knowledge about creativity, leadership, and ethics—than as syntheses of existing work. Parenthetically, I might point out that this sequence is unusual. In the sciences, younger workers are more likely to achieve creative breakthroughs, while older ones typically pen syntheses.

In general, we look to leaders, rather than to managers, for examples of creativity. The transformational leader creates a compelling narrative about the missions of her organization or polity; embodies that narrative in her own life; and is able, through persuasion and personal example, to change the thoughts, feelings, and behaviors of those whom she seeks to lead.

And what of the role of creativity in the workaday life of the professional? Major creative breakthroughs are relatively rare in accounting or engineering, in law or medicine. Indeed, one does well to be suspicious of claims that a radically new method of accounting, bridge building, surgery, prosecution, or generating energy has just been devised. Increasingly, however, rewards accrue to those who fashion small but significant changes in professional practice. I would readily apply the descriptor *creative* to the individual who figures out how to audit books in a country whose laws have been changed and whose currency has been revalued three times in a year, or to the attorney who ascertains how to protect intellectual property under conditions of monetary (or political or social or technological) volatility.

Respectful and Ethical

As I shift focus to the last two kinds of minds, a different set of analyses 20
becomes appropriate. The first three kinds of minds deal primarily with cognitive forms; the last two deal with our relations to other human beings. One of the last two (respectful) is more concrete; the other (ethical) is more abstract. Also, the differences across career specializations become less important: we are dealing with how human beings—be they scientists, artists, managers, leaders, craftspeople, or professionals—think and act throughout their lives. And so, here I shall try to speak to and for all of us.

Turning to respect, whether I am (or you are) writing, researching, or managing, it is important to avoid stereotyping or caricaturing. I must try to understand other persons on their own terms, make an imaginative leap when necessary, seek to convey my trust in them, and try so far as possible to make common cause with them and to be worthy of their trust. This stance does not mean that I ignore my own beliefs, nor that I necessarily accept or pardon all that I encounter. (Respect does not entail a "pass" for terrorists.) But I am obliged to make the effort, and not merely to assume that what I had once believed on the basis of scattered impressions is necessarily true. Such humility may in turn engender positive responses in others.

As I use the term, *ethics* also relates to other persons, but in a more abstract way. In taking ethical stances, an individual tries to understand his or her role as a worker and his or her role as a citizen of a region, a nation, and the planet. In my own case, I ask: What are my obligations as a scientific researcher, a writer, a manager, a leader? If I were sitting on the other side of the table, if I occupied a different niche in society, what would I have the right to expect from those "others" who research, write, manage, lead? And, to take an even wider perspective, what kind of a world would I like to live in, if, to use John Rawls's phrase, I were cloaked in a "veil of ignorance" with respect to my ultimate position in the world? What is my responsibility in bringing such a world into being? Every reader should be able to pose, if not answer, the same set of questions with respect to his or her occupational and civic niche.

For more than a decade, I have been engaged in a large-scale study of "good work"—work that is excellent, ethical, and engaging for the participants. In the latter part of the book I draw on those studies in my accounts of the respectful and the ethical minds.

Education in the Large

When one speaks of cultivating certain kinds of minds, the most immediate frame of reference is that of education. In many ways, this frame is appropriate: after all, designated educators and licensed educational institutions bear the most evident burden in the identification and training of young minds. But we must immediately expand our vision beyond standard educational institutions. In our cultures of today—and of tomorrow—parents, peers, and media play roles at least as significant as do authorized teachers and formal schools. More and more parents "homeschool" or rely on various extra-scholastic mentors or tutors. Moreover, if any cliché of recent years rings true, it is the acknowledgment that education must be lifelong. Those at the workplace are charged with selecting individuals who appear to possess the right kinds of knowledge, skills, minds—in my terms, they should be searching for individuals who possess disciplined, synthesizing, creating, respectful, and ethical minds. But, equally, managers and leaders, directors and deans and presidents, must continue perennially to develop all five kinds of minds in themselves and—equally—in those for whom they bear responsibility.

Discussion Questions

1. What are the five minds that Gardner discusses? Why does Gardner use the term "minds" instead of "intelligences"?
2. Gardner recalls the words of Benjamin Franklin, who says, "We must indeed all hang together, or, most assuredly, we shall all hang separately." What does this mean, and why does Gardner use it?
3. Which of the five minds do you think that you already possess? Which ones would you like to improve?
4. Why is respect and ethical consideration so important to Gardner? Can you think of situations in college when both of these ideas concerning social relations become important?
5. Gardner believes that schools are an important place where one develops the five minds. In what other institutions or places does this sort of development need to take place?

Writing Task

- Write an essay in which you give your own example of each of the five minds.

How to Bring Our Schools into the 21st Century

Claudia Wallis and Sonja Steptoe

Claudia Wallis graduated from Yale University in 1976 with a degree in philosophy. She began at *Time Magazine* as a writer in 1979, and served as its medical writer from 1982 through 1987. In 1987, she became the third woman in the magazine's history to be named a senior editor. Wallis is especially concerned with women's and children's issues, and she has written more than 20 cover stories for *Time*. Sonja Steptoe studied economics and journalism at the University of Missouri, and she earned a law degree from Duke University. She has written and served as editor at *Sports Illustrated*, *Time Magazine*, and *The Wall Street Journal*. Steptoe has won numerous awards for her journalism including two National Magazine Awards.

Pre-Reading

Can you think of ways new technologies could be used to improve your current educational experience?

There's a dark little joke exchanged by educators with a dissident streak: 1
Rip Van Winkle awakens in the 21st century after a hundred-year snooze and is, of course, utterly bewildered by what he sees. Men and women dash about, talking to small metal devices pinned to their ears. Young people sit at home on sofas, moving miniature athletes around on electronic screens. Older folk defy death and disability with metronomes in their chests and with hips made of metal and plastic. Airports, hospitals, shopping malls—every place Rip goes just baffles him. But when he finally walks into a schoolroom, the old man knows exactly where he is. "This is a school," he declares. "We used to have these back in 1906. Only now the blackboards are green."

American schools aren't exactly frozen in time, but considering the pace of change in other areas of life, our public schools tend to feel like throwbacks. Kids spend much of the day as their great-grandparents once did: sitting in rows, listening to teachers lecture, scribbling notes by hand, reading from textbooks that are out of date by the time they are printed. A yawning chasm (with an emphasis on yawning) separates the world inside the schoolhouse from the world outside.

For the past five years, the national conversation on education has focused on reading scores, math tests and closing the "achievement gap" between social classes. This is not a story about that conversation. This is a story about the big public conversation the nation is *not* having about education, the one that will ultimately determine not merely whether some fraction of our children get "left behind" but also whether an entire generation of kids will fail to make the grade in the global economy because they can't think their way through abstract problems, work in teams, distinguish good information from bad or speak a language other than English.

This week the conversation will burst onto the front page, when the New Commission on the Skills of the American Workforce, a high-powered, bipartisan assembly of Education Secretaries and business, government and other education leaders releases a blueprint for rethinking American education from pre-K to 12 and beyond to better prepare students to thrive in the global economy. While that report includes some controversial proposals, there is nonetheless a remarkable consensus among educators and business and policy leaders on one key conclusion: we need to bring what we teach and how we teach into the 21st century.

Right now we're aiming too low. Competency in reading and math—   5
the focus of so much No Child Left Behind (NCLB) testing—is the meager minimum. Scientific and technical skills are, likewise, utterly necessary but insufficient. Today's economy demands not only a high-level competence in the traditional academic disciplines but also what might be called 21st century skills. Here's what they are:

Knowing More About the World

Kids are global citizens now, even in small-town America, and they must learn to act that way. Mike Eskew, CEO of UPS, talks about needing workers who are "global trade literate, sensitive to foreign cultures, conversant in different languages"—not exactly strong points in the U.S., where fewer than half of high school students are enrolled in a foreign-language class and where the social-studies curriculum tends to fixate on U.S. history.

Thinking Outside the Box

Jobs in the new economy—the ones that won't get outsourced or automated—"put an enormous premium on creative and innovative skills, seeing patterns where other people see only chaos," says Marc Tucker, an author of the skills-commission report and president of the National Center on Education and the Economy. Traditionally that's been an American strength, but schools have become less daring in the back-to-basics climate of NCLB. Kids also must learn to think across disciplines, since that's where most new breakthroughs are made. It's interdisciplinary combinations—design and technology, mathematics and art—"that produce YouTube and Google," says Thomas Friedman, the best-selling author of *The World Is Flat*.

Becoming Smarter About New Sources of Information

In an age of overflowing information and proliferating media, kids need to rapidly process what's coming at them and distinguish between what's reliable and what isn't. "It's important that students know how to manage it, interpret it, validate it, and how to act on it," says Dell executive Karen Bruett, who serves on the board of the Partnership for 21st Century Skills, a group of corporate and education leaders focused on upgrading American education.

Developing Good People Skills

EQ, or emotional intelligence, is as important as IQ for success in today's workplace. "Most innovations today involve large teams of people," says former Lockheed Martin CEO Norman Augustine. "We have to emphasize communication skills, the ability to work in teams and with people from different cultures."

Can our public schools, originally designed to educate workers for agrarian life and industrial-age factories, make the necessary shifts? The skills commission will argue that it's possible only if we add new depth and rigor to our curriculum and standardized exams, redeploy the dollars we spend on education, reshape the teaching force and reorganize who runs the schools. But without waiting for such a revolution, enterprising administrators around the country have begun to update their schools, often with ideas and support from local businesses. The state of Michigan, conceding that it can no longer count on the ailing auto industry to absorb its poorly educated and low-skilled workers, is retooling its high schools, instituting what are among the most rigorous graduation requirements in the nation. Elsewhere, organizations like the Bill and Melinda Gates Foundation, the Carnegie Foundation for the Advancement of Teaching and the Asia Society are pouring money and expertise into model programs to show the way.

What It Means to Be a Global Student

Quick! How many ways can you combine nickels, dimes and pennies to get $2.04? That's the challenge for students in a second-grade math class at Seattle's John Stanford International School, and hands are flying up with answers. The students sit at tables of four manipulating play money. One boy shouts " 10 plus 10"; a girl offers "10 plus 5 plus 5," only it sounds like this: *"Ju, tasu, go, tasu, go."* Down the hall, third-graders are learning to interpret charts and graphs showing how many hours of sleep people need at different ages. *"¿Cuantas horas duerme un bebé?"* asks the teacher Sabrina Storile.

This public elementary school has taken the idea of global education and run with it. All students take some classes in either Japanese or Spanish. Other subjects are taught in English, but the content has an international flavor. The school pulls its 393 students from the surrounding highly diverse neighborhood and by lottery from other parts of the city. Generally, its scores on state tests are at or above average, although those exams barely scratch the surface of what Stanford students learn.

Before opening the school seven years ago, principal Karen Kodama surveyed 1,500 business leaders on which languages to teach (plans for Mandarin were dropped for lack of classroom space) and which skills and disciplines. "No. 1 was technology," she recalls. Even first-graders at Stanford begin to use PowerPoint and Internet tools. "Exposure to world cultures was also an important trait cited by the executives," says Kodama, so that instead of circling back to the Pilgrims and Indians every autumn, children at Stanford do social-studies units on Asia, Africa, Australia, Mexico and South America. Students actively apply the lessons in foreign language and culture by videoconferencing with sister schools in Japan, Africa and Mexico, by exchanging messages, gifts and joining in charity projects.

Stanford International shows what's possible for a public elementary school, although it has the rare advantage of support from corporations like Nintendo and Starbucks, which contribute to its $1.7 million-a-year budget. Still, dozens of U.S. school districts have found ways to orient some of their students toward the global economy. Many have opened schools that offer the international baccalaureate (LB.) program, a rigorous, off-the-shelf curriculum recognized by universities around the world and first introduced in 1968—well before globalization became a buzzword.

To earn an LB. diploma, students must prove written and spoken proficiency in a second language, write a 4,000-word college-level research paper, complete a real-world service project and pass rigorous oral and written subject exams. Courses offer an international perspective, so even a lesson on the American Revolution will interweave sources from Britain and France with views from the Founding Fathers. "We try to build something we call international mindedness," says Jeffrey Beard, director general of the International Baccalaureate Organization in Geneva, Switzerland. "These are students who can grasp issues across national borders. They have an understanding of nuances and complexity and a balanced approach to problem solving." Despite stringent certification requirements, LB. schools are growing in the U.S.—from about 350 in 2000 to 682 today. The U.S. Department of Education has a pilot effort to bring the program to more low-income students.

Real Knowledge in the Google Era

Learn the names of all the rivers in South America. That was the assignment given to Deborah Stipek's daughter Meredith in school, and her mom, who's dean of the Stanford University School of Education, was not impressed. "That's silly," Stipek told her daughter. "Tell your teacher that if you need to know anything besides the Amazon, you can look it up on Google." Any number of old-school assignments—memorizing the battles of the Civil War or the periodic table of the elements—now seem faintly absurd. That kind of information, which is poorly retained unless you routinely use it, is available at a keystroke. Still, few would argue that an American child shouldn't learn the causes of the Civil War or understand how the periodic table reflects the atomic structure and properties of the elements. As school critic E.D. Hirsch Jr. points out in his book, *The Knowledge Deficit*, kids need a substantial fund of information just to make sense of reading materials beyond the grade-school level. Without mastering the fundamental building blocks of math, science or history, complex concepts are impossible.

Many analysts believe that to achieve the right balance between such core knowledge and what educators call "portable skills"—critical thinking, making connections between ideas and knowing how to keep on learning—the U.S. curriculum needs to become more like that of Singapore, Belgium and Sweden, whose students outperform American students on math and science tests. Classes in these countries dwell on key concepts that are taught in depth and in careful sequence, as opposed to a succession of forgettable details so often served in U.S. classrooms. Textbooks and tests support this approach. "Countries from Germany to Singapore have extremely small textbooks that focus on the most powerful and generative ideas," says Roy Pea, co-director of the Stanford Center for Innovations in Learning. These might be the key theorems in math, the laws of thermodynamics in science or the relationship between supply and

15

demand in economics. America's bloated textbooks, by contrast, tend to gallop through a mind-numbing stream of topics and subtopics in an attempt to address a vast range of state standards.

Depth over breadth and the ability to leap across disciplines are exactly what teachers aim for at the Henry Ford Academy, a public charter school in Dearborn, Mich. This fall, 10th-graders in Charles Dershimer's science class began a project that combines concepts from earth science, chemistry, business and design. After reading about Nike's efforts to develop a more environmentally friendly sneaker, students had to choose a consumer product, analyze and explain its environmental impact and then develop a plan for re-engineering it to reduce pollution costs without sacrificing its commercial appeal. Says Dershimer: "It's a challenge for them and for me."

A New Kind of Literacy

The juniors in Bill Stroud's class are riveted by a documentary called *Loose Change* unspooling on a small TV screen at the Baccalaureate School for Global Education, in urban Astoria, N.Y. The film uses 9/11 footage and interviews with building engineers and Twin Towers survivors to make an oddly compelling if paranoid case that interior explosions unrelated to the impact of the airplanes brought down the World Trade Center on that fateful day. Afterward, the students—an ethnic mix of New Yorkers with their own 9/11 memories—dive into a discussion about the elusive nature of truth.

Raya Harris finds the video more convincing than the official version of the facts. Marisa Reichel objects. "Because of a movie, you are going to change your beliefs?" she demands. "Just because people heard explosions doesn't mean there were explosions. You can say you feel the room spinning, but it isn't." This kind of discussion about what we know and how we know it is typical of a theory of knowledge class, a required element for an international-baccalaureate diploma. Stroud has posed this question to his class on the blackboard: "If truth is difficult to prove in history, does it follow that all versions are equally acceptable?"

Throughout the year, the class will examine news reports, websites, propaganda, history books, blogs, even pop songs. The goal is to teach kids to be discerning consumers of information and to research, formulate and defend their own views, says Stroud, who is founder and principal of the four-year-old public school, which is located in a repurposed handbag factory.

Classes like this, which teach key aspects of information literacy, remain rare in public education, but more and more universities and employers

20

say they are needed as the world grows ever more deluged with information of variable quality. Last year, in response to demand from colleges, the Educational Testing Service unveiled a new, computer-based exam designed to measure information-and-communication-technology literacy. A pilot study of the test with 6,200 high school seniors and college freshmen found that only half could correctly judge the objectivity of a website. "Kids tend to go to Google and cut and paste a research report together," says Terry Egan, who led the team that developed the new test. "We kind of assumed this generation was so comfortable with technology that they know how to use it for research and deeper thinking," says Egan. "But if they're not taught these skills, they don't necessarily pick them up."

Learning 2.0

The chairman of Sun Microsystems was up against one of the most vexing challenges of modern life: a third-grade science project. Scott McNealy had spent hours searching the Web for a lively explanation of electricity that his son could understand. "Finally I found a very nice, animated, educational website showing electrons zooming around and tests after each section. We did this for about an hour and a half and had a ball—a great father-son moment of learning. All of a sudden we ran out of runway because it was a site to help welders, and it then got into welding." For McNealy the experience, three years ago, provided one of life's *aha!* moments: "It made me wonder why there isn't a website where I can just go and have anything I want to learn, K to 12, online, browser based and free."

His solution: draw on the Wikipedia model to create a collection of online courses that can be updated, improved, vetted and built upon by innovative teachers, who, he notes, "are always developing new materials and methods of instruction because they aren't happy with what they have." And who better to create such a site than McNealy, whose company has led the way in designing open-source computer software? He quickly raised some money, created a nonprofit and—*voila!*— Curriki.org made its debut January 2006, and has been growing fast. Some 450 courses are in the works, and about 3,000 people have joined as members. McNealy reports that a teenager in Kuwait has already completed the introductory physics and calculus classes in 18 days.

Curriki, however, isn't meant to replace going to school but to supplement it and offer courses that may not be available locally. It aims to give teachers classroom-tested content materials and assessments that are livelier and more current and multimedia-based than printed textbooks. Ultimately, it could take the Web 2.0 revolution to school, closing that yawning gap between how kids learn at school and how they do everything else.

Educators around the country and overseas are already discussing ways to certify Curriki's online course work for credit.

Some states are creating their own online courses. "In the 21st century, the ability to be a lifelong learner will, for many people, be dependent on their ability to access and benefit from online learning," says Michael Flanagan, Michigan's superintendent of public instruction, which is why Michigan's new high school graduation requirements, which roll out next year, include completing at least one course online.

A Dose of Reality

Teachers need not fear that they will be made obsolete. They will, however, feel increasing pressure to bring their methods—along with the curriculum—into line with the way the modern world works. That means putting a greater emphasis on teaching kids to collaborate and solve problems in small groups and apply what they've learned in the real world. Besides, research shows that kids learn better that way than with the old chalk-and-talk approach.

At suburban Farmington High in Michigan, the engineering-technology department functions like an engineering firm, with teachers as project managers, a Ford Motor Co. engineer as a consultant and students working in teams. The principles of calculus, physics, chemistry and engineering are taught through activities that fill the hallways with a cacophony of nailing, sawing and chattering. The result the kids learn helps them to apply academic principles to the real world, think strategically and solve problems.

Such lessons also teach students to show respect for others as well as to be punctual, responsible and work well in teams. Those skills were badly missing in recently hired high school graduates, according to a survey of over 400 human-resource professionals conducted by the Partnership for 21st Century Skills. "Kids don't know how to shake your hand at graduation," says Rudolph Crew, superintendent of the Miami-Dade school system. Deportment, he notes, used to be on the report card. Some of the nation's more forward-thinking schools are bringing it back. It's one part of 21st-century education that sleepy old Rip would recognize.

Discussion Questions

1. Discuss the reference to Rip Van Winkle. In what ways do you see school as "frozen in time"?
2. What skills do the authors believe American students need to learn to excel in the modern world? Can you give examples where these skills are taught?

3. What do the authors mean by "thinking outside the box"? Can you give examples where education is behind technology?
4. Why is it increasingly important for today's students to know more about the world? Can you give specific examples where such knowledge would be particularly helpful?
5. Why is it more important than ever to be able to distinguish the quality and credibility of new sources of information?
6. Define what Jeffrey Beard means by "international mindedness."
7. Discuss the difference between "core" knowledge and "portable skills." How should they work together?
8. In your view, what is a better method of learning: amassing a large supply of details about lots of topic or concentrating on key ideas and events?
9. What are the advantages and disadvantages of online learning?

Writing Tasks

- Discuss the advantages or disadvantages of on-line education as compared to the traditional model.
- Write an essay that takes on an issue debated on a web log or blog. Be sure to incorporate and evaluate the diverse opinions expressed in the blog discussion.

Making Connections

1. Consider the points that Howard Gardner raises in "Five Minds for the Future." Do you think that Claudia Wallis's and Sonja Steptoe's discussion of the evolution of education in a global context in "How to build a Student for the 21st Century" addresses his concerns? Explain in detail.
2. Drawing from the ideas in your readings, especially Bilal Rahmani's "Chronicles of a Once Pessimistic College Freshmen," discuss the ways that the educational system does not meet the needs of students who are going to college.
3. Write an argumentative essay in which you offer your own reflections on what makes a high performance school and a successful student. Be sure to address some of the issues raised in at least two of the articles in this chapter. Feel free to offer your own experiences to support and develop your positions.

CHAPTER 4

Urban Art and Design

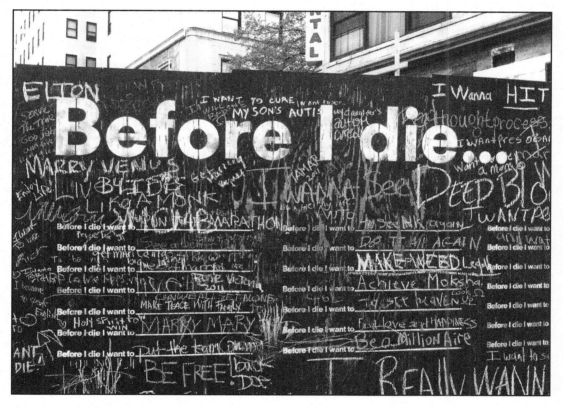

Sean Scanlan, "Before I die," 2011.

I think artists almost always end up turning to what's around them, what's in their environment or outside their window.

Susan Rothenberg, Artist

Historically, walls have exhibited the voice of the people. My earliest paintings were made on walls at night. [. . .] As my works evolved, be it paintings, signatures, or even the documentation of these early ephemeral artworks throughout the city walls, the works took on the nature of personal journals based on empirical experiences.

José Parlá, Artist

Art and design *and* New York City, what an enormous topic! There is simply too much to cover, because, first of all, art itself covers so many types and subtypes, from painting to sculpture to performing arts and museum culture. For many decades, New York City has been at the epicenter of U.S. arts and design, especially for fashion, theatre, music, and photography. And tourists from all over the world visit New York City to marvel at the vast array of architectural styles.

In short, New York is a global artistic, creative, and design hub. In this chapter we cannot possibly cover all the arts. Instead, we have selected four subjects as a way to raise awareness and promote further discussion: graffiti, photography, architecture, and music. We encourage students to continue to research art and design, and so, with this in mind, we have additional entries in the appendix of this book.

We start with graffiti. This form of writing, or drawing, is very old and very contentious. From the early cave paintings in Lascaux, France, to etchings on religious walls in Jerusalem, to street corners in Boston in the 1950s, to the brightly colored murals put up on subway trains in New York City in the 1970s, people have been writing on surfaces to send a message. It might not be a stretch to say that people have been writing on walls since there were walls. José Parlá started his graffiti career in Miami, but he has since moved to Brooklyn. Now, his work has crossed over from tags and quick throw-ups to huge, wall-sized canvases that display his expertise in calligraphy and in a hybrid form of diary-writing that pushes the boundaries of what is considered language and what is considered art. Parlá's essay, "Research and Memory," reveals the importance of "mixing documents of memory and research," which has the effect of helping him to affirm his "everlasting devotion to art as a form of spirituality." As for Joseph Anastasio, writing in New York meant a delicate dance between risk and reward, between desire and necessity. Anastasio writes "My Life in Graffiti" from the perspective of a former writer and current professional photographer of subway graffiti.

The three photographers in this section share a fascination with New York City. First, Berenice Abbott, a powerful creative force in the photography world during the 1930s and 40s, pushed the boundary of the proper subject of photography. While Abbott did photograph people, she was primarily interested in the designs and angles of urban geometry. Lewis Hine was primarily interested in labor: who worked? where did they work? and what kind of work did New Yorkers do? These questions were important to Hine. And lastly, we present two photographic portraits by Dinanda Nooney, one of the most important photographers of domestic scenes in Brooklyn. Nooney's carefully composed domestic portraits capture essential qualities about each of her subjects. The portrait of the Basquiat family may reward the careful observer who knows something about the history of Jean-Michel Basquiat, a high-profile pop artist discovered by Andy Warhol.

New York is an ideal place for artists, designers, and architects to not only experiment, but to experiment big. And what better proof is there of big designs than these two: the 1811 grid design for Manhattan and the Empire State Building? Of course, other large designs and structures abound, but, in "Prediction," Dutch architect Rem

Koolhaas believes that the preposterous prediction of the grid layout was the biggest and boldest—as big and bold as the city itself. Donald Reynolds' essay "The Making of an Icon" also describes a bold endeavor—a true colossus. What is so interesting about Reynolds' story of the Empire State Building is not just the sheer size of the skyscraper, but rather that all the parts had to come together in the building process: leadership, finance, planning, marketing, engineering, and architecture.

While we could have filled an entire book on the history, development, and evolution of music in New York, we decided on Mark Naison's essay "From Doo Wop to Hip Hop: The Bittersweet Odyssey of African-Americans in the South Bronx," because it captures the history and culture that serves as the foundation for much of today's hip hop music. Many readers will find that this essay is part sociology, part history, and part call-to-action. The inner city in the 1970s came to be associated with the lines of Grandmaster Flash in "The Message": "Broken glass everywhere, people pissing on the street, you know they just don't care." So, it is both ironic and hopeful that out of the ashes of that era of societal neglect, a vibrant art form and cultural movement arose. Now hip hop is more than music. It is art, design, fashion, culture, and perhaps it is also a form of politics. Naison believes that art and music are central to the mission of education and to the success of New York's neighborhoods; they are not simply frivolous extras.

Research and Memory

José Parlá

José Parlá was born in Miami, Florida in 1973 to parents who were Cuban exiles. He studied at the Savannah College of Art and recently set up his studio in Brooklyn. Parlá began writing graffiti in Miami and his current paintings exhibit aspects of graffiti, only heightened and refined. He calls his art "segmented reality" because his canvases seem to take small samples of real walls. Handwriting becomes what he calls "abstract storytelling," in which the line contains emotions, even if you cannot read the words. His influences include Marcel Duchamp, Cy Twombly, and different Asian calligraphy styles. His art is urban and layered; it invites viewers to try to read the city as palimpsest.

Pre-Reading

What message or messages do you get from "Nevins Street Jargon"?

Historically, walls have exhibited the voice of the people. My earliest 1 paintings were made on walls at night. My thought and impulse behind the gesture was as primitive as that of cavemen marking and drawing in their dwellings to assert their existence in a place and time. As my works evolved, be it paintings, signatures or even the documentation of these early ephemeral art works throughout city walls, the works took on the nature of personal journals based on empirical experiences. The organized black books and photo albums also became my diaries. This style of art became an influential sub-culture in many of the places I have traveled to and inspired the aesthetic in my cityscape paintings.

During the beginning, this was an art that was not accepted by society because it was seen as destructive, rebellious and anarchic. I felt a challenge to present art that originally existed outdoors—inside, like art displayed in museums, and this was an interesting problem for me that needed a solution. I wanted to create works that retained their roots. My new paintings could not abandon their environment. I then embarked on a journey to search out in detail the dialogue of decaying walls, the marks on them, and what it all meant to me. This would lead the paintings to become memory documents.

As a result, these works are time capsules, mixed documents of memory and research; part performance, as I impersonate the characters that leave their marks on walls. Time is a part of these paintings as their creative process simulates the passing of time on city walls and their layers of history with layers of paint, posters, writing, and re-construction. This process, like meditation, affirms my everlasting devotion to art as a form of spirituality, which exists in the present and pays homage to those who leave their traces behind.

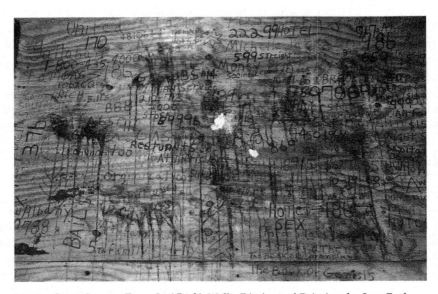

Nevins Street Jargon. From *José Parlá: Walls, Diaries, and Paintings* by Jose Parla. Copyright 2011 José Parlá All Rights Reserved. Member of ARSNY & DACS U.K.

Discussion Questions

1. Discuss the idea of layers and segmented reality in terms of Parlá's painting titled "Your History," which is the on the cover of this textbook.
2. Would you like to have either "Your History" or "Nevins Street Jargon" hanging in your home? Why or why not? What kinds of feelings and emotions do these pieces evoke?
3. Do you think that graffiti is art? Why or why not?
4. Does art have to be beautiful to be art?

Writing Tasks

- Photograph some examples of graffiti in New York City. Write a photo-essay in which you compare José Parlá's work to other, possibly anonymous, writing.
- Create your own tag or signature, and then write an essay discussing the importance of your name, tag, or design to your identity.

My Life in Graffiti

Joseph Anastasio

Joseph Anastasio is a writer and photographer. He has published three books related to New York City graffiti culture and the subway system: *Subway Solitude: One Man's Journey through the NYC Subway System* (2007); *Brooklyn Queens Freight: Graffiti along the Tracks* (2009); and *Yard Job NYC: Graffiti in the Freight Yards of NYC* (2009).

Pre-Reading

What is your passion? Do your career goals relate to it?

Ditmars

On the subway again. Morning. Rush hour. I get on every day at Ditmars in Queens. The clean silver train is always there waiting to go. The car cleaners have already swept off the litter, and the conductor is at the ready by the intercom. "Partner got the line up?" he blurts out, and the voice crackles back over the speakers and says, "Yes." "Next stop Astoria Blvd, stand clear of the closing doors." The dialog is always the same; the trains all look more or less the same. The passengers, well, they all look the same, too. Everything is always routine on a weekday-morning commute. Robotic, boring. Devoid of life, really.

There was a time when it wasn't quite this way . . .

I remember the 1980s, the good old days of New York, when each and every subway car bore an exterior top-to-bottom coating of layers upon layers of graffiti. Each car was a unique blend of colors. Some were painted from one end to the other with artistic "pieces," cloaked in bright letters and mystery. Even the windows were covered with paint, sometimes giving a cathedral-like quality to the interior lighting. There were ugly "toy" (beginner) tags with no stylistic merit, making the trains look a mess, and then there were tags that'd make even the best calligrapher wet herself. There were some ugly pieces, and then there were some that resembled oversized versions of something you'd see on a museum wall. Each car was unique. Each one colored with paint, sweat, and life itself.

1

I remember growing up and riding the subways a lot with my parents, and being inspired by all of this artwork. Graffiti looked and smelled a lot like being a rock star. If you did it good enough and got your name up enough, everyone in the city would know your name. When the book *Subway Art* came out back then, it put a public face on the movement. It showed the artwork and the people behind it, helping lay a path to art careers that some still enjoy today. If having your name up all over town wasn't Rock Star enough, getting your work in such a book sure did the trick. Part of me wanted to be a rock star. I'd never learn to play an instrument well enough, but I could draw damn good.

Sean Scanlan, "Graffiti Keeps Me Clean," 2010.

I remember hanging out in some of the tunnels for hours at a time.   5
I remember chilling out down there and watching these two guys paint a train that was parked on some unused track, being inspired by their boldness. I wasn't old enough to even walk into a hardware store to get some paint without raising an eyebrow, but time would soon take care of that.

30th Avenue

I remember tagging up on 30th Ave station. I was still young and brash, and more importantly I was free. I could stay out late no questions asked. My teen responsibility was to be irresponsible. I could get my hands on paint any time. I could get away with being a graffiti-writer now, and I went for mine.

Back when I was hitting this station, the graffiti in, on, and around the NYC subway system was dead, or so the MTA thought. Us writers weren't having it though. Rooftops became hot. To get up on a rooftop facing the elevated subway line was prime real estate, a surefire route to fame. The stations themselves became targets, too. The MTA just couldn't paint them as fast as kids were bombing them. Back then there were at least fifty to a hundred active writers in the neighborhood, some just wannabe toys, others more serious—and everyone was trying to get their tags up on these stations weekly. Those were the days; today you'd be lucky to see maybe a dozen people hit these stops during the course of a year.

Broadway

I remember 1991, when all the neighborhood writers hung out on the corner just outside Broadway station, and the cops would come around and harass us for no other reason than because you could tell everyone there was a bad apple. The first US invasion of Iraq had started, and one night the cops rolled up and started frisking the notorious writer Crime SWC. They felt a spray can in his jacket pocket and asked, "What's this?"

"It's a SCUD missile, motherfucker!" he replied. It may as well have been. Spray cans were the weapon, and we were at war with society. We were at war with other gangs and other writers. Fighting to make a name every single day.

Years later I learned that another infamous writer, Sane, was a station agent at this stop. I probably bought tokens from him and didn't even know it. That's how it was back then. Everyone was a writer, and a lot of the really hardcore dudes you'd never know about or recognize unless you ran in the right circles.

36th Avenue

I remember coming up here one night while I was still young but not entirely naive. I was with three other writers. They started tagging up the station and I was just thinking, "What are they, stupid?" We knew the Vandal Squad cops were hiding out in the "lay up" trains—subway cars parked in the middle track during off-peak hours. We knew the cops were watching, or at least I thought we all did. The cops were waiting to catch themselves some collars. Make some arrests, meet the "Performance Standard" (because there's no such a thing as a quota). One cop came up from the only exit on the station, the other from the tracks behind us. It was a trap, and in an instant it wasn't a game anymore. It was over. I was going to jail. My parents would disown me and I'd have to pay some big-ass fine I couldn't possibly afford...

They were big men with badges and guns, and they had us on the ground getting their frisk on. But they were human, and luck was on my side. Let's just say I was the only one to protest some of their search tactics, and that resulted in the cop not being very thorough. They never found the brand-new never-used can of pink Krylon up my coat sleeve. I suppose it helped too that I was a dirty-looking metal-head kid. Every writer I knew shared more or less the same fashion style: fade haircuts, phat sneakers I couldn't afford if I tried, triple-fat goose jackets, and of course beepers. Let's just say I didn't look that way. With my long hair, fucked-up jeans, construction-worker boots, spiky bracelets and .50-caliber bullet shell that I used for a necklace, I looked a lot more like someone out of a death-metal video than a hip-hoppin' graffiti-writer. When a train came, the cops told me to scram. Everyone on the train going home from work was looking out at these little kids in handcuffs on the station with these two big burly cops standing over them. Then the doors closed and suddenly everyone on the train was looking at me, white as a ghost.

I started walking through the train, got off at the next stop, and walked for miles that night. I couldn't go home. I had to wear off the adrenaline. I didn't want a criminal record or grief from my parents and all the other associated stigmas of getting caught. But then again I had a can in my hand, and I knew I had to empty that shit. I bombed and cleaned that can out, and then I retired from the game, or at least that's what I tried to tell myself.

Queens Plaza

I used to always catch tags on Queens Plaza, too. One night I was with my boy and these two guys came up to us—using the universal tagger greeting, "Yo, you guys write?" It was Seus and Spook. I remember them guys... Seus was coming out all over the neighborhood and in the subway tunnels in a big way. I remember a few weeks later when Spook was electrocuted on a power line while out graffiti-bombing some tunnel. He lasted a while in a coma before dying. He was just sixteen. A few years later I heard that Seus was randomly stabbed to death one night. The streets, the tunnels, this graffiti game... it takes a heavy toll sometimes. But when you're young, and when the economy sucks and the crack epidemic is in full swing, you just accept that death is waiting for you. Death might come on any given mission, any given night. You could get stabbed, mugged, beaten, or shot just corning home from hanging out on the subway. There were a dozen ways to Sunday to get fucked up real bad back then, so bombing and living every night like it was your last was just what you did—and you'd do it without regret.

At Queens Plaza, the train finally ducks underground. It leaves the station packed to the gills with passengers. Standing room only, and some of them people are standing uncomfortably close to each other. You'd think maybe people would find another way to get to work besides the subway-sardine option, but they don't. They're persistent, doing this shit day after day after day, just like some taggers. 15

I remember persistence. The word was defined by a name, and that name was Sane Smith. Throughout the '80s, no matter what part of the city you went to, you'd see a Sane or Smith tag, and if you didn't, you'd see some' of their boys, Ghost, JA, Bruz, etc. I was impressed by this persistence and the daring tactics some of these writers employed. 60th Street tunnel was a perfect example of this.

The "60th Street tube" is a long, straight, narrow unforgiving place. Unlike most subway tunnels, there's no place to hide down there should a train come. Smith and Bruz rocked it though, with tags under each light along the tunnel walls. With lights perhaps every 20 feet along this mile-long tunnel, you can do the math.

"It was a mission to hit every light," Smith says. "But we weren't going to leave any space for anyone else to get up. We wanted to claim it." Laying such a claim rarely comes without complications, though. "A worker train came, so we had to run to the next emergency exit—it was like a slow speed chase. We hid there behind a door and they just went by, and we went back to work." Persistence is the quality that makes mere mortals into legends of the graffiti game.

59th Street/Lexington Ave

Getting off the train at 59th Street/Lexington Ave, I look across—across the platform, past the newly assigned cop stuck in his little "Omega" guard booth in the middle of it, across the northbound track—and stare for a split second at the wall. It is dull, gray, and utterly lifeless.

I remember when Gridz hit that wall. It was a simple piece—white, blue, and green, but it shined like a pearl. That shit ran for months and always brought a smile to my face. It takes balls to get up right there on the platform—to do a quickie piece at such a busy station. 20

So much has changed since then. Post-9/11 paranoia mandated the police booth, guarding the cross-river tunnel as best they can. With this twenty-four-hour watch, you won't be seeing any new tags under them lights in the tube anytime soon, and you'll probably never see another piece on that dull gray wall again.

I go down the stairs and transfer to the downtown 5 train. It too consists of nothing but nice new shiny subway cars, complete with digital displays and automatic voice announcements of each stop. A more rote and predictable ride you cannot find. I board the train.

Grand Central Station

I remember the passage of time—the two years between my close call with "the man" and realizing I wasn't done yet. I came out of retirement, if one can ever truly quit this game. By this point I had been practicing on paper religiously and had developed my "handstyle" real good. I wasn't a toy-ass bastard anymore, and I had a new fast-acting super-sticky tag to slap all around town like your drunken mom's face at 4:00 AM.

I wouldn't do it alone, though. I was talking with this girl and she was all bent on adventure. I suggested taggin' up. I showed her some styles. Having an artistic flare, she took to writing like Koch to a crowd. It wasn't too long before we were bombing, taking the streets of Manhattan by storm. I think she even wrote "how 'm I doin'?" in one throwy.

The tag names we used, that's not important. What was important was   25
the fun and adventure we had, the smell of the paint, the adrenaline rush, the aerosol-junky life. Scamming cans wherever we could by day, going out and bombing the town by night. We hit it and hit it big for a hot minute, and when word was going around that the man had their eye on trying to find out about us, we quit it. We emptied out our last cans on a wall in an abandoned lot in Hell's Kitchen. Doing it on the down-low and never bragging about it at the time. That's the only way to really do graf and not get bagged by the man. Keep your mouth shut and do the work.

14th Street

I remember finally feeling satisfied after that. Like I had done what I wanted to do with graffiti and was done with it. I also remember bringing along a camera more and more. I had always been a photographer, but I never really had the cash for a lot of film. By now I was getting older, working, and realizing I could achieve the same effect of graffiti, saying, "Hey, I was there" by taking photos of some of these crazy places we went. For me, the camera replaced the spray can. My handstyle became my shutter style.

*

By this point the crowd on the train has thinned out a bit. The Lexington Avenue line that the 5 train runs on is considered to be one of the most overcrowded in the city. This crowding is due in no small part to the fact that the city has never completed building the Second Avenue line, which is eventually to run parallel to the Lex Ave line and hopefully absorb some of the riders from it.

I remember Second Avenue and meeting up with fellow photographer Mike Epstein and us being the first photographers to explore the abandoned northern half of the 63rd Street station. The station itself is part of the 63rd Street tunnel, though one can easily argue that the northern side of the platform was built as a provision for (and therefore a part of) the Second Avenue tunnel. Most people don't even know that there is a whole other half of a station laying abandoned behind the wall at 63rd and Lex, but sure enough it's there.

Just like everywhere else, a lot of graffiti artists had come and gone before us. According to Swatch, a graffiti artist who was the first to hit a lot of these Second Avenue spots, they went so far as to throw a New Year's party down here. The days of such parties are pretty much gone, but the tags remain. The taggers, thought they still go down there. A graffiti artist who recently went was Jedi 5. "Painting spots of this nature makes graffiti feel worthwhile," he told me. "I don't really care about street bombing, even though it's lots of fun. Coming to exclusive spots like this makes me feel I'm really putting effort into it."

Putting in the effort, finding the spots, and then rocking them in your own special way. Swatch and Tyke did it. Scope and Nuke did it a lot, and now Jedi & co are at it. Graffiti is a cycle, and it does not stop.

From *New York Calling: From Blackout to Bloomberg*, edited by Marshall Berman and Brian Berger. Copyright © Reaktion Books, 2007.

I also remember exploring the Chinatown segment of this Second Avenue subway line. I remember me and Clayton gearing up and going in. It was a nice feeling, being in a subway spot that so few have gotten to see. I remember the marvel of all the extra space they had built in there for utilities and ventilation.

What will happen to this spot when the Second Avenue tunnel is finally built is unknown. Several of the current plans for routing the tunnel downtown do not use this stretch of tunnel at all. It may very well become an orphan, disconnected from the system, a monument to the fiscal crisis of the '70s that brought an end to the construction of the original Second Avenue line.

*

The train keeps moving, now going past the abandoned Worth Street station.

I remember not that long ago going to Worth Street. I remember running down the tracks to photograph this station late one weekday night. We were originally going to go to 18th Street, but the track-workers were out and about. I remember how we had to hide from passing subways on the platform, and how I found an old set of block letters from Rebel.

Rebel remembers that spot well, too. "We came out of that tunnel filthy," he said. "I had soot in my *ears* from that place. We ran out at like 3:00 AM and thought the station we were coming out onto was empty, but there was a guy right there at the end, and when I stepped onto the platform I was right there in his face. He stepped back and almost had a fucking heart attack—this eyes were like dinner plates!" Every real graffiti artist who's ever rocked a can has dozens of memories like these. They are the best urban stories you'll ever hear.

*

Brooklyn Bridge

I remember exploring all the tunnels near Brooklyn Bridge just a few years ago. One night I was down there with Maria, a fellow photographer and a woman who just plain ain't afraid to get down and dirty. We were wandering around down there for a few hours and getting ready to leave. We were waiting for a train to leave the J-train platform so that there wouldn't be any MTA personnel staring at us once we climbed up and out of this hole, but the train just wouldn't leave—and when it finally was about to, we heard work bums walking down the tunnel right toward us. The gig was up and it was time to go—we started running alongside the J train as it headed northbound towards Canal Street. We kept pace with it somehow, arriving at Canal just as the train pulled out continuing northbound. We jumped on the platform and ran out of the station just as some extremely loud buzzer went off on the tracks. Some guy was by the token booth saying, "What's that alarm sound?" We got out onto the street and we ran, finally stopping a few blocks away in a parking lot, where I proceeded to cough up some of the steel dust we kicked up for a good five minutes. You just can't pay for an adventure like that. I remember the war on graffiti. I remember when they singled out people like the brothers SaneSmith and tried to vilify them as best they could. The battle continues today, only more so. Even toy kids these days are getting their names in the paper when they get caught for catching just a few tags around town. To the powers that be, graffiti is a sign not of art but of trouble, of crime and a loss of control over the mindless herd of citizens. It is a precursor to more crime. The broken-windows school of Gestapo-style law enforcement. Graffiti is ugly and destructive, and for some writers, that's just the point.

"I came out of retirement because I lived in a nice neighborhood and soon found I couldn't pay the rent," proclaims FE One, a man that used to tag the trains back when they were hot in the '80s. "I'm just trying to bring the property values down. At this rate of gentrification, they just keep pushing us back further and further to the outsides of the city—they're pushin' us out into the ocean, and I don't want to be livin' that *Waterworld* life!"

You could say that the graffiti artist's story is every New Yorker's story. It is a struggle to survive in a city of ever-increasing rents, ever-increasing luxury for the rich, while the poor just keep getting pushed aside.

Wall Street

I remember just last weekend, being on a rooftop in Brooklyn. It's a hot   40
spot, lots of tags in a prime location, and I was just sitting back, watching a new writer get his paint on. I was like a movie critic, thinking his tag's too long, takes too slow, his style isn't fully developed, and if he gets nabbed, how severe are the penalties? Before, you could get caught writing and get community service. Now, they're trying to stick even toy newbies with years in jail just for catching a tag.

On the one hand, graffiti get to be a frustrating game to watch as you get older. You see these kids coming up who don't practice enough, don't have skills, and don't know how to stay off the radar. For a cat like me, I *know* I could do it better. I could come out and rock shit pretty hard and get away with it. But I won't, and I don't, because the other part of getting is older is how much less doing stupid shit is worth the risks. You got bills to pay, a girl to keep happy, jobs you don't want to lose, a clean record, and let's be real, no matter how good you think you are, luck might turn out to be a bitch instead of a lady on any given night. It's easy to hate on the toys coming up, but hey, at least they're getting up, and getting up under increasingly risky circumstances.

I remember being on vacation looking at time-share property with my fiancée. Out of curiosity we looked through the catalog to see where their NYC property was located. I nearly had a heart attack when I recognized the address. Their nice new multi-million-dollar building was built right on the abandoned lot where perhaps ten years ago I dropped my last tags on a wall.

Investments, bills, falling in love, getting married, having kids, cars, babies—all of these are reasons why people like me stop being so bad... but the temptation... it's always there. And while maybe I won't be picking up a spray can anytime soon, I sure as fuck won't stop running around the tunnels and abandoned parts of town taking my photos any time soon either.

The subway car I'm in only has a few riders at this point. Bowling Green is the last stop in Manhattan, and it is where I get off. In another four or five minutes I'll be in the office, at my desk, putting in another eight or nine hours of routine, rote, boring work, passing the time really, waiting for the sun to set, the weekend to begin, and the next adventure to begin, because this, this commuting, this sitting in an office all day... this isn't life. Graffiti, exploring, going on crazy missions... that's what life is, and I'm gonna live my life every damn chance I get.

Discussion Questions

1. How would you define graffiti? Should it be legal or illegal?
2. Is graffiti a legitimate art form? Does Graffiti make the city beautiful or vice versa?
3. How would you feel if your classrooms were covered in graffiti? Discuss your reaction if you found your front door covered in graffiti.
4. Discuss the reasons that graffiti arose in the 1970s and then declined in the 1980s. Are the reasons that graffiti artists write today the same as they were forty years ago?
5. Joseph Anastasio says that "persistence is the quality that makes mere mortals into legends of the graffiti game." Can you think of other activities that require or reward persistence?

Writing Tasks

- Anastasio mentions persistence several times. Write an essay in which you discuss the value of persistence in a career or activity that interests you.
- Find something that is not in an art museum (graffiti, a lamppost, an abandoned building, etc.) and write an essay in which you treat it as if it was a famous work of art.
- Research and perhaps even interview an urban or street artist who is not well-known. Write an essay in which you introduce the work and the artist to the public.

Photographing the City

Berenice Abbott

Berenice Abbott (1898–1991) was influenced by modernist art forms and spent several years in Europe practicing sculpture and poetry before becoming a darkroom assistant for the famed photographer Man Ray. In 1929, Abbott returned to the U.S. and began photographing New York in an attempt to document the city. Her successful one-woman show at the Museum of the City of New York in 1934 helped to secure her lasting fame as a photographer and artist. She disliked sentimental artistry and instead called her images of urban and architectural subjects "straight photography." Abbott spent most of her career in New York City.

Pre-Reading

Is it possible to "read" a photograph like one reads an essay?

Berenice Abbott, "Seventh Avenue looking south from 35th Street, Manhattan," 1935
Photography Collection, Miriam and Ira D. Wallach Division of Art, Prints and Photographs, The New York Public Library, Astor, Lenox and Tilden Foundations.

Discussion Questions

1. What makes this view of Seventh Avenue artistic? Who might get to enjoy this perspective of the city?
2. What do you think Abbott means by "straight photography"? Use either of her two images to discuss her term.
3. If you were to take photographs of Seventh Avenue, how might your images be different from Abbott's images?

Pre-Reading

Does it matter what a bridge looks like? Why or why not? What is your favorite bridge?

Berenice Abbott, "Manhattan Bridge, From Bowery and Canal Street, Manhattan to Warren and Bridge Street, Brooklyn," 1936
Photography Collection, Miriam and Ira D. Wallach Division of Art, Prints and Photographs, The New York Public Library, Astor, Lenox and Tilden Foundations.

Discussion Questions

1. When you first look at this photograph, can you tell that it is a bridge? Why do you think that Abbott chose this particular angle and composition?
2. Do you think these images are beautiful? Why or why not?
3. When you think of New York City photographs, what iconic images come to mind?
4. How has photography changed since Abbott's time?

Writing Tasks

- Write an essay in which you compare Abbott's two images in terms of composition, movement, and geometry.
- Go to the New York Public Library's digital archives or the photo gallery of New York City at www.nyc.gov and find two photographs that catch your attention. Compare and contrast them.
- Write an essay in which you compare and contrast Berenice Abbott's photographs to those of Lewis Wickes Hine and Dinanda H. Nooney.

New York at Work

Lewis Wickes Hine

Lewis Wickes Hine (1874–1940) was a photographer and sociologist interested in people and their relation to work. Hine was especially interested in advocating for children and their rights, and his photographs often show workers toiling in industrial settings. He took many photographs for the Red Cross and for the Works Progress Administration (WPA). His images are widely republished, and over 5000 of his photos are held at the Library of Congress in Washington DC.

Pre-Reading

Is work an interesting subject for photography?

Lewis Wickes Hine, "Riveters attaching a beam," 1931
Photography Collection, Miriam and Ira D. Wallach Division of Art, Prints and Photographs, The New York Public Library, Astor, Lenox and Tilden Foundations.

Discussion Questions

1. Does this look like typical construction work? Why or why not?
2. How do you think that Hine was able to take this photograph?
3. How does this photograph make you feel about the risks of work and the risks that artists take?
4. Discuss the play of interior and exterior space in this photograph.

Lewis Wickes Hine, "Sweat shop, New York City," 1900-1937
Photography Collection, Miriam and Ira D. Wallach Division of Art, Prints and Photographs,
The New York Public Library, Astor, Lenox and Tilden Foundations.

Discussion Questions

1. What is a sweatshop? What makes the room shown here one?
2. Discuss the space in which these men and women are working. Does it look like a factory or like a living room?
3. Some of the workers are looking directly at the camera, while others are working. Discuss the idea of posing for photographs or taking candid snapshots.
4. Why are the men at the far end of the sweatshop?

Writing Task

-   Take photographs of people that you know at work or at play. Discuss your images.

Domestic Photographs of Brooklyn

Dinanda H. Nooney

Dinanda H. Nooney (1918–2004) was a documentary photographer who focused her artistic attention primarily on New York. Nooney's first extensive photographic project documented the collapsed West Side Highway in Manhattan in the mid 1970s. Her second major project was photographing Brooklyn families. From 1978 to 1979, Nooney traveled through dozens of Brooklyn neighborhoods from Greenpoint to Sea Gate, taking photographs of many families who then recommended other families for her to photograph. These two portraits are typical of Nooney's work; they reveal her attention to architecture, décor, and family relationships.

Pre-Reading

Does this photograph remind you of a typical dinner scene in modern-day Brooklyn?

Dinanda H. Nooney, "Home of Gerard Basquiat. 553 Pacific St., Park Slope, Brooklyn. March 5, 1978"
Photography Collection, Miriam and Ira D. Wallach Division of Art, Prints and Photographs, The New York Public Library, Astor, Lenox and Tilden Foundations. Reprinted by permission of The New York Public Library and the Estate of Dinanda H. Nooney.

Discussion Questions

1. Discuss the décor and the details present in this portrait.
2. Describe the people in the photo.
3. The empty chair most probably belongs to Gerald Basquiat's son, the famous artist Jean-Michel Basquiat (1960–1988), who left home before this photo was taken. How does knowing this detail change your understanding of the portrait?

Writing Task

- Search through your family photo albums, pick your favorite, and then write a photo-essay about it.

Pre-Reading

Does this photograph strike you as humorous or difficult to understand?

Dinanda H. Nooney, "Joe Roifer & friend. Apt. 9E, Turner
Tower. 135 Eastern Parkway, Prospect Heights, Brooklyn.
June 20, 1978"
Photography Collection, Miriam and Ira D. Wallach Division of Art,
Prints and Photographs, The New York Public Library, Astor, Lenox and
Tilden Foundations. Reprinted by permission of The New York Public
Library and the Estate of Dinanda H. Nooney.

Discussion Questions

1. Discuss the composition of the photograph.
2. Nooney uses detailed titles of her photographs. Why do you think that she uses her subject's full address?
3. Compare this domestic scene with the Basquiat dinner scene.
4. How do you read the large "Continued" sign above the men?

Writing Task

- Write an essay in which you consider what the images in this section hide or obscure.

Prediction

Rem Koolhaas

Born in 1944 in Rotterdam, Netherlands, Rem Koolhaas is an architect, theorist, and urban scholar. His architecture books *Delirious New York: A Retroactive Manifesto of New York* (1978) and *S, M, L, XL* (1995) are well known by both architects and urban critics. In 2000, Koolhaas received the Pritzker Prize, the highest international award for architecture. He has designed houses, stores, libraries, and government buildings throughout Europe, North America, and Asia. He is a visiting professor of architecture at Harvard's Graduate School of Design, and he is a founding partner of the Rotterdam-based architecture firm OMA.

Pre-Reading

Are squares and rectangles the best way to organize a city or a neighborhood?

In 1807 Simeon deWitt, Gouverneur Morris and John Rutherford are commissioned to design the model that will regulate the "final and conclusive" occupancy of Manhattan. Four years later they propose—above the demarcation that separates the known from the unknowable part of the city—12 avenues running north-south and 155 streets running east-west.

With that simple action they describe a city of $13 \times 156 = 2{,}028$ blocks (excluding topographical accidents): a matrix that captures, at the same time, all remaining territory and all future activity on the island. The Manhattan Grid.

Advocated by its authors as facilitating the "buying, selling and improving of real estate," this "Apotheosis of the gridiron"—"with its simple appeal to unsophisticated minds"—is, 150 years after its super-imposition on the island, still a negative symbol of the shortsightedness of commercial interests. In fact, it is the most courageous act of prediction in Western civilization: the land it divides, unoccupied; the population it describes, conjectural; the buildings it locates, phantoms; the activities it frames, nonexistent.

Discussion Questions

1. Discuss the layout of your neighborhood. Is it gridded like Manhattan?
2. What are the social and emotional effects of having such a rigid design for streets and blocks?
3. Do you agree with Koolhaas that the grid design is "still a negative symbol of the shortsightedness of commercial interests"?
4. Compare the planning of the Manhattan grid to the planning of "natural" spaces such as Central Park or Prospect Park.
5. Imagine that you were in charge of redesigning your neighborhood. What would you do about transportation, parks, buildings, housing, and commercial spaces?

Writing Tasks

- Write an essay that investigates what populations came to occupy New York and what activities have occurred over time.
- Collaborate with your classmates to design a futuristic version of New York City.

The Making of an Icon

Donald Reynolds

Donald Reynolds is an art historian, author, and teacher. From 1970 to 2003, he taught at Columbia University, where he earned his doctorate in art history. A frequent lecturer to corporations and urban groups, he is also the author of numerous books and articles on art and architecture. Two of his books include *The Architecture of New York City* (1994) and *Masters of American Sculpture* (1994). In addition, he is the founder and director of The Monument Conservancy.

Pre-Reading

What is your favorite skyscraper in New York?

© Cedric Weber, 2012. Used under license from Shutterstock, Inc.

The Empire State Building was the inspiration of John Jacob Raskob, a self-made man, who had risen from economically deprived circumstances in Lockport, New York—by way of a series of successful ventures with Pierre DuPont, his mentor (who had discovered him)—to enormous wealth and positions of influence as an officer and shareholder in General Motors. Active in politics, Raskob supported Al Smith for governor of New York and was Smith's campaign manager in his presidential race against Herbert Hoover in 1928. The friendship grew, and when Al Smith left public office, he played a major role in Raskob's success story with the Empire State Building.

From his automotive experience Raskob understood the importance of producing a superior product, the complexities of merchandising it, and the necessity of having the right people to achieve these ends. He applied his formula for success to the new building at Thirty-fourth Street and Fifth Avenue at a time when the country was experiencing its worst financial crisis, and he produced not only the tallest building in the world, but the most famous and revered skyscraper yet to be built. Even now that other commercial structures have reached far greater heights, the Empire State Building remains an icon that refuses to relinquish its special meaning.

Raskob produced the perfect skyscraper with the perfect image for its time and place: it was a building that did exactly what an executive office building ought to do with maximum efficiency and economy, and it was executed with superb artistry and superlative engineering in a tastefully modern style. Although the Empire State Building did what any office building was supposed to do for its tenants, it did it better and in a bigger way. At least that was Raskob's message, and people believed it.

Unlike the Woolworth, Chrysler, and Chanin buildings, named for men of remarkable achievement, Raskob's building was to be identified with the very embodiment of superlative achievement—New York. It was to become a symbol of the city. Being the tallest building in the world meant more than winning a race for Raskob; height was symbolically identified with the essential concept of the building.

It is the interdependence of the building's architectural preeminence and its symbolic content that relates the Empire State Building conceptually to such landmarks as the Eiffel Tower and that establishes it as a major image of modernity in the twentieth century. This successful confluence of form and content is also what has made the building an enduring symbol. What it looked like, what it was, and what it stood for all became identified in the minds of the public and the building's tenants.

Selection of the Architects

To produce this superior product, Raskob selected the architectural firm of Shreve, Lamb, and Harmon. A fairly new partnership, the group had good credentials and a practical approach to building that appealed to him. William Frederick Lamb was the designer of the building. The son of a New York builder, he had studied architecture at Columbia University in New York and the École des Beaux-Arts in Paris and had been a partner with Richmond Harold Shreve in Carrère and Hastings, Shreve, and Lamb. Shreve had studied architecture at Cornell and had taught there, before joining Carrère and Hastings. Arthur Loomis Harmon joined them in 1929 to form Shreve, Lamb, and Harmon. Harmon studied architecture at Columbia University and had been a designer with McKim, Mead, and White before practicing independently.

The Significance of the Design

Lamb's natural propensity was toward simplicity, and he preferred functional architecture, which was why the contemporary architect Raymond Hood's Daily News Building, built a year before the Empire State Building, appealed to him and influenced him. So Lamb envisioned a building shaped essentially by the practical factors of budget, time, zoning regulations, and technological necessities. Raskob wanted 36 million cubic feet of space on a lot 200 feet (Fifth Avenue) by 425 feet (Thirty-third and Thirty-fourth streets) for a construction budget of approximately $60 million. The building was to be completed by May 1, 1931, in order to make rental space available immediately (the day for signing commercial leases). That gave the architect a year and a half to complete the plans and erect the building.

Lamb reduced these requirements to their bare essentials for his design. A central core rising up the height of the building accommodates service and utility rooms, corridors, and shafts for four elevator banks of low and high-rise elevators. Around this core is a perimeter of rentable office space twenty-eight feet deep from window to corridor—at that time, the accepted formula for sufficient natural light. As the low-rise elevators drop away, the core space is reduced, which is expressed in the facades as setbacks.

The vertical composition of the building conforms to the traditional organization of skyscraper mass into base, shaft, and capital—the design, based on the divisions of the Classical column, that has its origins in New York's earliest elevator buildings of Post (Western Union Building) and Hunt (Tribune Building) in the 1870s.

A limestone tower rises from a 5-story base to the 86th floor observa-   10
tory and is capped by a monumental spire, a "mooring mast" of metal
and glass for dirigibles (which proved too dangerous to be used as such),
and the television antenna added much later. Atop the 5th-story base is a
60-foot-wide terrace created by setting the tower back to fulfill the zoning requirements. This terrace setback emphasizes the tower and its unprecedented height of 1,250 feet. Although it has 86 floors of offices, the
Empire State Building is often described as being 102 stories high, because
the mooring mast is equivalent in height to 14 stories and when the building's two basements are also counted, the total comes to 102 stories.

The grandeur of the Empire State Building—its height, materials, and
design, and the technological skills that produced it—immediately captured the minds and hearts of all Americans. To watch the building's steel
skeleton rise 102 stories into the sky in just over eight months was even
startling to the construction workers who put it up, as Harold L. McClain
wrote in his "Recollections of Working on the Empire State Building."

At the opening ceremonies, May 1, 1931, former New York Governor
Al Smith hailed the Empire State Building as the world's greatest monument to man's ingenuity, skill, mind, and muscle. Three weeks later, Earl
Musselman stood on the platform of the Empire State Building's obser-
vation tower. Looking at the tall buildings around him, he said, "I keep
wanting to put out my hand to feel them—so that I can tell what they really look like." Born blind, the twenty-two-year-old Musselman had only
two months before undergone an operation that gave him sight. His uncle
brought him to New York from Philadelphia to see the view from the top
of the Empire State Building, a view of sea and land that only three weeks
before was beyond the earth's horizon.

The great height of the Empire State Building has been celebrated in
such movie myths as *King Kong* and *Tarzan's New York Adventure*, and it
was the source of tragedy when Lt, Col. William F. Smith's B-25 Mitchell
bomber, with a crew member and a passenger aboard, crashed into the
north side of the fog-shrouded building at the seventy-ninth-floor level on
the morning of July 28, 1945. Fortunately, because it was a Saturday, there
were few people in the building; nonetheless, at least fourteen people perished along with the pilot and his crewman.

Now, through a modern lighting system, the top of the Empire State
Building is a great beacon honoring special events that was inaugurated on
October 12, 1977, when blue and white lights announced that the Yankees
had won the World Series. From the seventy-second floor to the top of the
TV antenna, colored lights in various combinations celebrate such significant days as St. Valentine's Day (red and white), Washington's Birthday
(red, white, and blue), St. Patrick's Day (green), and Columbus Day (red,

white, and green). And from Christmas to New Year's Day, festive combinations of red and green illuminate the top of the building.

The New Symbol

The main entrance on Fifth Avenue echoes the building's tripartite design.   15
Grand columns flank the entrance doors, and great black stone bases at
the ground level support reeded shafts which terminate in capitals of stylized American eagles that frame the massive attic on which is engraved
"EMPIRE STATE." At ground level, broad shop fronts of moulded aluminum and glass are set within black marble beneath a three-story screen of
masonry piers.

The time and budget within which the building had to be completed
dictated a system of fenestration and a method of handling the stonework
that eliminated traditional, but time-consuming, practices and fortuitously
resulted in enhancing the vertical emphasis of the building. By setting the
windows in framed strips of stainless steel, and projecting them in front of
the Indiana limestone cladding, the stone finishing usually needed at the
juncture of wall and window was eliminated, saving time and money. Furthermore, by using aluminum for the spandrels, instead of masonry, cross
bonding was avoided and resulted in a further economy.

The projected window units, grouped in bays of one, two, and three,
were visually united to read as continuous, slender, vertical units capped
by geometric crowns. The masonry cladding read as a skeleton of slender
alternating piers, reflecting the building's internal structure. Lamb's solution, which unifies the building's almost 6,500 windows into a coherent
design, was probably influenced by the way his friend Raymond Hood
handled the Daily News Building. Hood de-emphasized the windows by
an innovative recessed vertical strip and a continuous pier unbroken up to
the cresting.

The hubris that informs the design and ornamentation of New York's
Art Deco skyscrapers is uniquely expressed in the Empire State Building's
scale and the decorative features that enhance it, which are geometric and
carry almost no narrative content. The architects avoided didactic ornamentation except in the main lobby at the ground floor, where they celebrate the concept and image of the building in a program of restrained
symbolism coordinated with rich materials and dramatic lighting.

The design of the lobby was dictated by the same realities that guided the
general massing of the building. Here, the four banks of elevators in the central core of the building are subdivided by three east-west concourses and
connecting lateral corridors to facilitate traffic flow from the main Fifth Avenue entrance and the side entrances at Thirty-third and Thirty-fourth streets.

Moreover, the elevator banks are surrounded by shops with entrances   20
from both the lobby and the street and aluminum bridges (originally open,
now enclosed) over the east-west concourses connect offices at the second
story. Stairs led down (now escalators) from the ends of the concourses to
the lower level.

A grand entrance hall in gray marble, stainless steel, and glass extends from the main entrance to a wall of polished black granite, which
is the backdrop for a portrait of the building above the information desk.
The aluminum image of the building, emanating rays symbolic of man's
creative energy which merge with the rays of the sun—nature's energy—
is superimposed over a map of New York. The building's location is
marked, and at the lower left the dates of construction, March 17, 1930–
March 1, 1931, are inscribed in a medallion. At the right is a clock set in
a compass, symbolic of the coordinates of time and space that define the
position of the Empire State Building in the mural and in the modern
world. The panel, beneath the clock and over the aluminum information
desk, lists those responsible for constructing the building and includes
Pierre S. DuPont, Raskob's mentor and associate. South of the information desk is a scale model of the building in a display vitrine with base,
made in the Empire State Cabinet Shop by Oliver J. Brown and painted
by J. M. Rossi (1938).

Natural light pours into the great ceremonial space through the three
glazed and traceried vertical panels over the main entrance. Beneath
each panel and above the three doors is a round medallion with a stylized representation of Electricity (north), Masonry (middle), and Heating
(south). These are three of the eighteen medallions placed throughout the
lobby that identify the industries involved in producing the Empire State
Building.

To merchandise the building properly, Raskob sought to give it a strong
identity with New York and with an image of integrity associated with
high purpose. Raskob hired Al Smith to be the president of the Empire
State Company and to give his superior product a superior image. As the
building and its function were inseparable, so Al Smith became identified
with the building, and his personal popularity and reputation for integrity
imparted a sense of high purpose to the building, which was totally believ-
able. Moreover, through his lifelong connection with public affairs and the
Democratic party, Smith had consistent visibility at the public level; he was
always news. Thus, the Empire State Building had much greater exposure
through the press and news media than any building before it.

Raskob's judgment proved sound. Even though his building opened
during the Great Depression, it flourished, and by the 1940s it had 98 percent occupancy.

Discussion Questions

1. Who was the mastermind behind the Empire State Building, and what was his formula for success used to build it?
2. How long did it take to build the Empire State Building? Do you think that is fast or slow? Why might the answer be surprising given the cultural and economic situation of the nation at that time?
3. Have you ever been to the top of the Empire State Building? Have you seen it from a distance or in pictures or movies?
4. Do you get the impression that Donald Reynolds dislikes or likes the Empire State Building? Find examples of Reynolds' word choices and phrases to support your answer.

Writing Task

- Write an essay about your favorite building in New York. Include information such as who built it, why it was built, when it was built, and any challenges that the builders faced.

From Doo Wop to Hip Hop: The Bittersweet Odyssey of African-Americans in the South Bronx

Mark Naison

Mark Naison (b. 1946) is Professor of African and African-American Studies at Fordham University. He is also the Director of Fordham University's Urban Studies Program. He is the author of *Communists in Harlem during the Depression* (1983) and *White Boy: A Memoir* (2002). Professor Naison has also written articles on African-American culture and contemporary urban issues, including "Outlaw Culture in Black Culture," *Reconstruction* (Fall 1994). The following essay originally appeared in the *Bronx Country Historical Society Journal* in 2004. He is currently working on two book-length projects, and he maintains an active blog at withabrooklynaccent .blogspot.com

Pre-Reading

What is your favorite genre of music? What message do you believe it strives to get across?

Sometimes, music can be a powerful tool in interpreting historical events. [1] Played side by side, two of the most popular songs ever to come out of The Bronx, the Chantel's "Maybe" and Grandmaster Flash and the Furious Five's "The Message," dramatize an extraordinary shift in the culture, dreams and lived experience of African Americans in the South Bronx between the mid 1950s and the early 1980s. These songs, so different in tone, content and feeling, were produced by artists who lived less than six blocks away from one another in the Morrisania section of The Bronx, an important center of musical creativity in both the rhythm and blues and hip hop eras.[1]

The Chantels, the most successful "doo wop" group ever to come out of The Bronx, and one of the first of the "girl groups" ever to have a hit single, grew up singing together in the choir at St. Anthony of Padua elementary school, located at East 165th Street and Prospect Avenue. Their song "Maybe" appeared in 1957, a time when many African-Americans

---

Reprinted by permission of Bronx Historical Society.

in The Bronx were having a modest taste of postwar prosperity and were optimistic about their futures. Throughout the South Bronx neighborhoods they inhabited, new housing developments were going up at breakneck speed, allowing thousands of black and Latino families to move into clean airy apartments, with ample heat and hot water, which were a step up from the tenements many of them lived in when they first came to New York. They lived in neighborhoods where most families were intact, where children received strong adult guidance in their home, their block, and their school, and where adolescent violence was rarely life threatening.

Grandmaster Flash, one of three pioneering Bronx DJs credited with founding hip hop, also grew up in Morrisania—at 947 Fox Street, right off East 163rd Street—but it was a very different Morrisania than the one the Chantels grew up in. When Mel Melle, the MC for the group sang "Broken glass, everywhere, people pissing on the street, you know they just don't care" to a pounding, rhythmic backdrop, he was talking about a community buffeted by arson, building abandonment, drugs, gang violence, shattered families, the withdrawal of public services and the erosion of legal job opportunities. Surrounded by tenement districts that had been ravaged by fires, housing projects that were once centers of pride and optimism had become dangerous and forbidding. "Rats on the front porch, roaches in the back, junkies in the alley with a baseball bat." This was the world in which hip hop was created, a world where government was distant and remote, families were under stress, adult authority was weak, and young people had to find economic opportunity and creative outlets on their own in the most forbidding of circumstances.

How did this happen? How did the harmonic, optimistic environment evoked by the Chantels, the Chords (who came out of Morris High School), or Little Anthony and the Imperials, give way to the violent, danger filled world described, in clinical detail, by the Furious Five and, several years later by another brilliant South Bronx hip hop lyricist, KRS-1? And how did people respond to these community destroying forces? Did they give in? Leave? Try to resist? If they did resist, how effective was their resistance?

These are some of the issues that I will try to address in this article. Please keep in mind that what I am sharing with you is the product of preliminary research rather than a polished product. A little more than a year ago, The Bronx County Historical Society and the Department of African and African-American Studies at Fordham University came together to launch The Bronx African American History Project, an effort to document the experience of the more than five hundred thousand people of African descent who live in The Bronx. I decided to focus on the generation of African Americans who moved to the South Bronx from Harlem, the American South and the Caribbean during and after World War II, the generation of

5

people Colin Powell has written about in the early chapters of his autobiography, *An American Journey.*[2]

I began interviewing members of that pioneering generation and in the process came across a remarkable group of people who grew up in the Patterson Houses, a 17 building development bounded by Morris and Third avenues and East 139th and East 144th streets. These individuals, who come together every July for a Patterson Houses Reunion, are successful professionals in education, business, and the arts. They remember the Patterson Houses as a safe, nurturing place from the time it opened in 1950 until heroin struck in the early 60s. Their story, which challenges so much of what people think about public housing, the South Bronx, and black and Latino neighborhoods, is important not only because of its intrinsic value, but because it helps us understand the events that follow. Based on interviews and long discussions with Victoria Archibald-Good, Nathan "Bubba" Dukes, Adrian Best, Arnold Melrose, Joel Turner, Michael Singletary, Marilyn Russell and Allen Jones, I am going to bring back a time when public housing was a symbol of hope, not failure, and when working class black and Latino families, supported by strong, well-funded government services, helped each other raise their children with love, discipline, respect and a determination to achieve success in school, athletics and the arts. And though this story is about Patterson, the atmosphere it evokes also existed in the Melrose, St. Mary's and Forest Houses, the other large developments that opened in the South Bronx in the late 1940s and early 50s.

One of the first things that grabbed my attention when I began doing interviews was that African American families who moved into the Patterson Houses saw their arrival there as a "step up" from the crowded tenement neighborhoods where they had been living. Vicki Archibald-Good, whose parents moved to Patterson Houses from Harlem, recalled: "There wasn't a lot of affordable housing. I am not sure how long my parents were on the waiting list for public housing, but I do remember my mother saying they were living in one room in my grandmother's apartment before we moved. . . . By the time we moved from Harlem to The Bronx, I was born, my brother Tiny was born and my mother was pregnant with a third child."[3]

Nathan Dukes, whose family moved from a crowded building in the Morrisania section of The Bronx, where his father was superintendent, recalled: "It was basically like a migration, where people moved from the Tinton Avenue/Prospect Avenue area over into the Patterson Houses.... The projects were relatively new and they were accommodating." The new residents, Dukes claims, took tremendous pride in their surroundings. "Outsiders could not come into the Patterson Projects if we didn't know them," he remembers. "A lot of the older guys would question anybody who didn't look right who came into the projects late in the evenings. . . . They were basically patrolling. . . . They would walk around the neighborhood... making sure things were OK."[4]

When the project first opened, children who lived in Patterson experienced a level of communal supervision that is difficult to imagine today. The families who lived in the development, ninety percent of whom were black and Latino, took responsibility for raising one another's children. Not only did they help one another with babysitting and childcare, they carefully monitored the behavior of young people in hallways, from apartment windows and project benches, making public spaces of the huge development anything but anonymous. "You couldn't get away with anything," Nathan Dukes recalled, "The moms and the pops . . . they'd be out on the benches. . . . If you went in the wrong direction, by the time you came back, everybody in the neighborhood would know. And that was it. . . . You'd get a whooping."[5] Vicki Archibald-Good, who fondly recalled the "camaraderie and supportiveness and nurturing" she got from people who in her building "who weren't blood relatives," also remembered that people were quick to correct one another's children: ". . . they did not hesitate to speak to you about dropping garbage in the hallway or talking too loud or skating in the hallway. And all a neighbor had to do was say 'Don't let me tell your mother.' That's all it took for us to come back to reality..." Even childless people got in the act. Vicki remembered a "Miss Cassie" who used to "stand in that hallway, or sit by the window, or on the bench and everybody knew what was going on in 414..."[6]

This communal investment in child rearing was reinforced by publicly funded programs that provided children in the Patterson Houses with a extraordinary array of cultural and recreational opportunities. As Josh Freeman points out in his landmark book *Working Class New York,* residents of communities like Patterson Houses were the beneficiaries of a remarkable campaign by the city's postwar labor movement to have government invest in education, health care, recreation and youth services for working class families.[7] Children growing up in Patterson in 1950s had round the clock supervised activities in a community center housed in the local elementary school, PS 18, had first rate music instruction from teachers at the local junior high school, went on summer field trips to zoos and museums, and got free medical exams, vaccinations, and dental care in schools and in clinics. The experience made children in the projects feel at home in all of the city's major cultural sites. "We had a vacation day camp, every summer, for children in the projects," Vicki Archibald-Good recalled. "We went to... every single museum you could think of, to Coney Island, to baseball games, to the planetarium. . . . I knew The Bronx Zoo like the back of my hand. We went to Prospect Park, we went to the Botanical Garden. . . I don't think there was one spot in the city that we didn't cover."[8]

These programs were headed by teachers and youth workers who took a deep interest in the welfare of Patterson's children and were in regular communication with parents, reinforcing the communal investment in the neighborhood's young people. Nathan Dukes and Adrian Best both speak with reverence of the instruction and guidance they received from "Mr. Eddie Bonamere," the music teacher at Clark Junior High School, who headed the school's band. At that time, Clark, like most New York public schools, allowed students to take instruments home over the weekend, and Bonamere, a talented jazz pianist, used this opportunity to train hundreds of youngsters from the Patterson Houses to play the trumpet, trombone, flute and violin. Bonamere's extraordinary influence on his pupils—Nathan Dukes referred to him as the "love of my life"—was reinforced by his determination to expand the cultural horizons of everyone living in the neighborhood. At the end of every summer, Dukes recalled, Bonamere would sponsor a jazz concert in the schoolyard of PS 18 that included famous musicians like Willie Bobo and "everyone, I mean the entire projects, would be there."[9]

Supervised sports programs in the Patterson Houses, were, if anything, even more visible and influential. The community center at PS 18, which was directed by the former CCNY basketball star Floyd Lane and ex-Knickerbocker center Ray Felix, was kept open on weekends, holidays, and weekday afternoons and evenings. Not only did children have a chance to play knock hockey and checkers, do double dutch and play in organized basketball leagues, they had an opportunity to watch some of the greatest African-American basketball players in the nation play in the holiday basketball tournaments that Lane sponsored. Players like Wilt Chamberlain, Meadlowlark Lemon, Tom Thacker, and Happy Hairston showed up the PS 18 court. Similar programs existed in other South Bronx neighborhoods. Nat Dukes joined a community basketball program headed by Hilton White at a public park near Prospect Avenue, and played on a softball team called the Patterson Knights that was coached by a Burns security guard who lived in the Patterson Houses. Because of this array of sports programs, many young people who grew up in Patterson had successful careers in high school, college, and professional athletics, and one of them, Nate Tiny Archibald, became one of the greatest point guards ever to play in the NBA.[10]

This portrait of a time when black and Latino children in the Patterson Houses experienced strong adult leadership in every dimension of their lives so challenges the standard portrait of life in public housing that you might find it hard to believe. Wasn't the South Bronx in the 1950s the home of numerous street gangs, you might ask? Weren't its neighborhoods filled with illegal activities and a strong underground economy?

The answer to both of these questions is yes. Most of the people who lived in the Patterson Houses were poor and gang fighting and the underground economy were part of their lives. But except in rare cases, neither gangs nor illegal activities led to deadly violence. Boys in the Patterson Houses were constantly fighting kids from other neighborhoods and other projects, but most of the fighting was done with fists, and adults in the projects would step in if knives or zip guns became involved. The underground economy was huge, but its primary manifestation was the numbers and the major numbers entrepreneur in Patterson, Mr. Clay, carried himself more like a community banker than a thug. A "major donor in the church" and a sponsor of the community softball team, Mr. Clay dressed formally, did his entire business in his head and never worried about being robbed by his customers, even though he always carried hundreds of dollars in his pocket. Even those who acted outside the law seemed to operate within a powerful communal consensus.[11]

This remarkable period in the life of the Patterson Houses, which lasted   15
less than fifteen years, rested on a number of intersecting factors which would not exist in public housing from the mid 1960s on. First, the presence of intact families. All of the families with children who moved into Patterson in the 1950s had two parents present. Second, the ready availability of jobs in the local economy that men with high school educations and less could work at. Many of the men in the Patterson Houses worked in factories and small shops located in the South Bronx—Dukes' father was a furniture assembler, other men worked in milk bottling plants, or small metal shops. Third, schools and community centers near the Patterson Houses offered an impressive array of day camps, after-school centers and sports and music and arts programs that offered round the clock supervision and activity for young people in the projects. And fourth, and most importantly, most Patterson residents had a sense, reinforced by public policy and lived experience, that life was getting better, that people heading families were living better than their parents had, and that their children were going to do even better than they had.

In the 1960s, the comfort and security of people living in the Patterson Houses was to be cruelly shattered by a number of forces, creating an environment ruled by fear and mistrust in which children were too often forced to raise themselves. What changed? When people who grew up in Patterson try to explain why the environment that nurtured them fell apart, the two things they mention are heroin and the fragmentation of families.

For both Vicki Archibald-Good and Nathan Dukes, it was heroin use, which reached epidemic proportions in the early and mid 1960s, that did the most to erode bonds of community and trust in the Patterson Houses.

All of a sudden, young men who were bright, popular and ambitious, were transformed into dangerous and disoriented individuals who wouldn't hesitate to rob their neighbors or families to get their next fix. Vicki Archibald-Good, whose best friend's brother was the first person she knew to get hooked, saw heroin strike with the force of a "major epidemic." She recalled: "It was so completely different that it felt that I was living in a dream . . . . All of a sudden, everyone in the projects is talking about break-ins . . . people were saying these were inside jobs, that somebody was letting these folks in to burglarize people's apartments. Then I started hearing about folks that I grew up with getting thrown off rooftops because they were dealing. For the first time, I was starting to feel fear, not only for myself, but for the whole community."[12]

Nathan Dukes remembers heroin hitting with the force of a flood: ". . . there was just an abundance, it came out of nowhere . . . people that you thought would not become involved in narcotics became involved on a very heavy level." Dukes recalled being "devastated" during his first year in college by the news that one of his best friends had just gotten shot and killed while robbing a jewelry store.[13] By 1965 and 1966, Archibald-Good recalled, she didn't feel safe walking back from the subway by herself at night. The Patterson dream had become a nightmare: ". . . here I was in this huge housing complex and there was a story every day about somebody who overdosed or who was thrown off a roof . . . . So yes, it was a troublesome time for most of us."[14]

The impact of heroin on the Patterson community was so traumatic that Nathan Dukes remains convinced it was part of a government conspiracy to weaken the civil rights movement. But there were other forces eroding the community in the mid 60s that would have lasting impact on the projects and the neighborhood. The fragmentation of families also contributed to the atmosphere and disorder. During the early and mid 60s, Dukes recalled, more and more fathers began to desert their families, frustrated by their inability to support their wives and children at a time when the factory jobs they worked at were beginning to leave The Bronx.[15] During those same years, housing projects began to relax their admissions standards and open their doors to families on welfare, many of them recent migrants from Puerto Rico or the South, or refugees from urban renewal projects in the rest of the city. As a result of both of these developments, the adult male presence in the projects which had helped keep gang behavior and teenage violence under control, began to diminish sharply, leaving public space in control of drug dealers, junkies and teenage gangs.

The resulting violence and chaos led to a gradual exodus of families   20 that had managed to resist these corrosive forces, most to the West and North Bronx. As a result, sections of The Bronx which had once been primarily Jewish, Irish and Italian, such as Morris Heights, University Heights, South Fordham, and Williamsbridge, began to experience a rapid increase in their black population, while the housing projects of the South Bronx increasingly became places for those too poor, or troubled, to escape to safer areas. The exodus increased further with the wave of arson and disinvestment that spread through Melrose, Mott Haven, and Morrisania in the early 1970s, and later spread into Highbridge, Morris Heights and Crotona, exacerbated by a city fiscal crisis that led to dramatic cuts in public services. By the late 1970s, when The Bronx had become an international symbol of social decay, it would have been impossible for most people to imagine that housing projects in the South Bronx were once safe and nurturing places where children were watched over in every aspect of their lives and exposed to the best cultural opportunities the city had to offer.

In this moment of decay and despair, an improbable cultural movement would arise among young people in the South, West and East Bronx whose creative impulses were integrally linked to the atmosphere of social breakdown that surrounded them. That movement was hip hop, and its unique styles of dancing, visual arts, and musical expression were created in The Bronx in the face of skepticism, indifference, and occasionally hostility from adults inside and outside the communities they lived in. In fact, a good argument could be made that it was the breakdown of social order and adult authority that made this form of artistic innovation possible, especially in the formative years when hip hop had no commercial viability. The music writer Nelson George offered the following ironic observations of how the music fit the times:

> The New York that spawned hip hop spit me out, too. I came of age in the 70s.... But I'd be lying if I told you the 70s were a time of triumph.... It was, at times, a frightful experience to walk the streets, ride the subways, or contemplate the future. . . . But in chaos there is often opportunity, in pain a measure of pleasure and joy is just a stroke or two away from pain. The aesthetic industry now known as hip hop is a product of these blighted times, a child that walked, talked and partied amidst negativity.[16]

Hip hop developed at a time when the adult presence in the lives of young people in The Bronx had radically diminished. Not only had informal supervision by family members and neighbors become far less significant, but music instruction had disappeared from the public schools, parks and recreation staffing had been cut in half, afternoon and evening programs in the schools had been eliminated, and sports programs had been cut to the bone. More and more, young people had to bring up themselves, and the result was that gangs in The Bronx had become far larger and more violent than their 50s counterparts, rates of violent crime had quadrupled, and the underground economy had come to replace the legal economy as a source of employment for youth.

Along with gang activity came radical politics. In the late 60s and early 70s, more intellectually inclined Bronx youngsters were gravitating to the Black Panther Party and the Young Lords, the Nation of Islam and the Five Percenters, as well as the community action groups seeking to wrest political control of The Bronx from its Irish, Jewish and Italian leadership. These events occurred at the same time that black and Puerto Rican studies courses were being created on the CUNY campuses and elsewhere. Along with the gangs, drugs, disinvestment and crime, race conscious political activism, reinforced by open admissions in the City University system, was part of the unique chemistry that created hip hop as a cultural movement.

The birth of hip hop as a distinctive music form can be traced to the   25 year 1973, when a Jamaican immigrant nicknamed "Cool DJ Herc" began holding parties at the community center in his building, 1520 Sedgwick Avenue in the Morris Heights section of The Bronx. At that time, you could not hold a party in The Bronx without being concerned which of the gangs would show up and how they would respond—particularly the Savage Skulls and the Black Spades. Competition for territory and prestige by gangs dominated public space in many parts of The Bronx, with neither a fiscal crisis-decimated police force, nor local adults, able to control their activity. In addition to fighting, the competition had begun to take the form of graffiti writing and dancing, with gang members at clubs trying to outdo each other in launching acrobatic moves on the dance floors of clubs and parties they attended.

The innovation that Herc inaugurated was to take music that was no longer played on mass market radio—particularly heavily rhythmic music by James Brown, Sly and the Family Stone, and George Clinton—and use incredibly powerful speakers to accentuate the base line. In addition, two turntables were used so that the most danceable portions of the record— the break beats—could be played in consecutive order. The result was a sound that drove dancers wild and turned the competition on the floor between gang members into high theater. What soon became known as "break dancing" described the increasingly acrobatic moves that took place at Herc's parties at the Sedgwick community center, which people all over The Bronx flocked to see.

Soon, Herc was moving his events outdoors by hooking up his sound system to streetlights, and thousands of people were starting to attend them. He eventually found a commercial venue for his shows at "Club Hevalo" on Jerome Avenue between Tremont and Burnside avenues. By 1974 and 1975. Herc's style of dee jaying had started to spread through other neighborhoods of The Bronx, connecting with traditions of toasting and boasting, long established in black communities. To add variety to his shows and stir up the audience, Herc began to allow one of his partner DJs, Coke La Rock, "grab the mike and start to throw out his poetry." This innovation was so successful that Herc added other "MCs" to his shows, and they soon began to compete to see how well they could stir up the crowd. This, some people say, is where "rapping" (long a respected art in black communities) became a part of hip hop.

While Herc built a reputation in the West Bronx, even establishing a major venue near Fordham University at PAL (Police Athletic League) center on East 183rd Street and Webster Avenue, a former gang leader from the Bronx River Houses in Soundview who called himself Afrika Bambaataa began holding parties in the community center of his housing project that built on and in some respects expanded Herc's innovations. Influenced by the Nation of Islam and the Black Panthers, Bambaataa created an organization called the Zulu Nation aimed at bringing cooperation among Bronx gangs, using hip hop culture to attract them to his shows. Eclectic in his tastes, Bambaataa added rock and latin and jazz to the funk driven beats he was playing. He encouraged break dancers from all over The Bronx to come to his center, knowing they would be protected from violence by Bambaataa's bodyguards. He also encouraged poets and MCs to work alongside him, creating a more artistically varied product than Herc usually did. Bambaataa was explicitly political in his objectives. As he told Jim Fricke and Charlie Ahearn:

> I grew up in the southeast Bronx. It was an area where back in the late 60s, early 70s, there was "broken glass everywhere," like Mel Melle said in "The Message." But it was also an area where there was a lot of unity and social awareness going on, at a time when people of color was coming into their own, knowin' that they were black people, hearing records like James Brown's "Say It Loud—I'm Black and Proud," giving us awareness. . . . Seeing all the violence that was going on with the Vietnam War and all the people in Attica and Kent State, and being aware of what was going on in the late 60s, with Woodstock and the Flower Power. . . just being a young person and seeing all this happening around me put a lot of consciousness in my mind to get up and do something; it played a strong role in trying to say, "We've got to stop this violence with the street gangs."[17]

The final hip hop innovator was Grandmaster Flash, an electronic wizard who figured out ways of having turntables mingle break beats automatically. Flash, a graduate of Samuel Gompers Vocational High School, began performing in schoolyards (his biggest events took place outside PS 163 at East 169th Street and Boston Road), clubs and community centers in Morrisania—a neighborhood which had been devastated by fires, but was anchored by several large public housing projects. Flash became the dominant figure in the South Bronx neighborhoods of Melrose, Mott Haven and

30

Hunts Point, attracting a brilliant group of poets and rappers led by Mel Melle, the voice which is heard on Flash's signature song, "The Message."

What makes this entire movement remarkable is that it was created entirely by people under the age of thirty, with little support from parents, teachers, or the music industry. The music teachers who had once played a vital role in exposing an earlier generation to instrumental music, and sponsoring talent shows for vocal groups in after school centers, had been removed or reassigned during the fiscal crisis. Community center directors like Arthur Crier in the Tremont section, who sponsored parties and talent shows at which hip hop pioneers performed, were the only adults present at hip hop's genesis, but they had little influence on its musical content.[18]

Because hip hop was about rhythm, rather than harmony, and because turntables and records had replaced musical instruments and voice, many people brought up on gospel, blues, jazz and soul had difficulty regarding it as music, just as many people had difficulty regarding graffiti as art. But because so many young people had grown up in the fractured world that hip hop became the major form of community entertainment among young people in The Bronx and soon spread far beyond its borders.

The story of hip hop's rise is a testimony to the vitality of the human spirit, but it does not give my story a happy ending. Although hip hop has given young people in the South Bronx (and communities like it throughout the world) a vehicle and a moral compass that helps them describe the conditions in which they live, and has prevented the media and government from rendering them invisible, it has not been able to turn fractured neighborhoods into safe supportive communities like the one that Vicki Archibald-Good and Nathan Dukes grew up in.

The opportunities provided by growing up in The Bronx after World War II, however, provide us with insights as to how to improve the current situation for its people. We cannot replace the nuclear family and bring back the industrial jobs that left The Bronx in the 1950s, 60s and 70s, but we can restore music instruction to the public schools, rehire recreation supervisors in parks and playgrounds, and revive the after school programs and evening centers that were once a fixture of every elementary school in the city. Public housing was once a place where dreams of success and achievement were nurtured. There is no reason why public housing cannot play that role again, if we restore the round-the-clock youth programs Patterson children once benefitted from and make a generous investment in child care, education and medical care for working class children and families.

Notes

[1]On rhythm and blues in Morrisania, see Philip Groia, *They All Sang On the Corner: A Second Look at New York City's Rhythm and Blues Vocal Groups* (Port Jefferson, NY: Phillie Dee

Enterprises, 1983, 130–132.) PS 99, which sponsored evening talent shows as part of a night center directed by a legendary teacher named Vincent Tibbs, and Morris High School, were centers of musical creativity in the "doo wop" years. Groia writes: "After three o'clock, P.S. 99 and Morris High School became rehearsal halls for the simplest of musical instruments, the human voice. Both schools were major forces in keeping young people off the streets…"

[2]Colin Powell, with Joseph E. Persico, *My American Journey* (New York: Ballantine, 1995). Chapter One discusses Powell's experiences growing up in the South Bronx.

[3]Mark Naison, " 'It Take a Village to Raise a Child': Growing Up in the Patterson Houses in the 1950s and Early 1960s, An Interview with Victoria Archibald-Good," *The Bronx County Historical Society Journal*, 40, No. 1 (Spring 2003): 7

[4]Oral history interview with Nathan Dukes by Mark Naison, April 25, 2003. Transcript and videotape at The Bronx County Historical Society and at the Walsh Library of Fordham University.

[5]Ibid.

[6]Naison, "Interview with Victoria Archibald-Good," 8–9.

[7]Joshua B. Freeman *Working Class New York: Life and Labor Since World War II* (New York: New Press, 2000).

[8]Naison, "Interview with Victoria Archibald-Good," 8.

[9]Dukes oral history interview and oral history interview with Adrian Best by Mark Naison, July 1, 2003. Transcripts and videotapes at The Bronx County Historical Society and at the Walsh Library of Fordham University.

[10]Dukes oral history interview.

[11]Ibid.

[12]Naison, "Interview with Victoria Archibald-Good," 17–18.

[13]Dukes oral history interview.

[14]Naison, "Interview with Victoria Archibald-Good," 18.

[15]Dukes oral history interview.

[16]Jim Fricke and Charlie Aheam *"Yes Yes Y'All: The Experience Music Project Oral History of Hip Hop's First Decade* (New York: Da Capo Press, 2002), vii. Nelson George wrote the introduction to this remarkable book, which provides the best portrait of the rise of hip hop in The Bronx in the 1970s. The discussion of hip hop's origins draws on this book and other works documenting hip hop's Bronx years: Raquel Rivera, *New York Ricans In the Hip Hop Zone* (New York: Palgrave, 2003); Tricia Rose, *Black Noise: Rap Music and Black Culture in Contemporary America* (Hanover: Wesleyan University Press, 1994); Alan Light, ed. *The Vibe History of Hip Hop* (New York: Three Rivers Press, 1999); James D. Eure and James Spady, *Nation Conscious Rap* (New York: PC International Press, 1991); James G. Spady, Charles G. Lee, and H. Samy Alin, *Street Conscious Rap* (Philadelphia: Black History Museum, Umum/Loh Publishers, 1999).

[17]Frick and Ahearn *"Yes Yes Y'All,"* 44.

[18]In an interview with The Bronx African American History Project on January 30,2004, Crier, a singer, arranger, producer and songwriter who was one of the major figures in the Morrisania rhythm and blues scene in the 1950s and 60s, said that the talent shows at PS 99 in the 1950s were his inspiration when he began organizing talent shows at his community center in the middle and late 1970s.

Discussion Questions

1. Discuss how Naison uses the music of the Chantels and the rap lyrics of Grandmaster Flash to structure his overall argument.
2. What is the effect of interviewing actual people as evidence to support his argument?
3. How did the tenants of the Patterson houses in the 1950s view their new residences?
4. How were children treated at this time? What was available to them? What role did adults play in their lives?
5. What was the economy like for working-class families in the 1950s?
6. What was the effect of heroin use in the mid-1960s?
7. What role did the loss of jobs have? Do you think this is a larger social issue?
8. What was early hip hop like? What social and political agenda did it serve?
9. Why does Naison argue that the story of hip hop's rise "does not have a happy ending"? How did hip hop, according to Naison, change? Do you agree with his assessment?
10. What solutions does Naison offer to revitalize troubled neighborhoods? Can you suggest any other ones?

Writing Tasks

- Write an essay that discusses the history of your neighborhood and your own feelings about the current situation. If possible, interview someone who has lived in your neighborhood for quite some time about these changes.
- Choose a hip hop song and discuss the message it conveys.
- Research articles that defend and/or attack the value of hip hop as a musical genre or social influence. Write an essay that takes a stand in this debate and considers the merit of two contrasting perspectives.

Making Connections

1. What is your favorite type of art? How does your own interest in art connect to the subjects in this chapter? If you were deeply interested in some type of art or design, how would you go about becoming an expert?
2. Drawing from the ideas in your readings, discuss how both art and design are changing. Visit a local museum or gallery to answer this question.
3. Research the artists whose quotations begin this chapter. Write an essay that examines their different perceptions of New York City.
4. Suppose that your school must decide whether to devote a large sum of money to one of two projects that cost the same amount of money: commissioning an artist to paint a large mural or installing money-saving, energy-efficient

windows. Write an argumentative essay in which you consider both sides, but that makes a case for one project over the other.

5. Write an essay which offers suggestions to improve your school through art and design.

6. On your course website, create a montage or collage of the public art on or near your campus; this may involve taking pictures and putting them up for comment and discussion. This project can be expanded to include photographing local graffiti, urban spaces, and architecture.

CHAPTER 5

Current Issues

"Pro-immigrant Rally Crossing the Brooklyn Bridge in 2007"
© Seth Wenig/Reuters CORBIS

The experiment is how close can rich and poor live before the fabric completely falls apart? How close can you put ethnic groups that don't like one another much? How much can you promise people about a rich and privileged future, and then not be able to deliver before they rise up and say enough? And the answer here, over and over and over again, has been that the fabric becomes tattered, that sometimes the fabric even becomes torn, but the fabric survives.

Anna Quindlen, from *New York: A Documentary Film*

The 1890 publication of *How the Other Half Lives* by Jacob Riis called attention to the extreme poverty of more than half of all New Yorkers at the time. The polarizing division between the haves and the have-nots continues to this day. In a recent essay "As Income Gap Widens, New York Grows Apart," James Parrot points out "that New York City has extreme wealth and extreme poverty, and lots of both, [and it] seems like a law of nature, older than the Subway or the Brooklyn Bridge."

In various ways, this chapter explores the most pressing issues New York City faces. These essays explore the impacts of certain urban policies on the city's population, specifically the ways in which they intensify or alleviate class and social divisions, among other problems. The readings encourage students to engage in debates concerning gentrification, urban development, environmental planning, homelessness, poverty, crime, police brutality, and other issues. Some of the articles in this section come from *Gotham Gazette*, an online journal that specializes in a wide array of urban issues. We encourage students to visit this site, which has links to other local and national publications and reports, and to further explore topics and discussions beyond the scope of this chapter.

As Income Gap Widens, New York Grows Apart

James Parrott

James Parrott is Deputy Director and chief economist of the Fiscal Policy Institute. He has been studying and writing about the New York economy since he arrived in New York City a quarter of a century ago.

Pre-Reading

What are your concerns about the economy?

New York has the greatest disparities in income of any major U.S. city, with the top 1 percent of the population getting 44 percent of the income in the city.   1

That New York City has extreme wealth and extreme poverty, and lots of both, seems like a law of nature, older than the subway or the Brooklyn Bridge. While there is a lot of truth in that, the city has not always had the extremes to the extent it has them now. Today, the wealthiest 1 percent of city residents has 44 percent of all income in the city, a share nearly four times as great as 30 years ago.

Over the past three decades, the bulk of economic gains in the United States and New York has accrued to those at the very top of the income pyramid. The economy has grown significantly over this period, but those at the very top have taken a vastly disproportionate share of the gains, leaving very little for the rest.

The Big Change

The chart below, from a recent report on income concentration by the Fiscal Policy Institute, demonstrates that the first three decades after World War II—from the mid 1940s to the late 1970s—were a time when the share of total income going to the wealthiest 1 percent stayed remarkably steady. In 1947, the top 1 percent received 12 percent of the total, and three decades later, in 1978, that remained about the same—actually slightly lower—at 9 percent. The top 1 percent's share held at close to 10 percent throughout all three decades.

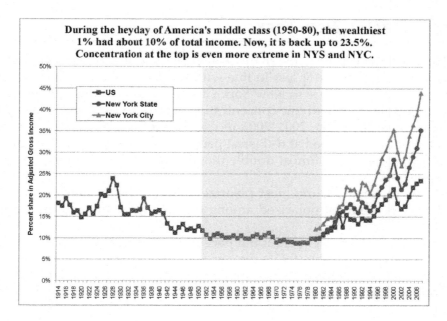

During the heyday of America's middle class (1950-80), the wealthiest 1% had about 10% of total income. Now, it is back up to 23.5%. Concentration at the top is even more extreme in NYS and NYC.

The post-war era is widely seen as a golden age of the middle class, with an economy fueled in significant part by middle-class spending. The middle class flourished. Its numbers expanded, and its living standards rose steadily. The U.S. economy grew, and that growth lifted millions of families out of poverty and into the middle class. Parents could expect their children to do even better than they had done.

The top 1 percent gained as well—executives and bankers enjoyed the success of the American economy as much as anyone. Their incomes grew steadily, but together with the rest of the country in a rising tide that lifted all boats, in New York and in the country as a whole. We grew together.

The picture since 1980 has changed dramatically. In 1980, the top 1 percent of households nationally held 10 percent of the total income. By 2007, that share had more than doubled, rising to 23.5 percent—a high previously attained only in 1928, the eve of the 1929 stock market crash that ushered in the Great Depression.

The economy has grown considerably in the three decades since 1980, albeit not as fast as in the 1950s through the 1970s. But growth after 1980 looked different than it had in the preceding era. The incomes of the top 1 percent and the top 5 percent grew faster, much faster, than in the post-war period, while the incomes of everyone else, those with low incomes as well as the broad middle class, faltered and stagnated. We grew apart.

Growing Apart in New York

In New York City in 1980, the share of all incomes going to the top 1 percent was 12 percent—more or less in line with the rest of the U.S. But by 1990 the top 1 percent's share in New York City had risen to almost 20 percent, and after a period of extreme concentration in the late 1990s reached nearly 35 percent in 2000. The 2001–2003 recession briefly pushed the top share down, but then it gained at its fastest pace over the past 30 years, climbing to 44 percent in 2007, almost double the historically high national level of 23.5 percent.

New York State is the most polarized among the 50 states, and New   10
York City is the most polarized among the 25 largest cities in the United States.

Today, most experts expect the pace of the nascent recovery from the Great Recession of 2008–09 to remain subdued in large part because of high household debt burdens, stagnant or declining wages, and a bleak job outlook. The recession was triggered by the bursting of the housing bubble and a speculative, excess-prone financial system, but it occurred in an economy with an increasingly shaky foundation characterized by weak job growth, continued export of middle-income jobs and wage growth that failed to keep pace with inflation and the growth in the productivity of labor.

This shaky foundation has a lot to do with the post-1980 hyper-concentration of income. The expansion from 2004 to 2007 was the first in which family incomes and median wages adjusted for inflation did not rise over the cycle to reach the peak of the previous business cycle. Despite economic growth, many Americans never saw their income return to the levels they had reached in 2000. Faced with this, families turned to debt, using credit cards and home equity borrowing to sustain their living standards. The crash of the financial and housing bubbles destroyed trillions of dollars in retirement and college savings that had been accumulated by middle- and low-income Americans, and decimated the value of their homes.

Rebuilding that wealth and economic security and restoring a sense of optimism for the next generation will be doubly difficult given the current polarized system of economic rewards and the bleak outlook for job and economic growth. The broadly shared prosperity that prevailed in the three decades after World War II is a distant memory. Are we destined to grow further apart?

Growth at the Top

The concentration of income growth at the top does not necessarily mean that those below the top will not see living standards improve. Incomes could rise up and down the income scale even as gains are disproportionately concentrated at the top. That, though, is not what has happened recently.

Over the period from 1980 to 2007, when inflation-adjusted income in   15 New York state grew an average of 2.1 percent a year after adjusting for population increase, incomes for those in the bottom half of the income spectrum (incomes below $33,000) generally declined. Incomes of people in the middle-range (incomes from $33,000 to $176,000) rose but at only a fraction of the pace of total income growth. Meanwhile, the real incomes of those in the top 1 percent (incomes over $580,000) grew 7 percent annually, over three times as fast as overall income growth. The rest of those in the top 5 percent (incomes from $176,000 to $580,000) saw their incomes rise a little faster than the pace of total income growth.

Most New York City workers and their families have experienced very little real income or wage growth over the past two decades. For example, as the table below shows, the inflation-adjusted median hourly wage fell by 8.6 percent from 1990 to 2007, and poverty came down very little during a period when the income share of the top 1 percent doubled from 21.5 percent to 44 percent.

There has been considerable growth in the NYC economy since 1990 (2.9% annually) and higher educational attainment, but it has not meant lower poverty, or higher real wages or higher family income for most New Yorkers

However, the income share of those at the top and average Wall Street pay have soared

	1990	2007	1990-2007
Real NYC Gross Domestic Product ($ billions)	$365.3	$595.0	62.9%
Percent of age 25-64 workforce with bachelor's degree or higher, NYC	26.0%	35.3%	+ 9.3 ppts
Poverty Rate, NYC (from U.S. Census Bureau)	19.3%	18.5%	- 0.8 ppts
Real Hourly Median Wage, NYC ($2007)	$17.00	$15.53	-8.6%
Real average annual Wall Street salary (including cash bonus) ($2007)	$190,400	$403,358	111.8%
Real Median Family Income, NYC ($2007)	$46,017	$45,000	-2.2%
Average earnings for full-time, year-round NYC worker with bachelor's degree or higher, age 25-34	$60,627	$57,000	-6.0%
Income Shares			
Share of Total NYC income received by the top 1 percent (in 2007, incomes above $642,700)	21.5%	44.0%	+ 22.5 ppts
Share of Total NYC income received by the top 5 percent (in 2007, incomes above $167,400)	30.0%	58.0%	+ 28.0 ppts
Share of Total NYC income received by the "middle" 45 percent (the 51st to the 95th percentile, in 2007, income range from $28,800 to $167,400)	53.2%	34.1%	- 19.1 ppts
Share of Total NYC income received by the "bottom" 50 percent (in 2007, incomes below $28,800)	15.8%	7.9%	- 7.9 ppts.

New York's Stark Split

In New York City, there are about 34,500 households, representing about 90,000 people, in the top 1 percent. On average, these households have annual incomes of $3.7 million. At the same time, about 900,000 people in New York City—about 10.5 percent of city residents—live in deep poverty. Deep poverty is half of the federal poverty line; for a four-person family, that means an income of $10,500. An annual income of $3.7 million trans-lates into a *daily* level of $10,137—more than the average *annual* family income of those living in deep poverty. According to state tax data, half of the households in New York City have annual incomes below $30,000, an amount that the top 1 percent receives over the course of a holiday weekend.

If New York City were a nation, its level of income concentration would rank 15th worst among 134 countries, between Chile and Honduras. Wall Street, with its stratospheric profits and bonuses, sits within 15 miles of the Bronx—the nation's poorest urban county.

Behind the Income Concentration

It is often argued that skills-based technological change largely explains the trend toward greater income polarization. According to this reasoning, the steady advance of technological change raises skill requirements. As a result, those who pursue higher education and obtain the skills needed to master new technologies receive greater economic rewards. Those lacking higher education see the demand slacken for their limited skills and their wages fall accordingly.

There is a certain appeal to this explanation, but it does not account for the intensified degree of income concentration that has taken place. One third of New Yorkers aged 25 to 64 in the workforce now have a four-year college degree or better, a considerable increase since 1990. Despite that, income gains have been concentrated among a much smaller segment of the population. In New York City, inflation-adjusted annual earnings of college-educated young workers have fallen 6 percent from 1990 levels. In addition, among the well-educated those with the highest incomes do not have the best education.

Something else must be at work since education, however important on an individual level, simply cannot serve as a compelling explanation for increased income concentration.

Moreover, skills-based technological change—and globalization for that matter—has occurred throughout the developed world. Yet no other coun-try has seen the heightened polarization of incomes that has taken place in

20

the United States. In the early 1970s, the richest 1 percent in the U.S. had a share of total income that was roughly in line with several other developed economies, including Canada, France, Japan and the United Kingdom. By 2000, however, the top 1 percent's share had risen much higher in the U.S. than in any other country. In Germany, there was almost no change in the income share of the top 1 percent. France even saw a decline in the share going to the richest 1 percent, and by 2000 that share was half what it was in the United States. Japan's top 1 percent received a slight gain in share, but that share also was only half that of the U.S. in 2000.

Jacob Hacker and Paul Pierson persuasively argue in their book, *Winner-Take-All Politics,* that incomes have risen so high at the top not because of education or other economic factors but because of national policy changes that have favored the wealthy and certain institutions, such as the largest financial companies. Hacker and Pierson point to several national policy changes involving labor markets and labor unions, financial deregulation and taxation that were largely unique to the U.S.

These changes—such as financial deregulation and the failure to limit executive compensation—have tremendously benefited large financial firms and corporate executives. Those developments have made a big difference in New York City. National policies that allowed the purchasing power of the minimum wage to seriously erode and that reduced the power of labor unions also have made a significant difference in depressing wages for middle- and low-income workers.

There is nothing inevitable in the operation of markets that generates extreme polarization in the distribution of economic rewards, but policy choices on how markets can operate and on taxes have everything to do with the distribution of economic rewards.

It has become increasingly understood that the many steps taken since the 1970s to deregulate financial markets played a key role in excessive speculation, poorly designed and unregulated financial innovations, and eventually, in the 2008 financial collapse. Deregulation gave financial institutions virtually a free hand to combine commercial and investment-banking, increase leverage and sell exotic financial instruments such as derivatives without regard for effective risk management. In financial bubble periods, such as the one based on commercial real estate lending in the 1980s and the dot.com boom of the late 1990s, financial firms reap enormous profits and pay their top bankers and traders huge bonuses. Nationally, in 2004, Hacker and Pierson point out, nearly 20 percent of America's super-wealthy (the top one-tenth of 1 percent) worked in finance; 40 percent were CEOs and other executives.

Federal tax policy also has contributed greatly. The moves to reduce top tax rates and capital gains tax rates—as Presidents Ronald Reagan and

25

George W. Bush did—and to maintain glaring loopholes have all had a major effect. Hacker and Pierson found that the average effective federal income tax rate on the top 1 percent fell by one third from 1970 to 2004.

States have much more limited authority. Despite that, several tax policy changes enacted by New York State have eased the tax burden at the top. New York's top state personal income tax rate was 15 percent in the early 1970s and in several steps it was reduced to 6.85 percent by 2009, when the state enacted a temporary surcharge. While the management fees referred to as "carried interest" received by hedge fund managers is taxed at the lower capital gains tax rate at the federal level, New York City exempts it from taxation altogether under the city's unincorporated business tax.

Can We Grow Together?

The Great Recession dramatically worsened an already highly polarized economy. Policy changes are needed at the state and national level to stimulate more robust growth and to reverse excessive income polarization. Not all of these changes are politically possible in the immediate term, but it is hard to see how the economy can fundamentally improve in the absence of significant changes that move us toward more broadly shared prosperity.

The kinds of policies that would help include: increasing the minimum   30
wage, strengthening the enforcement of labor standards, expanding living wage requirements, increasing labor union membership, making investments in economic growth rather than slashing government budgets, helping small businesses grow, provide real assistance on home foreclosures including keeping people in their homes as renters, and investing in public higher education.

At this moment, the most critical move to reverse extreme income polarization would be enacting progressive tax policies at all levels of government. In New York State, the top 1 percent pays a smaller share of their income in state and local taxes than all of those less well off, from the upper-middle, to the middle, to the poor. The story is similar in New York City. While the top one percent has 44 percent of city income and pay slightly over half of all local personal income taxes, they account for only one-third of total New York City tax revenue including personal income, city sales and residential property taxes.

At the national level, the income and estate tax changes agreed to by President Barack Obama and the Republican leadership will give 34 percent of the tax cuts going to all New Yorkers to the richest 1 percent. On average, the richest households will receive a tax cut averaging $124,000 in

2011. The middle fifth of New Yorkers will average a $1,500 tax cut, and the poorest 20 percent will get less than $300 on average.

There are many reasons to be concerned about New York's extreme income concentration. Among the most pressing is that the pronounced polarization in the distribution of the rewards of economic growth is holding back the nascent recovery. Growth is stalled because our system of rewarding economic effort is out of kilter. In the last three decades, the U.S. has become a country where average workers can no longer count on being paid for their productivity, while those at the top receive an income far out of proportion to what they contribute to our economy.

Discussion Questions

1. What were the important changes in income concentration over the last 70 years in the U.S.?
2. How does the income gap in New York City compare to the rest of the nation? How does this affect average New Yorkers?
3. How do Americans cope with reduced income growth?
4. What are the contributing factors to the widening income gap in New York City?
5. According to the author, what can be done to ensure better distribution of income? Do you agree with him? Can you think of other measures?

Writing Tasks

- Discuss how having or not having enough money has helped or hindered the choices you or somebody you know has made. If you can, try to imagine two or more scenarios.
- Write an essay that discusses the key elements for success in America. Consider the following possibilities: inherited wealth, knowing the right people, natural ability, a good education, and/or hard work.

Affordable Housing Policies May Spur Gentrification, Segregation

Brian Paul

Brian Paul is a fellow at the Hunter College Center for Community Planning & Development. He is currently working on an independent documentary film on real estate development and neighborhood change in Greenpoint and Williamsburg called *The Domino Effect*.

Pre-Reading

Have you witnessed gentrification in your neighborhood? How has it affected you?

Manuel Zuniga has lived in Greenpoint since 1982. Back then the neighborhood was pl gued with high crime, vacant buildings and a shortage of basic government services. But Zuniga was won over by the ease of the commute to Manhattan, the affordability and the close-knit immigrant community of mostly Latino and Polish residents.

Now with two kids in high school, Zuniga is thankful for the many improvements in the neighborhood over the last decade. "In Greenpoint, my kids got a shot at a good education . . . and safety-wise, the crime is almost non-existent in the neighborhood, now you can walk around at night without a problem," he said.

But not all the changes have been positive for longtime residents. Since 2000, average market rents have doubled in Greenpoint-Williamsburg, and rent-stabilized tenants face increasing pressure from landlords looking to flip their apartments to the affluent young people now flooding the neighborhood. "It makes me angry about it because the people that are running these things, they don't see the whole picture, they only see profit. . . . The only place I can afford if I move out of here, I can't take my family there, it's too dangerous," said Zuniga.

This was not supposed to happen. When Greenpoint-Williamsburg was rezoned in 2005, city officials and community advocates involved in the negotiations claimed that requiring developers to set aside 30 percent of new units on the waterfront for "affordable housing" would ensure that

1

Reprinted by permission of Brian Paul.

longtime residents like Zuniga would be able to stay in the neighborhood. They repeated the promise this year when they announced the deal for the redevelopment of the Domino Sugar Refinery site into a Battery Park City-style complex with 2,200 housing units.

Despite such promises, this public-private, affordable-luxury model   5
of development has not produced enough affordable housing to meet the needs of longtime, working class residents. The flood of new luxury units has far outpaced the trickle of affordability.

This story has been told before. But what has not been examined is the possibility that the city's market-based affordable housing system may actually contribute to, rather than alleviate, this pattern of gentrification and displacement.

The City's Model

In rapidly gentrifying neighborhoods like Greenpoint-Williamsburg, the city has promoted combining public and private investment, and linking affordable housing with luxury. The Bloomberg administration and many local nonprofits see this as an ideal compromise between real estate developers and communities.

The Community Preservation Corp., or CPC, is one of the city's largest private partners in this mission and is the developer of the Domino Sugar project. The corporation, a consortium of over 80 banks and insurance companies, receives city subsidies for affordable housing while also profiting from private market-rate real estate investments. In this way, it epitomizes the kind of hybrid entities that have grown out of the current affordable housing system.

CPC's record of investment in Brooklyn raises some disturbing questions about the results of these development practices. Despite the corporation's image as a developer of affordable housing, analysis of the city's public ACRIS property records reveals that since 2007, more than 65 percent of the $701 million invested in Brooklyn (including new loans and refinancing), have gone to market rate development. CPC has invested with some of Brooklyn's most notoriously unethical—and in some cases criminal—luxury developers. The investment in the luxury market is concentrated on the frontier of gentrification in neighborhoods like Williamsburg, Clinton Hill, South Park Slope and Prospect Heights.

On the other hand, CPC's lending for affordable housing is concen-   10
trated in neighborhoods on the outskirts of the borough like Brownsville and East New York, places of less interest to private for-profit developers.

Ironically, many of the community organizations and advocates one might expect to challenge this pattern of development actively support

CPC. These community-based nonprofit developers often depend on private sources of funding from entities like CPC and compete for political favor with the city to receive public grants. These ties could make it difficult for them to voice any criticism.

By financing luxury development in gentrifying neighborhoods, concentrating affordable housing investment in the outskirts, and influencing the politics of local nonprofit organizations and political figures through its lending, the Community Preservation Corp.—and the market-based affordable housing system it represents—may actually be a major contributor to the accelerating gentrification of Brooklyn.

Expert Public Relations

Although CPC was provided with the full ACRIS dataset and map of investments used for this article, the company declined to comment on the findings. And if one were to judge the company by its public testimonies and public relations, one would never know that CPC was anything but a generous funder and developer of affordable housing.

Every week, CPC publishes a newsletter celebrating its affordable housing projects and trumpeting the community benefits of its lending. But the numerous luxury condominium developments CPC has funded somehow never make these pages.

At the first public hearing on the Domino project in February 2010, CPC's project manager Susan Pollock stated, "The mission of the company is to build and preserve affordable housing. That's it, that's the mission."   15

During City Council hearings in August, representatives from several Brooklyn-based community development corporations and Catholic churches vouched for CPC. John Simon, director of housing at Catholic Charities, described CPC as "deeply committed to responsible community development." Reverend Julio Cruz Jr. from East Brooklyn Congregations proclaimed, "We have developed thousands of units of affordable housing with them, and we know that they provide the best possible and most affordable developments." And the executive director of Los Sures, a respected nonprofit affordable housing developer in Williamsburg, lauded CPC's "immaculate history."

These testimonials provided crucial public support for the approval of the controversial Domino development. And certainly CPC has funded many laudable affordable housing projects, such as the East Brooklyn Congregations' Nehemiah Houses and renovations of the Riverdale Osborne Towers, both in Brooklyn, and the Parkchester complex in the Bronx. But examining the complete record of CPC's lending in Brooklyn raises serious contradictions to its carefully cultivated image as a benevolent developer of affordable housing.

Luxury Investment on Gentrification's Frontier

New York's ACRIS system maintains a publicly accessible database of property transactions for every building and lot in the city. Analysis of CPC's transactions in Brooklyn since 2007 reveals that is a major player in financing luxury development in gentrifying neighborhoods.

From East Williamsburg down to Clinton Hill, Prospect Heights and Prospect-Lefferts Gardens, CPC's luxury investments form a trench down the frontier of Brooklyn gentrification. Over the past four years, these investments account for over 65 percent of CPC's lending in the borough. With condominium prices ranging from $300,000 to over a million dollars, this housing is completely unaffordable to the vast majority of New Yorkers.

Some of CPC's luxury development partners have histories that put them at odds with CPC's clean image. Isaac Katan, CPC's investment partner on the New Domino project, is a Brooklyn developer notorious for building super-sized luxury projects on brownstone blocks in South Park Slope. While he was able to successfully build a CPC-financed 11 story condominium at 162 16th Street, the planned "sister" building at 182 South 15th St was halted by the Board of Standards and Appeals. Neighborhood residents spent over $100,000 in legal fees to prove that Katan illegally began construction without a permit while trying to rush to complete the building before the neighborhood was rezoned to rule out such massive structures.

CPC financed a luxury project at 147 Classon Ave. in Clinton Hill developed by Moshe Junger, who served four months in prison for the 2001 death of his worker Rogelio Villaneuva-Daza. Junger violated a direct government order in proceeding to demolish a Williamsburg factory without first surveying its structural integrity. Daza died when the second floor collapsed and he was crushed by a falling beam. Other developers with questionable ethics whose projects have been financed by CPC include Eli Karp, Yitzchok Schwartz and Abe Betesh.

Many of CPC's luxury projects were initiated in the speculative boom of 2005 to 2007. In the past year, CPC has gone back and refinanced some of these developments with mortgages insured by the State of New York Mortgage Agency.

The state's justification for backing these troubled luxury condominium developments is that doing so will "help stabilize neighborhoods put at risk by the debt crisis." But it is widely recognized that speculative luxury construction and the "housing bubble" were major factors in causing the debt crisis in the first place.

State-insured refinancing of troubled luxury projects by lenders like CPC allows developers to avoid participating in the Housing Asset

20

Renewal Program, the city's experimental effort to encourage developers to convert ailing luxury projects to affordable housing. These refinancings enable the developers to warehouse the units in the hope that the market will recover; they are essentially a bailout. As a result, the Housing Asset Renewal Program has been a complete failure, with not a single empty luxury unit converted to affordable housing.

Where the Affordable Housing Is

In contrast to the plans for the New Domino, where 100 percent of the   25
affordable units will be on-site in Williamsburg, the vast majority of CPC's affordable housing investment has not been made in neighborhoods that are under threat of gentrification and displacement. It is instead concentrated in areas like East New York and Brownsville—heavily segregated neighborhoods with high rates of poverty and crime.

Taken together, the populations of East New York and Brownsville are over 90 percent black and Latino. Almost half of all households have incomes of less than $25,000 and almost half of adults over 16 years old are "not in the labor force." Commutes by public transit to Manhattan are roughly twice as long as they are in closer neighborhoods like Greenpoint-Williamsburg. And the crime rates are the highest in the city and on the rise for the first time since the early 1990s.

Manuel Zuniga can keep his family in Greenpoint because he has a rent-stabilized apartment and is friendly with his landlord. But thousands of other families are not so lucky and must go wherever affordable housing is available, even if it means leaving a relatively safe neighborhood with good schools for one with lots of crime and poorly performing schools.

CPC's pattern of concentrating affordable housing investment in marginalized neighborhoods is typical of a larger national trend. Since direct public development of public housing ended during the Reagan era, affordable housing creation has been tied to the principles of the real estate market. At the federal level, the Treasury Department's Internal Revenue Service oversees the Low Income Housing Tax Credit program, not the Department of Housing and Urban Development.

While the housing department operates under a mandate to further racial integration, the Treasury is not so bound. Its emphasis is to produce affordable housing at the lowest possible expense with little regard to location. Partly because of that, affordable units are concentrated in neighborhoods where property values are low and the for-profit market has little interest instead of in the gentrifying neighborhoods where they are needed the most.

Since the 1970s, urban planners and policymakers have emphasized   30
the value of "mixed-income" development and diverse neighborhoods. It is widely recognized that governments made a major mistake in the 1950s

and 1960s when they built huge public housing projects, concentrating and segregating large numbers of low-income people in neighborhoods with few economic opportunities and serious environmental problems.

Our current affordable housing policies may be repeating the same mistakes. Leaving affordable housing to entities like CPC that operate on market real estate principles leads to the majority of affordable homes being placed in the most disadvantaged neighborhoods in the city, helping to reinforce racial and economic segregation.

A Broken System

The reality of affordable housing policy in New York is rather less rosy than the public relations efforts of the developers and the Bloomberg administration would have us think. But in Brooklyn politics, "affordable housing" has become a term like "freedom"—something no one in his right mind could possibly oppose.

Affordable housing is desperately needed across the five boroughs, and the Bloomberg administration is constantly pledging to create more of it. But New York has actually experienced a loss of almost 200,000 affordable apartments, or 16.4 percent of the city's total between 2002 and 2008, according to the most recent city Housing and Vacancy Survey.

The single-minded pursuit of "deals" for a percentage of affordable housing in luxury projects like Domino Sugar may be leading non-profit community developers to overlook the role that the market-oriented affordable housing system is playing in gentrifying their communities. When confronted with these findings, John Simon from Catholic Charities said, "We supported the Domino project based simply on the fact that they guaranteed 30 percent affordable housing. . . .We didn't do any intricate analysis."

Speaking on behalf of East Brooklyn Congregations, Michael Gecan defended CPC for being a "central and pivotal part of investment and production" of affordable housing in New York City. "In an imperfect world . . . [deals like Domino Sugar] are the best solution. Others may disagree or believe in wishful thinking. We operate in reality," he said.   35

The reality of Brooklyn real estate today is indeed very different than it was in the late 1970s and early 1980s when neighborhoods like Williamsburg were ignored and redlined by private real estate investors. During that time, organizations like East Brooklyn Congregations and Los Sures had great success in organizing and pressuring the city for funding to rehabilitate thousands of abandoned buildings into tenant cooperatives and other forms of affordable housing.

Since the return of private market investment in the 1990s however, these organizations have had to compete and make deals with wealthy for-profit developers. Because government investment in affordable housing is tied into the public-private, luxury-affordable models, the community-based nonprofit developers need private dollars from entities like CPC to fund their work. All of the community development corporations and church affiliated groups that testified on CPC's behalf during the New Domino hearings have received loans from the company during the past four years, with the largest amount—over $30 million—going to the East Brooklyn Congregations' Nehemiah Houses project.

With the community housing organizations so heavily invested in this current "reality," there are few voices left to question whether this system—and the tremendous amount of public money that flows into it—really serves the best interest of all New Yorkers.

Since 2000, average rents have doubled in Williamsburg-Greenpoint and almost 40 percent of the Latino population has left the neighborhood likely because of the housing costs. Similar shifts are occurring all along the frontier of Brooklyn gentrification.

The market-based, public-private affordable housing system embodied   40
by CPC is helping to create and preserve thousands of affordable units across the city. But looking at the big picture and tracing the connections between affordable development and the explosion of luxury construction reveals that it also may be fueling gentrification and housing segregation—the very problems that the city and developers claim it is helping to solve.

Discussion Questions

1. According to the article, what are the positive and negative effects of gentrification in Greenpoint?
2. According to the author, what may be causing the accelerating gentrification of Brooklyn?
3. What is the stated mission of the Community Preservation Corporation? What does it do that seems to contradict its mission?
4. What were the mistakes in urban planning in the 1950s and 60s? What was done to rectify them?
5. What specific areas in Brooklyn are chosen to be sites for affordable homes? According to the author, what are the results of these decisions?

Writing Task

- Write a persuasive essay either supporting or arguing against gentrification in your neighborhood. Give examples of the possible effects of an increase of new residents and an influx of new businesses.

The Williamsburg Renaissance

Jessica Guerra

Jessica Guerra is a student at New York City College of Technology. This essay was written for her ENG 1101 course and was published in *City Tech Writer*.

The year is 1990. A newlywed couple has just moved into the railroad style 1-bedroom apartment across the hall. They'll like it here—the street is quiet, the building is clean. Your morning stroll down the block brings you to the corner of Roebling and North 7th Streets. But don't turn on North 7th just yet. Look down Roebling. See the factories? They're perfectly lined up on the left side, on the right side … all the way down to McCarren Park, to those large, looming trees in the distance. Pretty soon they'll be turning yellow, orange, red, then the colors will fall, spread themselves over the grassy patches and bumpy asphalt leaving the naked branches to prepare for the heavy snowfall ahead. Smell the bread baking? It's that factory right there. Now turn on North 7th. Walk past the three-story walkups. Greet the old man sitting on his stoop and his granddaughter riding her tricycle. Tell her how fast she's growing up, as if that matters to a two-year old. Walk briskly past the L train. Turn left on Bedford Avenue and head over to Pedro's Grocery Store. Go in, ask him how his wife is, buy a gallon of milk, some eggs … wish him a good day. Walk home perfunctorily—almost without looking, you cross the streets. Think about introducing yourself to the new neighbors. They seem nice.

Williamsburg in the 1990's was simply that, an industrial and residential area whose inhabitants were mostly of European and Hispanic descent. Affordable housing was in abundance and, although the apartments were small, the rent never surpassed $500 a month. The couple you read about are my parents. That railroad style apartment was their first place together after the honeymoon, and the place they would call home for the next eighteen years. Their '83 Buick Regal was parked in front of the narrow building; plenty of space available down the block and across the street as well. Little did they know that in just a few years, parking would become almost impossible to find.

Condos Cutting Corners

Fifteen years later, the couple has two daughters, one ten, the other twelve months old. You hear the baby crying in the distance. Must be hungry. See the sunlight coming in through the fire escape window and decide to go jogging in McCarren Park. Go down two flights, through the two metal doors, down the steps. Walk past the bread factory and stop for a while. Hear a bulldozer in the distance, look toward the construction workers across the street, the bright blue scaffolding on the next block, the new traffic light at the corner. You know, that's one of the last factories *left. They've been replaced with tall buildings. Condos, they call them. Spanning Kent Avenue from North 5th to North 10th, the brand new luxury condominiums hover at $1 million. The apartments start at $2,400 a month. You only paid $485 a month when you first moved in! The biggest of the waterfront complexes is called EDGE. You've heard some of the apartments are designated for lower income residents. The family across from you has already applied—maybe you will too.*

What sparked all the change? Developers noticed the proximity of Williamsburg to Manhattan. The L and J trains, which span the North and Southside neighborhoods, Bedford-Stuyvesant, and Bushwick areas, provide easy access to Manhattan, making the area attractive to those residents. By constructing luxury housing, Manhattan residents looking to spend less for equal luxury and still be close to work are instantly driven to Williamsburg. But it is not a coincidence that a bunch of developers suddenly noticed Williamsburg's potential. This is something the city had been planning for years. Expecting the population of Manhattan residents to increase, they had to prepare for the overflow of New Yorkers into the surrounding neighborhoods. Williamsburg, of course, was the chosen one. So developers not only buy factories, but three- and four-story buildings as well, paying sky-high prices to landlords and tenants so as to have the buildings vacant. Why? To demolish them, of course, replacing them with luxury apartments, co-ops, and condominiums. And the factories not worth tearing down are turned into lofts. These new developments are strictly designed for the incoming Manhattanites. They are mostly from the East Village, single women and single men—artists, they call themselves. Some are couples looking to start a family, yes, but that's what the very few 2-bedroom condos are for. However, EDGE is not the only new development. In recent months, high-rise buildings such as the Northside Piers, 80 Met, 568 Union, 88 South 1st, and 29 Montrose Avenue have seemingly popped up. And most recently, the Domino Sugar factory project was resurrected, an eleven-acre property bought by the Walentas real estate family for $185 million. The plan is to create 2,200 apartments, 70% being what we call "luxury" (Bagli).

Booming Businesses, Not Bodegas

The year is 2008. You cross Metropolitan Avenue looking both ways and subconsciously realize this is the boundary between the North and Southside neighborhoods. It seems as though Southside residents have somehow managed to keep their Hispanic culture alive. Maybe this condo thing hasn't hit them yet. But keep your eyes peeled. Remember that beverage distributor across the street from Kellogg's Diner? It says Sunac Natural Food. Nice building, big glass windows. Go in. Grab a cookie. Gluten-free, sugar-free, dairy-free, and fat-free. Price? Two dollars. Without so many ingredients, shouldn't it cost less? Leave the cookie on the shelf, walk out slowly. Take Havemeyer Street. Certainly C-Town hasn't *changed. Wrong. Notice the new floors, bright lighting, and wide aisles? Pick up a jar of peanut butter. Organic, it says. Pick up another. Organic again. Desperately look on the top shelves, bottom shelves. Isn't there any Jif? Oh, look. Skippy. Turn the jar over. $5.99. Almost drop it. Look behind you to see if anyone noticed. Put it back on the shelf carefully. Leave the store looking confused. Decide to pay a quick visit to Pedro's Grocery Store. Stand on the corner of North 8th and Bedford Avenue and look up. Where's the bodega? Quick, pretend you've lost your way from the train station, blend in with the crowd. Make your way back to Roebling Street without tripping over all the bikes parked on the curb. Wonder why Hub's Pub is where Pedro's Grocery Store used to be. Almost walk into a woman walking her three Labrador Retrievers on a leash. Jump when they all bark at you, blush at the woman's laughter. Find the family across from you bringing boxes down the steps. Ask them if they need help and put the boxes in the trunk of their Toyota Sienna. After wishing them the best, go up the stoop, but turn around to watch them leave. Catch the landlord crying. Jog up the stairs fighting back tears, put the key in your lock with a heaviness on your shoulders. Look across the hallway and notice the empty apartment. Let the tears roll down.*

After developers provide new housing and entrepreneurs establish their organic stores and "cute" little pubs in Williamsburg, residents are no longer oblivious to the change. In fact, many residents feel fear and helplessness. Who is going to be shopping in these places anyway? Cue the hipsters! An article from the *Village Voice*, popular among Northside residents, references a British newspaper that calls Williamsburg "the national capital for young hipsters" and depicts these new residents as having "beards, piercings, lots of tattoos, and belong[ing] to at least one band" (Coscarelli). A simple stroll down Berry Street and North 6th would provide sufficient evidence. But these hipsters, as they are called, have slowly made their way into the Southside as well, specifically Grand Street, converting a small food distributor into an expensive T-shirt shop, a DVD rental store into a candlelit café, and causing Key Food to be completely unaffordable for most residents of the area. An article published last year in the *Daily News*, very popular among Southside residents, spoke out for those who feel their neighborhood has been taken over. It starts off with "Hey hipsters, keep your skinny jeans out of my Southside Williamsburg neighborhood." The article goes on to interview many residents who share the same fear of being evicted from their own neighborhood. One man sums it up pretty well: "You wake up one morning and you see the corner bodega is now replaced by a fancy café or restaurant and you see your neighbors being pushed out because they can no longer afford the rent… You begin to wonder 'Am I next?'" Another gentleman who was interviewed grew up in the neighborhood years ago and remembers nostalgically a bodega that used to be on South 4th and Driggs Avenue. Today a small cardboard sign hangs behind the window with "Pies N Thighs" written in black marker (Morales, Nelson).

From the Outside Looking In

The family who moved out of the small apartment on Roebling Street four years ago is my family. By the time we moved out, rent was under $800, but the new tenants in the building were paying way over $1,000 a month. Fortunately, that wasn't a problem for them. Of course we would miss the area: the proximity of the L train (not that you could find your way to the train station anymore—bike racks and long lines for dollar pizza blurred it from view), the Mexican bodega that we always bought fresh tortillas from (not that it would be there much longer—the sign on the window said "For Sale"), the convenient laundromat on Driggs Avenue and North 6th, Northside Pharmacy on Bedford Avenue, the Deli Mart a few blocks down, Vinnie's Pizzeria, and Brothers Cleaners... but who knows how long they'd be there for. And our landlord did cry. She begged us to stay, but finally settled for a nice dinner sometime in the upcoming months. We hopped in the minivan on our way to Maspeth, Queens. It's not that we hadn't tried to apply for those nice apartments on the Northside. We did. Even in Bushwick there were new developments. But it was always a matter of waiting. And frankly, we could not wait any longer. The people from EDGE finally replied, but it was too late. We were already enjoying our new apartment.

Although I live in Maspeth, my grandma still lives in the Southside and my sister goes to school across the street from her house. I have seen more and more of these hipsters going in and out the brick six-story buildings that neatly line up her block and their new businesses on Grand Street where I wait for the bus. But, most importantly, I have taken note of the new elementary school that is gradually replacing the one my sister attends. It is the same school I went to: P.S. 19 Roberto Clemente. Back when my parents first moved in together, there were over 1,000 students in the school. Now there are only about 300. After continuous poor performance, the Department of Education decided to phase out the school, leaving only grades 3 - 5. This year they introduced P.S. 414 Brooklyn Arbor, where all the kids wear green shirts and khakis, and the entire faculty is Caucasian, with the exception of one paraprofessional who is African-American. P.S. 19, on the other hand, had a vastly diverse group of teachers, and good ones at that. Sadly, the Department of Education waited until it was too late to fire the person responsible for the school's downfall: the principal. Believe it or not, this has all been part of the plan. A church on Union Avenue and Stagg Street, for example, has recently been demolished to make room for a new luxury building and, surely, the people who will move in, along with all the new residents on Keap Street, will have children of their own looking for a "good" school to enroll their kids in. P.S. 19 Roberto Clemente brings an air of Hispanic pride, what the Southside used to be about, while

P.S. 414 Brooklyn Arbor has a more modern, eco-friendly feel to it. Appealing to whom? To those hip, young, fresh-from-the East River newcomers who have already infiltrated all of Williamsburg.

It's almost funny, actually. These new residents walk around with 100% recycled bags, shirts that promote saving the environment, and loads of groceries from their favorite organic, natural, and health food shops. Yet, if you stop by McCarren Park any weekend in July, you'll find yourself face to face with 6,500 men and women scurrying about the streets looking for the park's entrance, anxious to see a not-so-famous band blast their acoustics across the East River, leaving trails of trash behind them like an evil Hansel and Gretel. An article in the *New York Times* looked at these summer concerts through the eyes of a long-time resident in the area: "the rivers of trash strewn along the street and on her stoop, the thunderous noise, [and] the drunken revelers using the street as a toilet" (Leland). To make my point simple: How could a group of people so determined to "save the Earth" (think 1960's hippies with a more snobbish flair), be so inconsiderate to litter the sidewalks, relieve their necessities in the street, and walk around the residential areas of Williamsburg late at night completely intoxicated?

Calling It Gentrification

Instead of working to provide lower-class residents with better structures, lighting, green areas, and security, the city has simply pushed them to poorer areas, conglomerating already overpopulated neighborhoods like East New York, Brooklyn and Ridgewood, Queens. It's almost as if they are too undignified to live in neighborhoods near the city, as if Manhattan residents coming in might feel uncomfortable with them around. This is not the case. In fact, if anything, it's the other way around. It's not that Williamsburg residents are intolerant to these vibrant young artists, but to kick residents out by making them feel unwanted with the intention of making the area entirely upper-class is simply unacceptable. This type of gentrification is not about a mere displacement. It's about rebirthing Williamsburg, a renaissance if you will, transforming the environment into one that ostracizes the very people who gave birth to it in the first place, who worked tirelessly in the factories, who took care of their neighbors, who opened up delis and pizzerias and bakeries, and planted those beautiful trees that line Roebling Street.

Maybe we should've seen it coming. Maybe that summer night my next door neighbor's daughter and I bought ice cream while watching the fireworks on North 6th, we didn't realize those beautiful views of the Manhattan skyline would one day be blocked by high-rises and organic cleaners. Maybe while walking from the train station to my grandma's house one afternoon, I should have noticed the new sketchy-looking pub on Broadway and Hooper Street and realized it was the first of many. Maybe. But I didn't. And now it's too late. Let's just hope I can still find my way around Keap Street and Borinquen Place—so long as my favorite Caribbean food isn't replaced by another Duane Reade.

Works Cited

Bagli, Charles V. "Developer to Revive a Project in Brooklyn." *New York Times*. 21 June 2012. Web.

Coscarelli, Joe. "Williamsburg, Brooklyn Is the 'New Front Line' of Gentrification." *Village Voice*. 12 Dec. 2010. Web.

Leland, John. "In Williamsburg, Rocked Hard." *New York Times*. 28 May 2011. Web.

Nelson, Katie, and Mark Morales. "Brooklyn Gentrification Meets Resistance from Longtime Latino Residents in South Williamsburg." *Daily News*. 16 Sept. 2011. Web.

Discussion Questions

1. Guerra begins her essay like a short story. In the next paragraph, the font style changes as does the style of writing. Do you find this strategy to be effective? What other writing strategies does Guerra use in her essay?
2. What does Guerra mean by the phrase "Williamsburg Renaissance"? What are some of the neighborhood changes she discusses? How does she feel about them?
3. How does the author describe the newcomers to Williamsburg? Do you think she is entirely fair in her assessment and description of them?
4. Who receives the most blame for gentrification? What solutions to this phenomenon does the author offer? Do you agree with her recommendations? What is happening in your neighborhood that reflects some of the issues that Guerra raises?

Writing Task

- Write a short essay in which you consider the gentrification of a New York neighborhood and discuss its overall advantages and disadvantages.

The Homeless

Margaret Morton

Margaret Morton received her BFA from Kent State University and MFA from Yale University. Morton joined the faculty at Cooper Union in 1980, where she teaches Photography and Art of the Book. She has exhibited in over twenty-five solo photo shows and in over fifty group shows. In addition, she has received numerous awards including grants from the National Endowment for the Arts, New York State Council on the Arts, and New York Foundation for the Arts. Her book projects include *Glass House*; *Fragile Dwelling*; *The Tunnel: The Underground Homeless of New York City*; and *Transitory Gardens, Uprooted Lives* (co-authored with Diana Balmori).

Pre-Reading

What are your feelings toward the homeless problem in New York?

In 1989, when my documentation of New York City's homeless communi-   1
ties began, there were more homeless New Yorkers than at anytime since
the Great Depression. Twenty-five thousand homeless poor sought beds
in city shelters each night. Thousands more slept outside. Highly visible
homeless encampments filled vacant lots and public parks, lined the sea-
walls along the East River, and perched at the ends of the Hudson River's
crumbling piers. More than two thousand men and women lived beneath
the city's streets, hidden in subway and railroad tunnels.

The economic, political, and social shifts that led to this massive dislocation
are complex, but several key events of the 1970s accelerated the crisis. Tens of
thousands of chronically ill patients had been discharged from state mental institutions, many without provision for housing or community-based treatment.
People wandering the streets and sleeping in public places soon became visible
beyond the Bowery. The decade marked a dramatic reduction in manufactur-
ing jobs, particularly in New York City. Many low-skill jobs disappeared, casu-
alties of automation and the use of cheap labor abroad. Soaring unemployment
coincided with a sudden decline in the real-estate market. In the wake of the
city's 1975 fiscal crisis, stringent revisions to property-tax laws were instituted.
But the city's plan to increase revenue had an unexpected effect: a significant
number of landlords, particularly in the South Bronx and on the Lower East
Side, responded with arson or abandonment, leaving some five hundred vacant
properties in neighborhoods where low-rent housing was desperately needed.

From *New York Calling: From Blackout to Bloomberg*, edited by Marshall Berman and Brian Berger. Copyright © Reaktion Books, 2007.

By the end of the '70s, the real-estate market had begun to recover. Rapid gentrification in the city's low-income neighborhoods further reduced the number of affordable apartments and single-room-occupancy (SRO) hotels, thus inflating the housing market. While the economic expansion that continued through the 1980s brought a surge of wealth to the elite of New York, the outlook for the poor became dismal. Rules governing eligibility for welfare were tightened, especially for single adult men. Those who succeeded in navigating the tangled bureaucracy received public-assistance checks that were inadequate in the face of escalating apartment rents.

A landmark lawsuit filed against the city in 1981, settled as the Callahan consent decree, guaranteed single homeless men the right to shelter. Subsequent litigation extended this right to women and families with children. More than twenty-eight thousand children and adults were residing in shelters by March 1987. Converted armories, such as Fort Washington in Upper Manhattan and the Atlantic Avenue Armory in Brooklyn, slept as many as a hundred men, billeted on floors once used for military drills. The crowded and conditions led thousands more to sleep outside, huddled in plastic bags or discarded refrigerator boxes, seeking protection in empty doorways and finding warmth on top of sidewalk steam grates. As the situation worsened, a startling phenomenon occurred: homeless people began to improvise housing for themselves. Shantytowns soon became visible in vacant lots on the Lower East Side. These encampments also appeared in public parks, under highway along the rivers, and beneath the streets. Residents clustered their dwellings into small villages that provided a sense of community and security.

The largest of these encampments was in Tompkins Square Park in   5
the East Village, where 150 homeless people had set up tents by the late 1980s. The 10-acre park was also a nighttime gathering place for punk-music fans and activists resisting the neighborhood's gentrification. On the night of August 6, 1988, a large crowd lingered at the park's band shell after a concert. At a nearby entrance protesters rallied against news that the police would enforce a curfew. Police arrived. A bottle-throwing skirmish erupted into a bloody melee. Over a hundred complaints of police brutality were filed by protesters and bystanders, and over forty people, including more than a dozen police officers, were injured. Afterwards the homeless individuals quietly returned. They were again swept from the park by police in July and December 1989. Each time, they made their way back. But on June 3 1991, a phalanx of police in riot gear routed them from the park and closed it for renovation. When it reopened in August 1992, a curfew was imposed. The homeless commuty rebuilt.

Over the next six years, homeless New Yorkers continued to be pushed out of their fragile, self-made dwellings by politics, police, and bulldozers. Some homes were demolished after only a few weeks. Others survived for several years and gradually expanded into more permanent settlements.

The most longstanding of these communities existed for three years in an abandoned railroad tunnel stretching for 2½ miles under Manhattan's Riverside Park. Joe, an army veteran, found shelter there in 1973: "I know how it is to be a tunnel rat. I did that tour in Vietnam." Cathy, a woman he had met in Riverside Park, joined him. They made a home together, the equivalent of eight blocks into the tunnel, in a pre-existing cinder-block room. Joe added a door and furnished the room with a bed, a nightstand, and a cupboard that he scavenged from the streets "upstairs." In addition to furniture, the refuse discarded by residents of Upper West Side high-rise apartments supplied Joe with used books and magazines, which he sold along Broadway, and with beverage cans that he redeemed at nearby re-cycling centers. Cathy, who suffered from asthma and epilepsy, cared for their pets: eighteen stray cats and a pit bull named Buddy. Throughout the 1980s, other homeless men and women found their way into the tunnel. They clustered plywood shanties beneath air vents, where shafts of daylight punctuated the darkness. Visiting graffiti artists painted elaborate murals on light-washed walls. Loners perched themselves on narrow ledges high above the tracks. Meals were cooked over fires that also served to com-bat winter's damp chill. The community relied on an underground water source. When it was suddenly shut off, tunnel residents were forced to walk miles below and above ground to obtain water and food.

While Cathy and Joe's community burgeoned, Bernard Isaac, found his way into the tunnel through a broken gate twelve blocks north. He hand-picked other homeless people to share his refuge, and by the late 1980s his "camp" of seventeen men and women formed the nucleus of a separate tunnel community. Larry joined Bernard's group in 1986. "I was walking down by the river and I saw the gate was open," he said. "This has been my home for five years out of the nine or ten that I've been roaming the streets."

Esteban, who had fled Cuba during the 1980 Mariel Boatlift, worked as a security guard for a building on 90th Street where Bernard collected cans. "I'd been down here sometimes and had visited Bernard. But the job ended. Then everything ended." Esteban moved into the tunnel. Bernard befriended Bob at an Upper West Side soup kitchen where they both volun-teered as cooks. Underground, Bernard cooked all the meals over an open campfire.

In 1990, Amtrak crews discovered more than fifty people living in the tunnel. Many of the residents refused to leave, continuing to live in their underground homes until June 1995, when Amtrak police informed them that they were trespassing and threatened them with arrest. Cops pad-locked most of the entrances. Tunnel residents, undaunted, regained entry by digging "rabbit holes" and cutting the locks with hacksaws. In the late spring of 1996, through the combined efforts of Coalition for the Homeless and Project Renewal, twenty-six of the tunnel residents were offered Fed-eral housing vouchers. Cathy and Joe moved to a subsidized apartment in

10

Spanish Harlem. Bernard lives in north Harlem but returns to the Upper West Side to earn money assisting the superintendents of luxury buildings and walking dogs. Bob lives in an SRO near Times Square. Esteban still lives on the Upper West Side, but now he sleeps on the streets.

***

In the late 1980s, fourteen homeless men from Puerto Rico made a community in a vacant lot on East 4th Street. They cleared debris, searched for scrap building materials, and constructed plywood houses along a central path. The men continually embellished their homes with additions that stirred memories of the place they had left behind: a front porch, brightly painted rock gardens, an interior courtyard, an inflated plastic palm tree, a Puerto Rican flag. Pepe built the front porch out of red plastic bakery trays and framed his entrance gate with bedposts he had found in the trash. He connected his roof to his vegetable garden with a *marquesina*, or covered walkway, paved with marble left over from a local apartment renovation. Metal window grates cut from shopping carts protected his home from break-ins and vandalism. Pepe added a tool room where he made money repairing lamps, radios, TVs, and turntables for residents of tenements on 3rd Street and Avenue D. Over a period of four years, he transformed his plywood shack into a five-room home. Juan, one of the earliest residents of "Bushville," as the community came to known, built a 16-by-8-foot plywood house using the exterior of a deserted building as the fourth wall. Above the front door he nailed a prized wooden sign: SPICE ISLANDS.

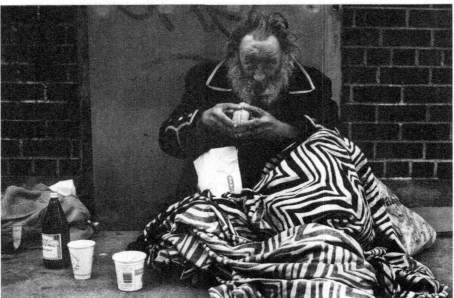

Homeless Man Eating on Street © Andrew Holbrooke/Corbis.

Juan was found dead inside his home in 1991, following an illness. Evelyn, his widow, sold his hut for $100 to Gumiscindo, a neighbor, who rented it to newcomers Duke and his companion Tanya for $40 a month. Duke, a Vietnam veteran, complained about paying rent to live in a homeless community, but he had already endured four evictions and needed to find more stable shelter than his cardboard-and-plastic lean-to along the FDR Drive.

Despite its look of permanence, the community could not last. After the abandoned apartment buildings that overlooked Bushville were renovated as housing for low-income families, the new tenants complained about the homeless. Early on December 15, 1993, Bushville was demolished. The residents had been warned of the impending destruction but had nowhere else to go. As the bulldozers arrived, people quickly gathered their belongings. The noise of the heavy equipment was deafening. Massive shovels wrenched the small houses from their foundations, held them high, then hurled them to the ground. Tanya and Duke lived for seven months in a stripped van up on blocks in a vacant lot on East Ninth Street before moving into an abandoned building in the neighborhood. Tanya's mother tends their baby. Pepe, the only Bushville resident offered subsidized housing, died four years later at age seventy. Another evicted resident, Mario, slept on the sidewalk around the corner from his former home until he died in 1998. He was sixty years old. The vacant lot is now a community garden.

***

Fourteen blocks southwest of Bushville, a group of sixteen homeless men and women pieced together homes on a triangular knoll that bordered the Canal Street off-ramp of the Manhattan Bridge. Bypassed by the steady stream of traffic from Brooklyn that pours into the heart of Chinatown, "the Hill" gained renown for its unusual dwellings.

At its crest, just before it narrows to a ravine and plummets toward Forsyth Street, stood the curious home of Mr Lee, an immigrant from Guangdong Province in China. Lee, who arrived at the encampment without a word in 1989 carrying his possessions in a sack, soon astonished his neighbors by constructing a house without pounding a nail or sawing a board. Instead, it was bound together with knots. Bright yellow plastic straps wrapped his soft, rounded hut, binding old mattresses and bedsprings into walls. The exterior was festooned with red bakery ribbons, paper lanterns, and castoff calendars that celebrated the Chinese New Year. Oranges, symbols of prosperity, had hardened in the bitter cold and hung from straps like ornaments. Mr Lee died in his home on May 29, 1992, in a fire set by an arsonist seeking revenge on another resident Detectives searching through the ashes found bundles of charred photographs of Chinese families, hand-crafted passports for invented relatives all named Lee, and a large slate inscribed with cryptic ideograms. In the months that followed, every attempt to build on the site of Mr Lee's house of mysterious knots and messages was also consumed by flames.

The community continued to evolve: some people left the Hill; others [15] arrived. Louie, the earliest resident, built houses for the newly homeless, charging $5 for each one, "Though no one ever paid me." But after another rash of fires, the city razed the settlement on August 17, 1993.

Louie piled a few possessions into a shopping cart and wheeled it down Forsyth Street to join a group of men and women who had pieced together a row of plywood shanties along the seawall bordering the East River between the Manhattan and Brooklyn Bridges. Most were refugees from homeless encampments that had been destroyed Several of the men had been evicted from Tompkins Square Park. Others had been expelled from vacant lots, public parks, or abandoned buildings. Two had fled the arched ramparts of the Brooklyn Bridge; another had been routed from an underground tunnel. Some sought respite from the city's shelters, others asylum from oppressive foreign regimes. Soon girlfriends arrived, and the population grew to thirty-five, and stray cats and dogs were adopted as pets.

Louie, who had been nicknamed "the architect" when he lived at the Hill, never built a hut for himself along the river. Instead, he shared the tents of friends or slept beneath mounds on the edge of the seawall. He lost his balance and drowned in the East River on May 18, 1995.

For others, the sense of community at the river offered stability. Wooden pallets, left behind by local delivery trucks, provided fuel and building supplies. Residents of neighboring projects disposed of an endless supply of cans that the men redeemed for a nickel apiece. As the years passed, the makeshift huts were transformed into more permanent structures that evoked memories of childhood homes: a roof of equal pitch, a rope porch railing, a nameplate over an entrance, a weather vane. On May 10, 1993 the city demolished "Little Puerto Rico," the north end of the encampment. Ten residents lost their homes. The sense of community was fractured and tensions erupted among the remaining men. The following spring Mark made plans to leave. "Of the original guys that came here, I'm the only one left. That's telling me it's time to go. With this new crew down here, I don't know. I just don't feel right with them." Mark was murdered, his body found at the bottom of a recycling cart on June 4, 1994. He was interred in the potters' field on Hart Island. He was forty years old. Bulldozers leveled die river encampment on July 1, 1996.

***

Other homeless men and women found refuge along the Hudson River. Angelo Aldi built his hut on a massive concrete pier that stretches out into the river at West 44th Street. To the north, tourists swarm over the *Intrepid,* a World War II aircraft carrier. To the south, visitors board the Circle Line sightseeing boat. Angelo and the six other men who lived on the wharf ignored these activities as they went about the work of building their homes.

Twenty-five blocks north, JR found refuge in a rusting metal structure that rises 45 feet above the Hudson at the end of a rotting pier. The reward for his perilous climb to the chamber atop the floating bridge, built 120 years ago to transfer boxcars arriving by barge to inland tracks, was solitude and a safe lookout against any intruders. But the bitter cold of January 1994 forced JR from his outpost and into the narrow confines of one of twenty-seven concrete vaults that lined a desolate stretch of railroad track nearby. Over the next three years, thirty-five more people found shelter in this ruin, all that remained of an elevated track once used by the New York Central Railroad. Police forced the residents to leave on February 26, 1997. Within hours, bulldozers had buried the last homeless community in Manhattan with dirt and debris excavated for construction of Donald Trump's luxury apartment complex, which now overlooks the rail yard.

***

Since then, the number of homeless poor has not diminished. In January 2006, Coalition for the Homeless announced that throughout the first half of the decade an average of 32,609 New Yorkers slept in homeless shelters each night, including 7,640 families and 13,616 children. Ironically, the city's building boom now provides temporary shelter for the dispossessed beneath construction scaffolding; cardboard boxes and bedding are concealed moments before morning work crews arrive. Only early-morning joggers, dog-walkers, and park employees see the homeless poor bending over water fountains to brush their teeth, shaking dirt from their sleeping bags, and bundling their possessions into backpacks. An all-night journey through the city finds urban nomads forever on the move: riding subways across the night, sleeping on the streets, tucking themselves into decaying structures along the waterfront and disappearing again before dawn. 20

Discussion Questions

1. What were some of the causes of increased homelessness during the 1970s and 80s?
2. Morton describes several homeless communities. Discuss some reasons that may drive homeless individuals to form such communities.
3. Which individuals in this essay stand out? What details make their stories so memorable?

Writing Tasks

- Read a recent report on homeless issues in a newspaper such as *The New York Times* or *Gotham Gazette*. Write an essay that explores their arguments and concerns.
- Based on both Morton's research and on your own ideas, write an essay that discusses ways that society could better help the homeless.

Youth Gangs

Mark Berkey-Gerard

Mark Berkey-Gerard earned his M.S. at the Columbia Graduate School of Journalism and now teaches courses at Rowan University. Previously, he worked as the city government editor for the *Gotham Gazette* in New York City. His research interests include interactive news and online storytelling. This article appeared in the *Gotham Gazette* in 2001.

Pre-Reading

Why do young people join gangs?

At a recent public forum at City Council, police, school officials, politicians, and other experts offered their best guesses as to why the number of gang members in the city has risen over 30 percent in the last year. "We live in a criminal environment," said one expert. "There are cops in our schools, the mayor is obsessed with crime, innocent people are being shot 41 times. It creates a mentality of crime in young people." This particular expert has first-hand experience with the question. She is 19 years old and a member of the Latin Queens, complete with the tattoo of a crown on her ankle. The city has spent increased amount of money and energy in recent years trying to crack down on gangs that recruit young people like her.

In 1997, the mayor stepped up his effort to combat gangs, focusing on them as criminal enterprises, not just as groups of juvenile delinquents. In 1998, the Board of Education agreed to give school security over to the police department with officers patrolling some hallways. And last year, a bill was introduced that would give police the power to arrest suspected gang members loitering on street corners.

Despite such efforts, gangs and their crimes are a routine part of news headlines. Recently 18 members of The Mexican Boys gang were arrested for carrying knives and guns on their way to a party of a rival gang in Brooklyn. The Albany County jail had the highest rate of violence in its history this year, with many of the incidents occurring between New York City and upstate gangs. And last month, three teenagers were arrested in connection with the shooting death of a man in Central Park, the first homicide there in two years. The teens claimed affiliation with both the Bloods and the Crips, though police later determined that they were lying. Clearly, gangs still hold some appeal.

The 19-year-old member of the Latin Queens, who asked that only her last name, Vargas, be used, suggested some reasons why. "There are no jobs, no programs for youth, our schools are falling apart," Vargas said. "Our youth bond together for protection and opportunity." While not everybody would agree with her—New York offers more cultural opportunities and youth programs, some say, than many other cities with gang problems—Councilmember Ken Fisher, chair of the Youth Services Committee, seemed to agree with Vargas at least in part. "I find it troubling that the same day we hear the police testify to an increase in gang members the mayor proposes a 20 million dollar cut in funding for youth services," said Fisher. Youth gangs have been a part of New York City life as long as young people have been hanging out on the streets looking for something to do. Unlike adult crimes, most juvenile crime is committed in groups. And gangs offer a sense of identity, camaraderie, and financial payoff for their loyalty.

The difference is that today's gangs are more widespread and more   5
dangerous. It is estimated that 94 percent of medium and large-cities in the U.S. have gang activity. And with easy access to guns and the drugs market, gangs present a more substantial criminal force. "These kids are not afraid of death or jail," said Robert DeSena who has worked with Brooklyn gangs since 1975. "Once a kid reaches that mindset, you've got a hard-core challenge."

Defining Image

Popular images of gang members range from Tony, who fell in love with a rival gang member's sister in *West Side Story,* to the violent gang-bangers who run the Los Angeles streets in the movie *Boyz 'N the Hood.* There are a wide range of perceptions, and misperceptions, of what youth gangs do and who is a part of them.

The New York Police Department defines a gang as a group that engages in criminal behavior and has a formal organizational structure, identifiable leadership, and territory. The U.S. Department of Justice estimates that there are approximately 750,000 gang members in 28,000 gangs in the U.S., although no one really knows how many there are because accurate counts are nearly impossible to make. It is estimated that females make up approximately 20 percent of the national gang population. And while the average age of gang members is 17, nearly half of all gang members range in age from 18 to 25 years.

The New York Police Department recently reported that the known   10
gang members in the city increased from 11,000 to 15,000 in the past year.
However, many researchers doubt the validity of such numbers. "I've
stayed away from New York statistics for years," said Malcolm Klein from
the Center for Research for Crime and Social Control, who has been studying gangs for over two decades. Prior to 1976, New York City's Youth Services Administration kept more dependable gang statistics in the city, but
in the fiscal problems of the city, the administration was disbanded and
tracking was handed over to police.

While the ethnic make-up of gangs, the streets they call "turf," and the
names they give themselves have changed over time, the common factor is
social class. Most gang members come from lower or working-class backgrounds, looking for a way to gain power in the social order.

History of Gotham Streets

Youth gangs have always been part of New York City life.

In 1807, members of the African Methodist Episcopal Zion Church in
lower Manhattan complained to the city about the gangs of white, working
class youths who harassed churchgoers, according to the book, *Gotham* by
Edwin G. Burroughs and Mike Wallace. By the 1820's, the authors explain,
young men "swaggered about the city after work and on Sundays, stak-
ing out territories, picking fights, defending the honor of their street and
trade." Until the mid-1900's, a majority of gangs in America were white,
composed of boys from various European backgrounds.

The postwar gangs in the 1940's-1960's were primarily "turf gangs
who defended their areas against neighboring ethnic groups and new
immigrants. In his recent book, *Vampires, Dragons, and Egyptian Kings,* Eric
Schneider presents Postwar gang life as a world of switchblades, zoot suits,
slums, and bebop music. Young men took on brash names like Enchant-
ers, Young Lords, Bishops, Greene Avenue Stompers, and the Latin Gents.
While youth gangs were often seen as "violent, short-lived, disorganized
collections of misfits whose main purpose was thrill seeking and immediate gratification," says Schneider, they provided a social structure for
working-class boys that provided a sense of identity, place, and masculinity.

By 1970, about four-fifths of gang members were either African-
American or Hispanic. And the late 1980's and early 1990's saw the growth
of West Coast gangs like the Crips and the Bloods, although most experts
dispute the notion that the gangs actually migrated across the country. Instead they are local, non-centralized gangs that go by the same names and
wear the same identifying colors.

Today in New York, the most prominent New York City gangs are the Bloods, Crips, Latin Kings, Nietas, Five Prisoners, Silenciosos, Matatones, Rat Hunters, and Zulu Nation. They are groups that span ethnicity, race, and neighborhoods.

From Turf to Drugs, From Fists to Guns

Two major changes in recent years have transformed the nature of youth gangs. First, the influx of illegal drugs—first heroin, then cocaine, and then crack cocaine—changed street gangs from social groups to economic enterprises. Instead of fighting over the geography of turf, gangs began to wage war over corners used to sell drugs. The institution of the Rockefeller drug laws in 1973 and stiffer prison penalties for adults, had a bitterly ironic result: Drug dealers began to recruit minors to do much of their selling on the streets. While gangs have become a significant part of the drug trade (a recent study that gangs are involved in about a quarter of the drug arrests), most researchers argue that youth gangs are not major drug traffickers. "Drug gangs separate themselves from street gangs," said Klein. "Drugs require tight corporate-like structure that youth do not have."

15

The second and perhaps the most devastating change is the availability of guns. It is estimated that gang related homicides increased nearly five times between 1987 and 1994. "Violence has always been around, usually concentrated amongst the poor," said Geoffrey Canada, who runs the non-profit Rheedlin Center for Children and Families in Harlem. "The difference is that we never had so many guns in our inner cities. The nature of the violent act has changed from the fist, stick, and knife to the gun."

The Riker's Island Gang Museum

To visit the offices of the Gang Unit at Riker's Island is to visit a virtual museum of gang paraphernalia. The walls are covered with photographs of gang member tattoos, red and blue bandanas from the Crips and the Bloods, and rosaries with black and yellow beads used by members of the Latin Kings. There is a display of home-made weaponry: knives made from pocket combs, razor blades fashioned from bottle caps, and even a small gun made from a toilet paper roll and rubber bands. And on the desk are computers used to enter the information into the city's gang database. It is all part of the Corrections Department's "zero tolerance" policy on gangs and the city's attempt to enhance its gang intelligence.

At Riker's Island, gang members are stripped of any kind of identifying clothing or trinkets, forced to live in the same rooms with rival gangs, and any act of violence automatically adds time to their sentence. The Correction's Department says it is working. The incidence of violence in the city's jail is at the lowest in over a decade.

The School Safety and Prevention Service's division of the New York City operates under a similar notion. If any student exhibits gang behavior—wearing colors, using hand signals, graffiti, or any criminal activity—they are immediately removed from school. Efforts to pass legislation to control gangs are generally more difficult. Most of the state legislation has to do with graffiti and tougher sentences for assault.

Last year in the city, Councilmembers John Sabini and Michel Abel   20
introduced a bill that would give police the power to arrest suspected gang members loitering on street corners. The legislation drew criticism from civil rights groups and others who thought the law would lead to police abuse. Currently the proposed legislation is still sitting in committee.

Finding Solutions

While legislators and police often take the credit for drops in gang related crime, the ebb and flow of gangs are more susceptible to other less tangible factors. There are several theories of why New York City has less of a problem with gangs than cities like Los Angeles and Chicago.

One is that today's gangs operate in an automobile culture that facilitates drive-by-shootings and drug dealing, and enables gangs to travel in greater anonymity. New York's mass transit system makes it more difficult for such activities. Another theory is that New York City has more opportunities for young people that fill the similar needs as a gang. "In New York you can be part of a religious group, an arts club, a cultural group, you can even be part of a doo-wop group," said Councilmember Ken Fisher, who is Chair of the Youth Services Committee. "There are more opportunities for someone to belong to something."

There are also a host of non-profits that work with gang members on a one-to-one basis. The main challenge for these groups is to offer something that replaces the protection, identity, and money young people gain from being part of a gang.

Robert DeSena, a retired schoolteacher and founder of Council for Unity, a group that works to bring rival gangs together, says many of the gang members he meets are looking for a way out. "Violence is exhausting and gangs realize they are unable to exterminate the opposition," said DeSena. DeSena works to build a network of protection and support that replaces gang life. The youth are responsible for running their own cultural events, support meetings, marketing the programs, soliciting members—using skills they had previously used on the street. The members are paired with alumni of the program who work as mentors, often hiring the youth to work at their companies. "You get an ex-gang member who works for Price Waterhouse to take an interest in a kid," said DeSena, "and the kids will take notice."

Discussion Questions

1. What point does Ken Fisher make when he connects increased gang problems with the mayor's proposal to cut 20 million dollars in funding for youth services?
2. According to the article, what contributes to the "criminal mindset" plaguing many young people today?
3. Do you think increased school security is the best way to combat teen violence?
4. According to the article, what is a common factor linking gangs throughout history? What does this say about one of the universal motivations for gang behavior?
5. What two changes have transformed the nature of youth gangs making them more violent than ever before?
6. Why does New York City tend to have fewer gang-related problems than other major cities? Do you agree with this assessment?
7. What can be done to get kids to stay out of gangs?

Writing Task

• Write an essay in which you analyze the high school you attended and how students treated each other. Were there cliques, gangs, or even violence? Why or why not?

Legalization and De-Legalization

Aarti Shahani

Aarti Shahani is a co-founder of Families for Freedom, a Brooklyn-based defense network for immigrant families facing deportation.

Pre-Reading

How do you feel about immigration? Do you have any personal experience with immigration or immigration policies?

As thousands of students walked out of their schools to protest pending immigration bills in Congress, 17-year-old Julio Beltre stood in front of New York's Federal Plaza last month to tell the story of his father, Juan Beltre: On a morning a year ago, in April 2005, before the sun rose, six agents from the Department of Homeland Security had woken up his father and dragged him away from their Bronx home, while his wife and four children—all U.S. citizens—watched in horror.

Why was he being seized? Juan Beltre had committed a single drug possession offense dating back to 1995. But in those ten long years, Beltre had completed probation, was a long-term greencard holder—and was now suffering from a brain tumor.

"Now my mom has to raise us alone," his son recounted at the demonstration. His father was deported back to the Dominican Republic.

The testimonies of Julio Beltre and a dozen other citizen-children with similar stories came in a week of marches, walkouts, hearings, and headlines. Immigration is *the issue* everywhere, from the hearts of protesters to the halls of the Capitol to the editorial pages of *The New York Times*.

More Legalization—Or More Deportations?

The debate is as complex as it is heated. On March 27th, the Senate Judiciary Committee approved an immigration bill that would, if passed into law:

- expand the grounds of deportation
- use domestic military bases for immigration detention

Reprinted by permission of Aarti Shahani.

- legalize the indefinite detention of noncitizens
- authorize New York City police and other local officers to enforce federal immigration laws
- erect a border fence
- enable Homeland Security agents to expel suspected foreigners indiscriminately
- create a national identification system for all workers.

Yet the following morning, the front page of New York's largest Spanish language paper, *El Diario*, exclaimed "TRIUMFAMOS." Meanwhile, restrictionist commentator Lou Dobbs campaigned against the bill on television and in Mexico.

This ironic role reversal stems from one section of the proposed bill, the guestworker legalization provisions. Under the leadership of Senator Arlen Specter of Pennsylvania, the Judiciary Committee voted 12-6 to approve a new visa program, devised by Senators Edward Kennedy and John McCain, under which undocumented workers would have to register with the government, maintain continuous employment for six years, pay back and future taxes, and pass civics and English lessons in order to apply for a green card. Some hail the Senate bill as a victory because, for the first time since the amnesty passed by President Ronald Reagan in 1986, undocumented workers would have a potential pathway to work and live lawfully in the U.S.

Fighting to Keep the Legalization Provisions

In the coming weeks, the Judiciary proposal faces the scrutiny of the full Senate. Advocates are fighting to prevent the "earned legalization" provisions from being watered down. The main variable is whether or not the visa granted to undocumented workers will lead to a green card and eventual citizenship.

We are now at a crossroads. While the nation's attention is focused on the legalization question, lawmakers have guaranteed only one thing: there will be no legalization-only bill. If the Senate ultimately approves anything, it will go to a closed-door conference committee to be resolved with the House bill passed in December 2005 under the leadership of Wisconsin Republican James Sensenbrenner. The House bill concedes no greencards. It's only common ground with the Senate provision is to expand detentions, deportations, and border police.

A shared history underlies the consensus. September 11th transformed immigration into a national security debate, with Democrats and Republicans both convinced that any immigration reform must come with tighter controls. But as the Beltre family illustrates, the New York congressional delegation has to resolve the national security agenda with a powerful reality: non-citizens are not the only affected population. Citizen spouses and children left behind are devastated because of decade-old deportation laws.

Ten Years of Deportations

It's not the act of terror we remember best. In April 1995, a white veteran of the first Gulf War blew up the Oklahoma City federal building. One year later, to memorialize that tragedy, then-President Bill Clinton signed a sweeping immigration enforcement measure: the Anti-Terrorism and Effective Death Penalty Act. A sister bill, the Illegal Immigration Reform and Immigrant Responsibility Act, passed just months later.

Together, the 1996 laws transformed the meaning of membership in America and substantially ramped up policing based on citizenship. There was no legalization or guestworker program. Instead, there were sweeping deportation measures that empowered the executive branch to more easily expel people already within our borders.

Prior to the 1996 laws, a New Yorker placed in deportation proceedings could typically go before an immigration judge and seek a pardon if she could demonstrate that she was no threat to society and had significant ties to her U.S. community. But the new laws instituted a system of mandatory deportation and detention whereby the vast majority of New Yorkers facing deportation are held in immigrant prisons without bail and have no opportunity to plead their case before an immigration judge. These judges are appointees of the U.S. attorney general, yet they cannot pardon or postpone the deportation of a noncitizen—even if they believe the punishment would harm U.S. citizen children and communities.

With detention and deportation as the new mandatory minimums, more than 1.3 million people have been expelled from the U.S. in the last 10 years, and immigrants have become the fastest-growing segment of our prison population. (Homeland Security does not make city-specific statistics available.) Taxpayers are footing the bill for the ever-growing deportation budget. American veterans, breadwinners, and people who have lived here since infancy have been deported through this process.

Just before September 11th, lawmakers on both sides of the aisle agreed that 1996 went too far. One of its leading proponents, former Republican Congressman Bill McCollum of Florida, called the unintended impacts on families a "manifest injustice." But such wisdom crumbled with the Twin Towers. America was left with the inflexible, even cruel legal infrastructure of 1996. Since the tragedy, the Bush Administration has poured billions into even more vigilant enforcement of these laws.

Plea Bargains Lead To Deportations

In New York as in other urban centers, the criminal justice system is a cornerstone of the immigration policing strategy. The criminal courts rely on a plea system to expedite the high volume of cases. Prosecutors issue lengthy indictments. Defense attorneys advise clients to plea to lesser charges, in order to secure a deal with little or no jail time.

Every week, hundreds of immigrant New Yorkers arrested for garden-variety crimes plead guilty under this plea-bargain system. But neither the judge nor attorney warn them that after they complete their sentence, a second punishment will follow: detention and deportation. As the federal immigration authorities' reliance on local criminal institutions grows, there is no countervailing process to ensure that the rights of immigrants are observed.

Connecting Past and Present Policy

The criminalization trends of 1996 pervade the bills in Congress today. Proposals consistently extend mandatory deportation and detention to a wider net of immigrants. Even the most progressive proposals bar immigrants who admit to crimes—like using a fake ID to get a job—from obtaining green cards.

The New York congressional delegation has been nearly mute on how America's immigration laws are harming families—with one recent exception. On March 28, 2006, Congressman Jose Serrano of the Bronx introduced the Child Citizen Protection Act, a bill to restore partial discretion to immigration judges in cases where removal of an immigrant is clearly against the best interests of a U.S. citizen child. Serrano called the bill "common-sense legislation" that would protect children and families from unnecessary separation. But the other members of Congress from New York are largely silent, despite the New York families who flood their district offices—families already devastated by deportation.

"Our leaders need to change the laws," Julio Beirre concluded his speeech during the demonstration at Federal Plaza, "before more young people like me get hurt." On April 24th, the 10-year anniversary of the 1996 laws, he and other New Yorkers will converge in Washington D.C. with families from other cities whose lives have changed because of deportation.

Discussion Questions

1. How does the anecdote of Julio Beltre's deportation set up this essay's central theme?
2. Why exactly is immigration *"the issue* everywhere" as Shahani claims? Do you see it as an important concern?
3. What is your response to the Senate Judiciary Committee's recommendations for an immigration bill?
4. What exactly is the "guestworker legalization provision"? How does this affect support for the Senate's immigration bill?
5. What has the effect of 9/11 been on immigration reform?
6. How did the immigration laws of 1996 affect illegal immigrants in this country?
7. What is the problem with the current plea bargain system for immigrants?

Writing Tasks

- Write an essay in which you argue either for stricter or more lenient immigration laws. Be sure to cite key legislation and bring in concrete examples that support your assertions.
- Research the current deliberations on immigration reform in America today. Where does the debate over legalization and de-legalization seem to be heading?
- Look up familiesforfreedom.org. Report on what articles and statistics you find there.

Despite Setbacks, Bloomberg Plan Has Made New York Greener

Courtney Gross

Courtney Gross is a reporter for *Gotham Gazette*. She specializes in health and environmental issues in New York City. The following article was published in April 2011.

Pre-Reading

What can you do as an individual to improve the city's environment?

At a joint announcement on climate change last week, former President Bill Clinton and Mayor Michael Bloomberg both boasted of how green they had become.   1

In an elaborately decorated parlor in Gracie Mansion, Mayor Michael Bloomberg and former President Bill Clinton last week each ticked off how he had personally become green.

Clinton bought a hybrid.

Bloomberg painted the roof of his Upper East Side townhouse white.

They both pushed for sustainable building.   5

"I'm devoting more time to the environment," said Bloomberg.

Bloomberg plans to encourage all New Yorkers to adopt those personal practices. And he's doing it through his environmental agenda: PlaNYC 2030. In December 2006, PlaNYC set out more than 120 initiatives, programs and goals to reduce carbon emissions by more than 30 percent over the next two decades and prepare the city for a population influx of 1 million people. It proposed regional parks, bike lanes, stormwater infrastructure, affordable housing and a green building code. According to Bloomberg's estimate, the city has already ticked off 97 percent of these initiatives.

"The vast bulk of these things we actually are doing, and they are making a difference," said Bloomberg.

Many advocates say the vast majority of the plan has been successful, but not all of it.

Since the plan's launch, the administration has been hit with several   10
major defeats (most notably, congestion pricing), while some adopted proposals (ahem, bike lanes) currently face renewed opposition.

This week, Bloomberg is expected to release a retooled plan, announce
new initiatives and incorporate the city's solid waste management strategy
into his sustainability agenda. As the city plans for PlaNYC 2.0, officials
and advocates question whether Bloomberg can accomplish all of the goals
of the original plan in the face of a staggering economy and third termitis.

The Disappointments

First came congestion pricing—the mayor's plan to charge drivers to enter
Manhattan during the workweek.

The linchpin of the entire environmental agenda, the pricing plan failed
to gain traction in Albany thanks to fierce opposition from legislators in the
outer boroughs.

That defeat was followed by a series of court decisions striking down
another PlaNYC proposal: the creation of an all-hybrid taxi fleet.

Then came the Great Recession and 10 rounds of budget cuts. Now,   15
thanks to the economy, some programs have been abandoned altogether.

"We had our wins and our losses," said Rohit Aggarwala, the former
head of the mayor's Office of Long-term Planning and Sustainability, who
left the Bloomberg administration last year. "The biggest achievement that
I'm most proud of is the green buildings package," Aggarwala said referring to legislation to reduce carbon emissions from buildings.

The administration has been thwarted in its efforts to convert to hybrid
taxi cabs.

But, he added, "Congestion pricing was obviously a tragic loss. The
hybrid taxis is kind of a mixed bag."

Some would call "mixed" generous.

The administration is set to select a new taxi model this month—none   20
of the cars under consideration are hybrids.

Beyond taxis, the city planned to open 43 sports fields across the city
to their communities. That proposal has been abandoned, according to the
latest PlaNYC status report.

By 2015, according to PlaNYC, the city would redevelop at least one
underutilized major park in every borough. Construction was supposed
to start on all eight by the end of 2010. Half—Fort Washington Park, High-
land Park, High Bridge and Soundview Park—have yet to see a shovel in
the ground.

The plan promised every New Yorker would live within walking distance of a park. Some advocates question whether that will ever happen.

"We thought we were going to get a waterfront park with an environmental education center and children's playground," said Elizabeth Yeampierre, the executive director of UPROSE, an environmental group in Sunset Park. "We thought we were going to get a greenway."

They have none of that, she said.   25

The city was supposed to complete 640 greenstreets, or thoroughfares with small islands with green space, by 2015. That number has been halved, according to a PlaNYC progress report. The administration originally committed to installing nighttime lights on 25 fields. That has been decreased to 19.

The plan called for encouraging home ownership and affordable housing. But the administration's preliminary budget has eliminated city funding for the Center for New York City Neighborhoods, which provides counseling for those at risk of foreclosure.

For its part, administration officials are quick to deflect blame and point fingers—sometimes at Wall Street and the economy, other times at Washington or Albany.

"For those things that are within the city government's unilateral control, the transportation initiatives have been successful," said David Bragdon, the new head of the city's sustainability office. "Where the transportation objectives haven't been met, it's largely a function of state and or federal inaction."

Bragdon, who took over the mayor's sustainability office last year, said   30
the administration is committed to seeing the plan through. Park construction is not eliminated, only delayed. As part of the city's budget cutting measures, the administration is stretching out projects over several more years.

In light of billion-dollar deficits, some advocates sympathized with Bloomberg, who has to weigh spending city funds on the creation of open space with keeping cops on the street.

"They've accomplished a lot already, and while it's frustrating that the progress has had to slow, it's still underway," said Alyson Beha, director of research, planning and programs at New Yorkers for Parks. "They are doing a fantastic job given the financial climate."

The Successes

Despite the setbacks, Bloomberg administration officials easily list the plan's accomplishments.

Just last week, the mayor lauded the 2-year old pedestrian plaza in Times Square for bringing down nitrogen dioxide and nitrogen oxide levels in the area (PlaNYC called for 10 to 15 public plazas across the city).

While major park construction has been delayed, the administration has   35
been successful at opening school playgrounds to the public. As of April,
177 have been opened and 34 are currently under construction, according
to a Bloomberg spokesperson.

Last month, Bloomberg and Council Speaker Christine Quinn
announced the launch of East River ferry service between Brooklyn,
Manhattan and Queens—after much delay—and committed $3.3. billion
to the city's waterfronts.

Back on land, the administration has successfully launched the nation's
first ever Office of Environmental Remediation—the only city run brownfield
cleanup program. The office aims to attract developers by providing start-
up capital to clean up contaminated land, which does not qualify for state
or federal programs. So far, said Daniel Walsh, the head of the office, eight
developers have signed on and the city has approved $800,000 in grants.

"For us, it's a very good story," Walsh told the *Gotham Gazette.* "The
economy has not stopped us from building programs and getting them in
place."

Despite earlier criticism, most advocates champion new laws approved
in 2009 to require buildings get energy audits. In an original version, the
proposal would have forced building owners to complete the audit's recommendations. In a compromise with the real estate industry, that provision was scratched.

Nonetheless, advocates say the legislation would still be extremely   40
effective at reducing pollution from buildings—which are responsible for
80 percent of all the city's carbon emissions.

"From our members' perspective, brownfields, the green infrastructure, stormwater management plan, the greater greener buildings plans
. . . every one of those have had a disproportionately positive effect for
environmental justice communities," said Eddie Bautista, a former member of the Bloomberg administration who now heads the Environmental
Justice Alliance. "Had PlaNYC not prioritized these type of programs
cumulatively, we would be talking about dirtier air, more un-remediated
soil, more CO_2 discharges."

But Bautista added: "The jury is out on moving forward in a budget
challenged, in a deficit era."

Moving to 2.0

The next version of PlaNYC, which will be unveiled Thursday, is already
getting mixed reviews.

"While on its face it looks like this great effort to address climate, it
doesn't really address the environmental health needs of communities that

really deserve it," said Yeampierre of UPROSE, who says projects in Manhattan are higher priorities than those in outer borough, poorer neighborhoods. "The more we learn about what's being proposed, the more we're concerned."

Some of the criticism from advocates like Yeampierre stems from the 45
administration's renewed exploration of waste-to-energy—otherwise known as the process of burning trash to create electricity. Solid waste management will be included in the plan for the first time, and some advocates fear communities already inundated with the city's garbage burden will face the prospect of new facilities.

Other environmentalists, like those at the New York League of Conservation Voters, are encouraging the administration to consider waste-to-energy facilities. Too much of the city's trash is taken to out of state landfills, said Marcia Bystryn, the group's executive director, at an extremely high financial and environmental cost.

Stakeholders do not anticipate a sea change this week considering the city's budget crunch. Advocates say it's a good sign the administration is willing to revisit the plan and consider new technologies that have emerged over the last five years. But they are far from claiming victory.

"The hard part of conveying this story is you can acknowledge the progress that has been made and still worry about the serious challenges yet to be addressed," said Eric Goldstein of the Natural Resources Defense Council. "Celebrating now would be premature."

Discussion Questions

1. What is PlaNYC 2030?
2. What are some of the setbacks and accomplishments of Mayor Bloomberg's environmental agenda? Have you benefited from his plan?
3. What was the Congestion Pricing Plan? Who were the main opponents to this plan?
4. What do critics and advocates have to say about the new version of PlaNYC? Do you agree with these proposals? Do you have other suggestions?

Writing Tasks

- Write an evaluation of some of the measures implemented under Mayor Bloomberg's environmental plan. Support your points with examples and evidence.
- Write a letter to the Mayor in which you propose a list of environmental improvements for your neighborhood.

Fighting Police Brutality in Global Brooklyn

Benjamin Shepard

Benjamin Shepard is Assistant Professor of Human Services at New York City College of Technology (CUNY). He is the author of *Play, Creativity and Social Movements: If I Can't Dance It's Not My Revolution*.

Pre-Reading

What is your relationship with the police in your neighborhood? Do you think police brutality is a problem where you live?

Today, Brooklyn residents are experiencing the negative dynamics of global forces in the form of uneven developments. On the one hand, positive developments include the influx of new immigrants, new cultures and customs, and new financial capital. And on the other, negative patterns of financial speculation, environmental degradation, gentrification, foreclosures, and aggressive policing have also emerged. But rather than cave in, Brooklyn residents have banded together to challenge these latter forces by building bike lanes, planting gardens, and creating innovative tactics of resistance. This essay asks a question: to what degree do community reactions to recent escalations of police brutality reflect new, interrelated regional and global pressures?

Over the years, Brooklyn has become a site in a class war between those who live, work, and play in public and those who seek to control this space and the people who live here. Shortly after his election as mayor in 1993, Giuliani's police chief William Bratton released a blueprint for policing that focuses on reclaiming New York's public spaces from the presence of the impoverished, the poor, and other social outsiders. This involved a "broken windows" style of policing which included no tolerance for the smallest of infractions. Histories of police brutality in New York City dedicate considerable attention to this aggressive policing approach. In recent years, police have continued to target specific communities, most notably, youth of color.

In 2007, for example, a group of thirty-two young African Americans and Latinos were arrested while going to attend the funeral of a friend, in Bushwick. Initially, Police Commissioner Ray Kelly claimed the teens were blocking traffic, damaging property, and participating in an "unlawful assembly," as they walked from a park to the subway station to attend the funeral of an alleged gang member. The Brooklyn district attorney claimed "they were not just walking on one car; they were trampling on all sorts of cars. It was almost as if they were inviting their arrest." Yet, no evidence supported the police claim that the students were blocking traffic or jumping on cars. "Witnesses who saw the kids, including one man who used his cell phone to take photos of some of them who were handcuffed on the sidewalk, said they had been orderly, quiet and well behaved," reported *New York Times* columnist Bob Herbert. Greer Martin, a witness to the arrests outside her front window, spoke on the record. "'[S]he felt the police officers had abused their power.'" "'I was shocked beyond shock,'" she explained. "'My windows were open, and it didn't look like the kids had done anything wrong.'"

In the wake of the event, citizens started mobilizing. Make the Road by Walking (a non-profit group dedicated to promoting economic justice, equity, and opportunity for all New Yorkers) helped the students get organized. The students formed a group called Student Coalition Against Racial Profiling (SCARP), which was able to get the charges thrown out for its members and procure a legal settlement, with several thousand dollars being paid to minors who had been held by police for a day and a half. Such patterns are not uncommon; in fact, "Stop and Frisk" ensnared over 684,000 New Yorkers in 2011, 90% of them African American and Latino.

The prolonged detention for minor infractions that the teens suffered   5
is a byproduct of the type of policing which has become part of life in global Brooklyn. It is also one of the battlefronts. While SCARP and Make the Road by Walking have fought for justice, their experiences suggest that structural violence continues to be a common experience for minority youth. According to Michael Scolnick, a lawyer for those arrested, "what I have been told by my clients is that their being stopped on the street merely for being on the street is about as common an occurrence in their lives as me getting up in the morning and brushing my teeth—and that's pretty outrageous."

These arrests reflect a larger pattern of the hyper-regulation of public space and preemptive action against any behavior deemed deviant by the NYPD. This policy involves no tolerance for the smallest of infractions. It is based on flexible deployment and new rules and regulations, which combine to micromanage public space. "[A]uthorities responded by criminalizing whole communities of impoverished and marginalized populations," notes globalization scholar David Harvey (48). Patterns of stops and frisks, racial profiling, and aggressive policing were thought necessary by certain authorities to support a better business climate for economic growth. But, if Global Brooklyn is to survive as a space that values diversity and difference, communities will need to continue to battle.

Works Cited

Harvey, David. *A Brief History of Neoliberalism*. New York: Oxford UP, 2005. Print.

Herbert, Bob. "Arrested While Grieving." *New York Times*. 26 May 2007. Web. 2 February 2012.

—. "No Cause for Arrest." *New York Times*. April 18, 2009. Web. 2 February 2012.

Discussion Questions

1. How does Shepard define the term "global Brooklyn"?
2. Do you see negative global forces affecting your neighborhood?
3. Discuss the "broken windows" style of policing.
4. What is Shepard's argument about who gets "ensnared" by "Stop and Frisk"? Do you think his argument is legitimate?
5. What do you believe is the best way to balance neighborhood safety against overly aggressive policing?

Writing Task

- Find other articles on racial profiling cases that occurred in Brooklyn to determine if this problem persists. Discuss your findings.

Making Connections

This assignment asks you to find at least three articles addressing an issue which you find interesting or important that concerns New York City and to then write on this topic. You may choose your topic from a variety of sources, including our textbook, the library databases, an online journal such as *Gotham Gazette,* or a New York newspaper such as *The New York Times.* The themes and topics you select may include but are not limited to the following possibilities:

1. The issues and history of a particular immigrant group living in New York.
2. The problem of unequal wealth distribution related to health care, education, mass transit, housing, etc.
3. The problems in the New York public school system and possible solutions.
4. A discussion of the issues and solutions relating to homelessness.
5. The problem of gang/teen violence or police brutality.
6. The debate over gentrification in certain New York neighborhoods.
7. An environmental concern such as air quality, water pollution, or industrial waste.
8. Problems related to mass transit: cost, efficiency, sanitation, handicap access, etc.
9. The role of technology in the city.
10. Other controversial issues relating to a neighborhood.

In this short research assignment, your job is to discuss specific aspects of a selected subject or issue by presenting and evaluating different viewpoints. Make sure that you communicate your own ideas and opinions in the paper. Be sure to properly document all of your sources.

CHAPTER 6

Exploring the Waterfront

Reprinted by permission of Robin Michals.

"Giovanni Verrazzano Discovers the New York Bay" (1524)

After proceeding one hundred leagues, we found a very pleasant situation among some steep hills, through which a very large river, deep at its mouth, forced its way to the sea; from the sea to the estuary of the river, any ship heavily laden might pass, with the help of the tide, which rises eight feet. But as we were riding at anchor in a good berth, we would not venture up in our vessel, without a knowledge of the mouth; therefore we took the boat, and entering the river, we found the country on its banks well peopled, the inhabitants not differing much from the others, being dressed out with the feathers of birds of various colours. They came towards us with evident delight, raising loud shouts of admiration, and showing us where we could most securely land with our boat. We passed up this river, about half a league, when we found it formed a most beautiful lake three leagues in circuit, upon which they were rowing thirty or more of their small boats, from one shore to the other, filled with multitudes who came to see us. All of a sudden, as is wont to happen to navigators, a violent contrary wind blew in from the sea, and forced us to return to our ship, greatly regretting to leave this region which seemed so commodious and delightful, and which we supposed must also contain great riches, as the hills showed many indications of minerals.

Exploring the Waterfront

This section aims to teach the importance of place, specifically the role that the industrial waterfront has played to make Manhattan and Brooklyn world famous.

We start by going back to early explorations with readings about the Italian navigator Giovanni da Verrazzano and Henry Hudson, an Englishman sailing for the Dutch. Both explorers were in search of the famous "Northwest Passage," a waterway that would lead directly to the silks, spices, and other riches of China. Instead, they found indigenous peoples thriving in a beautiful and bountiful water paradise. Soon after, the Dutch came to understand that a fortune could be made out of the fur trade. In 1626, they bought the entire island of Manhattan from the Native Americans for the equivalent of $26 and built Fort Amsterdam at the mouth of the East River. On the Brooklyn side of the river, they purchased additional land for their farms and mills, designed for grinding grain. The natural resources and advantages of living near a massive bay connected to two major waterways (the Hudson River and the East River) allowed Nieuw-Amsterdam and Breukleyn, as Manhattan and Brooklyn were then named, to prosper.

In the 1850s and 60s, the Brooklyn poet, Walt Whitman, marveled at the growth and majesty of his beloved city which he celebrates in his poems "Mannahatta" and "Crossing Brooklyn Ferry." Ernest Poole in the opening chapter of his novel *The Harbor* also focuses on the busy waterfront, teeming with warehouses, shipbuilding, and the beautiful ships themselves. Also helping both Manhattan and Brooklyn to expand during this time was the Brooklyn Bridge, completed in 1883, which Philip Lopate discusses in his article on the cultural history of the bridge.

In "Reading Lucy," students will read about another aspect of the waterfront that played a vital role in providing high-paying jobs for hundreds of thousands of Brooklynites, especially during World War II—the Brooklyn Navy Yard. From the 1850s to the 1950s, Brooklyn was the world's greatest center for shipbuilding. This period also saw its warehouses teem with goods imported from overseas or produced in the borough's many factories that took full advantage of being so near the East River waterfront.

At the same time, as Gloria Deák writes in her overview of Brooklyn, the borough is much more than just a place to work and produce goods. It is also a place to play, a place to fall in love and raise a family, a place to be proud of. In reading these essays, students will explore the rich history and excitement of life along the waterfront. We also encourage them to take a walking tour along the water's edge—to see Brooklyn and Manhattan with new eyes.

Henry Hudson: The Pollinator

Russell Shorto

Russell Shorto (b. 1959) is an American author, historian, and journalist, best known for his book on the Dutch origins of New York City, *The Island at the Center of the World* (2005).

To SEA THEN, launching from near the squat brick tower called the Schreier-storen, where the city walls [of Amsterdam] fronted the water and where generations of Dutch women had stood gazing nervously out, waiting for their men to return. Hudson made it by spring, in time for the sailing season of 1609. He had a new ship, the eighty-five-foot *Halve Maen* ("Half Moon"), and a crew of sixteen, half English and half Dutch. He had orders, too: to find a north*east-ern* route. He must have pushed strongly for the northwest, for they pushed back; in the accompanying instructions the Dutch merchants warned him "to think of discovering no other routes or passages" than the northeast. In his best fashion, he disobeyed them utterly. After taking a flier along the coast of Norway in the general direction of Russia, he went along with a gale blowing westward and then kept going. He was about to voyage three thousand miles in the opposite direction from what he had promised: inconceivable in another ship's captain; for him, pretty standard. Thus, his historic journey was truly of his own doing, even if its result was something beyond his intention.   1

Having convinced his crew to reverse course in mid-ocean, he had two options: to follow George Weymouth's journal, which suggested a true northwest passage, navigating the islands and ice floes of what is today northern Canada; or John Smith's notes, indicating that the passage was in fact not northwest at all, but southwest, straight through the North American continent. He followed Smith. After approaching Newfoundland, he hugged the coast southward for six weeks, until he came within ten miles of the Jamestown settlement of Virginia, and his friend. Then, abruptly, he stopped. He knew perfectly well where he was, for his English first mate recorded in his journal, "This is the entrance into the Kings River in Virginia, where our English-men are." They were at the mouth of the Chesapeake, where the Chesapeake Bay Bridge now crosses. Hudson was aware that he was sailing for a Dutch concern, and likely wouldn't have felt welcome or comfortable sailing into the English settlement. He had probably sailed here to orient himself. After swinging farther south to Cape Hatteras

"Landing of Henry Hudson in New York Harbor," by Robert Weir.

Island, he headed north, and on August 28 came into Delaware Bay, the first European ever to do so. No sooner had he entered the bay than the crew sighted treacherous shoals and sand bars. The captain quickly determined that this river could not be the wide, deep channel that led to Cathay.

And so they continued north: misty mornings, bloody sunsets, a stretch of coast like a long smooth cut; surf eternally pounding the belt of sand; wild silence beyond. They were aware that they were shouldering a new world, impossibly dark, utterly unknown, of imponderable dimension, and with no clear means of access.

And then they felt something happening. Rounding a hooked point, they were startled at what they perceived to be three rivers; cliffs rose up— the land "very pleasant and high, and bold to fall withal." They were in the outer reaches of New York Harbor, riding along the coast of Staten Island. Fish streamed thickly around them: salmon, mullet, wraith-like rays. They anchored and went ashore, marveling at primordial oaks and "an abundance of blue plums."

Then, just like that, people appeared. They came at them frankly, dressed in skins, peaceable, and with an air of dignity, offering corn bread and green tobacco. In 1801 the Moravian missionary John Heckewelder interviewed a Long Island Indian and published an account of Hudson's arrival from the Indian perspective. The story, supposedly handed down through generations of Delaware Indians, gibes with the account by Hudson's mate Robert Juet of the first encounter: peaceable, wary, curious. The Indian told of sighting "a large house of various colors" floating on the water (Dutch ships were indeed vividly painted with geometric motifs). As in Juet's version, the Indian

5

story has the first meeting taking place on land, with several of the visitors, including their leader, rowing ashore. The Indian story adds that the leader of the newcomers is dressed in a "red coat all glittering with gold lace"—a nice and by no means incongruous addition to the portrait of Hudson.

Out came the products. Hemp, dried currants, oysters, beans. Knives, hatchets, and beads. Over the next three days, as the ship explored an intricate mesh of islands, bays, and rivers, making the rounds of Brooklyn, Staten Island, and coastal New Jersey, there would be two violent encounters with Indians, which Juet claims were initiated by the Indians. People died. It's ironic that immediately upon entering the watery perimeter of what would become New York City, these two things take place: trade and violence.

Hudson then sailed his small, three-masted wooden vessel into the coliseum-like interior of the harbor—"a very good harbor for all windes." From his perch on the high poop-deck, looking down on his crew, he gave the order to proceed upriver. His heart must have quickened as the vista unfolded before him. "The River is a mile broad: there is very high Land on both sides," wrote Juet—as likely a channel into the other side of the world as one could hope for. Upriver, they encountered more natives: "a very loving people...and we were well taken care of." Hudson went ashore with them, visiting their circular houses made of bark. "The land is the finest for cultivation that I ever in my life set foot upon," he wrote. He and his men noted more offerings from the locals: furs.

Then it ended. The river grew narrow and shallow: no ship could pass through; Asia did not lie over there. They turned south again: more skirmishes with the Indians of the southern reaches of the river. It's not certain if Hudson was aware that the land they "rode quietly" past one rainy night was an island—in the first written record of the name, Juet refers to "the side of the river called *Manna hatar*." In any case, while Hudson dutifully noted the possibilities for trade—the grandness of the harbor and the river, the toehold they would provide onto the continent—his own gaze never left the horizon of his obsession. He headed for home, empty-handed.

Discussion Questions

1. In what direction was Henry Hudson initially ordered to travel? What direction does he ultimately take? What does this say about Hudson's personality?
2. What "wide, deep channel" was Hudson and his crew looking for? Why?
3. How did the Native Americans greet Hudson's crew? How were they treated in return?
4. What commodity interested the Dutch the most when Hudson returned to tell of his discoveries?
5. How are the Dutch origins of New Amsterdam different, say, from the origins of colonial New England or Virginia?

Mannahatta and Crossing Brooklyn Ferry

Walt Whitman

Walt Whitman (1819–1892), America's most famous poet, reveled in the "faces and streets" of Manhattan and Brooklyn, where he was born. He viewed the crowd as the embodiment of democracy and a spiritual force and wrote about his urban experiences incessantly. He was particularly fascinated with the spectacle of early mass transit such as the Brooklyn Ferry and the omni-buses on Broadway, which symbolized to him the relentless tide of human energy.

Bayley/Whitman Collection, Ohio Wesleyan University.

MANNAHATTA

I was asking for something specific and perfect for my city,   1
    Whereupon lo! upsprang the aboriginal name.
Now I see what there is in a name, a word, liquid, sane,
    unruly, musical, self-sufficient,
I see that the word of my city is that word from of old,   5

Because I see that word nested in nests of water-bays, superb,
Rich, hemm'd thick all around with sailships and steamships,
　　an island sixteen miles long, solid-founded,
Numberless crowded streets, high growths of iron, slender,
　　strong, light, splendidly uprising toward clear skies,　　　　10
Tides swift and ample, well-loved by me, toward sundown,
The flowing sea-currents, the little islands, larger adjoining
　　islands, the heights, the villas,
The countless masts, the white shore-steamers, the lighters,
　　the ferry-boats, the black sea-steamers well-model'd,　　　　15
The down-town streets, the jobbers' houses of business,
　　the houses of business of the ship-merchants and
　　money-brokers, the river-streets,
Immigrants arriving, fifteen or twenty thousand in a week,
The carts hauling goods, the manly race of drivers of　　　　20
　　horses, the brown-faced sailors,
The summer air, the bright sun shining, and the sailing
　　clouds aloft,
The winter snows, the sleigh-bells, the broken ice in the
　　river, passing along up or down with the flood-tide or
　　ebb-tide,　　　　25
The mechanics of the city, the masters, well-form'd,
　　beautiful-faced, looking you straight in the eyes,
Trottoirs* throng'd, vehicles, Broadway, the women, the
　　shops and shows,
A million people—manners free and superb—open voices—　　30
　　hospitality—the most courageous and friendly young men,
City of hurried and sparkling waters! City of spires and masts!
City nested in bays! my city!

_____
*Sidewalks

Discussion Questions

1. Why does the poet think Manhattan is so perfectly named? Why does he use its Native American spelling?
2. What is New York bay filled with at this time? Can you explain why?
3. What are the various people in the poem doing? Explain each job.
4. The mechanics, we are told, look "you straight in the eyes." What does this line say about Whitman's view of working-class people in general?
5. According to Whitman, what other attributes make New Yorkers worthy of high praise?
6. How many complete sentences are there in this poem? What is the literary effect of this choice?

CROSSING BROOKLYN FERRY

1

Flood-tide below me! I see you face to face!   1

Clouds of the west—sun there half an hour high—I see you
    also face to face.

Crowds of men and women attired in the usual costumes,
    how curious you are to me!   5

On the ferry-boats the hundreds and hundreds that cross,
    returning home, are more curious to me than you
    suppose,

And you that shall cross from shore to shore years hence
    are more to me, and more in my meditations, than you
    might suppose.   10

2

The impalpable sustenance of me from all things at all
    hours of the day,

The simple, compact, well-join'd scheme, myself
    disintegrated, every one disintegrated yet part of the
    scheme,

The similitudes of the past and those of the future,   15

The glories strung like beads on my smallest sights and
    hearings, on the walk in the street and the passage over
    the river,

The current rushing so swiftly and swimming with me far
    away,   20

The others that are to follow me, the ties between me and
    them,

The certainty of others, the life, love, sight, hearing of others.

Others will enter the gates of the ferry and cross from shore
    to shore,   25

Others will watch the run of the flood-tide,

Others will see the shipping of Manhattan north and west,
    and the heights of Brooklyn to the south and east,

Others will see the islands large and small;

Fifty years hence, others will see them as they cross, the   30
    sun half an hour high,

A hundred years hence, or ever so many hundred years
    hence, others will see them,

Will enjoy the sunset, the pouring-in of the flood-tide, the
    falling-back to the sea of the ebb-tide.   35

3

It avails not, time nor place—distance avails not,
I am with you, you men and women of a generation, or
     ever so many generations hence,
Just as you feel when you look on the river and sky, so I
     felt,
Just as any of you is one of a living crowd, I was one of a   40
     crowd,
Just as you are refresh'd by the gladness of the river and
     the bright flow, I was refresh'd,
Just as you stand and lean on the rail, yet hurry with the
     swift current, I stood yet was hurried,   45
Just as you look on the numberless masts of ships and
     thick-stemm'd pipes of steamboats, I look'd.
I too many and many a time cross'd the river of old,
Watched the Twelfth-month sea-gulls, saw them high in the
     air floating with motionless wings, oscillating their bodies   50
Saw how the glistening yellow lit up parts of their bodies
     and left the rest in strong shadow,
Saw the slow-wheeling circles and the gradual edging
     toward the south,
Saw the reflection of the summer sky in the water,   55
Had my eyes dazzled by the shimmering track of beams,
Look'd at the fine centrifugal spokes of light round the
     shape of my head in the sunlit water,
Look'd on the haze on the hills southward and south-
     westward,   60
Look'd on the vapor as it flew in fleeces tinged with violet,
Look'd toward the lower bay to notice the vessels arriving,
Saw their approach, saw aboard those that were near me,
Saw the white sails of schooners and sloops, saw the ships
     at anchor,   65
The sailors at work in the rigging or out astride the spars,
The round masts, the swinging motion of the hulls, the
     slender serpentine pennants,
The large and small steamers in motion, the pilots in their
     pilothouses,   70
The white wake left by the passage, the quick tremulous
     whirl of the wheels,
The flags of all nations, the falling of them at sunset,
The scallop-edged waves in the twilight, the ladled cups,
     the frolicsome crests and glistening,   75

The stretch afar growing dimmer and dimmer, the gray
    walls of the granite storehouses by the docks,
On the river the shadowy group, the big steam-tug closely
    flank'd on each side by the barges, the hay-boat, the
    belated lighter,   80
On the neighboring shore the fires from the foundry
    chimneys burning high and glaringly into the night,
Casting their flicker of black contrasted with wild red and
    yellow light over the tops of houses, and down into the
    clefts of streets.   85

4

These and all else were to me the same as they are to you,
I loved well those cities, loved well the stately and rapid river,
The men and women I saw were all near to me,
Others the same—others who look back on me because I
    look'd forward to them,   90
(The time will come, though I stop here to-day and to-night.)

5

What is it then between us?
What is the count of the scores or hundreds of years
    between us?
Whatever it is, it avails not—distance avails not, and place   95
    avails not,
I too lived, Brooklyn of ample hills was mine,
I too walk'd the street of Manhattan island, and bathed in
    the waters around it,
I too felt the curious abrupt questionings stir within me,   100
In the day among crowds of people sometimes they came
    upon me,
In my walks home late at night or as I lay in my bed they
came upon me,
I too had been struck from the float forever held in solution,   105
I too had receiv'd identity by my body,
That I was I knew was of my body, and what I should be I
    knew I should be of my body.

6

It is not upon you alone the dark patches fall,
The dark threw its patches down upon me also,   110
The best I had done seem'd to me blank and suspicious,

My great thoughts as I supposed them, were they not in
    reality meagre?
Nor is it you alone who know what it is to be evil,   115
I am he who knew what it was to be evil,
I too knitted the old knot of contrariety,
Blabb'd, blush'd, resented, lied, stole, grudg'd,
Had guile, anger, lust, hot wishes I dared not speak,
Was wayward, vain, greedy, shallow, sly, cowardly, malignant,
The wolf, the snake, the hog, not wanting in me,   120
The cheating look, the frivolous word, the adulterous wish,
    not wanting,
Refusals, hates, postponements, meanness, laziness, none
of these wanting,
Was one with the rest, the days and haps of the rest,   125
Was call'd by my nighest name by clear loud voices of
    young men as they saw me approaching or passing,
Felt their arms on my neck as I stood, or the negligent
    leaning of their flesh against me as I sat,
Saw many I loved in the street or ferry-boat or public   130
    assembly, yet never told them a word,
Lived the same life with the rest, the same old laughing,
    gnawing, sleeping.
Play'd the part that still looks back on the actor or actress,
The same old role, the role that is what we make it, as great   135
    as we like,
Or as small as we like, or both great and small.

7

Closer yet I approach you,
What thought you have of me now, I had as much of you—I
    laid in my stores in advance,   140
I consider'd long and seriously of you before you were born.
Who was to know what should come home to me?
Who knows but I am enjoying this?
Who knows, for all the distance, but I am as good as
    looking at you now, for all you cannot see me?   145

8

Ah, what can ever be more stately and admirable to me
    than masthemm'd Manhattan?
River and sunset and scallop-edg'd waves of flood-tide?
The sea-gulls oscillating their bodies, the hay-boat in the
    twilight, and the belated lighter?   150

What gods can exceed these that clasp me by the hand, and
    with voices I love call me promptly and loudly by my
    nighest name as I approach?
What is more subtle than this which ties me to the woman
    or man that looks in my face?   155
Which fuses me into you now, and pours my meaning
    into you?
We understand then do we not?
What I promis'd without mentioning it, have you not
    accepted?   160
What the study could not teach—what the preaching
    could not accomplish is accomplish'd, is it not?

9

Flow on, river! flow with the flood-tide, and ebb with the
    ebb-tide!
Frolic on, crested and scallop-edg'd waves!   165
Gorgeous clouds of the sunset! drench with your splendor
    me, or the men and women generations after me!
Cross from shore to shore, countless crowds of passengers!
Stand up, tall masts of Mannahatta! stand up, beautiful
    hills of Brooklyn!   170
Throb, baffled and curious brain! throw out questions and
    answers!
Suspend here and everywhere, eternal float of solution!
Gaze, loving and thirsting eyes, in the house or street or
    public assembly!   175
Sound out, voices of young men! loudly and musically call
    me by my nighest name!
Live, old life! play the part that looks back on the actor or
    actress!
Play the old role, the role that is great or small according a   180
    one makes it!
Consider, you who peruse me, whether I may not in
    unknown ways be looking upon you;
Be firm, rail over the river, to support those who lean idly,
    yet haste with the hasting current;   185
Fly on, sea-birds! fly sideways, or wheel in large circles
    high in the air;
Receive the summer sky, you water, and faithfully hold it
    till all downcast eyes have time to take it from you!
Diverge, fine spokes of light, from the shape of my head, or   190
    any one's head, in the sunlit water!

Come on, ships from the lower bay! pass up or down,
    white-sail'd schooners, sloops, lighters!
Flaunt away, flags of all nations! be duly lower'd at sunset!
Burn high your fires, foundry chimneys! cast black shadows   195
    at nightfall! cast red and yellow light over the tops of the
    houses!
Appearances, now or henceforth, indicate what you are,
You necessary film, continue to envelop the soul,
About my body for me, and your body for you, be hung our   200
    divinest aromas,
Thrive, cities—bring your freight, bring your shows, ample
    and sufficient rivers,
Expand, being than which none else is perhaps more
    spiritual,
Keep your places, objects than which none else is more   205
    lasting.
You have waited, you always wait, you dumb, beautiful
    ministers,
We receive you with free sense at last, and are insatiate
    henceforward,   210
Not you any more shall be able to foil us, or withhold
    yourselves from us,
We use you, and do not cast you aside—we plant you
    permanently within us,
We fathom you not—we love you—there is perfection in   215
    you also,
You furnish your parts toward eternity,
Great or small, you furnish your parts toward the soul.

From *The Collected Writings of Walt Whitman: Prose Works 1892,* Volume 2, New York University Press.

Discussion Questions

1. What is a "flood-tide"? Why start with this image?
2. What time of day is it? How can you tell? What is the narrator doing in the poem?
3. Why do you think the crowds seem "curious" to the narrator?
4. In the first five stanzas, who does the narrator mean by "you"? What is the effect of these shifting references?
5. Define "impalpable," "sustenance," "similitudes," and "disintegrated." How do these words help the reader to understand the theme(s) in the poem?

6. The poem makes several references to ships. What has replaced them today? What other changes have occurred along the waterfront?

7. "Twelfth-month seagulls" suggest what month? What is the symbolic significance of this fact? Can you find any other symbols in the poem?

8. Interpret the line: "It avails not, neither time nor place—distance avails not," (line 36).

9. How is Brooklyn described in the poem? How is Manhattan described (see lines 169–70)? What makes each borough different from each other today?

10. In section 7, why does the narrator confess so many of his failings? List them.

11. In section 8, line 158, what is it the narrator thinks we have come "to understand"?

12. What is the tone, or attitude, of the narrator in the final section? What lines support this?

The Harbor

Ernest Poole

The novelist Ernest Poole was born in Chicago on January 23, 1880. He attended Princeton University and moved to New York, where he worked as a muckraking journalist promoting social reform. In 1918, Poole was the first recipient of the Pulitzer Prize. *The Harbor* (1915) is his best known work, which follows the life of Billy who is born in Brooklyn Heights in a house overlooking the harbor. As a child, he is fascinated by the mystery of boats and the men who build and sail them. As a young adult, Billy moves to Europe to become an artist but returns to Brooklyn to write in support of union workers who are striking along the waterfront for better pay and conditions. Poole died on January 10, 1950.

CHAPTER I

"You chump," I thought contemptuously. I was seven years old at the time, and the gentleman to whom I referred was Henry Ward Beecher. What it was that aroused my contempt for the man will be more fully understood if I tell first of the grudge that I bore him.

1

I was sitting in my mother's pew in the old church in Brooklyn. I was altogether too small for the pew, it was much too wide for the bend at my knees; and my legs, which were very short and fat, stuck straight out before me. I was not allowed to move, I was most uncomfortable, and for this Sabbath torture I laid all the blame on the preacher. For my mother had once told me that I was brought to church so small in order that when I grew up I could say I had heard the great man preach before he died. Hence the deep grudge that I bore him. Sitting here this morning, it seemed to me for hours and hours, I had been meditating upon my hard lot. From time to time, as was my habit when thinking or feeling deeply, one hand would unconsciously go to my head and slowly stroke my bang. My hair was short and had no curls, its only glory was this bang, which was deliciously soft to my hand and shone like a mirror from much reflective stroking. Presently my mother would notice and with a smile she would put down my hand, but a few moments later up it would come and would continue its stroking. For I felt both abused and puzzled. What was there in the talk of the large white-haired old man in the pulpit to make my mother's eyes so queer, to make her sit so stiff and still? What good would it do me when I grew up to say that I had heard him?

"I don't believe I will ever say it," I reasoned doggedly to myself. "And even if I do, I don't believe any other man will care whether I say it to him or not." I felt sure my father wouldn't. He never even came to church.

At the thought of my strange silent father, my mind leaped to his warehouse, his dock, the ships and the harbor. Like him, they were all so strange. And my hands grew a little cold and moist as I thought of the terribly risky thing I had planned to do all by myself that very afternoon. I thought about it for a long time with my eyes tight shut. Then the voice of the minister brought me back, I found myself sitting here in church and went on with this less shivery thinking.

"I wouldn't care myself," I decided. "If I were a man and another man   5
met me on the street and said, 'Look here. When I was a boy I heard Henry Ward Beecher before he died,' I guess I would just say to him, 'You mind your business and I'll mind mine.'" This phrase I had heard from the corner grocer, and I liked the sound of it. I repeated it now with an added zest.

Again I opened my eyes and again I found myself here in church. Still here. I heaved a weary sigh.

"If you were dead already," I thought as I looked up at the preacher, "my mother wouldn't bring me here." I found this an exceedingly cheering thought. I had once overheard our cook Anny describe how her old father had dropped dead. I eyed the old minister hopefully.

But what was this he was saying! Something about "the harbor of life." The harbor! In an instant I was listening hard, for this was something I knew about.

"Safe into the harbor," I heard him say. "Home to the harbor at last to rest." And then, while he passed on to something else, something I *didn't* know about, I settled disgustedly back in the pew.

"You chump," I thought contemptuously. To hear him talk you would   10
have thought the harbor was a place to feel quite safe in, a place to snuggle down in, a nice little place to come home to at night. "I guess he has never seen it much," I snorted.

For I had. From our narrow brownstone house on the Heights, ever since I could remember (and let me tell you that seems a long time when you are seven years old), I had looked down from our back windows upon a harbor that to me was strange and terrible.

I was glad that our house was up so high. Its front was on a sedate old street, and within it everything felt safe. My mother was here, and Sue, my little sister, and old Belle, our nurse, our nursery, my games, my animals, my fairy books, the small red table where I ate my supper, and the warm fur rug by my bed, where I knelt for "Now I lay me."

But from the porch at the back of our house you went three steps down to a long narrow garden—at least the garden seemed long to me—and if you walked to the end of the garden and peered through the ivy-covered bars of the fence, as I had done when I was so little that I could barely walk alone, you had the first mighty thrill of your life. For you found that through a hole in the ivy you could see a shivery distance straight down through the air to a street below. You found that the two iron posts, one at either end of the fence, were warm when you touched them, had holes in the top, had smoke coming out—were chimneys! And slowly it dawned upon your mind that this garden of yours was nothing at all but the roof of a gray old building—which your nurse told you vaguely had been a "warehouse" long ago when the waters of the harbor had come 'way in to the street below. The old "wharves" had been down there, she said. What was a "wharf"? It was a "dock," she told me. And she said that a family of "dockers" lived in the building under our garden. They were all that was left in it now but "old junk." Who was Old Junk, a man or a woman? And what in the world were Dockers?

Pursuing my adventurous ways, I found at one place in the garden, hidden by flowers near a side wall, a large heavy lid which was painted brown and felt like tin. But how much heavier than tin. Tug as I might, I could not budge it. Then I found it had an iron hook and was hooked down tight to the garden. Yes, it was true, our whole garden was a roof! I put my ear down to the lid and listened scowling, both eyes shut. I heard nothing then, but I came back and tried it many times, until once I jumped up and ran like mad. For faintly from somewhere deep down under the flower beds I had heard a baby crying! What was this baby, a Junk or a Docker? And who were these people who lived under flowers? To me they sounded suspiciously like the goblins in my goblin book. Once when I was sick in bed, Sue came shrieking into the house and said that a giant had heaved up that great lid from below. Up had come his shaggy head, his dirty face, his rolling eyes, and he had laughed and laughed at the flowers. He was a drunken man, our old nurse Belle had told her, but Sue was sure he was a giant.

"You are wrong," I said with dignity. "He is either a Junk or a Docker."   15

The lid was spiked down after that, and our visitor never appeared again. But I saw him vividly in my mind's eye—his shaggy wild head rising up among our flowers. Vaguely I felt that he came from the harbor.

As the exciting weeks of my life went on I discovered three good holes in that ivy-covered fence of ours. These all became my secret holes, and through them I watched the street below, a bleak bare chasm of a street which when the trucks came by echoed till it thundered. Across the street rose the high gray front of my father's ware house. It was part of a solid line of similar gray brick buildings, and it was like my father, it was grim and silent, you could not see inside. Over its five tiers of windows black iron shutters were fastened tight. From time to time a pair of these shutters would fly open, disclosing a dark cave behind, out of which men brought barrels and crates and let them down by ropes into the trucks on the street below. How they spun round and round as they came! But most of the trucks drove rumbling into a tunnel which led through the warehouse out to my father's dock, out to the ships and the harbor. And from that mysterious region long lines of men came through the tunnel at noontime, some nearly naked, some only in shirts, men with the hairiest faces. They sat on the street with their backs to the warehouse wall, eating their dinners out of pails, and from other pails they took long drinks of a curious stuff all white on top. Some of them were always crossing the street and disappearing from my view into a little store directly underneath me. Belle spoke of this store as a "vile saloon" and of these men as "dockers." So I knew what Dockers were at last! In place of the one who lived under our garden and had burst up among the flowers, I saw now that there were hundreds and thousands of men like him down there on the docks. And all belonged to the harbor.

Their work I learned was to load the ships whose masts and spars peeped up at me over the warehouse roofs. From my nursery window above I could see them better. Sometimes they had large white sails and then they moved off somewhere. I could see them go, these tall ships, with their sails making low, mysterious sounds, flappings, spankings and deep boomings. The men on them sang the weirdest songs as they pulled all together at the ropes. Some of these songs brought a lump in your throat. Where were they going? "To heathen lands," Belle told me. What did she mean? I was just going to ask her. But then I stopped—I did not dare! From up the river, under the sweeping arch of that Great Bridge which seemed high as the clouds, came more tall ships, and low "steamers" belching smoke and "tugs" and "barges" and "ferry boats." The names of all these I learned from Belle and Anny the cook and my mother. And all were going "to heathen lands." What in the world did Belle mean by that?

Once I thought I had it. I saw that some of these smaller boats were just going across the river and stopping at the land over there, a land so crowded with buildings you could barely see into it at all. "Is that a heathen land?" I asked her. "Yes!" said Belle. And she laughed. She was Scotch and very religious. But later I heard her call it "New York" and say she was going there herself to buy herself some corsets. And so I was even more puzzled than ever. For some deep instinct told me you could buy no corsets in "heathen land"—least of all Belle's corsets.

She often spoke of "the ocean," too, another place where the tall ships   20
went. But what was the ocean? "It's like a lake, but mightier," Belle had said. But what was a lake? It was all so vague and confusing. Always it came back to this, that I had no more seen the "ocean" than I had seen a "heathen land," and so I did not know them.

But I knew the harbor by day and by night, on bright sunny days and in fogs and rains, in storms of wind, in whirling snow, and under the restful stars at night that twinkled down from so far above, while the shadowy region below twinkled back with stars of its own, restless, many-colored stars, yellow, green and red and blue, moving, dancing, flaring, dying. And all these stars had voices, too. By night in my bed I could hear them—hoots and shrieks from ferries and tugs, hoarse coughs from engines along the docks, the whine of wheels, the clang of bells, deep blasts and bellows from steamers. And closer still, from that "vile saloon" directly under the garden, I could hear wild shouts and songs and roars of laughter that came, I learned, not only from dockers, but from "stokers" and "drunken sailors," men who lived right inside the ships and would soon be starting for heathen lands!

"I wonder how I'd feel," I would think, "if I were out in the garden now—out in the dark all by myself—right above that vile saloon!"

This would always scare me so that I would bury my head in the covers and shake. But I often did this, for I liked to be scared. It was a game I had all by myself with the harbor.

And yet this old man in the pulpit called it a place where you went to rest!

Twenty-five years have gone since then, and all that I can remember   25
now of anything Henry Ward Beecher said was this—that once, just once, I heard him speak of something that I knew about, and that when he did he was wrong.

And though all the years since then have been for me one long story of a harbor, restless, heaving, changing, always changing—it has never changed for me in this—it has never seemed a haven where ships come to dock, but always a place from which ships start out—into the storms and the fogs of the seas, over the "ocean" to "heathen lands." For so I saw it when I was a child, the threshold of adventures.

Discussion Questions

1. Where is 7-year-old Billy when this chapter opens? How does he feel at that moment? Why is it so important for his mother that Billy is here?
2. What does Billy mean when he says about the minister Henry Ward Beecher, "I guess he has never seen it [the harbor] much"? What does the harbor represent to Billy?

3. Who does Billy think lives right below his outdoor garden? Who in fact does live there?
4. Looking out of the three holes in his fence, Billy can see his father's warehouse in the distance. Describe what else he sees.
5. Why do you think Billy imagines joining the men outside?
6. Billy speaks of the harbor as "restless, heaving, changing, always changing." How has the harbor changed since the time Poole was writing?

The Brooklyn Bridge

Phillip Lopate

Phillip Lopate is the author and editor of many books, including *The Art of the Personal Essay* (1994), *Writing New York: A Literary Anthology* (2000), and *Waterfront: A Journey Around Manhattan* (2004). He lives in Brooklyn and teaches at Columbia University.

CONFRONTING THE WORLD'S MOST RECOGNIZABLE, REPRODUCED MONU- 1
MENTS—THE EIFFEL TOWER, THE PYRAMIDS, THE ACROPOLIS, THE COLOSSEUM,
THE Brooklyn Bridge—the mind tends to go numb. So much devotion has
been lavished on these by-now primal shapes, they seem hard wired into our
imaginations, iconically omnipresent and therefore refractory to awe. Still, we
long to feel the same shiver our ancestors did; and sometimes we have what
approximates a religious experience in their proximity, either because of or
despite the programming we've received. The rest of the time we must scrape
away apathy and make a conscious effort to rekindle our wonderment, by exploring the historical ground against which they first stood out as miraculous.

Of all the world's grand monuments, the oddest, I would think, is the
Brooklyn Bridge, because it is so purely functional. This paradox was ar-
ticulated by America's first important architectural critic, Montgomery
Schuyler, when he wrote in 1883, the year it opened: "It so happens that
the work which is likely to be our most durable monument, and to convey
some knowledge of us to the most remote posterity, is a work of bare utility; not a shrine, not a fortress, not a palace, but a bridge."

The Brooklyn Bridge has remained celebrated and cherished, long after
its technological achievements have been superseded. It was not the first
successful suspension bridge in America; it is no longer the longest in the
country, or even necessarily the most beautiful in New York; some, like Le
Corbusier, would argue for the George Washington Bridge. Yet it is hard to
imagine the GW Bridge receiving the lavish national attention on its hun-
dredth birthday that the Brooklyn Bridge generated on its 1983 centenary.
Why has the Brooklyn span remained so alive in the popular culture?

Because it has had the capacity to make itself lovable. Beautiful it may
also be, but "lovable" is a different quality; it suggests the knack of inspiring tenderness. If the Brooklyn Bridge began as a magisterial, solitary alpine
range connecting the two great cities of Manhattan and Brooklyn, it soon

Reprinted by permission of Aaron Barlow.

enough had company across the East River: the Williamsburg Bridge opened in 1903, the Manhattan Bridge in 1905. These siblings forever gamboling at their elder brother's side, elbowing their raw profiles into view, meant that the Brooklyn Bridge had to be revered for something other than its riparian-spanning properties. Aesthetics and tradition both came to the rescue.

First, aesthetics: the Brooklyn Bridge is, without a doubt, soaringly, stubbornly handsome. There is the elegance of the catenary curve (the natural form taken by any rope or cable suspended from two points) as it swoops down to the center, and then scallops upward toward the towers; the visual cross-thatching of vertical cables and diagonal stays, yielding an effect that has been compared to a harp, a spider's web, angels' wings; the unearthly collision of materials: the airy steel wire of the cables and stays—it was the first bridge to rely solely on steel for such purposes—against the staunch granite towers. Its towers seemed at the time the one opportunity to make a consciously monumental statement. In an architecturally eclectic period, faced with the option of borrowing from any historical style (neoclassical, Gothic, French Renaissance), its makers chose Gothic for the gateways to the two cities. It was this very dissonance of sleek steel and old-fashioned granite that annoyed Montgomery Schuyler in his early, proto-modernist assessment, "The Brooklyn Bridge as Monument." After acknowledging that the bridge was

5

perhaps the finest, most enduring structure of the day, Schuyler took issue with the anachronistic heaviness of the Gothic stylings, wishing instead that the towers could have better "revealed" structurally the cables they contained within. It was as though he had in mind a pure steel structure like the George Washington Bridge, which is indeed more harmonious, from a modernist aesthetic viewpoint. But the Brooklyn Bridge is more endearing, more—lovable, precisely because it exemplifies that tension, held in stately balance, between old and new, handmade and industrial, granite and gossamer.

Adding to its endearing qualities are the heroic legends about its fourteen-year construction, which still cling to its girders. That Iliadic tale of the struggle to build the Brooklyn Bridge has been told many times, most definitively in David McCullough's fine book *The Great Bridge:* how the stern, brilliant German immigrant engineer John Augustus Roebling, ex-student of Hegel, having successfully solved the riddle of making suspension bridges safe (maximum stiffness), was offered the assignment to span the East River; how he became its first victim, his toes crushed in a pier accident, leading to tetanus and death; how his son, Washington Roebling, he of calm integrity and superhuman persistence, took over the task, assembled a loyal projects team, mostly fellow alumni from Rensselaer Polytechnic Institute, and set about resourcefully meeting each of the challenges with technological inventions; how they battled the elements and turbulent tides and geological surprises of the East River; how they built two enormous compressed-air foundations, or caissons, each weighing 6 million pounds, and sank them underwater to dredge and anchor the towers; how the laborers, working eight-hour shifts with primitive equipment (no power tools!) in these ill-lit, poorly ventilated, sweltering underwater conditions for two dollars a day, began to suffer from caisson sickness, or "the bends," which crippled them; how their boss, Washington Roebling, investigating a fire in the caisson, himself contracted the illness and became an invalid for life, forced to attend the bridge's construction from his window with a spyglass; how he developed, along with the physical disease, a nervous disorder—a neurotically unsociable manner close to misanthropy; how his devoted wife, Emily, played the "bridge" with his associates and employers, smoothing over public demands for her husband's resignation as chief engineer; how gluttonous William M. Tweed, ruler of Tammany Hall, saw this massive public work as a splendid opportunity for graft and almost took it, but the Tweed Ring was exposed and busted in the nick of time; how a corrupt supplier of steel wire, a bigamist mountebank who gained the contract through political kickbacks, managed to smuggle in substandard materials, despite Roebling's orders that every yard of wire be personally inspected; how it didn't matter, finally, because Roebling had already factored in that the bridge be built to six times its necessary strength; how it mattered only symbolically, in that there would always be invisible weak-nesses woven into the bridge's near-perfection, just as blood was admixed into its joints and bolts from the deaths of more than twenty workmen.

As Alan Trachtenberg has pointed out in his excellent study, *Brooklyn Bridge:* "For many Americans in 1883, Brooklyn Bridge proved the nation to be healed of its wounds of civil war and again on its true course: the peaceful mastery of nature." It was the age of engineer-heroes (de Lesseps, Roebling) and engineering feats, and nothing stirred the public's romantic sentiment more than bridges. "Babylon had her hanging garden, Egypt her pyramid, Athens her Acropolis, Rome her Atheneum; so Brooklyn has her Bridge," boasted a shopkeeper sign on the holiday of its opening. The bridge had been strung with lightbulbs, making it the first electrified span over water. But such innovations, again, are easily forgotten: what kept the Brooklyn Bridge alive in the minds of people was its significance in the mythos and daily life of New York City. The bridge unified two great cities as physically as a rope tied around their waists: it had been purposely designed in such a way as to connect New York's City Hall with the City Hall of Brooklyn; to extend, as it were, Broadway to Fulton Street. The success of the bridge preempted char-ter revision: it made the amalgamation of the five boroughs a few years later, in 1898, into one super-metropolis, a kind of inevitability, an afterthought.

"I hereby prophecy that in 1900 A.D. Brooklyn will be the city and New York will be the suburb," wrote George Templeton Strong in his di-ary in 1865. "It is inevitable if both go on growing as they have grown for the last forty years. Brooklyn has room to spread and New York has not." Brooklyn was the coming place; no one anticipated Manhattan would grow vertically. It was Brooklyn, then the fifth-largest city in the nation, that had agitated most for the bridge, thinking correctly that it would drive up the value of its Heights real estate and attract middle-class busi-nessmen, by making their commute easier than the unreliable, icebound ferries. It was Brooklyn that had supplied the vast majority of planning and political energies for the building of the bridge, and paid the lion's share of its construction costs. So it was only fair that what had been orig-inally called "the East River Bridge" would undergo a name change to honor its sponsoring agent. The irony is that the bridge both put Brook-lyn on the map and diminished it forever, by undermining its urban in-dependence. However much the residents of Kings County might cling to their faith that Brooklyn was still the emerging urban hub, its destiny was to be a provincial, if eccentric, bedroom borough to Manhattan.

For Manhattanites, the bridge became, as David McCullough put it, "a highway into the open air." One of Roebling's great design decisions had been to been to build an elevated promenade, which would arch ever so slightly, so as to bow *above* the traffic. The walker would have the freedom of the city: to look down at vehicles crossing the bridge (first horse-carriages and elevated trains; later cars), or else to ignore them and gaze uninterruptedly in every direction, at the water, the boats (innumerable, during the East River's heyday as a port), the skyline, and the sky itself.

From where else can one see the whole city today? From skyscraper   10 observatories, certainly, such as the Empire State Building, but one has to pay a fee, and then, once aloft, the pacing possibilities have distinct limits; whereas the Brooklyn Bridge promenade is an extension of the street system, a great free thoroughfare.

Governor Al Smith, in his autobiography, *Up to Now,* recalled: "In those early days the bridge served as more than a utility for transportation between the two cities. It soon became a place of recreation and of pleasure. So much so that it was referred to in songs and poularized on the variety stage. I can still sing 'Danny by my side.'

> The Brooklyn Bridge on Sunday is known as lover's lane,
> I stroll there with my sweetheart, oh, time and time again;
> Oh, how I love to ramble, oh, yes, it is my pride,
> Dressed in my best, each day of rest, with Danny by my side."

The lordly position of the pedestrian on the promenade must have suited Washington Roebling, who refused to enter a motorcar in his lifetime (he died in 1920). On the other hand, there is irony in the fact that this superb public space was built by a man who, after his bout with caisson sickness, hated to be in crowds, and found it a torment to socialize with anyone but his wife for more than a few minutes.

The bridge was also inspiration to poets and loners. Lewis Mumford, in his autobiography, *Sketches from Life,* told how the Brooklyn Bridge figured in a key experience of his dawning manhood. On a March day, the then-youthful Mumford was walking into Manhattan at twilight, and "as I reached the middle of the Brooklyn Bridge, the sunlight spread across the sky, forming a halo around the jagged mountain of skyscrapers, with the darkened loft buildings and warehouses huddling below in the foreground. The towers, topped by the golden pinnacles of the new Woolworth Building, still caught the light even as it began to ebb away. Three-quarters of the way across the bridge I saw the skyscrapers in the deepening darkness become slowly honeycombed with lights until, before I reached the Manhattan end, these buildings piled up in a dazzling mass against the indigo sky.

"Here was my city, immense, overpowering, flooded with energy and   15 light....And there was I, breasting the March wind, drinking in the city and the sky, both vast, yet contained in me, transmitting through me the great mysterious will that made them and the promise of the new day that was still to come." Mumford, looking backward half a century, remembers being filled with an exaltation he compares to "the wonder of an orgasm in the body of one's beloved." He says: "In that sudden revelation of power and beauty all the confusions of adolescence dropped from me, and I trod the narrow, resilient boards of the footway with a new confidence that came, not from my isolated self alone but from the collective energies I had confronted and risen to."

Here the Brooklyn Bridge is a cradle for self-creation. Like Rastignac in Balzac's *Père Goriot*, waving his fist at Paris below and swearing he will conquer it someday, Mumford vows to extract the fullest from his talents, and to affect the city stretched tantalizingly around him. The bridge's elevated, 360-degree vantage point inspired feelings of wholeness bordering on omnipotence.

The Russian poet Vladimir Mayakovsky, in his poem "Brooklyn Bridge," compared the structure to a dinosaur, one of those "huge giant lizards" from which future geologists could re-create our world, and whose bones alone would survive the apocalyptic twentieth century. Henry James, returning to his native city after years abroad, recorded with something like horror, in his travel book *The American Scene*, his reaction to the span as an enormous steam engine and power loom, as well as a sort of Frankenstein monster: "One has the sense that the monster grows and grows, flinging abroad its loose limbs even as some unmannered young giant at his 'larks,' and that the binding stitches must forever fly further and faster and draw harder; the future complexity of the web, all under sky and above the sea, becoming thus that of some colossal set of clockworks, some steel-souled machine-room of brandished arms and hammering fists and opening and closing jaws."

For James, writing in 1907, the Brooklyn Bridge was still too new—too suggestive of the ominous threat of industrialized conformity—to be cherished as a work of local genius. But Hart Crane saw and understood the lonely grandeur and achievement of the bridge from a more sympathetic, historically removed perspective. He had researched the Roeblings with an eye toward writing their biography. To inhabit their inner world, he rented the same apartment on Hicks Street, in Brooklyn Heights, from which Washington Roebling had overseen the bridge's construction. "Brooklyn Bridge," wrote Crane to his family, is "the most superb piece of construction in the modern world, I'm sure, with strings of lights crossing it like glowing worms as the Ls and surface cars pass each other coming and going." He chose it as his symbol of American affirmation in *The Bridge* (1927–30), his response to Eliot's *The Waste Land*. Among its many gorgeous, exhilarating lines are these in the prologue, addressed directly "To Brooklyn Bridge":

O harp and altar, of the fury fused,
(How could mere toil align thy choiring strings!)

Reprinted by permission of Aaron Barlow.

Crane encircles the bridge with spiritual connotations: a "curveship," like an alien spaceship dropped down from the galaxies, it redeems the prophet's pledges, sets up heavenly choirs, lifts night in its arms, condenses eternity, and, to top it all, lends its own myth to a God who seems in need of one, in our secular age.

It is interesting that so many of the most memorable paeans to the Brooklyn Bridge, in poetry (Crane, Mayakovsky, García Lorca), prose (John Dos Passos, Thomas Wolfe, Henry Miller), and paint (Joseph Stella, John Marin, Albert Gleizes, Marsden Hartley), were fashioned just after the First World War through the twenties and thirties, when the structure had already been standing for a number of decades. It no longer was a technological novelty, but its glamour had, if anything, skyrocketed. Why this should be may have as much to do with the development of modernism—and American modernism in particular—as with any singularities of the Brooklyn Bridge.

In his 1924 *Port of New York*, Paul Rosenfeld gathered a collection of his essays on fourteen American moderns, who included Arthur Dove, John Marin, William Carlos Williams, Alfred Stieglitz, Georgia O'Keeffe, and Marsden Hartley. He analyzed what he called "the drama of cultural   20 awakening" in America of the 1920s, using the Port of New York as a central organizing image. No longer was it necessary for bohemians and artists to go abroad, Rosenfeld argued. "For what we once could feel only by quitting New York—the fundamental oneness we have with the place and the people in it—that is sensible to us today in the very jostling, abstracted streets of the city. We know it here, our relationship with this place in which we live. The buildings cannot deprive us of it. For they and we have suddenly commenced growing together." If the buildings were entwining roots into the artists' souls, how much more so their beloved Bridge, the mother of local modernism, which spanned this selfsame, essential Port of New York?

Such fervent, mythifying worship could not continue at the same heat. It was too much to put on any bridge, even the most awesomely endearing. The literary tributes fell away, though Roebling's wonder continued to be the most photographed bridge in the world.

Crossing it today, you are made aware of the tense play of light and shadow in the Brooklyn Bridge's form: the granite arches that loom like minarets beckoning the traveler to prayer; the haunting shadow of the bridge on water; the serpentine plunge of the span's railing, like a roller-coaster descending into the high-rise city. Then there is the relationship between the bridge and the metropolis: on one side, flamboyant, vertical Manhattan; on the other, a more horizontal, spread-out Brooklyn.

I remember admiring the terrifying acrobatic cool of ironworkers, these sky-walkers who function, as the saying goes, without a net, when they repaired the bridge some years back. (The nets that were strung up, incidentally, were installed to protect the vehicles and pedestrians, not the repair workers.) How calm they looked in their hardhats as they perched over the river, one misstep away from catastrophe, drinking their coffee through ski masks necessitated by the bitter cold.

"When the perfected East River bridge shall permanently and uninterruptedly connect the two cities," predicted a reporter for the *Brooklyn Eagle*, Thomas Kinsella, with some regret, "the daily thousands who cross it will consider it a sort of natural and inevitable phenomenon, such as the rising and setting of the sun, and they will unconsciously overlook the preliminary difficulties surmounted before the structure spanned the stream, and will perhaps undervalue the indomitable courage, the absolute faith, the consummate genius which assured the engineer's triumph." Seeing those ironworkers restoring the bridge returned me to the original romance of its making. "How could mere toil align thy choiring strings!" demanded Hart Crane. But apparently mere toil did—and does, in a mutual dependency between nature and humanity, stone and sweat, that is as ancient to monuments as it is noble.

Discussion Questions

1. According to the author, what is so unusual about the Brooklyn Bridge's status as one of the world's most recognizable monuments?
2. Why do you think the Brooklyn Bridge is so celebrated? What is your own relationship to it?
3. The author uses a powerful vocabulary and writes many elegant sentences. Which sentences do you think are especially noteworthy?
4. For Lopate, what elements make the Brooklyn Bridge an aesthetic masterpiece?
5. What engineering challenges did John Augustus Roebling face in designing and constructing the bridge? What other problems did he and his son, Washington, need to solve?
6. What was the effect of the Bridge on Brooklynites? Why do so many tourists enjoy it today?
7. Discuss the variety of ways that poets and essayists such as Mumford, Mayakovsky, James, and Crane have written about the bridge.

Reading Lucy

Jennifer Egan

Jennifer Egan was born on September 6, 1962 in San Francisco, CA. She studied English at the University of Pennsylvania and is the author of numerous prize-winning short stories and novels. In 2011, she won the Pulitzer Prize for her novel *A Visit From the Goon Squad*, a genre-bending work about the passage of time and the importance of music. She currently lives in the Fort Greene neighborhood of Brooklyn. "Reading Lucy," an essay about a woman named Lucille Kolkin who worked at the Brooklyn Navy Yard during World War II, first appeared in the edited collection *Brooklyn Was Mine* (2007).

LAST SPRING I formed a brief, powerful friendship with a woman named   1
Lucille Kolkin. She was a Brooklynite, like me. For two months, Lucy and I spent a couple of hours together at the Brooklyn Historical Society every Wednesday and Friday, while my son was at preschool in the neighborhood. I say two months, but in Lucy's life it was actually five—from April to September 1944, when she moved to California and we lost touch.

We met for professional reasons. I was researching a novel I'm writing about a woman who worked at the Brooklyn Navy Yard during World War II, and Lucy actually *worked* at the navy yard for almost two years, as a mechanic in the shipfitting shop. When she started, in the fall of 1942, she was Lucille Gewirtz, but within a year she'd met Alfred Kolkin, from the mechanical shop, and married him after a brief courtship she once jokingly referred to as "Maidenhood to Marriage in Three Easy Months." The speed doesn't surprise me; Lucy was passionate. It's one of the things I love about her.

By the time I got to know her personally, I'd already spent time with the lecture notes she took at the navy yard shipfitting school. She wrote in blue pen in a small loose-leaf binder, defining countless acronyms (WL=waterline; AE=after end; FE=forward end) and neatly diagramming ships in cross-section. Since I, too, was trying to learn the basics of battleships, I began copying down much of what Lucy had copied, including details like: "Construction is started at midship and continued on both sides of it. Balances weight." But I also encountered flashes of the life attached to the notes I was cribbing from:

> *Buy–Bag*
> *Shoes*
> *Bras*

Fix–

> *gray dress*
> *blue suit*
> *stocks*

From cleaners—coat

Who was this woman whose to-do lists looked so much like mine? I knew that the historical society had a collection of correspondence between Lucy and her husband, beginning in April 1944, when he joined the navy. I requested the first group of letters she'd written to Alfred when he left for boot camp in Sampson, New York. That was when our friendship began.

Lucy wrote to Alfred almost daily—often on the street-car she took from Twentieth Avenue in Bensonhurst, where she ate supper at her mother's house before beginning her night shift at the navy yard. "We're approaching Pacific St. again—(wish I had a longer ride)" was a typical sign-off, accompanied by endearments: "Oodles of love and about 7 little kisses," or "So I'll throw in another kiss and just an inchy winchy pinch on the aft end." She was wildly in love with her husband. "You're a huge success, fella," she wrote to him on May 4, 1944. "Not only I—but the other thousand girls in the yard think you're handsome. See, I've been sporting a new picture of you and in my characteristically 'proud of my husband' feeling, no one can escape seeing it." 5

On an undated letter in May, she kissed the paper she was writing on in a spectacular shade of pink lipstick. It was shocking to see the impression of her lips, every crease still visible after sixty-two years, as if she'd left it ten minutes before.

Lucy described herself as a shipfitter 3/c, meaning third class, ("buzz: soon, to be 2/c I think," she told Alfred in June), and she often seemed to have the aid of a "helper," also female. A shipfitter fabricates and lays out the metal structural parts of a ship—a job that it would have been laughable to think of a woman performing before the war. But as male employees at the yard were drafted or enlisted, someone had to replace them; the Brooklyn Navy Yard was the largest shipbuilding facility in the world during World War II. It built seventeen battleships and repaired five thousand, including Allied ships from all over the world. And by January 1945, there were 4,657 women at the yard, working in nearly every phase of shipbuilding and repair.

I was hungry for detailed descriptions of Lucy's shipfitting work, but as is often the case when someone talks to a fellow "insider," her remarks about work were mostly in passing: "stenciled 120 pieces for a job" or "I was put back on the flow this afternoon—and I didn't like it nohow." She liked being the timekeeper, which apparently happened every two weeks and allowed her to stay in the office and write letters to Alfred. She complained often of sore feet (later mitigated by a pair of rubber-soled shoes) and described her hands as "kind of scratched." In one of her longest descriptions of actual work, from July 17, she wrote: "First it's 4, then it's 1, then it's 6. No, I ain't talking about babies—or even the time. You see, I'm a shipfitter and I'm making up some more kingposts and booms. 'Make up 4.' So I start making up the fittings for four ships. 'Cancel 3, they're duplications.' So I put some fittings for three ships away in case I get the job again. Then I make up the rest of the fittings—enough 1 ship. 'New order. Make up six.' So I start pc#1, pc#2 all over again. It's not a bad job otherwise." She included a diagram of a kingpost, with an arrow indicating a "5 × 5 H Beam about 9' lg."

When it came to life in the navy yard *around* the job itself, Lucy was superb. "I just learned of a wonderful way to lose friends—and get a lot of laughs—or do you already know the funnel trick?" she wrote in an undated letter. "Near closing time this morning, the boys said that for 10c a try a fellow could put a half dollar on his fore-head, a funnel in his pants and if he got the 50c piece into the funnel by bending his head it was his. Well of course when he put his head back to balance the coin, a container of water was poured into the funnel. Some level of humor!"

She had a particular interest in union organizing (she referred occasionally to "union friends") and also in the plight of "negroes," whom she viewed with great sympathy. Here's an anecdote from her letter of May 3:

"Yesterday, Minnie, a negro tacker who has been in the yard as long as I and interested in becoming a fitter, became disgusted and signed up for welding school. Another victory for Haack [Lucy's supervisor] and his ilk. Poor gal—she hates welding and is all upset. She knows she's not doing the right thing by giving up the fight but she insists there's nothing else to do. A couple of negro girls and I were trying to talk her out of it. But she persists in the idea that not only does she have to fight as a woman, but as a negro. She was practically in tears…She's a former teacher and math genius—and Gee! Butch, it's such a God damn shame."

Four days later, she wrote: "Just learned Minnie (remember?) is not quitting shipfitting. Our little talk with her took effect."

Amid the news, anecdotes, and political and cultural observations that Lucy somehow managed to pack into these daily missives, I learned the basics of her life: she and Alfred were Jewish. Lucy had gone to college— at Hunter—while Alfred had not, which occasioned from his wife occasional pep talks about how little college really mattered: "I went to college. So what. I look for a job and people say, 'Yes, yes but what can you do?' 'Nuttin' say I.'" She also had a habit of footnoting words whose meanings Alfred might not know—like *querulous*—and providing definitions. In one letter she included a lengthy tutorial on how to read music. The instruction apparently went both ways; in another letter, she asked Alfred for directions on how to wire a room.

I found these letters deeply absorbing; not only did hours pass without my noticing, so that I often found myself huffing, flustered, to pick up my son, but often it felt like sixty-two *years* had passed without my noticing—such was the ringing immediacy of Lucy's voice. In some ways our worlds felt close together: we walked the same streets (I live in Fort Greene, a few blocks from the navy yard); we both worked hard and struggled to find time for practical necessities like cleaning and shopping. Like me, Lucy hated buying clothes; "I'll brand myself, I'll go before a firing squad—anything," she wrote to Alfred in April. "Only I won't try on another dress." She loved movies and live performances, which in her case meant Duke Ellington, Paul Draper, Danny Kaye's *Up in Arms*, and countless other movies. And she often reported on her avid reading: Dorothy Parker, Howard Fast, Boris Voyetekhov's *The Last Days of Sevastopol*.

Of course, Lucy was much younger than I am—in her midtwenties,   15
in the early phase of her adult life. Part of the pleasure of reading her letters was wondering how her life would turn out; would Alfred return to Brooklyn, or would they put a down payment on a house in San Francisco, as Lucy fantasized? Would she continue to work, or leave that behind for motherhood? Would she have children? Would her love for Alfred remain as heedless as it was in this first year? I mused with an odd sense that these answers couldn't be known—as if Lucy's life, like mine, were still a thing in motion, with many outcomes uncertain. That's how close she seemed.

Sometimes, while crossing the street or jogging over the Brooklyn Bridge, I would have the thought that I might actually *see* Lucy, not as she was now—however that might be—but the Lucy of 1944: wisecracking, a talker, drinking a strawberry malted. I was dying to hear her speaking voice (I imagined it deep and a little crackly) and to see what she looked like beyond that fuchsia print of her lips. All of Brooklyn seemed full of her.

On May 7, Lucy wrote, "Butchie—guess what! I had a dream last night about our having a baby—a couple of months old—cute + blond—and dressed in a regular basque shirt + shorts. You were diapering him and I suggested it was about time you taught me how to diaper him, etc, etc. I should know better than to disclose my dreams, but it was too nice to keep to myself. Anyway, I guess the dream belonged to you too."

After reading that sentence, I stood up suddenly, walked to one of the historical society computers and typed "Lucille Kolkin" into Google. Within a second or two, I was reading her obituary. She'd died suddenly, in 1997, at age seventy-eight. She'd had two daughters, two grand children, and lived in New York. After fifty-three years of marriage, Alfred had survived her.

I returned to my seat, shaken. It was one of those moments when technology crushingly outpaces cognitive reach; I couldn't seem to make the transition from the handwritten pages in front of me, full of blindness and hope, to the obituary on the screen. It was several minutes before I resumed reading Lucy's letters, and when I did, it was at a slightly treacherous remove, as if I were withholding information from her—like faking surprise at an outcome you already know.

After that, I found Lucy's letters poignant in a way that they hadn't   20
seemed before. As she prattled to Alfred about bicycling in Prospect Park or rubbing bicarbonate of soda on the sunburn she'd gotten on a trip to Coney Island with her girlfriends, it would cross my mind that I knew the time and place of the death that awaited her. And I felt a corollary awareness as I walked the Brooklyn streets, holding my little sons' hands; how old would they be when I died? Would they have had children of their own? How would they remember me? Lying in bed with my husband, the big tree swaying outside, I thought about Lucy's words to Alfred: "the glorious blossoms on the tree facing our window—that is the tree in Brooklyn. The last thing I say good-morning to before sleeping." It made me eerily conscious of a point of view from which our lives would look quaint, and a long time ago.

Meanwhile, in 1944, events in Lucy's life were rapidly unfolding: Alfred began radio technician training in Chicago, and Lucy gave up the little apartment they had shared and moved in with her mother. There was much speculation about where Alfred might be stationed next, and the news came in August 1944: he was moving to a naval base in Del Monte, California. "The news of your new destination is not too bad," Lucy wrote to him. "I understand the climate there is very much like heaven...Perhaps I can go to the Yard in that state—altho it's about 150 miles from where you'll be. They work on 8 hour shifts there—and I imagine I'll be able to see you every week-end."

Two days later, she deemed the California Navy Yard "no good—too far away," but shortly after that, she revived the idea of a transfer. "I'm pretty certain I could get a transfer to the Calif. Navy Yard," she wrote on August 6. "If you can't sleep out and the Yard is within a 150 mile radius— I almost think it pays to get a transfer. The Yard is near San Fran.—a nice place to live—and 150 miles is really not too far to travel. What do you think?"

The reaction from Alfred must have been cool, because six days later, Lucy wrote, "Butch, do you really object if I feel like you? After all, you wanted to enlist even tho it meant leaving me. Well, I feel I have an important job too. And I don't feel like dropping everything and working in Del Monte just now—especially since I'll hardly be able to see you anyway. But if I work in San Fran. I can continue the work I'm doing and be able to see you besides."

I already knew the outcome of this debate from the biographical note accompanying the letters: Lucy would follow Alfred to Del Monte and work as a waitress. There would be no letters for almost a year, although they would begin again when Alfred shipped out in 1945. Still, as I read, I found myself mentally exhorting her the other way, as if the decision still hung in the balance, as if I could yank her, physically, from her time into mine. *Go to the yard*, I imagined telling her. *Savor this fluke of independence before the clamp of 1950s domesticity closes around you. Bank some more skills to capitalize on when the sexual revolution hits in twenty years. Please, Lucy, get the transfer! Go to San Francisco. I grew up there; it's gorgeous.*

The resolution came three days later: 25

". . . went to see my doctor—first time in about 5 weeks," she wrote, apparently referring to a therapist. "I was discussing my confused ideas about going to Calif. And thru association we discovered why I was confused—but my sub-conscious seems bent on going. Ain't this silly talk? But I like it. And so I'm still going. I plan to leave about the middle of September. Are you happy?"

The remainder of this section of Lucy's correspondence was mostly consumed with the details of her departure: packing with her girlfriends, the decision of whether to go by Pullman (expensive) or coach; the good-bye presents she was given by the women she worked with at the navy yard (books); the composition of her luggage. She mentioned a referral from the navy yard that she could present to the San Francisco Navy Yard, should she choose to. On September 5, on her way to Chicago—the first leg of her cross-country train trip—she wrote: "I showed some of your pictures to one of the girls on the train. She's seventeen and thought, 'you're a dream.' Yeah? Not for long, Butch. Soon you'll be a reality and then we'll both be happy."

Then, the letters stop. In the first days without her raucous writing voice and her panoramic gaze, I felt a little lost. I found myself contemplating tracking down some of her living relatives—her two daughters and maybe Alfred, if he was still alive—so I could talk to them about the rest of her life: the time between age twenty-six, where I'd left her, and seventy-eight. But that seemed a strange expenditure of time and energy, given that I was supposed to be researching the Brooklyn Navy Yard. In the end I settled on reading some of Alfred's letters to Lucy, beginning at the same time that hers had begun, in April of 1944. And as soon as I began reading, I felt relief: Alfred was a hoot. He had all of Lucy's humor and intelligence; his riotous account of learning to swim in navy boot camp made me laugh out loud. I'd conjured Alfred as a faceless 1950s drone, but I should have trusted Lucy—she would never have picked a guy like that. Soon after beginning Alfred's letters, I felt myself begin letting go, preparing to leave these two extraordinary people to live out their lives together.

The last letter I read of Alfred's involved plans for his furlough to Brooklyn in early May:

"I'm looking forward to those five days together Lucy," he wrote. "I   30
want us to cram a lot of things into it. It'll be easy if we plan it a little bit...

"I'll take you swiming in Hotel St. George Pool and you can see what progress I've made. I'll show you how a sailor rows a boat. I'll show you what a 'boot' can do to a good home-cooked meal. And you'll see that I can dance as flatfootedly as ever.

"You'll see!"

Discussion Questions

1. What type of work was Jennifer Egan engaged in when she "met" Lucille Kolkin? Where was Egan doing this work?
2. What qualities drew the author to Lucy? In what ways are their lives similar?
3. What did Lucy write to Alfred about, once he was assigned to boot camp?
4. What job did Lucy do at the Navy Yard? Why was she asked to do this kind of work? From the reading, who else worked at the Navy Yard?
5. What effect does Lucy's letters have on the author?
6. Why does Egan secretly wish that Lucy had not chosen to follow her husband to Del Monte, California to work as a waitress?
7. What does Egan discover when she finally reads Alfred's letters?

The People, Parks, and Ambience of Brooklyn

Gloria Deák

Gloria Deák is an independent scholar of American cultural affairs. She is the author of several books including *Picturing New York: The City From Its Beginnings to the Present* (2000), which won the 1989 Outstanding Publication Award of the American Historical Print Collectors Society.

"What do your Lordships understand regarding the Ferry between this   1 City [of] New Amsterdam and Breucklen—is it granted to this city or Not?" The question was put, by mail, to the colonial directors in Holland in 1654. Underlying it was a scramble for city revenue. A lively ferry service had developed between the two fledgling cities on either side of the East River. People were ferried across; cattle, horses, oxen, wagons, carts, trunks, boxes, bundles, and the destinies of entire families were ferried across the East River as settlers made their way to the bucolic heights across from Manhattan. But the ferry service was in private—and mischievous—hands, and the local burgomasters saw no reason why this should be so. Besides, the crossing was so miserable, so much a matter of whim and weather that the situation was in dire need of being regularized. Passengers were sometimes stranded out in the open for whole days and nights because of winds, blizzards, tides, fog, storms, ice jams, or because of disputes with the ferryman who might ask double the fare. Or he might row his clients over in a crowded or risky boat, separate passengers and possessions, or decide not to make the crossing at all, if the weather threatened or the tavern beckoned.

To remedy these vexations, Peter Stuyvesant issued the first ferry ordinance wherein fees and crossings were regulated. The authorized lessee was to have a sufficient number of boats and boatmen and, for the shelter of his passengers, he was to provide a covered shed or lodge on both sides of the river. He was not bound to convey anyone over "in a tempest, or when the Windmill hath lowered its sail in consequence of storm or otherwise." Eventually, the wooden lodge ordered by Stuyvesant was replaced on the Brooklyn side of the water at Fulton Street by a two-story house of stone and brick. There, men and horses might have "good Accommodation att

Reasonable Rates" and there the ferry agent was ordered to keep a "publick house of Entertainment."

The site of the "publick house" had already taken on a good bit of local color as seventeenth-century settlers, grouping themselves into six small towns, made constant use of a ferry service that was vital to their farming interests. Five of the six towns that came into being on the western end of Long Island were Dutch: Breucklyn, New Amersford (Flatlands), Midwout (Flat-bush), New Utrecht, and Boswick (Bushwick), to each of which a magistrate was assigned directly responsible to the colony's director-general. A good part of colonial Long Island harbored English settlers, as did Connecticut and Westchester, a fact most worrisome to the Dutch. Lying in the shadow of English colonies to the north, east, and south of them, they were always struggling for clear title to their territories. The sixth town that formed part of the present Brooklyn area was founded in 1645 by English Anabaptists under the leadership of Lady Deborah Moody. It was named Gravesend and was the only one of the six towns to boast a properly laid out settlement.

Reports circulated time and again that the Dutch were plotting to plunder and kill off English inhabitants in the area with the connivance of French and Indian assassins hired for the purpose. An investigation of these reports held that they were propagated by English refugees from New England with the intent of causing disaffection. Stuyvesant issued an ordinance in 1654 for the apprehension of the propagators and offered an award to anyone bringing about an arrest and conviction. Ten years later, the problem was completely resolved in favor of the English: they vanquished the entire New Netherland colony. The six small towns, formed before the takeover, were now grouped under the jurisdiction of Kings County. This administrative unit was conceived during English colonial rule to define what were now the Duke of York's holdings in all the "territoryes towards Connecticut" for which "true and exact Mapps" were to be sent forthwith to the duke. By this time, the town of Breucklyn had already taken a lead in establishing a weekly market as well as an annual autumn fair for cattle and agricultural products. When the first census was taken in 1690, the population of the entire county stood at two thousand, with blacks numbering just under three hundred of the total.

It was the area of Gravesend that witnessed one of the most dramatic of all battles during the Revolutionary War. British warships that had been anchored off Staten Island under Admiral Sir Richard Howe made their way northward to Kings County on August 22, 1776, landing troops along the shore between Gravesend and New Utrecht. By noon of that day, almost fifteen thousand men, the horses of the dragoons, and at least forty cannon had been put ashore; they were joined a few days later by two brigades of Hessian troops.

The ensuing military engagements culminated in the disastrous defeat of George Washington's forces. American soldiers, fighting in the hills of what would later become Prospect Park, were crushed in a vise of enemy soldiers twenty times their number. When possible, they fled down the slopes through muddy swamps hoping to make it to the American forts at Boerum Hill and Fort Greene. Some of the heaviest fighting took place near Baker's Tavern, close to the intersection of modern Fulton Street and Flatbush Avenue. "On Tuesday last [August 27] we got a severe flogging on Long Island," admitted Henry P. Johnston in a letter to his wife; he was an American officer who had taken part in the battle. Washington, reporting on September 19 to the president of the Massachusetts assembly, crisply commented: "In respect to the attack . . . the publick papers will furnish you with accounts nearly true. I shall only add, that . . . we lost about eight hundred men, more than three-fourths of which were taken prisoners."

A victorious end to the conflict allowed traffic over the mile-wide East River crossing to pick up in volume as the decades went by, with Brooklyn and its environs playing the role of Manhattan's breadbasket. From the east side of the river were ferried pigs, sheep, game, chickens, great quantities of fruit, vegetables, and grains, as well as eggs, fish, and oysters. Flat-bottomed boats carried wagons, carts, plows, and cattle to the opposite side. Much was at stake in the transport of these cargoes and in the carrying of passengers, yet maritime mishaps were still part of the scene when the eighteenth century came to a close. Ferrymen were just as often drunk, and capricious weather played havoc with the lightly crafted boats, "We were doused with a wave so large," moaned Médéric–Louis–Elie Moreau de St. Méry, a French exile who often made the crossing in 1794, "that I arrived at my New York lodging soaked and shivering with cold. I . . . only could end this shivering state by swallowing a large glass of sassafras liqueur fortified with brandy." Ferry charges could be paid in money or in kind, the French aristocrat observed, as he watched farmers pay their fare with eggs: two out of each hundred eggs they were transporting was the bartering price.

From the beginning, Brooklyn felt itself a location quite distinct from its raucous, seafaring neighbor across the river. It, too, had a generous stretch of waterfront but it also had abundant farms, wide reaches of bucolic splendor, and more than enough room for residential expansion. As elsewhere in the former colonial territories of the surrounding area, slavery was an essential part of economic life, with roughly one of every four residents of Kings County enslaved in the eighteenth century. From early on, Brooklyn wore a proud, independent air and intended to keep it that way. Moreau de St. Méry had the impression that Manhattan benefitted greatly from its proximity to Brooklyn in a variety of ways: "Thousands of people from New York go for walks in Brooklyn where they eat and exhaust all the fruit, even unripe, that they can reach.... Everyone carries away as much as he wishes." Earlier chroniclers were of the same opinion with regard to the lure of the wondrous, water–lapped area forming the western end of Long Island.

Because the town of Brooklyn was just opposite Manhattan near the ferry, it was the most visited among the towns in the Kings County chain. It accordingly made the greatest strides in cultivating a cosmopolitan identity beginning in the early nineteenth century. The designation of a U.S. Navy shipyard in 1801 on Wallabout Bay, the inauguration of Fulton's steamboat service in 1814, and the opening of the Erie Canal in 1825 were major elements in sparking an industrial bustle along its waterfront. Robert Fulton's genius had been locally acclaimed in 1815 when the first warship powered by steam, the *Fulton,* was built in the Brooklyn Navy Yard. For the rest of the century, Brooklynites were busy both as participants and spectators in a steady parade of innovations that enhanced their lives and insured the kind of prosperity that would eventually allow their once diminutive village of Breucklyn to annex all its Kings County neighbors. A newspaper reporter for the local *Daily Eagle* named Walt Whitman watched the rapid expansion of his town with elation, chronicling local happenings in both prose and poetry. In his elegiac *Song of Myself,* Walt Whitman affirmed:

This is the city and I am one of the citizens,
Whatever interests the rest interests me, politics, wars, markets,
    newspapers, schools,
The mayor and councils, banks, tariffs, steamships, factories, stocks,
    stores, real estate and personal estate.

Under the poet's very eyes, nineteenth-century Brooklyn rapidly expanded in several directions. Brooklyn City Hall was completed in 1849; gaslight was introduced, the Brooklyn Academy of Music founded in 1859, and a network of transport lines reinforced. Already, the imposing Green-Wood Cemetery, commissioned in 1838, had became the most renowned burial ground serving the New York area. Well before its enhancement with Gothic revival gates designed by Richard Upjohn in 1861, the cemetery's fame as a wondrous expanse of tranquility had set in motion plans for Manhattan's Central Park. A proud self-consciousness marking the distinct character of the borough took enough hold by 1863 for the creation of the Long Island Historical Society to which Brooklynites entrusted their historic memorabilia. Looming on the horizon as grandiose projects for the post–Civil War era were the Brooklyn Museum (1893) and the Brooklyn public library system (1897). Perhaps what brought the greatest swell of pride to the area meanwhile was the introduction of two major amenities

10

that streamed from impulses quite unjoined: Prospect Park and the Brooklyn Bridge. In both instances, art and engineering combined to produce stunning results.

The landscaping of the great greensward of Prospect Park was completed in 1874 under the imaginative direction of Calvert Vaux and Frederick Law Olmsted, a team that had only lately been hailed for their design of Central Park in Manhattan. Their conversion of 126 acres in west central Brooklyn into rolling green lawns, ravines, pavilions, meadows, arbors, and bridges was considered by the two men, as well as by an admiring public, their greatest achievement. That no detail escaped their attention is captured in a letter written by the architects to Brooklyn's park commissioner in which they insist that, for a pastoral effect in the stretch of meadow they had created, it would "of course be necessary that sheep and cattle should be allowed to graze in the meadows; beautiful specimens of fine breeds should be selected." Much later, when the poet Marianne Moore assumed the volunteer rank of Prospect Park custodian, she declared it "my only mortal entanglement."

Before another decade passed, the Brooklyn Bridge was completed. Not since the tower of Babel and the great pyramids of Egypt had there been a construction conceived in such massive proportions, went the excited talk among Brooklynites when the bridge was opened to traffic. As an engineering feat, the bridge was the achievement of John and Washington Roebling and the devices by which father and son would make the high suspension possible were examined with interest and awe at the Philadelphia Centennial Fair. Once construction got under way, there were the usual mishaps, the running out of money, the death of the older Roebling, hesitations, jealousies, accidents, and the shattered health of the son. But on May 14, 1883, all that wire, stone, steel, and wood, so long shuffled in random piles, had at last been skillfully woven into a soaring arch. The poet Hart Crane, born as he said "with one toe in the 19th century" (the year was 1889), praised the "swift / Fractioned idiom" of the awesome architecture in "To Brooklyn Bridge":

And thee, across the harbor, silver-paced
As though the sun took step of thee, yet left
Some motion ever unspent in thy stride,—
Implicitly thy freedom staying thee!

Crane had actually spent little time in Brooklyn, unlike the older Whitman who had made it his home for a great portion of his life. Before living out his final years in the New Jersey town of Camden, Walt Whitman had witnessed the influx of ever-continuing waves of European immigrants who crossed over from landing points in Manhattan to start life anew. Thousands and thousands of Old World families peopled Brooklyn in a sympathetic bonding that rendered the borough a pulsating mosaic of ethnic groups. Blacks pouring in from the South added to the African Americans already there. The influx continued well after the year 1898 when Brooklyn, despite its fierce independence, became one of the five boroughs making up the mighty profile of Greater New York.

Not that all Brooklynites were pleased with this marriage of boroughs or with opening their doors to more newcomers. Anticonsolidationists like the Reverend Richard Salter Storrs of the Church of the Pilgrims spoke of the "political sewage of Europe" now discernible in the more recent migrant waves that his borough would have to absorb. Others of his elitist, Protestant leanings feared the influence of Manhattan's corrupt underworld and of its Tammany Hall. St. Clair McKelway, editor of Whitman's paper the *Brooklyn Eagle,* was certain that benefits would flow only one way inasmuch as "our Brooklyn is so lovely and domestic that...New York wants it as a moral and spiritual infusion." The nagging question was, Did Brooklyn really need consolidation for its growth? After all, in 1897 it was the fourth-largest city in the country with a yearly quotient of two thousand ships moored in its docks. In the end, consolidation was voted by the slimmest of margins 644,467 against; 644,744 in favor. Those on the losing side were certain that Brooklyn would now live in the cursed shadow of Manhattan. One of the politicians who helped draft the charter for a Greater New York City was Seth Low, a native Brooklynite and a one-time Brooklyn mayor; he would become the second mayor of the grandly expanded city.

Newcomers continued to pour into Brooklyn after its loss of independence for the very reasons touted by those opposed to their increasing numbers. There they could find "American customs and institutions—including the public schools—[which] are maintained free from evil influence," as Mayor Frederick W. Wurster put it in 1896. They could also find there the resources for a new life in the many churches that conspicuously dotted the landscape, the ever-expanding cultural amenities, the small houses on tree-lined streets, and the exhilarating pleasures of thirty-five miles of beach.

Ah, the beaches! Ah, Coney Island! Was there ever such a fantasy land accessible to pleasure seekers right at their doorstep? Extending five miles (8 km) from east to west, this finger of an island flung out in the Atlantic to the south of Gravesend began its history as a summer resort in the 1830s. When a host of zany pleasures were later added to the natural attraction of the sandy beaches, untold thousands were lured there, especially from the 1890s to the 1950s. "They are going to Coney Island this afternoon," wrote Delmore Schwartz in a fictional story about the 1909 courting days of his parents, "although my mother considers that such pleasures are inferior...being beneath the dignity of so dignified a couple." The underworld, the rich, the prosperous, the undignified, and the poor all found their place there at one time or another. When the subway line was extended to Coney Island in 1920 and the automobile had lured the rich elsewhere, it became the favorite playground for those with less than a dollar to spare. "I had been in America for eighteen months," wrote Isaac Bashevis Singer of his arrival in the 1930s, "but Coney Island still surprised me.... From the beach came a roar [of people] even louder than the ocean."

The roar did not last. The public lost many of the attractions of its democratized playground when a series of catastrophes and an urban renewal program in the 1960s, led by Parks Commissioner Robert Moses, changed the demographics of the area. Steeplechase Park, Luna Park, and Dreamland—three of the highly popular amusement centers that were forerunners of Disneyland—were forced to close, leaving behind a deep nostalgia for the legendary stretch of beach. For some New Yorkers, the memories are indelible. Writing of Coney Island as the poor man's paradise of his youth, the novelist Joseph Heller conjures up in his autobiographical memoir *Now and Then: From Coney Island to Here* (1998) the tantalizing taste lures of his lost Brooklyn playground. "It was futile," he insists, "to search anywhere in the universe for a tastier potato knish than Shatzkin's."

If Coney Island was one of the great turn-of-the-century attractions, the Brooklyn Dodgers ran a close second. The antics of these baseball players, as well as the antics of their fans, made them one of the most popular teams in the country. Dodger personalities were truly esteemed by their public; particularly beloved was Jackie Robinson, the first black National League player. A loud, boroughwide wail followed the eventual transfer of the Dodgers in 1958 to a home base in Los Angeles. It was a dark patch in the lives of Brooklynites. But they could take sustained cheer in the many cultural diversions of the borough, particularly in the expanded offerings of the Brooklyn Academy of Music, whose highly applauded Next Wave Festival was launched in 1981. Located in the Fort Greene neighborhood, the neo-Italianate structure (1908) was once host to Enrico Caruso, Isadora Duncan, and Arturo Toscanini. BAM has since become a magnetic performing arts center for dance, theater, and music that ventures audaciously into the new and the bold. Audacious, too, was the exhibit put on by the Brooklyn Museum of Art in the fall of 1999. Entitled *Sensation,* it forced Manhattan as well as the rest of the nation to sit up and take notice. Brooklynites can take sustained cheer as well in the accolades awarded their borough over the years by a host of writers and poets. Walt Whitman claimed that the nineteenth-century "Brooklyn of ample hills was mine." Carson McCullers found living there in 1941 akin to the company of "a comfortable and complacent duenna" compared with life in Manhattan, "her more brilliant and neurotic sister." The stylish Truman Capote who had worried that Brooklyn was not altogether a fashionable address, opened a literary homily of 1959 with words flung out like a gauntlet: "I live in Brooklyn. By choice. Those ignorant of its allures are entitled to wonder why." In the closing years of the twentieth century, Hope Cooke chose Brooklyn Heights as her home after a long sojourn in Asia as Queen of Sikkim. "Though borough it may be," declared the *Brooklyn Eagle* at the time of consolidation, "Brooklyn it is, Brooklyn it remains, and Brooklynites are we!"

Discussion Questions

1. What was the original role of the Brooklyn ferry? What ferry service issues did passengers face?
2. Why do you think the Dutch, English, and Native Americans did not coexist so well together?
3. In the seventeenth and eighteenth centuries, how were Brooklyn and Manhattan different?
4. Discuss the debate over the merging of the city of Brooklyn with New York.
5. What role did Coney Island play for New Yorkers?
6. What were some of the causes leading to the decline of Brooklyn in the 1960s?
7. Discuss Truman Capote's quote: "I live in Brooklyn. By choice. Those ignorant of its allures are entitled to wonder why."
8. What are some recent changes to Brooklyn? Are they for the most part good or bad?

Research Assignments

1. Research the history and role of ferries in New York. Alternately, write about the history of New York transit and transportation such as its subway system or the construction of its roads, bridges, or tunnels.
2. Read more about Walt Whitman's life and write about his most famous work of poetry "Song of Myself," which appears in *Leaves of Grass*.
3. Research the construction of the Brooklyn Bridge. Elaborate on the many challenges the bridge's engineers and promoters faced.
4. Investigate further the life and work of one of the many New York writers or artists Phillip Lopate mentions in his article.
5. Visit and research the newly constructed Brooklyn Bridge Park and discuss its innovative features.
6. Visit the Brooklyn Navy Yard museum and conduct additional research on any aspect of the Yard's rich history.
7. Visit the Brooklyn Historical Society and explore its extensive archives, letters, and maps. Also, consider reviewing a recent exhibition or a topic featured on its website.

8. Visit Plymouth Church of the Pilgrims in Brooklyn Heights and research Henry Ward Beecher's role as its minister. Consider focusing on the issues he helped promote such as abolitionism and the rights of women.

9. Research the history of your neighborhood. Consider street names, important buildings, and the changing demographics of its inhabitants.

10. Read a local paper (print or online) and find out more about a current issue facing your particular neighborhood.

11. Research the history of Native Americans and/or the Dutch in New York.

12. Research the Battle of Brooklyn which took place during the Revolutionary War.

13. Other interesting research topics include: Green-Wood Cemetery, Prospect Park, the African American community of Weeksville, Brooklyn's Underground Railroad, Lady Moody and Gravesend, Jackie Robinson and the Brooklyn Dodgers, Red Hook and its labor history (especially the film *On the Waterfront*).

SECTION II:
Literary New York

Edward Hopper, American, 1882–1967, *Nighthawks*, 1942, Oil on canvas, 84.1 × 152.4 cm (33⅛ × 60 in.), Friends of American Art Collection, 1942.51, The Art Institute of Chicago. Photograph © The Art Institute of Chicago.

The city seen from the Queensborough Bridge is always the city seen for the first time, in its wild promise of all the mystery and the beauty in the world.

F. Scott Fitzgerald (from *The Great Gatsby*)

Writing is the hardest work in the world not involving heavy lifting.

Pete Hamill

Literary New York

New York inspires great writing like no other city in the world. A quick perusal of some of the city's finest classics provides an outline of a place that is simultaneously real, glorified, and disparaged. From the poetry of Walt Whitman, to the down-and-out reportage of Stephen Crane in *Maggie: A Girl of the Streets*, to the memorable vivisections of the upper crust in Henry James' *Washington Square*, Edith Wharton's *The House of Mirth*, and F. Scott Fitzgerald's *The Great Gatsby*, to exciting exposés of the marginalized in Ann Petry's *The Street*, Ralph Ellison's *Invisible Man* and Jack Kerouac's *The Subterraneans*, to the lyrical poetry of Langston Hughes, Edna St. Vincent Millay, and Li-Young Lee, to modern classics like Tom Wolfe's *Bonfire of the Vanities*, Chang-Rae Lee's *Native Speaker*, and Jonathan Lethem's *The Fortress of Solitude*, New York has been, and still is, the unrivalled setting for fiction and poetry, a setting that entertains and instructs on both a personal and universal level. Indeed, the setting for enduring writers like Whitman has to be New York. Nowhere else, after all, can one find such energy, diversity, spectacle, tension, and movement as in this most "unruly, musical, self-sufficient city—My City!"

The selections collected here are but a microcosm of a much larger field, but they are representative of the types of themes and approaches New York fiction and poetry often contain. In them, we find moments of pure feeling; histories of desperation; songs of hope; musings on loneliness, connection, isolation, and joy. We have organized the fiction chronologically: from Victorian literature of the nineteenth century to Jazz Age modernism, and from Harlem Renaissance representations to postmodernism.

Although the poetry section is arranged chronologically, we also pursued themes that relate to the issues in the earlier chapters, with the idea that artistic reflection and imagination are never wholly separate from actual political, social, and economic concerns. For example, the pieces by Taiyo Na, Honest Abe, and GangStarr are spoken word and hip hop expressions, a musical and cultural form that speaks to the struggles and triumphs associated with the urban condition. The last three poems are what could be called "9/11 poems." The falling of the Twin Towers brought with it feelings of loss, mourning, and melancholy which permeate these poems. The literature of the place where we dwell forever surprises us, broadening our perspectives and changing who we are.

Bartleby, the Scrivener: A Story of Wall Street

Herman Melville

Herman Melville (1819–1891) was born in New York City and spent close to twenty-five years working as a customs inspector at the port. In addition to writing one of the greatest novels in world literature, *Moby-Dick* (which begins in Manhattan), he is also author of what is arguably the greatest New York story of them all, "Bartleby, the Scrivener." This enigmatic story explores the world of Wall Street as it was emerging in the 1850s and points to the effects of modern life on the human soul. It is a story that remains as relevant today as it was then.

Part I

I am a rather elderly man. The nature of my avocations for the last thirty   1
years has brought me into more than ordinary contact with what would
seem an interesting and somewhat singular set of men, of whom, as yet,
nothing that I know of has ever been written—I mean the law-copyists,
or scriveners. I have known very many of them, professionally and pri-
vately, and, if I pleased, could relate divers histories at which good-natured
gentlemen might smile and sentimental souls might weep. But I waive the
biographies of all other scriveners for a few passages in the life of Bartleby,
who was a scrivener, the strangest I ever saw or heard of. While of other
law-copyists I might write the complete life, of Bartleby nothing of that
sort can be done. I believe that no materials exist for a full and satisfactory
biography of this man. It is an irreparable loss to literature. Bartleby was
one of those beings of whom nothing is ascertainable. . . .

Ere introducing the scrivener as he first appeared to me, it is fit I make
some mention of myself, my employees, my business, my chambers and
general surroundings, because some such description is indispensable to
an adequate understanding of the chief character about to be presented.

Imprimis: I am a man who, from his youth upwards, has been filled
with a profound conviction that the easiest way of life is the best. Hence,
though I belong to a profession proverbially energetic and nervous even to
turbulence at times, yet nothing of that sort have I ever suffered to invade

Bartleby, the Scrivener by Herman Melville, 1853.

my peace. I am one of those unambitious lawyers who never addresses a jury or in any way draws down public applause, but, in the cool tranquillity of a snug retreat, do a snug business among rich men's bonds, and mortgages, and title deeds. All who know me consider me an eminently *safe* man....

My chambers were upstairs at No.____ Wall Street. At one end they looked upon the white wall of the interior of a spacious skylight shaft, penetrating the building from top to bottom. This view might have been considered rather tame than otherwise, deficient in what landscape painters call "life." But, if so, the view from the other end of my chambers offered at least a contrast, if nothing more. In that direction, my windows commanded an unobstructed view of a lofty brick wall, black by age and everlasting shade...pushed up to within ten feet of my windowpanes.

At the period just preceding the advent of Bartleby, I had two persons   5
as copyists in my employment, and a promising lad as an office boy. First, Turkey; second, Nippers; third Ginger Nut. These may seem names the like of which are not usually found in the Directory. In truth, they were nicknames, mutually conferred upon each other by my three clerks, and were deemed expressive of their respective persons or characters. Turkey was a short, pursy Englishman, of about my own age—that is, somewhere not far from sixty. In the morning, one might say, his face was of a fine florid hue, but after twelve o'clock—his dinner hour—it blazed like a grate full of Christmas coals; and continued blazing till six o'clock, P.M. There are many singular coincidences I have known in the course of my life, not the least among which was the fact, that, exactly when Turkey displayed his fullest beams from his red and radiant countenance, just then, too, at that critical moment, began the daily period when I considered his business capacities as seriously disturbed for the remainder of the twenty-four hours. Not that he was absolutely idle or averse to business then; far from it. The difficulty was, he was apt to be altogether too energetic. There was a strange, inflamed, flurried, flighty recklessness of activity about him. He would be incautious in dipping his pen into his inkstand. All his blots upon my documents were dropped there after twelve o'clock. Indeed, not only would he be reckless and sadly given to making blots in the afternoon, but some days he went further and was rather noisy....He made an unpleasant racket with his chair; in mending his pens, impatiently split them all to pieces and threw them on the floor in a sudden passion; stood up and leaned over his table, boxing his papers about in a most indecorous manner, very sad to behold in an elderly man like him. Nevertheless, as he was in many ways a most valuable person to me, and all the time before twelve o'clock was the quickest, steadiest creature, too, accomplishing a great deal of work in a style not easily to be matched—for these reasons I was willing to overlook his eccentricities, though indeed, occasionally, I remonstrated with him....

Nippers, the second on my list, was a whiskered, sallow, and upon the whole rather piratical-looking young man of about five and twenty. I always deemed him the victim of two evil powers—ambition and indigestion. The ambition was evinced by a certain impatience of the duties of a mere copyist, an unwarrantable usurpation of strictly professional affairs, such as the original drawing up of legal documents. The indigestion seemed betokened in an occasional nervous testiness and grinning irritability, causing the teeth to audibly grind together over mistakes committed in copying; unnecessary maledictions, hissed rather than spoken, in the heat of business; and especially by a continual discontent with the height of the table where he worked. . . .

Ginger Nut, the third on my list, was a lad some twelve years old. His father was a carman, ambitious of seeing his son on the bench instead of a cart before he died. So he sent him to my office, as student at law, errand boy, cleaner and sweeper, at the rate of one dollar a week. . . . Copying law papers being proverbially a dry, husky sort of business, my two scriveners . . . sent Ginger Nut very frequently for that peculiar cake—small, flat, round, and very spicy—after which he had been named by them.

There was now great work for scriveners. Not only must I push the clerks already with me, but I must have additional help. In answer to my advertisement, a motionless young man one morning stood upon my office threshold, the door being open, for it was summer. I can see that figure now—pallidly neat pitiably respectable, incurably forlorn! It was Bartleby.

After a few words touching his qualifications, I engaged him, glad to have among my corps of copyists a man of so singularly sedate an aspect, which I thought might operate beneficially upon the flighty temper of Turkey and the fiery one of Nippers.

I should have stated before that ground-glass folding doors divided my premises into two parts, one of which was occupied by my scriveners, the other by myself. According to my humor, I threw open these doors or closed them. I resolved to assign Bartleby a corner by the folding doors, but on my side of them so as to have this quiet man within easy call, in case any trifling thing was to be done. I placed his desk close up to a small side window in that part of the room, a window which originally had afforded a lateral view of certain grimy back yards and bricks, but which, owing to subsequent erections, commanded at present no view at all, though it gave some light. Within three feet of the panes was a wall, and the light came down from far above, between two lofty buildings, as from a very small opening in a dome. Still further to a satisfactory arrangement, I procured a high green folding screen, which might entirely isolate Bartleby from my sight, though not remove him from my voice. And thus, in a manner, privacy and society were conjoined.

At first, Bartleby did an extraordinary quantity of writing. As if long famishing for something to copy, he seemed to gorge himself on my documents. There was no pause for digestion. He ran a day and night line, copying by sunlight and by candlelight. I should have been quite delighted with his application, had he been cheerfully industrious. But he wrote on silently, palely, mechanically.

It is, of course, an indispensable part of a scrivener's business to verify the accuracy of his copy, word by word. Where there are two or more scriveners in an office, they assist each other in this examination, one reading from the copy, the other holding the original. It is a very dull, wearisome, and lethargic affair. I can readily imagine that, to some sanguine temperaments, it would be altogether intolerable....

Now and then, in the haste of business, it had been my habit to assist in comparing some brief document myself, calling Turkey or Nippers for this purpose. One object I had in placing Bartleby so handy to me behind the screen was to avail myself of his services on such trivial occasions. It was on the third day, I think, of his being with me, and before any necessity had arisen for having his own writing examined, that, being much hurried to complete a small affair I had in hand, I abruptly called to Bartleby. In my haste and natural expectancy of instant compliance, I sat with my head bent over the original on my desk, and my right hand sideways, and somewhat nervously extended with the copy, so that, immediately upon emerging from his retreat, Bartleby might snatch it and proceed to business without the least delay.

In this very attitude did I sit when I called to him, rapidly stating what it was I wanted him to do—namely, to examine a small paper with me. Imagine my surprise, nay, my consternation, when, without moving from his privacy, Bartleby, in a singularly mild, firm voice, replied, "I would prefer not to."

I sat awhile in perfect silence, rallying my stunned faculties. Immediately it occurred to me that my ears had deceived me, or Bartleby had entirely misunderstood my meaning. I repeated my request in the clearest tone I could assume; but in quite as clear a one came the previous reply, "I would prefer not to."

"Prefer not to," echoed I, rising in high excitement, and crossing the room with a stride. "What do you mean? Are you moon-struck? I want you to help me compare this sheet here—take it," and I thrust it towards him.

"I would prefer not to," said he.

I looked at him steadfastly. His face was leanly composed; his gray eyes dimly calm. Not a wrinkle of agitation rippled him. Had there been the least uneasiness, anger, impatience or impertinence in his manner; in other words, had there been anything ordinarily human about him, doubtless I should have violently dismissed him from the premises. I stood gazing at

15

him awhile, as he went on with his own writing, and then reseated myself at my desk. This is very strange, thought I. What had one best do? But my business hurried me. I concluded to forget the matter for the present, reserving it for my future leisure. So calling Nippers from the other room, the paper was speedily examined.

A few days after this, Bartleby concluded four lengthy documents, being quadruplicates of a week's testimony taken before me in my High Court of Chancery. It became necessary to examine them. It was an important suit, and great accuracy was imperative. Having all things arranged, I called Turkey, Nippers, and Ginger Nut, from the next room, meaning to place the four copies in the hands of my four clerks, while I should read from the original. Accordingly, Turkey, Nippers, and Ginger Nut had taken their seats in a row, each with his document in his hand, when I called to Bartleby to join this interesting group.

"Bartleby! quick, I am waiting."   20

I heard a slow scrape of his chair legs on the uncarpeted floor, and soon he appeared standing at the entrance of his hermitage.

"What is wanted?" said he, mildly.

"The copies, the copies," said I, hurriedly. "We are going to examine them. There"—and I held towards him the fourth quadruplicate.

"I would prefer not to," he said, and gently disappeared behind the screen.

For a few moments I was turned into a pillar of salt, standing at the head   25
of my seated column of clerks. Recovering myself, I advanced towards the screen and demanded the reason for such extraordinary conduct.

"*Why* do you refuse?"

"I would prefer not to."

With any other man I should have flown outright into a dreadful passion, scorned all further words, and thrust him ignominiously from my presence. But there was something about Bartleby that not only strangely disarmed me, but, in a wonderful manner, touched and disconcerted me. I began to reason with him.

"These are your own copies we are about to examine. It is labor saving to you, because one examination will answer for your four papers. It is common usage. Every copyist is bound to help examine his copy. Is it not so? Will you not speak? Answer!"

"I prefer not to," he replied in a flutelike tone. It seemed to me that,   30
while I had been addressing him, he carefully revolved every statement that I made; fully comprehended the meaning; could not gainsay the irresistible conclusion; but, at the same time, some paramount consideration prevailed with him to reply as he did.

"You are decided, then, not to comply with my request—a request made according to common usage and common sense?"

He briefly gave me to understand that on that point my judgment was sound. Yes: his decision was irreversible.

It is seldom the case that, when a man is browbeaten in some unprecedented and violently unreasonable way, he begins to stagger in his own plainest faith. He begins, as it were, vaguely to surmise that, wonderful as it may be, all the justice and all the reason is on the other side. Accordingly, if any disinterested persons are present, he turns to them for some reinforcement for his own faltering mind.

"Turkey," said I, "what do you think of this? Am I not right?"

"With submission, sir," said Turkey, in his blandest tone, "I think that   35
you are."

"Nippers," said I, "what do *you* think of it?"

"I think I should kick him out of the office."

"Ginger Nut," said I, willing to enlist the smallest suffrage in my behalf, "what do *you* think of it?"

"I think, sir, he's a little *luny*," replied Ginger Nut, with a grin.

"You hear what they say," said I, turning towards the screen, "come   40
forth and do your duty."

But he vouchsafed no reply. I pondered a moment in sore perplexity. But once more business hurried me. I determined again to postpone the consideration of this dilemma to my future leisure. . . . Meanwhile Bartleby sat in his hermitage, oblivious to everything but his own peculiar business there.

Part II

Nothing so aggravates an earnest person as a passive resistance. . . . Even so, for the most part, I regarded Bartleby and his ways. Poor fellow! thought I, he means no mischief; it is plain he intends no insolence; his aspect sufficiently evinces that his eccentricities are involuntary. He is useful to me. I can get along with him. . . . But one afternoon the evil impulse in me mastered me, and the following little scene ensued:

"Bartleby," said I, "when those papers are all copied, I will compare them with you."

"I would prefer not to."

"How? Surely you do not mean to persist in that mulish vagary?"   45
No answer.

"Bartleby," said I, "Ginger Nut is away; just step around to the Post Office, won't you? (it was but a three minutes' walk), and see if there is anything for me."

"I would prefer not to."

"You *will* not?"

"I *prefer* not."   50

I staggered to my desk and sat there in a deep study. My blind inveteracy returned. Was there any other thing in which I could procure myself to be ignominiously repulsed by this lean, penniless wight?—my hired clerk? What added thing is there, perfectly reasonable, that he will be sure to refuse to do? "Bartleby!"

No answer.

"Bartleby," in a louder tone.

No answer.

"Bartleby," I roared.   55

Like a very ghost, agreeably to the laws of magical invocation, at the third summons he appeared at the entrance of his hermitage.

"Go to the next room, and tell Nippers to come to me."

"I prefer not to," he respectfully and slowly said, and mildly disappeared.

"Very good, Bartleby," said I, in a quiet sort of serenely severe self-possessed tone, intimating the unalterable purpose of some terrible retribution very close at hand. At the moment I half intended something of the kind. But upon the whole, as it was drawing towards my dinner hour, I thought it best to put on my hat and walk home for the day, suffering much from perplexity and distress of mind. . .

Now, one Sunday morning I happened to go to Trinity Church, to hear   60
a celebrated preacher, and finding myself rather early on the ground I thought I would walk round to my chambers for a while. Luckily I had my key with me, but upon applying it to the lock, I found it resisted by something inserted from the inside. Quite surprised, I called out, when to my consternation a key was turned from within, and, thrusting his lean visage at me, and holding the door ajar, the apparition of Bartleby appeared, in his shirt sleeves . . . saying quietly that he was sorry but he was deeply engaged just then, and—preferred not admitting me at present. In a brief word or two, he moreover added, that perhaps I had better walk about the block two or three times, and by that time he would probably have concluded his affairs. . . .

Full of a restless curiosity, at last I returned to the door. Without hindrance I inserted my key, opened it, and entered. Bartleby was not to be seen. I looked round anxiously, peeped behind his screen; but it was very plain that he was gone. Upon more closely examining the place, I surmised that for an indefinite period Bartleby must have ate, dressed, and slept in my office, and that too without plate, mirror, or bed. The cushioned seat of a rickety old sofa in one corner bore the faint impress of a lean, reclining form. Rolled away under his desk, I found a blanket; under the empty grate, a blacking box and brush; on a chair, a tin basin, with soap and a ragged towel; in a newspaper a few crumbs of ginger-nuts and a morsel of cheese. Yet, thought I, it is evident enough that Bartleby has been making his home here, keeping bachelor's hall all by himself. Immediately then the thought came sweeping across me, What miserable friendliness and loneliness are here revealed! His poverty is great; but his solitude, how horrible!

That morning...I walked homeward, thinking what I would do with Bartleby. Finally, I resolved upon this—I would put certain calm questions to him the next morning touching his history, etc., and if he declined to answer them openly and unreservedly (and I supposed he would prefer not) then to give him a twenty-dollar bill over and above whatever I might owe him, and tell him his services were no longer required; but that if in any other way I could assist him, I would be happy to do so, especially if he desired to return to his native place, wherever that might be, I would willingly help to defray the expenses. Moreover, if, after reaching home, he found himself at any time in want of aid, a letter from him would be sure of a reply. The next morning came. "Bartleby," said I, gently calling to him behind his screen. No reply.

"Bartleby," said I, in a still gentler tone, "come here—I am not going to ask you to do anything you would prefer not to do—I simply wish to speak to you."

Upon this he noiselessly slid into view.

"Will you tell me, Bartleby, where you were born?"   65

"I would prefer not to."

"Will you tell me *anything* about yourself?"

"I would prefer not to."

"But what reasonable objection can you have to speak to me? I feel friendly towards you."

He did not look at me while I spoke, but kept his glance fixed upon my   70 bust of Cicero, which, as I then sat, was directly behind me, some six inches above my head.

"What is your answer, Bartleby," said I.

"At present I prefer to give no answer," he said, and retired into his hermitage.

It was rather weak in me I confess, but his manner, on this occasion, nettled me. Not only did there seem to lurk in it a certain calm disdain, but his perverseness seemed ungrateful, considering the undeniable good usage and indulgence he had received from me.

Again I sat ruminating what I should do. Mortified as I was at his behavior, and resolved as I had been to dismiss him when I entered my office, nevertheless I strangely felt something superstitious knocking at my heart, and forbidding me to carry out my purpose, and denouncing me for a villain if I dared to breathe one bitter word against this forlornest of mankind. At last, familiarly drawing my chair behind his screen, I sat down and said: "Bartleby, never mind, then, about revealing your history; but let me entreat you, as a friend, to comply as far as may be with the usages of this office. Say now, you will help to examine papers tomorrow or next day: in short, say now, that in a day or two you will begin to be a little reasonable: —say so, Bartleby."

"At present I would prefer not to be a little reasonable," was his mildly   75 cadaverous reply....

The next day I noticed that Bartleby did nothing but stand at his window in his dead-wall reverie. Upon asking him why he did not write, he said that he had decided upon doing no more writing.

"Why, how now? what next?" exclaimed I, "do no more writing?"

"No more."

"And what is the reason?"

"Do you not see the reason for yourself?" he indifferently replied.   80

I looked steadfastly at him, and perceived that his eyes looked dull and glazed. Instantly it occurred to me that his unexampled diligence in copying by his dim window for the first few weeks of his stay with me might have temporarily impaired his vision.

I was touched. I said something in condolence with him, I hinted that of course he did wisely in abstaining from writing for a while; and urged him to embrace that opportunity of taking wholesome exercise in the open air. This, however, he did not do. A few days after this, my other clerks being absent, and being in a great hurry to dispatch certain letters by the mail, I thought that, having nothing else earthly to do, Bartleby would surely be less inflexible than usual, and carry these letters to the Post Office. But he blankly declined. So, much to my inconvenience, I went myself.

Still added days went by. Whether Bartleby's eyes improved or not, I could not say. To all appearance, I thought they did. But when I asked him if they did, he vouchsafed no answer. At all events, he would do no copying. At last, in reply to my urgings, he informed me that he had permanently given up copying.

"What!" exclaimed I; "suppose your eyes should get entirely well— better than ever before—would you not copy then?"

"I have given up copying," he answered, and slid aside.   85

He remained as ever, a fixture in my chamber. Nay—if that were possible—he became still more of a fixture than before. What was to be done?

Part III

Since he will not quit me, I must quit him. I will change my offices; I will move elsewhere, and give him fair notice that if I find him on my new premises I will then proceed against him as a common trespasser.

Acting accordingly, next day I thus addressed him: "I find these chambers too far from the City Hall; the air is unwholesome. In a word, I propose to remove my offices next week, and shall no longer require your services. I tell you this now, in order that you may seek another place."

He made no reply, and nothing more was said.

On the appointed day I engaged carts and men, proceeded to my chambers, and, having but little furniture, everything was removed in a few hours. Throughout, the scrivener remained standing behind the screen, which I directed to be removed the last thing. It was withdrawn; and, being folded up like a huge folio, left him the motionless occupant of a naked room. I stood in the entry watching him a moment, while something from within me upbraided me.   90

I re-entered, with my hand in my pocket and my heart in my mouth.

"Good-bye, Bartleby; I am going—good-bye; and God some way bless you; and take that," slipping something in his hand. But it dropped upon the floor, and then—strange to say—I tore myself from him whom I had so longed to be rid of....

Several days passed, and I heard nothing more; and, though I often felt a charitable prompting to call at the place and see poor Bartleby, yet a certain squeamishness, of I know not what, withheld me.

All is over with him, by this time, thought I at last, when, through another week, no further intelligence reached me. But, coming to my room the day after, I found several persons waiting at my door in a high state of nervous excitement.

"That's the man—here he comes," cried the foremost one, whom I recognized as the lawyer who had previously called upon me alone.   95

"You must take him away, sir, at once," cried a portly person among them, advancing upon me, and whom I knew to be the landlord of No.____ Wall Street. "These gentlemen, my tenants, cannot stand it any longer. Mr. B____," pointing to the lawyer; "has turned him out of his room, and he now persists in haunting the building generally, sitting upon the banisters of the stairs by day, and sleeping in the entry by night. Everybody is concerned; clients are leaving the offices; some fears are entertained of a mob; something you must do, and that without delay."

Aghast at this torrent, I fell back before it, and would fain have locked myself in my new quarters. In vain I persisted that Bartleby was nothing to me—no more than to anyone else. In vain—I was the last person known to have anything to do with him, and they held me to the terrible account. Fearful, then of being exposed in the papers (as one person present obscurely threatened), I considered the matter, and at length said that if the lawyer would give me a confidential interview with the scrivener, in his (the lawyer's) own room, I would, that afternoon, strive my best to rid them of the nuisance they complained of.

Going upstairs to my old haunt, there was Bartleby silently sitting upon the banister at the landing.

"What are you doing here, Bartleby?" said I.

"Sitting upon the banister," he mildly replied. 100

I motioned him into the lawyer's room, who then left us.

"Bartleby," said I, "are you aware that you are the cause of great tribulation to me, by persisting in occupying the entry after being dismissed from the office?"

No answer.

"Now one of two things must take place. Either you must do something, or something must be done to you. Now what sort of business would you like to engage in? Would you like to re-engage in copying for someone?"

"No; I would prefer not to make any change." 105

"Would you like a clerkship in a dry-goods store?"

"There is too much confinement about that. No, I would not like a clerkship; but I am not particular."

"Too much confinement," I cried; "why you keep yourself confined all the time!"

"I would prefer not to take a clerkship," he rejoined, as if to settle that little item at once.

"How would a bartender's business suit you? There is no trying of the 110 eyesight in that."

"I would not like it at all; though, as I said before, I am not particular."

His unwonted wordiness inspirited me. I returned to the charge.

"Well, then, would you like to travel through the country collecting bills for the merchants? That would improve your health."

"No, I would prefer to be doing something else."

"How, then, would going as a companion to Europe to entertain some 115 young gentleman with your conversation—how would that suit you?"

"Not at all. It does not strike me that there is anything definite about that. I like to be stationary. But I am not particular."

"Stationary you shall be, then," I cried, now losing all patience, and, for the first time in all my exasperating connection with him, fairly flying into a passion. "If you do not go away from these premises before night, I shall feel bound—indeed, I *am* bound—to—to—to quit the premises myself!" I rather absurdly concluded, knowing not with what possible threat to try to frighten his immobility into compliance.

"Bartleby," said I, in the kindest tone I could assume under such exciting circumstances, "will you go home with me now—not to my office, but my dwelling—and remain there till we can conclude upon some convenient arrangement for you at our leisure? Come, let us start now, right away."

"No; at present I would prefer not to make any change at all."

I answered nothing, but, effectually dodging everyone by the suddenness and rapidity of my flight, rushed from the building, ran up Wall Street towards Broadway, and, jumping into the first omnibus, was soon removed from pursuit...So fearful was I of being again hunted out by the incensed landlord and his exasperated tenants that, surrendering my business to Nippers for a few days, I drove about the upper part of the town and through the suburbs in my rockaway [carriage]; crossed over to Jersey City and Hoboken, and paid fugitive visits to Manhattanville and Astoria. In fact, I almost lived in my rockaway for the time.

When again I entered my office, a note from the landlord lay upon the desk. I opened it with trembling hands. It informed me that the writer had sent to the police, and had Bartleby removed to the Tombs[1] as a vagrant. Moreover, since I knew more about him than anyone else, he wished me to appear at that place and make a suitable statement of the facts....

The same day I received the note, I went to the Tombs, or to speak more properly, the Halls of Justice. Seeking the right officer, I stated the purpose of my call, and was informed that the individual I described was indeed within. I then assured him that Bartleby was a perfectly honest man, and greatly to be compassionated, however unaccountably eccentric. I narrated all I knew, and closed by suggesting the idea of letting him remain in as indulgent confinement as possible till something less harsh might be done—though, indeed, I hardly knew what. At all events, if nothing else could be decided upon, the almshouse must receive him. I then begged to have an interview.

Being under no disgraceful charge, and quite serene and harmless in all his ways, they had permitted him freely to wander about the prison, and, especially, in the inclosed grass-platted yards thereof. And so I found him there, standing all alone in the quietest of the yards, his face towards a high wall, while all around, from the narrow slits of the jail windows I thought I saw peering out upon him the eyes of murderers and thieves.

"Bartleby!"

"I know you," he said, without looking round—"and I want nothing to say to you."

"It was not I that brought you here, Bartleby," said I, keenly pained at his implied suspicion. "And, to you, this should not be so vile a place.

120

125

---

[1] A well-known New York City prison in the 19th century.

Nothing reproachful attaches to you by being here. And see, it is not so sad a place as one might think. Look, there is the sky, and here is the grass."

"I know where I am," he replied, but would say nothing more, and so I left him.

As I entered the corridor again, a broad meatlike man in an apron accosted me, and, jerking his thumb over his shoulder said—"Is that your friend?"

"Yes."

"Does he want to starve? If he does, let him live on the prison fare, that's all."   130

"Who are you?" asked I, not knowing what to make of such an unofficially speaking person in such a place.

"I am the grubman. Such gentlemen as have friends here hire me to provide them with something good to eat."

"Is this so?" said I, turning to the turnkey.

He said it was.

"Well, then," said I, slipping some silver into the grubman's hands (for   135
so they called him), "I want you to give particular attention to my friend there; let him have the best dinner you can get. And you must be as polite to him as possible."

"Introduce me, will you?" said the grubman, looking at me with an expression which seemed to say he was all impatience for an opportunity to give a specimen of his breeding.

Thinking it would prove of benefit to the scrivener, I acquiesced, and, asking the grubman his name, went up with him to Bartleby.

"Bartleby, this is a friend; you will find him very useful to you."

"Your sarvant, sir, your sarvant," said the grubman, making a low salutation behind his apron. "Hope you find it pleasant here, sir; nice grounds—cool apartments—hope you'll stay with us some time—try to make it agreeable. What will you have for dinner today?"

"I prefer not to dine today," said Bartleby, turning away. "It would dis-   140
agree with me; I am unused to dinners." So saying, he slowly moved to the other side of the inclosure and took up a position fronting the dead-wall.

"How's this?" said the grubman, addressing me with a stare of astonishment. "He's odd, ain't he?"

"I think he is a little deranged," said I, sadly.

Some few days after this, I again obtained admission to the Tombs, and went through the corridors in quest of Bartleby; but without finding him.

"I saw him coming from his cell not long ago," said a turnkey, "maybe he's gone to loiter in the yards."

So I went in that direction.   145

"Are you looking for the silent man?" said another turnkey, passing me. "Yonder he lies—sleeping in the yard there. Tis not twenty minutes since I saw him lie down."

The yard was entirely quiet. It was not accessible to the common prisoners. The surrounding walls, of amazing thickness, kept off all sounds behind them. The Egyptian character of the masonry weighed upon me with its gloom.

Strangely huddled at the base of the wall, his knees drawn up and lying on his side, his head touching the cold stones, I saw the wasted Bartleby. But nothing stirred. I paused, then went close up to him, stooped over, and saw that his dim eyes were open; otherwise he seemed profoundly sleeping. Something prompted me to touch him. I felt his hand, when a tingling shiver ran up my arm and down my spine to my feet.

The round face of the grubman peered upon me now. "His dinner is ready. Won't he dine today, either? Or does he live without dining?"

"Lives without dining," said I, and closed the eyes.   150

"Eh!—He's asleep, ain't he?"

"With kings and counselors,"[2] murmured I.

***

There would seem little need for proceeding further in this history. Imagination will readily supply the meager recital of poor Bartleby's internment. But ere parting with the reader, let me say, that if this little narrative has sufficiently interested him, to awaken curiosity as to who Bartleby was, and what manner of life he led prior to the present narrator's making his acquaintance, I can only reply, that in such curiosity I fully share, but am wholly unable to gratify it. Yet here I hardly know whether I should divulge one little item of rumor, which came to my ear a few months after the scrivener's decease. Upon what basis it rested, I could never ascertain; and hence, how true it is I cannot now tell. But inasmuch as this vague report has not been without a certain strange suggestive interest to me, however sad, it may prove the same with some others; and so I will briefly mention it. The report was this: that Bartleby had been a subordinate clerk in the Dead Letter Office at Washington,[3] from which he had been suddenly removed by a change in the administration. When I think over this rumor, I cannot adequately express the emotions which seize me. Dead letters! Does it not sound like dead men? Conceive a man by nature and misfortune prone to a pallid hopelessness, can any business seem more fitted to heighten it than

---

[2] From Job's Lament in the Bible: Bartleby is now dead, delivered from his troubled existence.

[3] The Dead Letter office is where letters go when recipients cannot be found.

that of continually handling these dead letters and assorting them for the flames? For by the cart-load they are annually burned. Sometimes from out of the folded paper the pale clerk takes a ring:—the finger it was meant for, perhaps, moulders in the grave; a bank-note sent in swiftest charity:—he whom it would relieve, nor eats nor hungers any more; pardon for those who died despairing; hope for those who died unhoping; good tidings for those who died stifled by unrelieved calamities. On errands of life, these letters speed to death.

Ah, Bartleby! Ah, humanity!

A Dark-Brown Dog

Stephen Crane

Stephen Crane (1871–1900) had a short but brilliant life. He is best known for two masterpieces of naturalistic literary fiction, *The Red Badge of Courage,* about a young private's experience in the Civil War, and *Maggie: A Girl of the Streets,* a novella set in New York City that follows the misfortunes of a young girl once she is kicked out of her tenement household. "A Dark-Brown Dog" is one of many stories also set in New York's Lower East Side at the turn of the nineteenth century, an area densely populated and known for its vice and harsh living conditions. This shocking tale speaks to the cruelty—and cruel lives—of the impoverished and neglected of the city at the time.

A CHILD was standing on a street-corner. He leaned with one shoulder against a high board fence and swayed the other to and fro, the while kicking carelessly at the gravel. 1

Sunshine beat upon the cobbles, and a lazy summer wind raised yellow dust which trailed in clouds down the avenue. Clattering trucks moved with indistinctness through it. The child stood dreamily gazing.

After a time, a little dark-brown dog came trotting with an intent air down the sidewalk. A short rope was dragging from his neck. Occasionally he trod upon the end of it and stumbled.

He stopped opposite the child, and the two regarded each other. The dog hesitated for a moment, but presently he made some little advances with his tail. The child put out his hand and called him. In an apologetic manner the dog came close, and the two had an interchange of friendly pattings and waggles. The dog became more enthusiastic with each moment of the interview, until with his gleeful caperings he threatened to overturn the child. Whereupon the child lifted his hand and struck the dog a blow upon the head.

This thing seemed to overpower and astonish the little dark-brown dog, and wounded him to the heart. He sank down in despair at the child's feet. When the blow was repeated, together with an admonition in childish sentences, he turned over upon his back, and held his paws in a peculiar manner. At the same time with his ears and his eyes he offered a small prayer to the child. 5

He looked so comical on his back, and holding his paws peculiarly, that the child was greatly amused and gave him little taps repeatedly, to keep him so. But the little dark-brown dog took this chastisement in the most serious way and no doubt considered that he had committed some grave crime, for he wriggled contritely and showed his repentance in every way that was in his power. He pleaded with the child and petitioned him, and offered more prayers.

At last the child grew weary of this amusement and turned toward home. The dog was praying at the time. He lay on his back and turned his eyes upon the retreating form.

Presently he struggled to his feet and started after the child. The latter wandered in a perfunctory way toward his home, stopping at times to investigate various matters. During one of these pauses he discovered the little dark-brown dog who was following him with the air of a footpad.

The child beat his pursuer with a small stick he had found. The dog lay down and prayed until the child had finished, and resumed his journey. Then he scrambled erect and took up the pursuit again.

On the way to his home the child turned many times and beat the dog,   10 proclaiming with childish gestures that he held him in contempt as an unimportant dog, with no value save for a moment. For being this quality of animal the dog apologized and eloquently expressed regret, but he continued stealthily to follow the child. His manner grew so very guilty that he slunk like an assassin.

When the child reached his doorstep, the dog was industriously ambling a few yards in the rear. He became so agitated with shame when he again confronted the child that he forgot the dragging rope. He tripped upon it and fell forward.

The child sat down on the step and the two had another interview. During it the dog greatly exerted himself to please the child. He performed a few gambols with such abandon that the child suddenly saw him to be a valuable thing. He made a swift, avaricious charge and seized the rope.

He dragged his captive into a hall and up many long stairways in a dark tenement. The dog made willing efforts, but he could not hobble very skillfully up the stairs because he was very small and soft, and at last the pace of the engrossed child grew so energetic that the dog became panic-stricken. In his mind he was being dragged toward a grim unknown. His eyes grew wild with the terror of it. He began to wiggle his head frantically and to brace his legs.

The child redoubled his exertions. They had a battle on the stairs. The child was victorious because he was completely absorbed in his purpose, and because the dog was very small. He dragged his acquirement to the door of his home, and finally with triumph across the threshold.

No one was in. The child sat down on the floor and made overtures to   15 the dog. These the dog instantly accepted. He beamed with affection upon his new friend. In a short time they were firm and abiding comrades.

When the child's family appeared, they made a great row. The dog was examined and commented upon and called names. Scorn was leveled at him from all eyes, so that he became much embarrassed and drooped like a scorched plant. But the child went sturdily to the center of the floor, and, at the top of his voice, championed the dog. It happened that he was roaring protestations, with his arms clasped about the dog's neck, when the father of the family came in from work.

The parent demanded to know what the blazes they were making the kid howl for. It was explained in many words that the infernal kid wanted to introduce a disreputable dog into the family.

A family council was held. On this depended the dog's fate, but he in no way heeded, being busily engaged in chewing the end of the child's dress.

The affair was quickly ended. The father of the family, it appears, was in a particularly savage temper that evening, and when he perceived that it would amaze and anger everybody if such a dog were allowed to remain, he decided that it should be so. The child, crying softly, took his friend off to a retired part of the room to hobnob with him, while the father quelled a fierce rebellion of his wife. So it came to pass that the dog was a member of the household.

He and the child were associated together at all times save when the child slept. The child became a guardian and a friend. If the large folk kicked the dog and threw things at him, the child made loud and violent objections. Once when the child had run, protesting loudly, with tears raining down his face and his arms outstretched, to protect his friend, he had been struck in the head with a very large saucepan from the hand of his father, enraged at some seeming lack of courtesy in the dog. Ever after, the family were careful how they threw things at the dog. Moreover, the latter grew very skilful in avoiding missiles and feet. In a small room containing a stove, a table, a bureau and some chairs, he would display strategic ability of a high order, dodging, feinting and scuttling about among the furniture. He could force three or four people armed with brooms, sticks and handfuls of coal, to use all their ingenuity to get in a blow. And even when they did, it was seldom that they could do him a serious injury or leave any imprint.

But when the child was present these scenes did not occur. It came to be recognized that if the dog was molested, the child would burst into sobs, and as the child, when started, was very riotous and practically unquenchable, the dog had therein a safeguard.

However, the child could not always be near. At night, when he was asleep, his dark-brown friend would raise from some black corner a wild, wailful cry, a song of infinite loneliness and despair, that would go

20

shuddering and sobbing among the buildings of the block and cause people to swear. At these times the singer would often be chased all over the kitchen and hit with a great variety of articles.

Sometimes, too, the child himself used to beat the dog, although it is not known that he ever had what truly could be called a just cause. The dog always accepted these thrashings with an air of admitted guilt. He was too much of a dog to try to look to be a martyr or to plot revenge. He received the blows with deep humility, and furthermore he forgave his friend the moment the child had finished, and was ready to caress the child's hand with his little red tongue.

When misfortune came upon the child, and his troubles overwhelmed him, he would often crawl under the table and lay his small distressed head on the dog's back. The dog was ever sympathetic. It is not to be supposed that at such times he took occasion to refer to the unjust beatings his friend, when provoked, had administered to him.

He did not achieve any notable degree of intimacy with the other   25
members of the family. He had no confidence in them, and the fear that he would express at their casual approach often exasperated them exceedingly. They used to gain a certain satisfaction in underfeeding him, but finally his friend the child grew to watch the matter with some care, and when he forgot it, the dog was often successful in secret for himself.

So the dog prospered. He developed a large bark, which came wondrously from such a small rug of a dog. He ceased to howl persistently at night. Sometimes, indeed, in his sleep, he would utter little yells, as from pain, but that occurred, no doubt, when in his dreams he encountered huge flaming dogs who threatened him direfully.

His devotion to the child grew until it was a sublime thing. He wagged at his approach; he sank down in despair at his departure. He could detect the sound of the child's step among all the noises of the neighborhood. It was like a calling voice to him.

The scene of their companionship was a kingdom governed by this terrible potentate, the child; but neither criticism nor rebellion ever lived for an instant in the heart of the one subject. Down in the mystic, hidden fields of his little dog-soul bloomed flowers of love and fidelity and perfect faith.

The child was in the habit of going on many expeditions to observe strange things in the vicinity. On these occasions his friend usually jogged aimfully along behind. Perhaps, though, he went ahead. This necessitated his turning around every quarter-minute to make sure the child was coming. He was filled with a large idea of the importance of these journeys. He would carry himself with such an air! He was proud to be the retainer of so great a monarch.

One day, however, the father of the family got quite exceptionally 30
drunk. He came home and held carnival with the cooking utensils, the furniture and his wife. He was in the midst of this recreation when the child,
followed by the dark-brown dog, entered the room. They were returning
from their voyages.

The child's practised eye instantly noted his father's state. He dived under
the table, where experience had taught him was a rather safe place. The dog,
lacking skill in such matters, was, of course, unaware of the true condition of
affairs. He looked with interested eyes at his friend's sudden dive. He inter-
preted it to mean: Joyous gambol. He started to patter across the floor to join
him. He was the picture of a little dark-brown dog en route to a friend.

The head of the family saw him at this moment. He gave a huge howl
of joy, and knocked the dog down with a heavy coffee-pot. The dog, yelling in supreme astonishment and fear, writhed to his feet and ran for cover.
The man kicked out with a ponderous foot. It caused the dog to swerve as
if caught in a tide. A second blow of the coffee-pot laid him upon the floor.

Here the child, uttering loud cries, came valiantly forth like a knight.
The father of the family paid no attention to these calls of the child, but
advanced with glee upon the dog. Upon being knocked down twice in
swift succession, the latter apparently gave up all hope of escape. He rolled
over on his back and held his paws in a peculiar manner. At the same time
with his eyes and his ears he offered up a small prayer.

But the father was in a mood for having fun, and it occurred to him that
it would be a fine thing to throw the dog out of the window. So he reached
down and, grabbing the animal by a leg, lifted him, squirming, up. He
swung him two or three times hilariously about his head, and then flung
him with great accuracy through the window.

The soaring dog created a surprise in the block. A woman watering 35
plants in an opposite window gave an involuntary shout and dropped
a flower-pot. A man in another window leaned perilously out to watch
the flight of the dog. A woman who had been hanging out clothes in a
yard began to caper wildly. Her mouth was filled with clothes-pins, but
her arms gave vent to a sort of exclamation. In appearance she was like a
gagged prisoner. Children ran whooping.

The dark-brown body crashed in a heap on the roof of a shed five stories below. From thence it rolled to the pavement of an alleyway.

The child in the room far above burst into a long, dirge-like cry, and
toddled hastily out of the room. It took him a long time to reach the alley,
because his size compelled him to go downstairs backward, one step at a
time, and holding with both hands to the step above.

When they came for him later, they found him seated by the body of
his dark-brown friend.

Mrs. Manstey's View

Edith Wharton

Edith Wharton (1862–1937) is recognized today as one of the most important writers of the early twentieth century. In novels such as *The House of Mirth* and *The Age of Innocence,* she wrote about wealthy New Yorkers, often times criticizing their customs and attitudes. "Mrs. Manstey's View" is an early tale by Wharton written when she was just beginning to discover New York as a rich subject for stories. Though written over a century ago, its focus on anger and despair over urban development is a theme that still resonates with present day New Yorkers.

The view from Mrs. Manstey's window was not a striking one, but to her   1
at least it was full of interest and beauty. Mrs. Manstey occupied the back room on the third floor of a New York boardinghouse, in a street where the ash-barrels lingered late on the sidewalk and the gaps in the pavement would have staggered a Quintus Curtius [a famous Roman historian]. She was the widow of a clerk in a large wholesale house, and his death had left her alone, for her only daughter had married in California, and could not afford the long journey to New York to see her mother. Mrs. Manstey, perhaps, might have joined her daughter in the West, but they had now been so many years apart that they had ceased to feel any need of each other's society, and their intercourse had long been limited to the exchange of a few perfunctory letters, written with indifference by the daughter, and with difficulty by Mrs. Manstey, whose right hand was growing stiff with gout. Even had she felt a stronger desire for her daughter's companionship, Mrs. Manstey's increasing infirmity, which caused her to dread the three flights of stairs between her room and the street, would have given her pause on the eve of undertaking so long a journey; and without perhaps, formulating these reasons she had long since accepted as a matter of course her solitary life in New York.

She was, indeed, not quite lonely, for a few friends still toiled up now and then to her room; but their visits grew rare as the years went by. Mrs. Manstey had never been a sociable woman, and during her husband's lifetime his companionship had been all-sufficient to her. For many years she had cherished a desire to live in the country, to have a hen-house and a garden; but this longing had faded with age, leaving only in the breast of the uncommunicative old woman a vague tenderness for plants and animals. It was, perhaps, this tenderness which made her cling so fervently to her view from her window, a view in which the most optimistic eye would at first have failed to discover anything admirable.

Mrs. Manstey, from her coign of vantage (a slightly projecting bow-window where she nursed an ivy and a succession of unwholesome-looking bulbs), looked out first upon the yard of her own dwelling, of which, however, she could get but a restricted glimpse. Still, her gaze took in the topmost boughs of the ailanthus below her window, and she knew how early each year the clump of dicentra strung its bending stalk with hearts of pink.

But of greater interest were the yards beyond. Being for the most part attached to boarding-houses they were in a state of chronic untidiness and fluttering, on certain days of the week, with miscellaneous garments and frayed table-cloths. In spite of this Mrs. Manstey found much to admire in the long vista which she commanded. Some of the yards were, indeed, but stony wastes, with grass in the cracks of the pavement and no shade in spring save that afforded by the intermittent leafage of the clotheslines. These yards Mrs. Manstey disapproved of, but the others, the green ones, she loved. She had grown used to their disorder; the broken barrels, the empty bottles and paths unswept no longer annoyed her; hers was the happy faculty of dwelling on the pleasanter side of the prospect before her.

In the very next enclosure did not a magnolia open its hard white flowers against the watery blue of April? And was there not, a little way down the line, a fence foamed over every May with lilac waves of wistaria? Farther still, a horse-chestnut lifted its candelabra of buff and pink blossoms above broad fans of foliage; while in the opposite yard June was sweet with the breath of a neglected syringa, which persisted in growing in spite of the countless obstacles opposed to its welfare.

But if nature occupied the front rank in Mrs. Manstey's view, there was much of a more personal character to interest her in the aspect of the houses and their inmates. She deeply disapproved of the mustard-colored curtains which had lately been hung in the doctor's window opposite; but she glowed with pleasure when the house farther down had its old bricks washed with a coat of paint. The occupants of the houses did not often show themselves at the back windows, but the servants were always in sight. Noisy slatterns, Mrs. Manstey pronounced the greater number; she knew their ways and hated them. But to the quiet cook in the newly painted house, whose mistress bullied her, and who secretly fed the stray cats at nightfall, Mrs. Manstey's warmest sympathies were given. On one occasion her feelings were racked by the neglect of a housemaid, who for two days forgot to feed the parrot committed to her care. On the third day, Mrs. Manstey, in spite of her gouty hand, had just penned a letter, beginning: "Madam, it is now three days since your parrot has been fed," when the forgetful maid appeared at the window with a cup of seed in her hand.

But in Mrs. Manstey's more meditative moods it was the narrowing perspective of far-off yards which pleased her best. She loved, at twilight, when the distant brown-stone spire seemed melting in the fluid yellow of the west, to lose herself in vague memories of a trip to Europe, made years ago, and now reduced in her mind's eye to a pale phantasmagoria of indistinct steeples and dreamy skies. Perhaps at heart Mrs. Manstey was an artist; at all events she was sensible of many changes of color unnoticed by the average eye, and dear to her as the green of early spring was the black lattice of branches against a cold sulphur sky at the close of a snowy day. She enjoyed, also, the sunny thaws of March, when patches of earth showed through the snow, like inkspots spreading on a sheet of white blotting-paper; and, better still, the haze of boughs, leafless but swollen, which replaced the clear-cut tracery of winter. She even watched with a certain interest the trail of smoke from a far-off factory chimney, and missed a detail in the landscape when the factory was closed and the smoke disappeared.

Mrs. Manstey, in the long hours which she spent at her window, was not idle. She read a little, and knitted numberless stockings; but the view surrounded and shaped her life as the sea does a lonely island. When her rare callers came it was difficult for her to detach herself from the contemplation of the opposite window-washing, or the scrutiny of certain green points in a neighboring flower-bed which might, or might not, turn into hyacinths, while she feigned an interest in her visitor's anecdotes about some unknown grandchild. Mrs. Manstey's real friends were the denizens of the yards, the hyacinths, the magnolia, the green parrot, the maid who fed the cats, the doctor who studied late behind his mustard-colored curtains; and the confidant of her tenderer musings was the church-spire floating in the sunset.

One April day, as she sat in her usual place, with knitting cast aside and eyes fixed on the blue sky mottled with round clouds, a knock at the door announced the entrance of her landlady. Mrs. Manstey did not care for her landlady, but she submitted to her visits with ladylike resignation. To-day, however, it seemed harder than usual to turn from the blue sky and the blossoming magnolia to Mrs. Sampson's unsuggestive face, and Mrs. Manstey was conscious of a distinct effort as she did so.

"The magnolia is out earlier than usual this year, Mrs. Sampson," she   10
remarked, yielding to a rare impulse, for she seldom alluded to the absorbing interest of her life. In the first place it was a topic not likely to appeal to her visitors and, besides, she lacked the power of expression and could not have given utterance to her feelings had she wished to.

"The what, Mrs. Manstey?" inquired the landlady, glancing about the room as if to find there the explanation of Mrs. Manstey's statement.

"The magnolia in the next yard—in Mrs. Black's yard," Mrs. Manstey repeated.

"Is it, indeed? I didn't know there was a magnolia there," said Mrs. Sampson, carelessly. Mrs. Manstey looked at her; she did not know that there was a magnolia in the next yard!

"By the way," Mrs. Sampson continued, "speaking of Mrs. Black reminds me that the work on the extension is to begin next week."

"The what?" it was Mrs. Manstey's turn to ask.   15

"The extension," said Mrs. Sampson, nodding her head in the direction of the ignored magnolia. "You knew, of course, that Mrs. Black was going to build an extension to her house? Yes, ma'am. I hear it is to run right back to the end of the yard. How she can afford to build an extension in these hard times I don't see; but she always was crazy about building. She used to keep a boarding-house in Seventeenth Street, and she nearly ruined herself then by sticking out bow-windows and what not; I should have thought that would have cured her of building, but I guess it's a disease, like drink. Anyhow, the work is to begin on Monday."

Mrs. Manstey had grown pale. She always spoke slowly, so the landlady did not heed the long pause which followed. At last Mrs. Manstey said: "Do you know how high the extension will be?"

"That's the most absurd part of it. The extension is to be built right up to the roof of the main building; now, did you ever?"

"Mrs. Manstey paused again. "Won't it be a great annoyance to you, Mrs. Sampson?" she asked.

"I should say it would. But there's no help for it; if people have got   20
a mind to build extensions there's no law to prevent 'em, that I'm aware of." Mrs. Manstey, knowing this, was silent. "There is no help for it," Mrs. Sampson repeated, "but if I *am* a church member, I wouldn't be so sorry if it ruined Eliza Black. Well, good-day, Mrs. Manstey; I'm glad to find you so comfortable."

So comfortable—so comfortable! Left to herself the old woman turned once more to the window. How lovely the view was that day! The blue sky with its round clouds shed a brightness over everything; the ailanthus had put on a tinge of yellow-green, the hyacinths were budding, the magnolia flowers looked more than ever like rosettes carved in alabaster. Soon the wistaria would bloom, then the horse-chestnut; but not for her. Between her eyes and them a barrier of brick and mortar would swiftly rise; presently even the spire would disappear, and all her radiant world be blotted out. Mrs. Manstey sent away untouched the dinner-tray brought to her that evening. She lingered in the window until the windy sunset died in bat-colored dusk; then, going to bed, she lay sleepless all night.

Early the next day she was up and at the window. It was raining, but even through the slanting gray gauze the scene had its charm—and then the rain was so good for the trees. She had noticed the day before that the ailanthus was growing dusty.

"Of course I might move," said Mrs. Manstey aloud, and turning from the window she looked about her room. She might move, of course; so might she be flayed alive; but she was not likely to survive either operation. The room, though far less important to her happiness than the view, was as much a part of her existence. She had lived in it seventeen years. She knew every stain on the wall-paper, every rent in the carpet; the light fell in a certain way on her engravings, her books had grown shabby on their shelves, her bulbs and ivy were used to their window and knew which way to lean to the sun. "We are all too old to move," she said.

That afternoon it cleared. Wet and radiant the blue reappeared through torn rags of cloud; the ailanthus sparkled; the earth in the flower-borders looked rich and warm. It was Thursday, and on Monday the building of the extension was to begin.

On Sunday afternoon a card was brought to Mrs. Black, as she was 25 engaged in gathering up the fragments of the boarders' dinner in the basement. The card, black-edged, bore Mrs. Manstey's name.

"One of Mrs. Sampson's boarders; wants to move, I suppose. Well, I can give her a room next year in the extension. Dinah," said Mrs. Black, "tell the lady I'll be upstairs in a minute."

Mrs. Black found Mrs. Manstey standing in the long parlor garnished with statuettes and antimacassars; in that house she could not sit down.

Stooping hurriedly to open the register, which let out a cloud of dust, Mrs. Black advanced on her visitor.

"I'm happy to meet you, Mrs. Manstey; take a seat, please," the landlady remarked in her prosperous voice, the voice of a woman who can afford to build extensions. There was no help for it; Mrs. Manstey sat down.

"Is there anything I can do for you, ma'am?" Mrs. Black continued. 30 "My house is full at present, but I am going to build an extension, and—"

"It is about the extension that I wish to speak," said Mrs. Manstey, suddenly. "I am a poor woman, Mrs. Black, and I have never been a happy one. I shall have to talk about myself first to—to make you understand."

Mrs. Black, astonished but imperturbable, bowed at this parenthesis.

"I never had what I wanted," Mrs. Manstey continued. "It was always one disappointment after another. For years I wanted to live in the country. I dreamed and dreamed about it; but we never could manage it. There was no sunny window in our house, and so all my plants died. My daughter married years ago and went away—besides, she never cared for the same things. Then my husband died and I was left alone. That was seventeen years ago. I went to live at Mrs. Sampson's, and I have been there ever since. I have grown a little infirm, as you see, and I don't get out often; only on fine days, if I am feeling very well. So you can understand my sitting a great deal in my window—the back window on the third floor—"

"Well, Mrs. Manstey," said Mrs. Black, liberally, "I could give you a back room, I dare say; one of the new rooms in the ex—"

"But I don't want to move; I can't move," said Mrs. Manstey, almost 35 with a scream. "And I came to tell you that if you build that extension I shall have no view from my window—no view! Do you understand?"

Mrs. Black thought herself face to face with a lunatic, and she had always heard that lunatics must be humored.

"Dear me, dear me," she remarked, pushing her chair back a little way, "that is too bad, isn't it? Why, I never thought of that. To be sure, the extension *will* interfere with your view, Mrs. Manstey."

"You do understand?" Mrs. Manstey gasped.

"Of course I do. And I'm real sorry about it, too. But there, don't you worry, Mrs. Manstey. I guess we can fix that all right."

Mrs. Manstey rose from her seat, and Mrs. Black slipped toward the door. 40

"What do you mean by fixing it? Do you mean that I can induce you to change your mind about the extension? Oh, Mrs. Black, listen to me. I have two thousand dollars in the bank and I could manage, I know I could manage, to give you a thousand if—" Mrs. Manstey paused; the tears were rolling down her cheeks.

"There, there, Mrs. Manstey, don't you worry," repeated Mrs. Black, soothingly. "I am sure we can settle it. I am sorry that I can't stay and talk about it any longer, but this is such a busy time of day, with supper to get—"

Her hand was on the door-knob, but with sudden vigor Mrs. Manstey seized her wrist.

"You are not giving me a definite answer. Do you mean to say that you accept my proposition?"

"Why, I'll think it over, Mrs. Manstey, certainly I will. I wouldn't annoy 45 you for the world—"

"But the work is to begin to-morrow, I am told," Mrs. Manstey persisted.

Mrs. Black hesitated. "It shan't begin, I promise you that; I'll send word to the builder this very night." Mrs. Manstey tightened her hold.

"You are not deceiving me, are you?" she said.

"No—no," stammered Mrs. Black. "How can you think such a thing of me, Mrs. Manstey?"

Slowly Mrs. Manstey's clutch relaxed, and she passed through the open 50 door. "One thousand dollars," she repeated, pausing in the hall; then she let herself out of the house and hobbled down the steps, supporting herself on the cast-iron railing.

"My goodness," exclaimed Mrs. Black, shutting and bolting the hall-door, "I never knew the old woman was crazy! And she looks so quiet and ladylike, too."

Mrs. Manstey slept well that night, but early the next morning she was awakened by a sound of hammering. She got to her window with what haste she might and, looking out saw that Mrs. Black's yard was full of workmen. Some were carrying loads of brick from the kitchen to the yard, others beginning to demolish the oldfashioned wooden balcony which adorned each story of Mrs. Black's house. Mrs. Manstey saw that she had been deceived. At first she thought of confiding her trouble to Mrs. Sampson, but a settled discouragement soon took possession of her and she went back to bed, not caring to see what was going on.

Toward afternoon, however, feeling that she must know the worst, she rose and dressed herself. It was a laborious task, for her hands were stiffer than usual, and the hooks and buttons seemed to evade her.

When she seated herself in the window, she saw that the workmen had removed the upper part of the balcony, and that the bricks had multiplied since morning. One of the men, a coarse fellow with a bloated face, picked a magnolia blossom and, after smelling it, threw it to the ground; the next man, carrying a load of bricks, trod on the flower in passing.

"Look out, Jim," called one of the men to another who was smoking a   55
pipe, "if you throw matches around near those barrels of paper you'll have the old tinder-box burning down before you know it." And Mrs. Manstey, leaning forward, perceived that there were several barrels of paper and rubbish under the wooden balcony.

At length the work ceased and twilight fell. The sunset was perfect and a roseate light, transfiguring the distant spire, lingered late in the west. When it grew dark Mrs. Manstey drew down the shades and proceeded, in her usual methodical manner, to light her lamp. She always filled and lit it with her own hands, keeping a kettle of kerosene on a zinc-covered shelf in a closet. As the lamp-light filled the room it assumed its usual peaceful aspect. The books and pictures and plants seemed, like their mistress, to settle themselves down for another quiet evening, and Mrs. Manstey, as was her wont, drew up her armchair to the table and began to knit.

That night she could not sleep. The weather had changed and a wild wind was abroad, blotting the stars with close-driven clouds. Mrs. Manstey rose once or twice and looked out of the window; but of the view nothing was discernible save a tardy light or two in the opposite windows. These lights at last went out, and Mrs. Manstey, who had watched for their extinction, began to dress herself. She was in evident haste, for she merely flung a thin dressing-gown over her night-dress and wrapped her head in a scarf; then she opened her closet and cautiously took out the kettle of kerosene. Having slipped a bundle of wooden matches into her pocket she proceeded, with increasing precautions, to unlock her door, and a few moments later she was feeling her way down the dark staircase, led by a glimmer of gas from the lower hall. At length she reached the bottom of the stairs and began the more difficult descent into the utter darkness of the basement. Here, however, she could move more freely, as there was less danger of being overheard; and without much delay she contrived to unlock the iron door leading into the yard. A gust of cold wind smote her as she stepped out and groped shiveringly under the clothes-lines.

That morning at three o'clock an alarm of fire brought the engines to Mrs. Black's door, and also brought Mrs. Sampson's startled boarders to their windows. The wooden balcony at the back of Mrs. Black's house was ablaze, and among those who watched the progress of the flames was Mrs. Manstey, leaning in her thin dressing-gown from the open window.

The fire, however, was soon put out, and the frightened occupants of the house, who had fled in scant attire, reassembled at dawn to find that little mischief had been done beyond the cracking of window panes and smoking of ceilings. In fact, the chief sufferer by the fire was Mrs. Manstey, who was found in the morning gasping with pneumonia, a not unnatural result, as everyone remarked, of her having hung out of an open window at her age in a dressing-gown. It was easy to see that she was very ill, but no one had guessed how grave the doctor's verdict would be, and the faces gathered that evening about Mrs. Sampson's table were awestruck and disturbed. Not that any of the boarders knew Mrs. Manstey well; she "kept to herself," as they said, and seemed to fancy herself too good for them; but then it is always disagreeable to have anyone dying in the house and, as one lady observed to another: "It might just as well have been you or me, my dear."

But it was only Mrs. Manstey; and she was dying, as she had lived, lonely if not alone. The doctor had sent a trained nurse, and Mrs. Sampson, with muffled step, came in from time to time; but both, to Mrs. Manstey, seemed remote and unsubstantial as the figures in a dream. All day she said nothing; but when she was asked for her daughter's address she shook her head. At times the nurse noticed that she seemed to be listening attentively for some sound which did not come; then again she dozed.

The next morning at daylight she was very low. The nurse called Mrs. Sampson and as the two bent over the old woman they saw her lips move.

"Lift me up—out of bed," she whispered.

They raised her in their arms, and with her stiff hand she pointed to the window.

"Oh, the window—she wants to sit in the window. She used to sit there all day," Mrs. Sampson explained. "It can do her no harm, I suppose?"

"Nothing matters now," said the nurse.

They carried Mrs. Manstey to the window and placed her in her chair. The dawn was abroad, a jubilant spring dawn; the spire had already caught a golden ray, though the magnolia and horsechestnut still slumbered in shadow. In Mrs. Black's yard all was quiet. The charred timbers of the balcony lay where they had fallen. It was evident that since the fire the builders had not returned to their work. The magnolia had unfolded a few more sculptural flowers; the view was undisturbed.

It was hard for Mrs. Manstey to breathe; each moment it grew more difficult. She tried to make them open the window, but they would not understand. If she could have tasted the air, sweet with the penetrating ailanthus savor, it would have eased her; but the view at least was there—the spire was golden now, the heavens had warmed from pearl to blue, day was alight from east to west, even the magnolia had caught the sun.

Mrs. Manstey's head fell back and smiling she died.

That day the building of the extension was resumed.

The Making of a New Yorker

O. Henry

O. Henry (1862–1910) was a prolific American short-story writer, a master of surprise endings, who wrote about the life of ordinary people in New York City. A twist of plot, which turns on an ironic or coincidental circumstance, is typical of O. Henry's stories.

Besides many things, Raggles was a poet. He was called a tramp; but that was only an elliptical way of saying that he was a philosopher, an artist, a traveller, a naturalist, and a discoverer. But most of all he was a poet. In all his life he never wrote a line of verse; he lived his poetry. His Odyssey would have been a Limerick, had it been written. But, to linger with the primary proposition, Raggles was a poet.   1

Raggles's specialty, had he been driven to ink and paper, would have been sonnets to the cities. He studied cities as women study their reflections in mirrors; as children study the glue and sawdust of a dislocated doll; as the men who write about wild animals study the cages in the zoo. A city to Raggles was not merely a pile of bricks and mortar, peopled by a certain number of inhabitants; it was a thing with soul, characteristic and distinct; an individual conglomeration of life, with its own peculiar essence, flavor, and feeling. Two thousand miles to the north and south, east and west, Raggles wandered in poetic fervor, taking the cities to his breast. He footed it on dusty roads, or sped magnificently in freight cars, counting time as of no account. And when he had found the heart of a city and listened to its secret confession, he strayed on, restless, to another. Fickle Raggles!—but perhaps he had not met the civic corporation that could engage and hold his critical fancy. . . .

One day Raggles came and laid siege to the heart of the great city of Manhattan. She was the greatest of all; and he wanted to learn her note in the scale; to taste and appraise and classify and solve and label her and arrange her with the other cities that had given him up the secret of their individuality. And here we cease to be Raggles's translator and become his chronicler.

Raggles landed from a ferry-boat one morning and walked into the core of the town with the blasé air of a cosmopolite. He was dressed with care to play the role of an "unidentified man." No country, race, class,

From *The Four Million* by O' Henry.

clique, union, party clan, or bowling association could have claimed him. His clothing, which had been donated to him piece-meal by citizens of different height, but same number of inches around the heart, was not yet as uncomfortable to his figure as those specimens of raiment, self-measured, that are railroaded to you by transcontinental tailors with a suit case, suspenders, silk handkerchief and pearl studs as a bonus. Without money—as a poet should be—but with the ardor of an astronomer discovering a new star in the chorus of the milky way, or a man who has seen ink suddenly flow from his fountain pen, Raggles wandered into the great city.

Late in the afternoon he drew out of the roar and commotion with a look of dumb terror on his countenance. He was defeated, puzzled, discomfited, frightened. The greetings of the other cities he had known—their homespun kindliness, their human gamut of rough charity, friendly curses, garrulot curiosity, and easily estimated credulity or indifference. This city Manhattan gave him no clue; it was walled against him. Like a river of adamant, it flowed past him in the streets. Never an eye was turned upon him; no voice spoke to him. His heart yearned for the clap of Pittsburg's sooty hand on his shoulder; for Chicago's menacing but social yawp in his ear; for the pale and eleemosynary stare through the Bostonian eyeglass—even for the precipitate but unmalicious boot-toe of Louisville or St. Louis.   5

On Broadway Raggles, successful suitor of many cities, stood, bashful, like any country swain. For the first time he experienced the poignant humiliation of being ignored. And when he tried to reduce this brilliant, swiftly changing, ice-cold city to a formula he failed utterly. Poet though he was, it offered him no color similes, no points of comparison, no flaw in its polished facets, no handle by which he could hold it up and view its shape and structure, as he familiarly and often contemptuously had done with other towns. The houses were interminable ramparts loop-holed for defence; the people were bright but bloodless spectres passing in sinister and selfish array.

The thing that weighed heaviest on Raggles's soul and clogged his poet's fancy was the spirit of absolute egotism that seemed to saturate the people as toys are saturated with paint. Each one that he considered appeared a monster of abominable and insolent conceit. Humanity was gone from them; they were toddling idols of stone and varnish, worshipping themselves and greedy for though oblivious of worship from their fellow graven images. Frozen, cruel, implacable, impervious, cut to an identical pattern, they hurried on their ways like statues brought by some miracle to motion, while soul and feeling lay unaroused in the reluctant marble.

Gradually Raggles became conscious of certain types. One was an elderly gentleman with a snow-white, short beard, pink, unwrinkled face, and stony, sharp blue eyes, attired in the fashion of a gilded youth, who seemed to personify the city's wealth, ripeness and frigid unconcern. Another type was a woman, tall, beautiful, clear as a steel engraving, goddess-like, calm, clothed like the princesses of old, with eyes as coldly blue as the reflection of sunlight on a glacier. And another was a by-product of this town of marionettes—a broad, swaggering, grim, threateningly sedate fellow, with a jowl as large as a harvested wheat field, the complexion of a baptized infant, and the knuckles of a prize-fighter. This type leaned against cigar signs and viewed the world with frappéd contumely.

A poet is a sensitive creature, and Raggles soon shriveled in the bleak embrace of the undecipherable. The chill, sphinx-like, ironical, illegible, unnatural, ruthless expression of the city left him downcast and bewildered. Had it no heart? Better the woodpile, the scolding of vinegar-faced housewives at back doors, the kindly spleen of bartenders behind provincial free-lunch counters, the amiable truculence of rural constables, the kicks, arrests, and happy-go-lucky chances of the other vulgar, loud, crude cities than this freezing heartlessness.

Raggles summoned his courage and sought hand-outs from the populace. Unheeding, regardless, they passed on without the wink of an eyelash to testify that they were conscious of his existence. And then he said to himself that this fair but pitiless city of Manhattan was without a soul; that its inhabitants were mannikins moved by wires and springs, and that he was alone in a great wilderness.

Raggles started to cross the street. There was a blast, a roar, a hissing and a crash as something struck him and hurled him over and over six yards from where he had been. As he was coming down, like the stick of a rocket, the earth and all the cities thereof turned to a fractured dream.

Raggles opened his eyes. First an odor made itself known to him—an odor of the earliest spring flowers of Paradise. And then a hand soft as a falling petal touched his brow. Bending over him was the woman clothed like the princess of old, with blue eyes, now soft and humid with human sympathy. Under his head on the pavement were silks and furs. With Raggles's hat in his hand and with his face pinker than ever from a vehement outburst of oratory against reckless driving, stood the elderly gentleman who personified the city's wealth and ripeness. From a near-by café hurried the by-product with the vast jowl and baby complexion, bearing a glass full of crimson fluid that suggested delightful possibilities.

"Drink dis, sport," said the by-product, holding the glass to Raggles's lips.

Hundreds of people huddled around in a moment, their faces wearing the deepest concern. Two flattering and gorgeous policemen got into the circle and pressed back the overplus of Samaritans. An old lady in a black shawl spoke loudly of camphor; a newsboy slipped one of his papers

10

beneath Raggles's elbow, where it lay on the muddy pavement. A brisk young man with a notebook was asking for names.

A bell clanged importantly, and the ambulance cleaned a lane through   15
the crowd. A cool surgeon slipped into the midst of affairs.

"How do you feel, old man?" asked the surgeon, stooping easily to his task. The princess of silks and stains wiped a red drop or two from Raggles's brow with a fragrant cobweb.

"Me?" said Raggles, with a seraphic smile, "I feel fine."

He had found the heart of his new city.

In three days they let him leave his cot for the convalescent ward in the hospital. He had been in there an hour when the attendants heard sounds of conflict. Upon investigation they found that Raggles had assaulted and damaged a brother convalescent—a glowering transient whom a freight train collision had sent in to be patched up.

"What's all this about?" inquired the head nurse.   20

"He was runnin' down me town," said Raggles.

"What town?" asked the nurse.

"Noo York," said Raggles.

Ferryslip

John Dos Passos

John Dos Passos (1896–1970) was one of the most famous writers of the "Lost Generation," a group of writers—including Ernest Hemingway and F. Scott Fitzgerald—who wrote about modern life using modern, experimental literary forms. Dos Passos wrote poetry, drama, and non-fiction essay, but he is most well-known for his more than forty novels. The section below is the first chapter of his 1925 novel *Manhattan Transfer*, an experimental novel that sought to capture the Jazz Age in New York City, a time of radical change and colliding forces. Over 130 short sections, or vignettes, make up this novel; and rather than writing about one or two characters, Dos Passos portrays dozens of characters who move into and out of the reader's main focus at rapid speed.

Three gulls wheel above the broken boxes, orangerinds, spoiled cabbage heads that heave between the splintered plank walls, the green waves spume under the round bow as the ferry, skidding on the tide, crashes, gulps the broken water, slides, settles slowly into the slip. Handwinches whirl with jingle of chains. Gates fold upwards, feet step out across the crack, men and women press through the manuresmelling wooden tunnel of the ferryhouse, crushed and. Jostling like apples fed down a chute into a press. 1

THE NURSE, holding the basket at arm's length as if it were a bedpan, opened the door to a big dry hot room with greenish distempered walls where in the air tinctured with smells of alcohol and iodoform hung writhing a faint sourish squalling from other baskets along the wall. As she set her basket down she glanced into it with pursed-up lips. The newborn baby squirmed in the cottonwool feebly like a knot of earthworms.

On the ferry there was an old man playing the violin. He had a monkey's face puckered up in one corner and kept time with the toe of a cracked patent-leather shoe. Bud Korpenning sat on the rail watching him, his back to the river. The breeze made the hair stir round the tight line of his cap and dried the sweat on his temples. His feet were blistered, he was leaden-tired, but when the ferry moved out of the slip, bucking the little slapping scalloped waves of the river he felt something warm and tingling shoot suddenly through all his veins. "Say, friend, how fur is it into the city from where this ferry lands?" he asked a young man in a straw hat wearing a blue and white striped necktie who stood beside him.

The young man's glance moved up from Bud's roadswelled shoes to the red wrist that stuck out from the frayed sleeves of his coat, past the skinny turkey's throat and slid up cockily into the intent eyes under the brokenvisored cap.

"That depends where you want to get to."

"How do I get to Broadway?...I want to get to the center of things."   5

"Walk east a block and turn down Broadway and you'll find the center of things if you walk far enough."

"Thank you sir. I'll do that."

The violinist was going through the crowd with his hat held out, the wind ruffling the wisps of gray hair on his shabby bald head. Bud found the face tilted up at him, the crushed eyes like two black pins looking into his. "Nothin," he said gruffly and turned away to look at the expanse of river bright as knifeblades. The plank walls of the slip closed in, cracked as the ferry lurched against them; there was rattling of chains, and Bud was pushed forward among the crowd through the ferryhouse. He walked between two coal wagons and out over a dusty expanse of street towards yellow streetcars. A trembling took hold of his knees. He thrust his hands deep in his pockets.

EAT on a lunchwagon halfway down the block. He slid stiffly onto a revolving stool and looked for a long while at the pricelist.

"Fried eggs and a cup o coffee."   10

"Want 'em turned over?" asked the redhaired man behind the counter who was wiping off his beefy freckled forearms with his apron. Bud Korpenning sat up with a start.

"What?"

"The eggs? Want em turned over or sunny side up?"

"Oh sure, turn 'em over." Bud slouched over the counter again with his head between his hands.

"You look all in, feller," the man said as he broke the eggs into the siz-   15
zling grease of the frying pan.

"Came down from upstate. I walked fifteen miles this mornin."

The man made a whistling sound through his eyeteeth. "Comin to the big city to look for a job, eh?"

Bud nodded. The man flopped the eggs sizzling and netted with brown out onto the plate and pushed it towards Bud with some bread and butter on the edge of it. "I'm goin to slip you a bit of advice, feller, and it won't cost you nutten. You go an git a shave and a haircut and brush the hayseeds out o yer suit a bit before you start lookin. You'll be more likely to git something. It's looks that count in this city."

"I kin work all right. I'm a good worker," growled Bad with his mouth full.

"I'm tellin yez, that's all," said the redhaired man and turned back to   20
his stove.

When Ed Thatcher climbed the marble steps of the wide hospital entry
he was trembling. The smell of drugs caught at his throat. A woman with a
starched face was looking at him over the top of a desk. He tried to steady
his voice.

"Can you tell me how Mrs. Thatcher is?"

"Yes, you can go up."

"But please, miss, is everything all right?"

"The nurse on the floor will know anything about the case. Stairs to the   25
left, third floor, maternity ward."

Ed Thatcher held a bunch of flowers wrapped in green waxed paper.
The broad stairs swayed as he stumbled up, his toes kicking against the
brass rods that held the fiber matting down. The closing of a door cut off a
strangled shriek. He stopped a nurse.

"I want to see Mrs. Thatcher, please."

"Go right ahead if you know where she is."

"But they've moved her."

"You'll have to ask at the desk at the end of the hall."   30

He gnawed his cold lips. At the end of the hall a redfaced woman
looked at him, smiling.

"Everything's fine. You're the happy father of a bouncing baby girl."

"You see it's our first and Susie's so delicate," he stammered with blink-
ing eyes.

"Oh yes, I understand, naturally you worried....you can go in and talk
to her when she wakes up. The baby was born two hours ago. Be sure not
to tire her."

Ed Thatcher was a little man with two blond wisps of mustache and   35
washedout gray eyes. He seized the nurse's hand and shook it showing all
his uneven yellow teeth in a smile.

"You see it's our first."

"Congratulations," said the nurse.

Rows of beds under bilious gaslight, a sick smell of restlessly stirring
bedclothes, faces fat, lean, yellow, white; that's her. Susie's yellow hair lay
in a loose coil round her little white face that looked shriveled and twisted.
He unwrapped the roses and put them on the night table. Looking out
the window was like looking down into water. The trees in the square
were tangled in blue cobwebs. Down the avenue lamps were coming on
marking off with green shimmer brickpurple blocks of houses, chimney
pots and water tanks cut sharp into a sky flushed like flesh. The blue lids
slipped back off her eyes.

That you Ed?...Why Ed they are Jacks. How extravagant of you?

"I couldn't help it dearest. I knew you liked them."   40

A nurse was hovering near the end of the bed.

"Couldn't you let us see the baby, miss?"

The nurse nodded. She was a lanternjawed grayfaced woman with tight lips.

"I hate her," whispered Susie. "She gives me the fidgets that woman does; she's nothing but a mean old maid."

"Never mind dear, it's just for a day or two." Susie closed her eyes.   45

"Do you still want to call her Ellen?"

The nurse brought back a basket and set it on the bed beside Susie.

"Oh isn't she wonderful!" said Ed. "Look she's breathing....And they've oiled her." He helped his wife to raise herself on her elbow; the yellow coil of her hair unrolled, fell over his hand and arm. "How can you tell them apart nurse?"

"Sometimes we cant," said the nurse, stretching her mouth in a smile. Susie was looking querulously into the minute purple face.

"You're sure this is mine."   50

"Of course."

"But it hasn't any label on it."

"I'll label it right away."

"But mine was dark." Susie lay back on the pillow, gasping for breath.

"She has lovely little light fuzz just the color of your hair."   55

Susie stretched her arms out above her head and shrieked: "It's not mine. It's not mine. Take it away....That woman's stolen my baby."

"Dear, for Heaven's sake! Dear, for Heaven's sake!" He tried to tuck the covers about her.

"Too bad," said the nurse, calmly, picking up the basket. "I'll have to give her a sedative."

Susie sat up stiff in bed. "Take it away," she yelled and fell back in hysterics, letting out continuous frail moaning shrieks.

"O my God!" cried Ed Thatcher, clasping his hands.   60

"You'd better go away for this evening, Mr. Thatcher....She'll quiet down, once you've gone....I'll put the roses in water."

On the last flight he caught up with a chubby man who was strolling down slowly, rubbing his hands as he went. Their eyes met.

"Everything all right, sir?" asked the chubby man.

"Oh yes, I guess so," said Thatcher faintly.

The chubby man turned on him, delight bubbling through his thick voice.   65
"Congradulade me, congradulade me; mein vife has giben birth to a poy."

Thatcher shook a fat little hand. "Mine's a girl," he admitted, sheepishly.

"It is fif years yet and every year a girl, and now dink of it, a poy."

"Yes," said Ed Thatcher as they stepped out on the pavement, "it's a great moment."

"Vill yous allow me sir to invite you to drink a congradulation drink mit me?"

"Why with pleasure."   70

The latticed halfdoors were swinging in the saloon at the corner of Third Avenue. Shuffling their feet politely they went through into the back room.

"Ach," said the German as they sat down at a scarred brown table, "family life is full of vorries."

"That it is sir; this is my first."

"Vill you haf beer?"

"All right anything suits me."   75

"Two pottles Culmbacher imported to drink to our little folk." The bottles popped and the sepia-tinged foam rose in the glasses. "Here's success.... Prosit," said the German, and raised his glass. He rubbed the foam out of his mustache and pounded on the table with a pink fist "Vould it be indiscreet meester...?"

"Thatcher's my name."

"Vould it be indiscreet, Mr. Thatcher, to inquvire vat might your profession be?"

"Accountant. I hope before long to be a certified accountant."

"I am a printer and my name is Zucher—Marcus Antonius Zucher."   80

"Pleased to meet you Mr. Zucher."

They shook hands across the table between the bottles.

"A certified accountant makes big money," said Mr. Zucher.

"Big money's what I'll have to have, for my little girl."

"Kids, they eat money," continued Mr. Zucher, in a deep voice.   85

"Won't you let me set you up to a bottle?" said Thatcher, figuring up how much he had in his pocket. Poor Susie wouldn't like me to be drinking in a saloon like this. But just this once, and I'm learning, learning about fatherhood.

"The more the merrier," said Mr. Zucher. "...But kids, they eat money.... Dont do nutten but eat and vear out clothes. Vonce I get my business on its feet.... Ach! Now vot mit hypothecations and the difficult borrowing of money and vot mit vages going up und these here crazy tradeunion socialists and bomsters..."

"Well here's how, Mr. Zucher." Mr. Zucher squeezed the foam out of his mustache with the thumb and forefinger of each hand. "It aint every day ve pring into the voirld a papy poy, Mr. Thatcher."

"Or a baby girl, Mr. Zucher."

The barkeep wiped the spillings off the table when he brought the new   90
bottles, and stood near listening, the rag dangling from his red hands.

"And I have the hope in mein heart that ven my poy drinks to his poy, it vill be in champagne vine. Ach, that is how things go in this great city."

"I'd like my girl to be a quiet homey girl, not like these young women nowadays, all frills and furbelows and tight lacings. And I'll have retired by that time and have a little place up the Hudson, work in the garden evenings. . . . I know fellers downtown who have retired with three thousand a year. It's saving that does it."

"Aint no good in savin," said the barkeep. "I saved for ten years and the savings bank went broke and left me nutten but a bankbook for my trouble. Get a close tip and take a chance, that's the only system."

"That's nothing but gambling" snapped Thatcher.

"Well sir it's a gamblin game," said the barkeep as he walked back to   95
the bar swinging the two empty bottles.

"A gamblin game. He aint so far out," said Mr. Zucher, looking down into his beer with a glassy meditive eye. "A man vat is ambeetious must take chances. Ambeetions is vat I came here from Frankfort mit at the age of tvelf years, and now that I haf a son to vork for . . . Ach, his name shall be Vilhelm after the mighty Kaiser."

"My little girl's name will be Ellen after my mother." Ed Thatcher's eyes filled with tears.

Mr. Zucher got to his feet. "Veil goodpy Mr. Thatcher. Happy to have met you. I must go home to my little girls."

Thatcher shook the chubby hand again, and thinking warm soft thoughts of motherhood and fatherhood and birthday cakes and Christmas watched through a sepia-tinged foamy haze Mr. Zucher waddle out through the swinging doors. After a while he stretched out his arms. Well poor little Susie wouldn't like me to be here. . . . Everything for her and the bonny wee bairn.

"Hey there yous how about settlin?" bawled the barkeep after him   100
when he reached the door.

"Didnt the other feller pay?"

"Like hell he did."

"But he was t-t-treating me. . . ."

The barkeep laughed as he covered the money with a red lipper. "I guess that bloat believes in savin."

A small bearded bandylegged man in a derby walked up Allen Street,   105
up the sunstriped tunnel hung with skyblue and smoked-salmon and mustardyellow quilts, littered with second hand ginger bread-colored furniture. He walked with his cold hands clasped over the tails of his frockcoat, picking his way among packing boxes and scuttling children. He kept gnawing his lips and clasping and unclasping his hands. He walked without

hearing the yells of the children or the annihilating clatter of the L trains overhead or smelling the rancid sweet huddled smell of packed tenements.

At a yellowpainted drugstore at the corner of Canal, he stopped and stared abstractedly at a face on a green advertising card. It was a high-browed cleanshaven distinguished face with arched eyebrows and a bushy neatly trimmed mustache, the face of a man who had money in the bank, poised prosperously above a crisp wing collar and an ample dark cravat. Under it in copybook writing was the signature King C. Gillette. Above his head hovered the motto NO STROPPING NO HONING. The little bearded man pushed his derby back off his sweating brow and looked for a long time into the dollarproud eyes of King C. Gillette. Then he clenched his fists, threw back his shoulders and walked into the drugstore.

His wife and daughters were out. He heated up a pitcher of water on the gasburner. Then with the scissors he found on the mantel he dipped the long brown locks of his beard. Then he started shaving very carefully with the new nickelbright safety razor. He stood trembling running his fingers down his smooth white cheeks in front of the stained mirror. He was trimming his mustache when he heard a noise behind him. He turned towards them a face smooth as the face of King C. Gillette, a face with a dollarbland smile. The two little girls' eyes were popping out of their heads. "Mommer...it's popper," the biggest one yelled. His wife dropped like a laundrybag into the rocker and threw the apron over her head.

"Oyoy! Oyoy!" she moaned rocking back and forth.

"Vat's a matter? Dontye like it?" He walked back and forth with the safety razor shining in his hand now and then gently fingering his smooth chin.

Prologue to "Invisible Man"

Ralph Ellison

Ralph Ellison (1914–1994) wrote reviews, essay, and short stories, but he became famous for his novel *Invisible Man*, published in 1952. After teaching at various universities, he became the Albert Schweitzer Professor in the Humanities at New York University (1970–9). He was awarded the Presidential Medal of Freedom in 1969. Ellison was an experimental writer who used modern writing techniques to tell stories of the daily lives of African Americans who lived with the legacy of slavery and had to negotiate modern racial politics. In this selection from *Invisible Man*, readers follow the story of an unnamed narrator who is living underground.

I am an invisible man. No, I am not a spook like those who haunted Edgar   1
Allan Poe; nor am I one of your Hollywood-movie ectoplasms. I am a man of substance, of flesh and bone, fiber and liquids—and I might even be said to possess a mind. I am invisible, understand, simply because people refuse to see me. Like the bodiless heads you see sometimes in circus sideshows, it is as though I have been surrounded by mirrors of hard, distorting glass. When they approach me they see only my surroundings, themselves, or figments of their imagination—indeed, everything and anything except me.

Nor is my invisibility exactly a matter of a biochemical accident to my epidermis. That invisibility to which I refer occurs because of a peculiar disposition of the eyes of those with whom I come in contact. A matter of the construction of their *inner* eyes, those eyes with which they look through their physical eyes upon reality. I am not complaining, nor am I protesting either. It is sometimes advantageous to be unseen, although it is most often rather wearing on the nerves. Then too, you're constantly being bumped against by those of poor vision. Or again, you often doubt if you really exist. You wonder whether you aren't simply a phantom in other people's minds. Say, a figure in a nightmare which the sleeper tries with all his strength to destroy. It's when you feel like this that, out of resentment, you begin to bump people back. And, let me confess, you feel that way most of the time. You ache with the need to convince yourself that you do exist in the real world, that you're a part of all the sound and anguish, and you strike out with your fists, you curse and you swear to make them recognize you. And, alas, it's seldom successful.

One night I accidentally bumped into a man, and perhaps because of the near darkness he saw me and called me an insulting name. I sprang at him, seized his coat lapels and demanded that he apologize. He was a tall blond man, and as my face came close to his he looked insolently out of his blue eyes and cursed me, his breath hot in my face as he struggled. I pulled his chin down sharp upon the crown of my head, butting him as I had seen the West Indians do, and I felt his flesh tear and the blood gush out, and I yelled, "Apologize! Apologize!" But he continued to curse and struggle, and I butted him again and again until he went down heavily, on his knees, profusely bleeding. I kicked him repeatedly, in a frenzy because he still uttered insults though his lips were frothy with blood. Oh yes, I kicked him! And in my outrage I got out my knife and prepared to slit his throat, right there beneath the lamplight in the deserted street, holding him in the collar with one hand, and opening the knife with my teeth—when it occurred to me that the man had not *seen* me, actually; that he, as far as he knew, was in the midst of a walking nightmare! And I stopped the blade, slicing the air as I pushed him away, letting him fall back to the street. I stared at him hard as the lights of a car stabbed through the darkness. He lay there, moaning on the asphalt; a man almost killed by a phantom. It unnerved me. I was both disgusted and ashamed. I was like a drunken man myself, wavering about on weakened legs. Then I was amused: Something in this man's thick head had sprung out and beaten him within an inch of his life. I began to laugh at this crazy discovery. Would he have awakened at the point of death? Would Death himself have freed him for wakeful living? But I didn't linger. I ran away into the dark, laughing so hard I feared I might rupture myself. The next day I saw his picture in the *Daily News,* beneath a caption stating that he had been "mugged." Poor fool, poor blind fool, I thought with sincere compassion, mugged by an invisible man!

Most of the time (although I do not choose as I once did to deny the violence of my days by ignoring it) I am not so overtly violent. I remember that I am invisible and walk softly so as not to awaken the sleeping ones. Sometimes it is best not to awaken them; there are few things in the world as dangerous as sleepwalkers. I learned in time though that it is possible to carry on a fight against them without their realizing it. For instance, I have been carrying on a fight with Monopolated Light & Power for some time now. I use their service and pay them nothing at all, and they don't know it. Oh, they suspect that power is being drained off, but they don't know where. All they know is that according to the master meter back there in their power station a hell of a lot of free current is disappearing somewhere into the jungle of Harlem. The joke, of course, is that I don't live in Harlem but in a border area. Several years ago (before I discovered the advantages of being invisible) I went through the routine process of buying service and paying their outrageous rates. But no more. I gave up all that, along with my apartment, and my old way of life: That way based upon the fallacious assumption that I, like other men, was visible. Now, aware of my invisibility, I live rent-free in a building rented strictly to whites, in a section of the basement that was shut off and forgotten during the nineteenth century, which I discovered when I was trying to escape in the night from Ras the Destroyer. But that's getting too far ahead of the story, almost to the end, although the end is in the beginning and lies far ahead.

The point now is that I found a home—or a hole in the ground, as you will. Now don't jump to any conclusion that because I call my home a "hole" it is damp and cold like a grave; there are cold holes and warm holes. Mine is a warm hole. And remember, a bear retires to his hole for the winter and lives until spring; then he comes strolling out like the Easter chick breaking from its shell. I say all this to assure you that it is incorrect to assume that, because I'm invisible and live in a hole, I am dead. I am neither dead nor in a state of suspended animation. Call me Jack-the-Bear, for I am in a state of hibernation.

My hole is warm and full of light. Yes, *full* of light. I doubt if there is a brighter spot in all New York than this hole of mine, and I do not exclude Broadway. Or the Empire State Building on a photographer's dream night. But that is taking advantage of you. Those two spots are among the darkest

Jeff Wall, After *Invisible Man* by Ralph Ellison, the Preface, 1999–2001, transparency in lightbox, 174 × 250.5 cm. Courtesy of the artist.

of our whole civilization—pardon me, our whole *culture* (an important distinction, I've heard)—which might sound like a hoax, or a contradiction, but that (by contradiction, I mean) is how the world moves: Not like an arrow, but a boomerang. (Beware of those who speak of the *spiral* of history; they are preparing a boomerang. Keep a steel helmet handy.) I know; I have been boomeranged across my head so much that I now can see the darkness of lightness. And I love light. Perhaps you'll think it strange that an invisible man should need light, desire light, love light. But maybe it is exactly because I *am* invisible. Light confirms my reality, gives birth to my form. A beautiful girl once told me of a recurring nightmare in which she lay in the center of a large dark room and felt her face expand until it filled the whole room, becoming a formless mass while her eyes ran in bilious jelly up the chimney. And so it is with me. Without light I am not only invisible, but formless as well; and to be unaware of one's form is to live a death. I myself, after existing some twenty years, did not become alive until I discovered my invisibility.

The Inheritance of Loss

Kiran Desai

Kiran Desai was born in India in 1971, she moved to the USA when she was fifteen. She attended Bennington College, Hollins University, and Columbia University, where she studied creative writing. She published in the *The New Yorker* and is the author of *Hullabaloo in the Guava Orchard* (1998) and *The Inheritance of Loss* (2006), which won the Booker Prize. The following excerpt is about the experience of an Indian immigrant who lives illegally in New York.

Ten

Biju had started his second year in America at Pinocchio's Italian Restaurant, stirring vats of spluttering Bolognese, as over a speaker an opera singer sang of love and murder, revenge and heartbreak.   1

"He smells," said the owner's wife. "I think I'm allergic to his hair oil." She had hoped for men from the poorer parts of Europe—Bulgarians perhaps, or Czechoslovakians. At least they might have something in common with them like religion and skin color, grandfathers who ate cured sausages and looked like them too, but they weren't coming in numbers great enough or they weren't coming desperate enough, she wasn't sure....

The owner bought soap and toothpaste, toothbrush, shampoo plus conditioner, Q-tips, nail clippers, and most important of all, deodorant, and told Biju he'd picked up some things he might need.

They stood there embarrassed by the intimacy of the products that lay between them.

He tried another tactic: "What do they think of the pope in India?"   5

By showing his respect for Biju's mind he would raise Biju's self-respect, for the boy was clearly lacking in that department.

"You've tried," his wife said, comforting him a few days later when they couldn't detect any difference in Biju. "You even *bought* the soap," she said.

Biju approached Tom & Tomoko's—"No jobs."
McSweeney's Pub—"Not hiring."
Freddy's Wok—"Can you ride a bicycle?"
Yes, he could.

Szechuan wings and French fries, just $3.00. Fried rice $1.35 and $1.00 for pan-tried dumplings tat and tight as babies—slice them open and flood your plate with a run of luscious oil. In this country poor people eat like kings! General Tso's chicken, emperor's pork, and Biju on a bicycle with the delivery bag on his handlebars, a tremulous figure between heaving buses, regurgitating taxis—what growls, what sounds of flatulence came from this traffic. Biju pounded at the pedals, heckled by taxi drivers direct from Punjab—a man is not a caged thing, a man is wild *wild* and he must drive as such, in a bucking yodeling taxi. They harassed Biju with such blows from their horns as could split the world into whey and solids: paaaaaaWWW!

One evening, Biju was sent to deliver hot-and-sour soups and egg foo yong to three Indian girls, students, new additions to the neighborhood in an apartment just opened under reviewed city laws to raised rents. Banners reading "Antigentrification Day" had been hauled up over the street by the longtime residents for a festival earlier in the afternoon when they had played music, grilled hot dogs in the street, and sold all their gritty junk. One day the Indian girls hoped to be gentry, but right now, despite being unwelcome in the neighborhood, they were in the student stage of vehemently siding with the poor people who wished them gone.

The girl who answered the buzzer smiled, shiny teeth, shiny eyes through shiny glasses. She took the bag and went to collect the money. It was suffused with Indian femininity in there, abundant amounts of sweet newly washed hair, gold strung Kolhapuri slippers lying about. Heavyweight accounting books sat on the table along with a chunky Ganesh brought all the way from home despite its weight, for interior decoration plus luck in money and exams.

"Well," one of them continued with the conversation Biju had interruptde, discussing a fourth Indian girl not present, "why doesn't she just go for an Indian boy then, who'll understand all that temper tantrum stuff?"

"She won't look at an Indian boy, she doesn't want a nice Indian boy who's grown up chatting with his aunties in the kitchen."

"What does she want then?"

"She wants the Marlboro man with a Ph.D."

They had a self-righteousness common to many Indian women of the English-speaking upper-educated, went out to mimosa brunches, ate their Dadi's roti with adept fingers, donned a sari or smacked on elastic shorts for aerobics, could say "*Namaste*, Kusum Auntie, *aayiye, baethiye, khayiye!*" as easily as "Shit!" They took to short hair quickly, were eager for Western-style romance, and happy for a traditional ceremony with lots of jewelry: green set (meaning emerald), red set (meaning ruby), white set (meaning diamond). They considered themselves uniquely positioned to lecture everyone on a variety of topics: accounting professors on accounting, Vermonters on the fall foliage, Indians on America, Americans on India, Indians on India, Americans on America. They were poised; they were impressive; in the United States, where luckily it was still assumed that Indian women were downtrodden, they were lauded as extraordinary—which had the unfortunate result of making them even more of what they already were.

Fortune cookies, they checked, chili sauce, soy sauce, duck sauce, chopsticks, napkins, plastic spoons knives forks.

"*Dhanyawad. Shukria.* Thank you. Extra tip. You should buy topi-muffler-gloves to be ready for the winter."

The shiny-eyed girl said it many ways so that the meaning might be conveyed from every angle—that he might comprehend their friendliness completely in this meeting between Indians abroad of different classes and languages, rich and poor, north and south, top caste bottom caste.

Standing at that threshold, Biju felt a mixture of emotions: hunger, respect, loathing. He mounted the bicycle he had rested against the railings and was about to go on, but something made him stop and draw back. It was a ground-floor apartment with black security bars, and he put two fingers to his lips and whistled into the window at the girls dunking their spoons into the plastic containers where the brown liquid and foggy bits of egg looked horrible against the plastic, *twe tweeeeee twhoo*, and before he saw their response, he pedaled as fast as he could into the scowling howling traffic down Broadway, and as he pedaled, he sang loudly, "*O, yeh ladki zara si deewani lagti hoi....*'

Old songs, best songs.   20

But then, in a week, five people called up Freddy's Wok to complain that the food was cold. It had turned to winter.

The shadows drew in close, the night chomped more than its share of hours. Biju smelled the first of the snow and found it had the same pricking, difficult smell that existed inside the freezer; he felt the Thermocol scrunch of it underfoot. On the Hudson, the ice cracked loudly into pieces, and within the contours of this gray, broken river it seemed as if the city's inhabitants were being provided with a glimpse of something far and forlorn that they might use to consider their own loneliness.

Biju put a padding of newspapers down his shirt—leftover copies from kind Mr. Iype the newsagent—and sometimes he took the scallion pancakes and inserted them below the paper, inspired by the memory of an uncle who used to go out to the fields in winter with his lunchtime *parathas* down his vest. But even this did not seem to help and once, on his bicycle, he began to weep from the cold, and the weeping unpicked a deeper vein of grief—such a terrible groan issued from between the whimpers that he was shocked his sadness had such depth.

When he returned home to the basement of a building at the bottom of Harlem, he fell straight into sleep.

The building belonged to an invisible management company that listed   25
its address as One and a Quarter Street and owned tenements all over the neighborhood, the superintendent supplementing his income by illegally renting out basement quarters by the week, by the month, and even by the day, to fellow illegals. He spoke about as much English as Biju did, so between Spanish, Hindi, and wild mime, Jacinto's gold tooth flashing in the late evening sun, they had settled the terms of rental. Biju joined a shifting population of men camping out near the fuse box, behind the boiler, in the cubby holes, and in odd-shaped corners that once were pantries, maids' rooms, laundry rooms, and storage rooms at the bottom of what had been a single-family home, the entrance still adorned with a scrap of colored mosaic in the shape of a star. The men shared a yellow toilet; the sink was a tin laundry trough. There was one fuse box for the whole building, and if anyone turned on too many appliances or lights, *PHUT*, the entire electricity went, and the residents screamed to nobody, since there was nobody, of course, to hear them.

Biju had been nervous there from his very first day. "Howdy," a man on the steps of his new abode had said, holding out his hand and nodding, "my name's Joey, and I just had me some WHEES-KAY!" Power and hiss. This was the local homeless man at the edge of his hunting and gathering territory, which he sometimes marked by peeing a bright arc right across the road. He wintered here on a subway grate in a giant plastic-bag igloo that sagged, then blew taut with stale air each time a train passed. Biju had taken the sticky hand offered, the man had held tight, and Biju had broken free and run, a cackle of laughter following him.

"The food is cold," the customers complained. "Soup arrived cold! Again! The rice is cold each and every time."

"I'm also cold," Biju said losing his temper.

"Pedal faster," said the owner.

"I cannot."   30

It was a little after 1 A.M. when he left Freddy's Wok for the last time, the street lamps were haloes of light filled with starry scraps of frozen vapor, and he trudged between snow mountains adorned with empty takeout containers and solidified dog pee in surprised yellow. The streets were empty but for the homeless man who stood looking at an invisible watch on his wrist while talking into a dead pay phone. "Five! Four! Three! Two! One—TAKEOFF!!" he shouted, and then he hung up the phone and ran holding onto his hat as if it might get blown off by the rocket he had just launched into space.

Biju turned in mechanically at the sixth somber house with its tombstone facade, past the metal cans against which he could hear the unmistakable sound of rat claws, and went down the flight of steps to the basement.

"I am very tired," he said out loud.

A man near him was frying in bed, turning this way, that way. Someone else was grinding his teeth.

By the time he had found employment again, at a bakery on Broadway 35 and La Salle, he had used up all the money in the savings envelope in his sock.

It was spring, the ice was melting, the freed piss was flowing. All over, in city cafés and bistros, they took advantage of this delicate nutty sliver between the winter, cold as hell, and summer, hot as hell, and dined al fresco on the narrow pavement under the cherry blossoms. Women in baby-doll dresses, ribbons, and bows that didn't coincide with their personalities indulged themselves with the first fiddleheads of the season, and the fragrance of expensive cooking mingled with the eructation of taxis and the lascivious subway breath that went up the skirts of the spring-clad girls making them wonder if *this* was how Marilyn Monroe felt—somehow not, somehow not....

The mayor found a rat in Gracie Mansion.

And Biju, at the Queen of Tarts bakery, met Saeed Saeed, who would become the man he admired most in the United States of America.

"I am from Zanzibar, *not* Tanzania," he said, introducing himself.

Biju knew neither one nor the other. "Where is that?" 40

"Don't you know?? Zanzibar full of Indians, man! My grandmother— she is Indian!"

In Stone Town they ate samosas and *chapatis, jalebis,* pilau rice....Saeed Saeed could sing like Amitabh Bachhan and Hema Malini. He sang, "*Mera joota hai japani.. .."* and "Bombay *se aaya mera dost—Oi!*" He could gesture with his arms out and wiggle his hips, as could Kavafya from Kazakhstan and Omar from Malaysia, and together they assailed Biju with thrilling dance numbers. Biju felt so proud of his country's movies he almost fainted.

Twenty-two

Brigitte's, in New York's financial district, was a restaurant hall of mirrors so the diners might observe exactly how enviable they were as they ate. It was named for the owners' dog, the tallest, flattest creature you ever saw; like paper, you could see her properly only from the side.

In the morning, Biju and the rest of the staff began bustling about, the owners, Odessa and Baz, drank Tailors of Harrowgate darjeeling at a corner table. Colonial India, free India—the tea was the same, but the romance was gone, and it was best sold on the word of the past. They drank tea and diligently they read the *New York Times* together, including the international news. It was overwhelming.

Former slaves and natives. Eskimos and Hiroshima people, Amazonian 45 Indians and Chiapas Indians and Chilean Indians and American Indians and Indian Indians. Australian aborigines, Guatemalans and Colombians and Brazilians and Argentineans, Nigerians, Burmese, Angolans, Peruvians, Ecuadorians, Bolivians, Afghans, Cambodians, Rwandans, Filipinos, Indonesians, Liberians, Borneoans, Papua New Guineans, South Africans, Iraqis, Iranians, Turks, Armenians, Palestinians, French Guyanese, Dutch Guyanese, Surinamese, Sierra Leonese, Malagasys, Senegalese, Maldivians, Sri Lankans, Malaysians, Kenyans, Panamanians, Mexicans, Haitians, Dominicans, Costa Ricans, Congoans, Mauritanians, Marshall Islanders, Tahitians, Gabonese, Beninese, Malians, Jamaicans, Botswanans, Burundians, Sudanese, Eritreans, Uruguayans, Nicarguans, Ugandans, Ivory Coastians, Zambians, Guinea-Bissauans, Cameroonians, Laotians, Zaireans coming at you screaming colonialism, screaming slavery, screaming mining companies screaming banana companies oil companies screaming CIA spy among the missionaries screaming it was Kissinger who killed their father and why don't you forgive third-world debt; Lumumba, they shouted, and Allende; on the other side, Pinochet, they said, Mobutu; contaminated milk from Nestlé, they said; Agent Orange; dirty dealings by Xerox. World Bank, UN, IMF, everything run by white people. Every day in the papers another thing!

Nestlé and Xerox were fine upstanding companies, the backbone of the economy, and Kissinger was at least a patriot. The United States was a young country built on the finest principles, and how could it possibly owe so many bills?

Enough was enough.

Business was business. Your bread might as well be left unbuttered were the butter to be spread so thin. The fittest one wins and gets the butter.

"Rule of nature," said Odessa to Baz. "Imagine if we were sitting around saying, 'So-and-so-score years ago, Neanderthals came out of the woods, attacked my family with a big dinosaur bone, and now you give back.' Two of the very first iron pots, my friend, and one toothsome toothy daughter from the first days of agriculture, when humans had larger molars, and four samples of an early version of the potato claimed, incidentally, by both Chile and Peru."

She was very witty, Odessa. Baz was proud of her cosmopolitan style, 50 loved the sight of her in her little wire-rimmed glasses. Once he had been shocked to overhear some of their friends say she was black-hearted, but he had put it out of his mind.

"These white people!" said Achootan, a fellow dishwasher, to Biju in the kitchen. "Shit! But at least this country is better than England," he said. "At least they have some hypocrisy here. They believe they are good people and you get some relief. There they shout at you openly on the street, 'Go back to where you came from.'" He had spent eight years in Canterbury, and he had responded by shouting a line Biju was to hear many times over, for he repeated it several times a week: "Your father came to *my* country and took *my* bread and now I have come to *your* country to get *my* bread back."

Achootan didn't want a green card in the same way as Saeed did. He wanted it in the way of revenge.

"Why do you want it if you hate it here?" Odessa had said angrily to Achootan when he asked for sponsorship.

Well, he wanted it. Everyone wanted it whether you liked it or you hated it. The more you hated it sometimes, the more you wanted it.

This they didn't understand.   55

The restaurant served only one menu: steak, salad, fries. It assumed a certain pride in simplicity among the wealthy classes.

Holy cow. Unholy cow. Biju knew the reasoning he should keep by his side. At lunch and dinner the space filled with young uniformed buisiness-people in their twenties and thirties.

"How would you like that, ma'am?"

"Rare."

"And you, sir?"   60

"Still mooin'."

Only the fools said, "Well done, please." Odessa could barely conceal her scorn. "Sure about that? Well, all right, but it's going to be tough."

She sat at the corner table where she had her morning tea and aroused the men by tearing into her steak.

"You know, Biju," she said, laughing, "isn't it ironic, nobody eats beef in India and just look at it—it's the shape of a big T-Bone."

But here there were Indians eating beef. Indian bankers. Chomp chomp. 65
He fixed them with a concentrated look of meaning as he cleared the plates. They saw it. They knew. He knew. They knew he knew. They pretended they didn't know he knew. They looked away. He took on a sneering look. But they could afford not to notice.

"I'll have the steak," they said with practiced nonchalance, with an ease like a signature that's a thoughtless scribble that you *know* has been practiced page after page.

Holy cow unholy cow.

Job no job.

One should not give up one's religion, the principles of one's parents and their parents before them. No, no matter what.

You had to live according to something. You had to find your dignity. 70
The meat charred on the grill, the blood beaded on the surface, and then
the blood also began to bubble and boil.

Those who could see a difference between a holy cow and an unholy
cow would win.

Those who couldn't see it would lose.

So Biju was learning to sear steaks.

Blood, meat, salt, and the cannon directed at the plates: "Would you
like freshly ground pepper on that, sir?"

"You know we may be poor in India, but there only a dog would eat 75
meat cooked like this," said Achootan.

"We need to get aggressive about Asia," the businessmen said to each
other. "It's opening up, new frontier, millions of potential consumers, big
buying power in the middle classes, China, India, potential for cigarettes,
diapers, Kentucky Fried, life insurance, water management, cell phones—
big family people, always on the phone, all those men calling their mothers, all those mothers calling all their many, many children; this country is
done, Europe done, Latin America done, Africa is a basket case except for
oil; Asia is the next frontier. Is there oil anywhere there? They don't have
oil, do they? They must...."

The talk was basic. If anyone dared to call them *Fool!* they could just
point at their bank accounts and let the numbers refute the accusation.

Biju thought of Saeed Saeed who still refused to eat a pig, "They dirty,
man, they messy. *First* I am Muslim, then I am Zanzibari, *then* I *will BE* American." Once he'd shown Biju his new purchase of a model of a mosque with
a quartz clock set into the bottom that was programmed, at the five correct
hours, to start agitating: *"Allah hu Akhar, La ilhaha illullah, wal lah hu akbar...."*
Through the crackle of the tape from the top of the minaret came ancient sand-
weathered words, that keening cry from the desert offering sustenance to create a man's strength, his faith in an empty-bellied morning and all through the
day, that he might not fall through the filthy differences between nations. The
lights came on encouragingly, flashing in the mosque in disco green and white.

"Why do you want to leave?" Odessa was shocked. A chance like they
had given him! He surely didn't know how lucky he was.

"He'll never make it in America with that kind of attitude," said Baz 80
hopefully.

Biju left a new person, a man full to the brim with a wish to live within
a narrow purity.

"Do you cook with beef?" he asked a prospective employer.

"We have a Philly steak sandwich."

"Sorry. I can't work here."

"They worship the cow," he heard the owner of the establishment tell   85
someone in the kitchen, and he felt tribal and astonishing.

Smoky Joe's.

"Beef?"

"Honey," said the lady, "Ah don't mean to ahffend you, but Ah'm a
steak eater and Ah AAHM beef."

Marilyn. Blown-up photographs of Marilyn Monroe on the wall, Indian owner at the desk!

The owner was on the speaker phone.   90

"Rajnibhai, *Kem chho?*"

"What?"

"Rajnibhai?"

"Who aez thees?" Very Indian-trying-to-be-American accent.

"Kem chho? Saaru chho? Teme samjo chho?"   95

"WHAAT?"

"Don't speak Gujerati, sir?"

"No."

"You are Gujerati, no?"

"No."   100

"But your name is Gujerati??"

"Who are you??!!"

"You are *not* Gujerati?"

"Who are you??!!"

"AT&T, sir, offering special rates to India."   105

"Don't know anyone in India."

"Don't know anyone???? You must have some relative?"

"Yeah," American accent growing more pronounced, "but I don' taaalk
to my relateev...."

Shocked silence.

"Don't talk to your relative?"   110

Then, "We are offering forty-seven cents per minute."

"Vhaat deeference does that make? I haeve aalready taaald you," he
spoke s l o w as if to an idiot, "no taleephone caalls to Eeendya."

"But you are from Gujerat?" Anxious voice.

"Veea Kampala, Uganda, Teepton, England, and Roanoke state of Vaer-
geenia! One time I went to Eeendya and, laet me tell you, you canaat pay
me to go to that caantreey agaen!

Slipping out and back on the street. It was horrible what happened to   115
Indians abroad and nobody knew but other Indians abroad. It was a dirty
little rodent secret. But, no, Biju wasn't done. His country called him again.
He smelled his fate. Drawn, despite himself, by his nose, around a corner,
he saw the first letter of the sign, *G*, then an *AN*. His soul anticipated the

rest: *DHI.* As he approached the Gandhi Café, the air gradually grew solid. It was always unbudgeable here, with the smell of a thousand and one meals accumulated, no matter the winter storms that howled around the corner, the rain, the melting heat. Though the restaurant was dark, when Biju tested the door, it swung open.

There in the dim space, at the back, amid lentils splattered about and spreading grease transparencies on the cloths of abandoned tables yet uncleared, sat Harish-Harry, who, with his brothers Gaurish-Gary and Dhan-sukh-Danny, ran a triplet of Gandhi Cafés in New York, New Jersey, and Connecticut. He did not look up as Biju entered. He had his pen hovering over a request for a donation sent by a cow shelter outside Edison, New Jersey.

If you gave a hundred dollars, in addition to such bonus miles as would be totted up to your balance sheet for lives to come, "We will send you a free gift; please check the box to indicate your preference":

1. A preframed decorative painting of Krishna-Lila: "She longs for her lord and laments."
2. A copy of the *Bhagvad Gita* accompanied by commentary by Pandit so-and-so (B A., MPhil., Ph.D., President of the Hindu Heritage Center), who has just completed a lecture tour in sixty-six countries.
3. A CD of devotional music beloved by Mahatma Gandhi.
4. A gift-coupon to the Indiagiftmart: "Surprise the special lady in your life with our special *choli* in the colors of onion and tender pink, coupled with a butter *lehnga*. For the woman who makes your house a home, a set of twenty-five spice jars with vacuum lids. Stock up on Haldiram's Premium Nagpur Chana Nuts that you must have been missing...."

His pen hovered. Pounced.

To Biju he said: "Beef? Are you crazy? We are an all-Hindu establishment. No Pakistanis, no Bangladeshis, those people don't know how to cook, have you been to those restaurants on Sixth Street? *Bilkul bekaar....*"

One week later, Biju was in the kitchen and Gandhi's favorite tunes 120 were being sung over the sound system.

New York Day Women

Edwidge Danticat

Edwidge Danticat was born in Haiti and moved to the United States when she was twelve. She is the author of several books, including *Breath, Eyes, Memory, Krik? Krak!*; and *The Farming of Bones*, an American Book Award winner. She is also the editor of *The Butterfly's Way: Voices from the Haitian Diaspora in the United States*.

Today, walking down the street, I see my mother. She is strolling with a happy gait, her body thrust toward the DON'T WALK sign and the yellow taxicabs that make forty-five-degree turns on the corner of Madison and Fifty-seventh Street.

I have never seen her in this kind of neighborhood, peering into Chanel and Tiffany's and gawking at the jewels glowing in the Bulgari windows. My mother never shops outside of Brooklyn. She has never seen the advertising office where I work. She is afraid to take the subway, where you may meet those young black militant street preachers who curse black women for straightening their hair.

Yet, here she is, my mother, who I left at home that morning in her bathrobe, with pieces of newspapers twisted like rollers in her hair. My mother, who accuses me of random offenses as I dash out of the house.

***

Would you get up and give an old lady like me your subway seat? In this state of mind, I bet you don't even give up your seat to a pregnant lady.

***

My mother, who is often right about that. Sometimes I get up and give my seat. Other times, I don't. It all depends on how pregnant the woman is and whether or not she is with her boyfriend or husband and whether or not *he* is sitting down.

As my mother stands in front of Carnegie Hall, one taxi driver yells to another, "What do you think this is, a dance floor?"

My mother waits patiently for this dispute to be settled before crossing the street.

***

In Haiti when you get hit by a car, the owner of the car gets out and kicks you for getting blood on his bumper.

***

My mother who laughs when she says this and shows a large gap in her mouth where she lost three more molars to the dentist last week. My mother, who at fifty-nine, says dentures are okay.

***

You can take them out when they bother you. I'll like them. I'll like them fine.

***

Will it feel empty when Papa kisses you?

***

Oh no, he doesn't kiss me that way anymore.

***

My mother, who watches the lottery drawing every night on channel 11 without ever having played the numbers.

***

A third of that money is all I would need. We would pay the mortgage, and your father could stop driving that taxicab all over Brooklyn.

***

I follow my mother, mesmerized by the many possibilities of her journey. Even in a flowered dress, she is lost in a sea of pinstripes and gray suits, high heels and elegant short skirts, Reebok sneakers, dashing from building to building.

My mother, who won't go out to dinner with anyone.

***

If they want to eat with me, let them come to my house, even if I boil water and give it to them.

***

My mother, who talks to herself when she peels the skin off poultry.

***

Fat, you know, and cholesterol. Fat and cholesterol killed your aunt Hermine.

***

My mother, who makes jam with dried grapefruit peel and then puts in cinnamon bark that I always think is cockroaches in the jam. My mother, whom I have always bought household appliances for, on her birthday. A nice rice cooker, a blender.

I trail the red orchids in her dress and the heavy faux leather bag on her shoulders. Realizing the ferocious pace of my pursuit, I stop against a wall to rest. My mother keeps on walking as though she owns the sidewalk under her feet.

As she heads toward the Plaza Hotel, a bicycle messenger swings so close to her that I want to dash forward and rescue her, but she stands dead in her tracks and lets him ride around her and then goes on.

My mother stops at a corner hot-dog stand and asks for something. The vendor hands her a can of soda that she slips into her bag. She stops by another vendor selling sundresses for seven dollars each. I can tell that she is looking at an African print dress, contemplating my size. I think to myself, Please Ma, don't buy it. It would be just another thing that I would bury in the garage or give to Goodwill.

***

Why should we give to Goodwill when there are so many people back home who need clothes? We save our clothes for the relatives in Haiti.

***

Twenty years we have been saving all kinds of things for the relatives in Haiti. I need the place in the garage for an exercise bike.

***

You are pretty enough to be a stewardess. Only dogs like bones.

***

This mother of mine, she stops at another hot-dog vendor's and buys a frankfurter that she eats on the street. I never knew that she ate frankfurters. With her blood pressure, she shouldn't eat anything with sodium. She has to be careful with her heart, this day woman.

***

I cannot just swallow salt. Salt is heavier than a hundred bags of shame.

***

She is slowing her pace, and now I am too close. If she turns around, she might see me. I let her walk into the park before I start to follow again.

My mother walks toward the sandbox in the middle of the park. There a woman is waiting with a child. The woman is wearing a leotard with biker's shorts and has small weights in her hands. The woman kisses the child good-bye and surrenders him to my mother; then she bolts off, running on the cemented stretches in the park.

The child given to my mother has frizzy blond hair. His hand slips into hers easily, like he's known her for a long time. When he raises his face to look at my mother, it is as though he is looking at the sky.

My mother gives this child the soda that she bought from the vendor on the street corner. The child's face lights up as she puts in a straw in the can for him. This seems to be a conspiracy just between the two of them.

My mother and the child sit and watch the other children play in the sandbox. The child pulls out a comic book from a knapsack with Big Bird on the back. My mother peers into his comic book. My mother, who taught herself to read as a little girl in Haiti from the books that her brothers brought home from school.

My mother, who has now lost six of her seven sisters in Ville Rose and has never had the strength to return for their funerals.

***

Many graves to kiss when I go back. Many graves to kiss.

***

She throws away the empty soda can when the child is done with it. I wait and watch from a corner until the woman in the leotard and biker's shorts returns, sweaty and breathless, an hour later. My mother gives the woman back her child and strolls farther into the park.

I turn around and start to walk out of the park before my mother can see me. My lunch hour is long since gone. I have to hurry back to work. I walk through a cluster of joggers, then race to a *Sweden Tours* bus. I stand behind the bus and take a peek at my mother in the park. She is standing in a circle, chatting with a group of women who are taking other people's children on an afternoon outing. They look like a Third World Parent-Teacher Association meeting.

I quickly jump into a cab heading back to the office. Would Ma have said hello had she been the one to see me first?

As the cab races away from the park, it occurs to me that perhaps one day I would chase an old woman down a street by mistake and that old woman would be somebody else's mother, who I would have mistaken for mine.

***

Day women come out when nobody expects them.

***

Tonight on the subway, I will get up and give my seat to a pregnant woman or a lady about Ma's age.

My mother, who stuffs thimbles in her mouth and then blows up her cheeks like Dizzy Gillespie while sewing yet another Raggedy Ann doll that she names Suzette after me.

***

I will have all these little Suzettes in case you never have any babies, which looks more and more like it is going to happen.

***

My mother who had me when she was thirty-three— *I'dge du Christ*—at the age that Christ died on the cross.

***

That's a blessing, believe you me, even if American doctors say by that time you can make retarded babies.

***

My mother, who sews lace collars on my company softball T-shirts when she does my laundry.

***

Why, you can't you look like a lady playing softball?

***

My mother, who never went to any of my Parent-Teacher Association meetings when I was in school.

***

You're so good anyway. What are they going to tell me? I don't want to make you ashamed of this day woman. Shame is heavier than a hundred bags of salt.

***

A Good Fall

Ha Jin

Ha Jin is the pen name of Xuefei Jin, born February 21, 1956, in China's Liaoning Province, He grew up during the turbulent years of the Cultural Revolution, served in the army, and completed bachelor's and master's degrees in his home country before coming to the United States in 1985 to pursue his doctorate in English at Brandeis University. Ha Jin is currently a professor of creative writing at Boston University. He is the author of numerous works, including the poetry volumes *Facing Shadows* (1996) and *Wreckage* (2001), and the short-story collections *Ocean of Words: Army Stories* (1996), *Under the Red Flag* (1997), *The Bridegroom* (2001), and *A Good Earth* (2009). Jin has also published the novels *In the Pond* (1998), *Waiting* (1999), *The Crazed* (2002), *War Trash* (2004), *A Free Life* (2007), and *Nanjiang Requiem* (2011). "A Good Fall" is based on a true story of a Chinese monk in Flushing, New York.

AGAIN GANCHIN COLLAPSED in the kung fu class he was teaching. Seated on the floor, he gasped for breath and couldn't get up. A student stepped over to give him a hand, but Ganchin waved to stop him. He forced himself to announce, "Let's call it a day. Please come back tomorrow afternoon." The seventeen boys and girls were collecting their bags in a corner and exiting the exercise hall. Some kept glancing at their teacher's contorted face.   1

Late that afternoon Master Zong called Ganchin into the small meditation room. They sat down on the floor, and the heavy-jawed master poured a cup of tea for him and said, "Brother, I'm afraid we have to let you go. We've tried but cannot get your visa renewed." He placed Ganchin's passport on the coffee table, beside the teacup.

Stunned, Ganchin opened his mouth, but no words came out. Indeed, he had been sick for weeks and couldn't teach the kung fu classes as well as before, yet never had he imagined that Master Zong would dismiss him before his contract expired. Ganchin said, "Can you pay me the salary the temple owes me?"

"We don't owe you anything," Zong answered, his hooded eyes glued to Ganchin's pale face.

"Our contract says clearly that you'll pay me fifteen hundred dollars a month. So far you haven't paid me a cent."   5

"Like I said, that was just a formality—we had to put down a figure to get the visa for you."

"Master Zong, I worked for you for more than two years and never made any trouble. Now that you fired me, you should give me at least my salary so I can go back and clear the debts I owe."

"We've provided lodging and board for you. This is New York, where everything's expensive. As a matter of fact, we paid you a lot more than fifteen hundred a month."

"But without some cash in hand I can't go home. I spent a fortune to get this teaching position, bribing the elders in charge of international exchanges at my monastery."

"We have no money for you."   10

"Then I cannot leave."

Zong picked up Ganchin's passport and inserted it into his robe. "I can't let you have your papers if you stay on illegally. From now on you're on your own, and you must move out tomorrow. I don't care where you go. Your visa has expired and you're already an illegal alien, a lawbreaker."

Zong got up from the floor and went out to the backyard, where his midnight blue BMW was parked. Ganchin was still sitting cross-legged in the room as the car pulled away. He knew the master was going home to Long Island, where he had recently bought a house in Syosset. Zong and his woman had just had a baby, but they couldn't marry because as the master of the temple he dared not take a wife openly. He'd kept his former residence, a town house in lower Manhattan, where he often put up his friends and the friends of his friends.

The temple felt deserted despite the tiny halos of candles on the rows of small tables in the service hall, at the end of which sat a tall statue of the Buddha smiling serenely, with his hands resting palms up on his knees. Ganchin closed the windows and bolted the front door. Since he had become ill, he had been more afraid of the night, when he felt more desolate and homesick. Originally he'd thought that by the time his three-year stint here was over he could return loaded with gifts and dollars. But now, penniless, he couldn't imagine going back. His father had written that some creditors had shown up to pester his family. The old man urged him not to rush home, not until he made enough money.

Ganchin cooked himself some rice porridge and ate it with two pre-   15
served eggs. After the meal he forced himself to drink some boiled water to keep down the acid gastric juice that was surging up into his throat. He decided to call Cindy, who had once learned martial arts from him when she visited Tianjin City, where his monastery and kung fu school were located. She was an "ABC" (American-born Chinese) but could speak Mandarin.

Ever since she'd met him again in Flushing, she had been friendly and often invited him to tea downtown.

They agreed to meet at Lovely Melodies, a bar at the northern end of Alexis Street. It was an out-of-the-way place where few could recognize Ganchin as a monk of Gaolin Temple. On arrival, he didn't go in, but waited for Cindy because he had no money. Within a minute she showed up. Together they entered the bar, found a table in a corner, and ordered their drinks. There were only about a dozen customers, but the music was loud. A young man near the front was belting out a karaoke song as if heartbroken:

What I miss most is your big smile
That still sweetens my dreams.
Although I run into you all the while,
Your face no longer beams...   20

"He really meant to get rid of you?" Cindy asked Ganchin about Master Zong, sipping her margarita with a straw.

"No doubt about it. I'll have to move out tomorrow." He gave a feeble sigh and set his glass of Sprite on the table.

"Where are you going to stay?"

"I have a friend, a fellow townsman, who might agree to take me in."

"You know, you can always use my place. I'm on trips most of the time   25
anyway." A small-framed woman of twenty-five with a sunny face, she was a flight attendant and often flew abroad. Sometimes she was away for a whole week.

"Thanks. I may be able to stay with my friend for the time being. To be honest, never have I felt this low—I can neither stay on nor go back."

"Why can't you live here?"

"Master Zong said I was already an illegal alien. He kept my passport."

"You shouldn't worry so much, sweetie. If worse comes to worst, you should consider marrying a woman, a U.S. citizen." She snickered, gazing at his lean face, her big eyes warm and brave.

He knew she was fond of him, but he said, "I'm a monk and can't think   30
of anything like that."

"Why not return to this earthly life?"

"Well, I'm already trapped in the web of dust. People say the temple is a place without strife, worry, or greed. It's not true. Master Zong lives like a CEO. I guess he must spend more than ten thousand dollars a month just for his house-hold expenses."

"I know. I saw him drive a brand-new car."

"That's why I am angry with him, for not paying me my salary."

"How much would be enough for you to go back?"   35

"At least twenty thousand dollars. He owes me forty thousand."

"I'm afraid he might never pay you that much."

Ganchin sighed. "I know. I'm upset but can't do a thing. He has a lot of pull back home. A cousin of his is the head the municipal police. Sometimes I wish I were an illegal coolie here, so that I could restart my life and wouldn't have to deal with any crook. But I've never worked outside a temple and don't have any skill. I'm useless here."

"Come on—you can teach martial arts."

"For that I'll have to know some English, won't I?"   40

"You can always learn it."

"Also, I'll need a work permit."

"Don't worry so much. Try to get better. Once you're well, there'll be ways for you to get by here."

He didn't want to talk more, unable to imagine making a living in America.

When they were leaving the bar, she asked him to contact her when-   45
ever he needed help. She was going to fly to Tokyo and would be back the next week. The night was slightly hazy and most shops were closed. Some young couples strolled along the sidewalks hand in hand or arm in arm. A car honked about two hundred feet away. At the blast a linden sapling nearby shuddered a little, its leaves rusting. Ganchin had a fit of wheezing coughing and wiped his mouth with a tissue. Cindy patted him on the back and urged him to rest in bed for a few days. He grimaced, his face wry. They said good night, and in no time her sylphlike figure in its orange skirt faded into the dark.

Fanku wasn't really Ganchin's friend. They had come to know each other about six months ago at a celebration of the Spring Festival. Ganchin had been delighted to find the man to be a fellow townsman, from the same county. Fanku worked as a line cook at an eatery. When Ganchin asked to stay with him for a few days, Fanku welcomed him, saying he was proud to help a friend.

His studio apartment was in the basement of a nine-story tenement, close to downtown Flushing. It had a tiny bathroom but no kitchenette, and was furnished with only a cot and a pair of metal chairs standing on either side of a narrow table. When Ganchin had arrived, Fanku pulled a bundle out of the closet and spread the thin sponge mattress on the floor. "Here, you can sleep on this," he told the guest. "I hope this is all right."

"Very good, thanks," Ganchin replied.

In the morning he would roll up the mattress and stow it in the closet again. The sleeping arrangement satisfied both of them, but Ganchin's hacking cough troubled Fanku, who asked him several times about the true nature of his illness. Ganchin assured him that it was not tuberculosis, that he must have hurt his lungs during his kung fu practice, and that the illness had been aggravated by the anger and anguish he'd gone through lately. Even so, Fanku often examined the water in a pickle bottle—into which the monk spat—to see if there was blood. So far he'd found nothing abnormal. Still, Ganchin's constant coughing disturbed him, especially at night.

Fanku let his guest use whatever food he had in the studio for free, while he himself ate at work. There were a few packs of ramen noodles and a half sack of jasmine rice in the cabinets, and he urged Ganchin to eat something more nutritious so that he could recuperate, but the monk had no money. He asked Fanku for a loan of two hundred dollars, but Fanku was almost as broke as Ganchin. He'd overstayed his business visa and had to pay horrendous attorney's fees, as he had been trying to get his illegal status changed. He lent Ganchin sixty dollars instead. Fanku often brought back food for Ganchin, a box of rice mixed with pork roast, or a bag of fish croquettes, or a bunch of egg rolls and spareribs. By now, Ganchin had started eating meat and seafood; it was hard to remain vegetarian when he had no idea where he would have his next meal. Fanku said he could get those food items at a discount, but Ganchin wondered if they were leftovers. Yet whenever the thought popped into his mind, he'd push it aside and remind himself to be grateful.

Then one morning Fanku said, "Look, Ganchin, I don't mean to pressure you, but I can't continue paying for the food I bring back. My lawyer asked me to give him thirty-five hundred dollars by the end of this month. I'm totally broke."

Lowering his eyes, Genchin said, "Please keep a record of the money you've spent on me. I'll pay it back."

"You misunderstood me, brother. I simply don't have enough cash now. Goodness knows if my lawyer really can help me. A girl at Olivia Salon has spent more than eighty thousand dollars for attorney's fees but still can't get a green card. Sometimes I'm so desperate for cash that I feel like mugging someone. You know, I have to send money to my wife and daughter back home as well."

"Can you help me find work at your restaurant? I can wash dishes and mop floors."

"You're so ill, no place would dare to use you. The best you can do is rest well and try to recover."

Ganchin turned silent for a few seconds, then replied, "I'll try to get some money."

Fanku said no more. He yawned, having slept poorly since Ganchin had been here. Fanku was only forty-one but looked wizened like an old man with a pimpled bald crown. He must have lived in fear and worry all

50

55

the time. He spread his hand towel on a clotheshorse in a corner and left for work.

After breakfast, which was two cold buns stuffed with red-bean paste and a cup of black tea, Ganchin set out for Gaolin Temple. His legs were a little shaky as he walked. A shower had descended the previous night, so the streets were clean and even the air smelled fresher, devoid of the stink of rotten fish and vegetables. He turned onto a side street. On the pavement seven plump sparrows were struggling with spilled popcorn, twittering fretfully and hardly able to break the fluffy kernels. Regardless of humans and automobiles, the birds were all working hard at the food. Approaching the temple, Ganchin heard people shouting and stamping their feet in unison inside the brick building. A new coach was teaching a kung fu class.

At the sight of Ganchin, Master Zong put on a smile and said, "You've gained some color. I hope you're well now." He led him to the back of the building, walking with a slight stoop.

Seated on a bamboo mat in the meditation room, Ganchin said, "Master, I came to see if there's some way you can pay me my salary. I can't stay on illegally—you know that—and neither can I go home without enough cash to clear my debts."   60

Zong's smile didn't stop, displaying a mouth of gleaming teeth, which had often made Ganchin wonder what kind of toothpaste the master used. Zong said, "Let me repeat, our temple doesn't owe you a thing."

"Master, you've pushed me to the edge of a cliff—I have no way out now and may have to follow Ganping's example." Ganping had been a monk at the temple, who, after three years' work, wouldn't go back on account of the unpaid salary. Master Zong had ordered him to leave, but the monk went to a park and hanged himself instead.

"You're not like Ganping," Zong said calmly, his fleshy face sleek. "He was insane and stupid, couldn't even do a clean job of hanging himself. That's why he is in jail now." People had spotted Ganping the moment he dangled from a piece of cloth tied to a bough of an oak, his legs kicking, and they'd called the police, who brought him back to the temple. Soon afterward he was sent back to China. But he went crazy because his girlfriend had taken a lover during his absence. He strangled the woman, with whom he ought not to have started a romantic relationship in the first place.

Ganchin felt like weeping but took hold of himself. He said, "Don't underestimate me, Master. If life is no longer worth living, one can end it without remorse."

"You have your old parents, who are looking forward to seeing you home. You shouldn't think of such a cowardly way out."   65

"If I went back empty-handed, I'd be a great disappointment to them. I'd prefer to die here."

"Don't talk about death. We monks must cherish every life. Life is given us only once, and it's a sin to destroy it. You know all this; no need for me to dwell on it."

"Master, farewell. See you in the next world."

"Stop bluffing. To be honest, according to my agreement with your monastery, I'm responsible for sending you home, but I won't force you. You can choose what to do." The master let out a huge burp.

"I only hope my soul can reach home. Good-bye now." Ganchin got up   70
from the bamboo mat and made for the door.

"Pighead," Zong said.

Ganchin stepped out of the temple. Forks of lightning cracked the sky in the south, where dark clouds were billowing, piling on one another. The wind was rising as shop signs along the street were flapping. Pedestrians were rushing back and forth to avoid the thickening rain, a stocky woman running with a newspaper over her head, but Ganchin just strolled back to Fanku's place. Big raindrops pattered on tree leaves and on his face while his robe fluttered.

Cindy came to see him the next afternoon. His cough had turned harsher, thanks to the rain that had drenched him. He was also thinner than the previous week. She took him to Little Pepper, a Sichuan restaurant, and ordered a vegetarian firepot for both of them.

He had no appetite for vegetables and would have preferred meat or seafood. He spoke listlessly while she tried to cheer him up. "Don't think you're down and out," she said. "You're still young and can always restart."

"How do you mean?" He looked at her heart-shaped face blankly.   75

"I mean it's foolish to think you're done for. Lots of people here are illegal aliens. They live a hard life but still can manage. In a couple of years there might be an amnesty that allows them to become legal immigrants." She cut a cube of tofu in two with her chopsticks and put a half into her mouth, chewing it with her lips closed.

"I really don't know what to do. I hope I can go home soon."

"Continue to be a monk?" She gave a pixieish smile.

"I've never been someone else since I grew up."

"You can always change. This is America, where it's never too late to   80
turn over a new page. That's why my parents came here. My mom hated her ex-mother-in-law—that's my grandmother—and wanted to restart her life far away from the old woman."

He grimaced again, having no idea what to say. He thought of borrowing money from Cindy to clear the debt of sixty dollars he owed Fanku, but refrained. He would prefer to leave her only good memories of him.

"You look better with your crew cut, you know." She pointed at his head, which used to be shaved bald.

"I didn't mean to keep it this way at all."

"You should let your hair grow longer. That will make your face look stronger—more masculine, I mean. Are you okay at your current place?"

He took a bite of a fake meatball made of minced mushroom and soy flour and answered, "It's all right for now. I don't know how long I can stay with Fanku. I might already be a burden to him."

"Keep in mind you can always use my place, I live on planes and in hotels these days."

"Thank you." His eyes went moist, but he averted his face and squeezed his lids. "If only I had been born here," he sighed.

"Except for the Indians, nobody's really a native in the United States. You mustn't think of yourself as a stranger—this country belongs to you if you live and work here."

"I'm too old to change."

"How can you say that? You're just twenty-eight!"

"But my heart is very, very old."

"You still have fifty years to go, at least." She giggled and patted his hand. He smiled and shook his head as if to admit he was beyond help.

After talking with Cindy, he realized that Master Zong had kept his passport with an eye to preventing him from changing his status, because illegal aliens had to produce their papers when the U.S. president issued an amnesty. It would be impossible to apply for a green card in good time if you couldn't prove your country of origin and your date of entry into the United States. Zong must be determined to get him back to China.

Fanku told Ganchin to stay in the next morning, because the superintendent of the tenement would come around eleven to check the smoke detector. Ganchin promised not to go out before the man showed up. He was lying on the cot, thinking about whether he should ask for a smaller amount of cash from Master Zong, say twenty-five thousand, since apparently the temple had never paid any monk a salary. How he regretted having tried so hard to come here! He'd been misled by the people who bragged about the opportunity found in America and wouldn't reveal the hardship they'd gone through here. They all wanted to appear rich and successful in their hometowns' eyes. Silly, how silly. If he went back, he would tell the truth—the American type of success was not for everyone. You must learn how to sell yourself there and must change yourself to live a new life.

As he was musing, someone knocked on the door. He got up to answer it. The instant he opened it a crack two men burst in. One was Master Zong and the other a brawny young fellow Ganchin had never met. They grabbed his arms. "Don't resist," Zong hissed. "We won't hurt you. We're just helping you go home, to keep you from deteriorating into a bum."

"Where are you taking me?" Ganchin gasped.

"To the airport," Zong said, as they hauled him away. Ganchin was too weak to struggle and so he obeyed them.

They shoved him into the back of the BMW, buckled him up, and dropped on his lap two paper napkins for his phlegm. Then they got into the front seats, and the car pulled away. In a placid voice Zong explained to him, "Don't be upset. I bought the plane ticket for you and will give you some cash for your travel expenses. When you check in at the counter, I'll let you have your passport."

"You've kidnapped me. This is against the law."

The men both guffawed. The squint-eyed young fellow said, "Please   100 don't accuse us like this. You're a Chinese and soon will board a plane for China."

"Yes, you can grouse as much as you like to the elders of your monastery," Zong told him.

Realizing it was useless to argue, Ganchin clammed up the rest of the way, though he was thinking hard about how to break loose.

They parked in a garage and then took him to Air China. A large uniformed black woman stood at the entrance to the ticketing counter; Ganchin wondered if he should shout to get her attention, but thought better of it. The three of them entered the zigzag cordoned lane filled with people. This wasn't personal, Master Zong kept telling him. They just didn't want to sully China's image by letting an ocher-robed monk roam the streets of New York. That would tarnish the temple's reputation as well.

What should Ganchin do? He could get rid of his robe as he had slacks underneath. Should he go to the men's room and see if he could find a way to escape from there? No, they would see through him. How about calling to the fully armed security guards with the big German shepherd near the checkpoint? No. Master Zong might still be able to get him on the plane, claiming he was mentally ill, dangerous like a terrorist, and must be sent home for treatment.

As he was wondering, a passenger cart with three rows of seats on it   105 was coming up, an old couple sitting in the first row. Ganchin glanced at his kidnappers—both of them were looking at the counter, where two young women were lugging a family's baggage onto the conveyor belt. Ganchin lifted the blue cordon beside him, slunk out of the lane, and leapt upon the last row of seats on the cart, then rolled down into the legroom. He pulled in his feet so his kidnappers couldn't see him. The battery-powered vehicle was running away when he heard Zong shout, "Ganchin, Ganchin, where are you?"

"Come here, Ganchin, you dickhead!" another voice barked.

"Ganchin, come over, please! We can negotiate," Zong cried.

Ganchin realized they didn't know he was on the vehicle, which veered off and headed for another terminal. He stayed put, letting it take him as far away as possible.

Finally the cart stopped, and he raised his head to look around. "Hey, this is for disability only," the black driver told him, flashing a smile while helping the old couple off.

Ganchin didn't know what the man meant, and just said, "Thank you."   110
That was all the English he had besides "goodbye." He got off and went into a men's room, where he shed his robe. He dumped it into a trash can and came out wearing black slacks and an off-white sweatshirt.

He managed to get back to Flushing by a hotel shuttle, following the suggestion of a middle-aged Taiwanese woman. Terrified, he could not return to Fanku's place. Evidently that man and Master Zong were in cahoots. Where to go now? Where was a safe place? Never had Ganchin imagined that Zong would resort to force to fly him back. A pain tightened his chest and he coughed again.

He still had a few dollars in his pocket, so he slouched into Teng's Garden, which wasn't far from Gaolin Temple. A trim little man in shirtsleeves, apparently the owner of the restaurant, greeted him and, raising his forefinger, said heartily, "One?" He was about to take him into the interior.

"Just a minute. Can I use your phone?" Ganchin asked.

"There's a pay phone down the street. Why not use that one?" The man waved in the direction of the temple.

"I don't know how to use a pay phone."   115

"Similar to a regular one—drop in a quarter and dial the number you want to call. We're talking about a local call, right?"

"Actually, I don't have to use a phone. I'm Ganchin, a monk of Gaolin Temple, and I'd like to leave a word for Master Zong there. Can you pass it for me?"

"I don't know you."

"Look, this is me." Ganchin produced a laminated photo and showed it to the man. In it Ganchin, wearing black cloth shoes, struck a pose like an eagle about to hop off; above his shiny shaved head a golden banner was floating in a breeze; he looked like a movie star, a hero, full of spunk.

The little man squinted at the picture and then at him. "Yes, it's you.   120
What do you want me to tell your master?"

"Tell him to say prayers and make offerings for my soul tomorrow morning before sunrise."

"What are you talking about? Like you're already a ghost."

"I'm going to die soon. Tell Master Zong to pray to redeem my soul before six o'clock tomorrow morning, all right?"

"Young brother, you shouldn't think like this. You mustn't give up so easily. Come with me, let's talk and see if this old man can be any help."

Ganchin followed him into an inner room; in its center stood a round   125
dining table with a revolving, two-level tray on it. Apparently this was a place for banquets. The moment they sat down at the immense table, Ganchin said he'd decided to kill himself today. He was sick and penniless, while Master Zong tried to send him back to China without paying him the salary the temple owed him. The little man listened, wordless. The more Ganchin rambled, the more heartbroken he became, until he couldn't continue anymore and collapsed into sobbing.

The restaurant owner sighed and shook his broad head. He said, "You wait here and I'll be back in a minute."

By now Ganchin had calmed down some, though was still tearful. He believed this was his last day on earth. Thinking about his old parents, he felt his insides writhing. How devastated they would be by his death! And without him, their only son, how miserable their remaining years would become. But he simply had no way out. If he died here, at least some of the creditors might take pity on his parents and forgive the debts. Oh, this was the only way he could help his family!

The little man came back with a large bowl of rice topped with sautéed seafood and vegetables. He said to Ganchin, "Young brother, I can see you're hungry. Eat this and you might think differently afterward. Gosh, I totally forgot you're a monk, a vegetarian! Sorry about this. I'm gonna—"

"I eat seafood," Ganchin said.

"Then eat this. Keep in mind, yours is not the worst sorrow. Life is   130
precious and full of wonderful things in spite of all the bitterness and sufferings."

"Thank you, Uncle," he mumbled. "I will put in a good word for you when I meet the Buddha in the other world." He broke the connected chopsticks and began eating.

Oh, it tasted so good! This was the most delicious meal he'd had in recent years, and he picked up the shrimp and scallops one after another and swallowed them as if they did not require chewing. The snow peas were crisp, the bamboo shoots crunchy, and the portabella mushrooms succulent, perfectly done. He ate and ate, and in no time finished the whole thing. Then he lifted the bowl, about to drink up the remaining sauce, but caught himself and put it down.

"Uncle," he said, "I know you're kind and generous. You gave ear to a stranger's grievance, you didn't ask me but guessed I was hungry, and you have a compassionate soul. Here's a bit of cash. Please keep this." He pulled all the money out of his pants pocket and left it on the table, one five and three singles.

Waving his stubby fingers, the man protested, "I didn't mean to sell you any food. I don't want your money. Just think about all the good things in this life, okay? Don't let your grief crush you."

"Please tell Master Zong to pray for me before sunrise tomorrow morning. Good-bye, Uncle." Ganchin hurried out the door and dragged himself away, feeling the restaurateur's gaze at his back. 135

Where should he go? He wanted to find a building out of which he could jump and kill himself. How about the temple? No, it had only two stories. Too low. How about the elementary school? No, his ghost might frighten the children if he died there, and people would condemn him.

Having crossed Northern Boulevard, he saw a brick building to his right, partly boarded up. He took a brief measure of it—it was high enough, five stories. Also, this was a deserted spot and his death might not disturb many people in the neighborhood. So he decided to use this building, which must once have been a factory and still had metal ventilators on its roof.

As he was laboring up the sagging stairs, a flock of pigeons took off, their wings flickering explosively, and a few bats flitted about, catching mosquitoes while emitting tinny squeaks in the glow of the sinking sun. The distant houses and the spires of the churches were obscured, half hidden in the golden smog. At a landing the floor was strewn with needleless syringes, takeout containers, cigarette butts, beer cans. He wondered if some people lived in here at night. Well, if they did, they shouldn't continue using this place when it got cold. On the top floor he leaned over a few unboarded windows to survey the base of the building. Down there in the empty parking lot a lone seagull with black wing tips was wrestling with a paper bag, dragging out balled-up napkins and plastic cups and plates to pick up bits of fries. Ganchin decided to use the backyard to avoid the traffic on the front street. He propped two thick boards on a windowsill that had lost its wood and was just lined with bricks. He pictured himself running all the way up the boards and springing out of the building headfirst. That would do the job for sure. He backed up a dozen steps, ready to dash.

Suddenly his stomach churned and sent up a chunk of scallop and a few rice grains that he hadn't chewed thoroughly. Oh, they still tasted good! He swallowed the morsel while tears were trickling down his cheeks. He started running, up and up, until he hurled himself into the air. As he was falling facedown, somehow all the years of training in martial arts at once possessed him. His body instinctively adjusted itself and even his arms spread out, swinging to ensure that he wouldn't hurt himself fatally. With a thump his feet landed on the ground. "Ow!" he yelled, thunderstruck that he had just cheated death. A tearing pain shot up from his left thigh while his right leg twitched.

"Ow, help me! Help!" he hollered.   140

How ludicrous this whole thing turned out! He kept yelling, and some people came over, most of them high school students playing basketball nearby. A man dialed 911 and another comforted him, saying, "Don't move. Everything's cool, man. I know this hurts, must hurt like hell, but help's on the way."

"Oh, let me die, let me finish myself!" Eyes shut, Ganchin was screaming and shaking his head, but nobody understood his Mandarin.

In addition to a broken leg, the doctors found, he also suffered from tracheitis. No wonder he was running a temperature and coughing non-stop. They kept him in the hospital for three days until his fever was gone. Meanwhile, his attempted suicide had become news in the Chinese communities across North America, reported by numerous small newspapers; a charitable organization offered to pick up his medical bills; and even the owner of Teng's Garden got famous for a week, having appeared twice on local TV. Everyone knew that the master of Gaolin Temple had exploited young monks and pocketed their salaries. Many declared that they would never donate anything to the temple again. A pretty thirtysome-thing named Amy Lok, running for a seat in the state senate, paid Ganchin a visit and told him to contact her office if he needed any assistance. Several lawyers called, eager to represent him in a lawsuit against the temple. All the notoriety befuddled and unnerved Ganchin.

Cindy took him in after he was released from the hospital with a pair of crutches, and she persuaded him to let her speak with the attorneys on his behalf so that they might not take advantage of him. She urged him to use Jon Mah, an older man who spoke both Mandarin and Korean and was known for handling this kind of case. Ganchin was worried about the legal fee, but Mr. Mah told him, "You don't need to pay before you get the damages from the defendant."

Cindy said to Ganchin, "They'll get a third of the money the court   145
awards you."

"This is America," Mr. Mah resumed, "a land ruled by law, and nobody is entitled to abuse others with impunity. Rest assured, you're in safe hands."

After the attorney left, Ganchin was still antsy. He asked Cindy, "What will the INS do to me? If they deport me, can I get enough money for the debts back home?"

"Now there'll be ways for you to avoid deportation—you can apply for political asylum, or marry a citizen or a legal resident. You know, you'll be rich, but not filthy rich like a millionaire who doesn't have to work."

Amazed, Ganchin thought about her words, then sighed. "I guess I'm not a monk anymore, and no temple will ever take me in."

"That also means you're free to date a girl." She giggled, rubbing her nose with a knuckle. 150

"Well, I hope that's something I can learn." He gazed at her and smiled.

The Bridge

Hart Crane

Hart Crane (1899–1932) was inspired by the modernist poetry of T.S. Eliot and wrote similarly difficult and highly stylized work. His most ambitious work, was *The Bridge* (1930). This poem depicts an epic vision of American life with the Brooklyn Bridge as a central image. The section reprinted below, entitled "To Brooklyn Bridge," is the poem's prologue.

THE BRIDGE

How many dawns, chill from his rippling rest   1
The seagull's wings shall dip and pivot him,
Shedding white rings of tumult, building high
Over the chained bay waters Liberty—

Then, with inviolate curve, forsake our eyes   5
As apparitional as sails that cross
Some page of figures to be filed away;
—Till elevators drop us from our day...

I think of cinemas, panoramic sleights
With multitudes bent toward some flashing scene   10
Never disclosed, but hastened to again,
Foretold to other eyes on the same screen;

And Thee, across the harbor, silver-paced
As though the sun took step of thee, yet left
Some motion ever unspent in thy stride,—   15
Implicitly thy freedom staying thee!

Out of some subway scuttle, cell or loft
A bedlamite speeds to thy parapets,
Tilting there momently, shrill shirt ballooning,
A jest falls from the speechless caravan.   20

Down Wall, from girder into street noon leaks,
A rip-tooth of the sky's acetylene;

All afternoon the cloud-flown derricks turn...
Thy cables breathe the North Atlantic still.

And obscure as that heaven of the Jews, 25
Thy guerdon...Accolade thou dost bestow
Of anonymity time cannot raise:
Vibrant reprieve and pardon thou dost show.

O harp and altar, of the fury fused,
(How could mere toil align thy choiring strings!) 30
Terrific threshold of the prophet's pledge,
Prayer of pariah, and the lover's cry,—

Again the traffic lights that skim thy swift
Unfractioned idiom, immaculate sigh of stars,
Beading thy path—condense eternity: 35
And we have seen night lifted in thine arms.

Under thy shadow by the piers I waited;
Only in darkness is thy shadow clear.
The City's fiery parcels all undone,
Already snow submerges an iron year... 40

O Sleepless as the river under thee,
Vaulting the sea, the prairies' dreaming sod,
Unto us lowliest sometime sweep, descend
And of the curveship lend a myth to God.

In a Station of the Metro

Ezra Pound

Ezra Pound (1885–1972) is considered one of the founding fathers of modern poetry, which sought to reduce writing to its essential features. His poem "In the Station of the Metro" is an excellent example of "imagist" writing, which strives to convey meaning concisely and vividly. Pound attended Hamilton College in New York and lived much of his life abroad. He is best known for *The Cantos,* a collection of poems he worked on throughout much of his life.

IN A STATION OF THE METRO[1]

The apparition of these faces in the crowd;
Petals on a wet, black bough.

1913–1916

From PERSONAE by Ezra Pound, 1909.

George Tooker (1920–2011), *The Subway*, 1950, egg tempera on gesso panel, 18⅛ × 36⅛ in., Whitney Museum of American Art, New York, purchased with funds from the Juliana Force Purchase Award, 50.23. Courtesy of DC Moore Gallery, New York.

---

[1] The Paris subway.

Recuerdo

Edna St. Vincent Millay

Edna St Vincent Millay (1892–1950) was born in Rockland, Maine. When Edna was twenty her poem, *Renascence,* was published in *The Lyric Year.* As a result of this poem, Edna won a scholarship to Vassar. In 1917, the year of her graduation, Millay published her first book, *Renascence and Other Poems.* After leaving Vassar she moved to New York's Greenwich Village where she befriended writers such as Floyd Dell, John Reed, and Max Eastman. The three·men were all involved in the left-wing journal, *The Masses,* and she joined in their campaign against Americans involvement in the First World War.

RECUERDO

We were very tired, we were very merry—
We had gone back and forth all night on the ferry.
It was bare and bright, and smelled like a stable—
But we looked into a fire, we leaned across a table,
We lay on a hill-top underneath the moon;   1
And the whistles kept blowing, and the dawn came
     soon.
We were very tired, we were very merry—
We had gone back and forth all night on the ferry;
And you ate an apple, and I ate a pear,
From a dozen of each we had bought somewhere;   5
And the sky went wan, and the wind came cold,
And the sun rose dripping, a bucketful of gold.
We were very tired, we were very merry,
We had gone back and forth all night on the ferry.
We hailed, "Good morrow, mother!" to a shawl-covered   10
     head,
And bought a morning paper, which neither of us read;
And she wept, "God bless you!" for the apples and pears,
And we gave her all our money but our subway fares.

From *Collected Poems* by Edna St. Vincent Millay, 1922

The Taxi

Amy Lowell

Amy Lowell (1874–1925) was an American Imagist poet. She grew up in a sophisticated and literary environment, yet she did not attend college and was largely self-educated. Although her writing career spanned just twelve years, she wrote over 600 poems. Lowell lectured about and wrote free-verse poetry; that is, poetry that does not follow strict rules of form. Her poetry used common speech, as she wanted to be free to communicate directly about any subject. In the poem below, published in 1914 in the collection *Sword Blades and Poppy Seeds*, readers get the impression of a city and of loss. For what things does the speaker in this poem yearn?

THE TAXI

When I go away from you   1
The world beats dead
Like a slackened drum.
I call out for you against the jutted stars
And shout into the ridges of the wind.   5
Streets coming fast,
One after the other,
Wedge you away from me,
And the lamps of the city prick my eyes
So that I can no longer see your face.   10
Why should I leave you,
To wound myself upon the sharp edges of the night?

Lenox Avenue: Midnight

Langston Hughes

Langston Hughes (1902–1967) was one of the most important figures of the Harlem Renaissance. Although widely respected, he was often criticized for publishing stories and poetry that included violence and imperfect characters. In this poem, published in 1926, the speaker combines musical terms with a specific street to evoke a certain mood.

LENOX AVENUE: MIDNIGHT

The rhythm of life   1
Is a jazz rhythm,
Honey,
The gods are laughing at us.
The broken heart of love,   5
The weary, weary heart of pain—
    Overtones,
    Undertones,
To the rumble of street cars,
To the swish of rain.
Lenox Avenue,
Honey,   10
Midnight,
And the gods are laughing at us.

New York Subway

Hilda Morley

Hilda Morley (1919–1998) had a long and distinguished career as a poet and teacher. She taught for many years in New York City. In the poem below, published in the collection titled *To Hold My Hand: Selected Poems 1955–1983*, we read about a subway event that might still happen today. Readers might notice that many different people come together to help someone. Do these acts of kindness still take place?

NEW YORK SUBWAY

The beauty of people in the subway   1
that evening, Saturday, holding the door for whoever
was slower or
left behind
    (even with   5
      all that Saturday-night
      excitement)
& the high-school boys from Queens, boasting,
joking together
proudly in their expectations
& power, young frolicsome
bulls,   10
    & the three office-girls
each strangely beautiful, the Indian
with dark skin & the girl with her haircut
very short and fringed, like Joan
at the stake,   the corners
of her mouth laughing   15
    & the black girl delicate
as a doe, dark-brown in pale-brown clothes
& the tall woman in a long caftan, the other
day,
serene & serious & the Puerto Rican
holding the door for more than 3 minutes for   20
the feeble, crippled, hunched little man who
could not raise his head,
    whose hand I held, to
help him into the subway-car—
    so we were
joined in helping him   & someone,   25
seeing us, gives up his seat,
    learning
from us what we had learned from each other.

The City in Which I Love You

Li-Young Lee

Li-Young Lee was born in 1957 in Jakarta, Indonesia, of Chinese parents. His father, who was a personal physician to Mao Zedong while in China, relocated his family to Indonesia, where he helped found Gamaliel University. In 1959 the Lee family fled the country to escape anti-Chinese sentiment and after a five-year trek through Hong Kong, Macau, and Japan, they settled in the United States in 1964. He is the author of *Book of My Nights, The City in Which I Love You* (1991), *Rose* (1986), as well as a memoir entitled *The Winged Seed: A Remembrance* (1995).

THE CITY IN WHICH I LOVE YOU

Morning comes to this city vacant of you. 1
Pages and windows flare, and you are not there.
Someone sweeps his portion of sidewalk,
wakens the drunk, slumped like laundry,
and you are gone. 5
You are not in the wind
which someone notes in the margins of a book.
You are gone out of the small fires in abandoned lots
where human figures huddle,
each aspiring to its own ghost. 10
Between brick walls, in a space no wider than my face,
a leafless sapling stands in mud.
In its branches, a nest of raw mouths
gaping and cheeping, scrawny fires that must eat.
My hunger for you is no less than theirs. 15

Meditation on a Brooklyn Bench

Harvey Shapiro

Harvey Shapiro is described by *The New York Times* as the "reigning laureate of New York's vox populi," i.e. the people's poet. He has written over a dozen volumes of poetry including *The Sights Along the Harbor.* His poetry encompasses a broad spectrum of subjects, including New York streets and locales, the Brooklyn waterfront, love, and the brutality of war.

MEDITATION ON A BROOKLYN BENCH

I was by myself on the promenade,   1
facing the massive city. Pleasure craft
cut white trails in the water.
The lady with the lamp dim green
in the dim green afternoon.   5
A Circle Line boat, looking sprightly,
hurrying up river toward the Bridge,
and the old paddle steamer from
the South Street Seaport meandering
past Battery. The kind of day you   10
needn't take responsibility for, sitting
in the shade, like an elderly citizen,
wondering where it all went—the wife
and kids, the years of work. Covered over
by the waters of the East River. Not a river,   15
a tidal basin, and the tide coming in now,
full force, dangerous, looking for me.

Lost Son's Self-Assessment

Abraham Benjamin

Abraham Benjamin, a.k.a. Honest Abe, was born in Brooklyn, NY. He is a spoken word artist who has recently published a book of poems, *Unlocked Thoughts of a Prophet's Temple: Humble Beginnings* as well as the indie album, *Brooklyn's Lost Son: Prelude to the Road 2 Redemption.*

Lost Son's Self-Assessment

In this disease of Nature we call life   1
I've been feeling out of place since birth
And I've been trying to realize my purpose
More times than not contemplated suicide
Now wondering if it's really worth this.   5
To quote one of my brothers in words & knowledge, 'Mar Hill,
"I didn't choose poetry. Poetry choose Me!!"
So I was pulled into this
Through a force of nature I couldn't control
Was never one to throw stones   10
With my nose to the grindstone
Since I first touched a microphone.
At times, the journey has felt so cold,
So I looked at myself
At the man in the mirror   15
And asked myself: Am I the only one?
After all the twists and turns in this roller coaster ride in
Spoken Word,
I guess that's why I dubbed myself, "Brooklyn's Lost Son."
Finding my path on this road to redemption   20
To finally accept the solace of my mind, body, soul,
I was taught to speak my mind
Even if it meant being so damn bold!
Trying to rebuild the bridges
I done burned,   25
Hoping the Almighty and Universe offer a
Clean slate.

Burn notices tend to leave scars of life lessons
When they've been nailed to your chest
By the hammer of Karma,   30
So you can endure the next test
Of change you need to make, and to change the needs to come.
Father Time seems to play the role of universal parent and
Wisdom teacher,
While Mother Nature is the soul doctor   35
Birthing spoken healers like myself
Delivering Flintstone vitamin strength of knowledge
To my people
So you know better in dealing smarter about
Who you play with or who you lay with.   40
The acolytes with swindler sell-out tendencies
Offer to buy your self-worth
With a price high enough to kill
To leave bankrupt your morality
In your memory banks that used to secure them.   45
The doors of opportunity for me—
They've always had loose hinges
Bringing determination with track star kicks.
So when they close too soon with my .44 pen waving,
I'd kick them in.   50
I didn't enter Spoken Word for "Slams" to win;
This is just the vehicle I discovered to repent my sins.
I've been accused as a blasphemer with my words.
But with no remorse to blast FEMA for B.S. 'n after Katrina.
Maybe all this is just the design of a prophet's torment 51
With the pain of the world on his shoulders
And one of the strifes my man Black Ice
Didn't mention of a lone soldier.

Immigrant Mother (Lovely to Me)

Taiyo Na

Honored by Governor David A. Paterson and the State of New York for his "legacy of leadership to the Asian American community and the Empire State" in May 2010, Taiyo Na is a singer, songwriter, MC, and producer. His debut album *Love is Growth* (Issilah Productions, 2008) features the song "Lovely To Me (Immigrant Mother)," whose music video was heralded by MTV's Iggy as "the realest thing seen in a while." In June 2010, he released an album *Home: Word* with hip hop duo Magnetic North. The title track off that album was released as a single in Japan in March 2011 and hit #2 on Japan's iTunes Hip-Hop charts.

IMMIGRANT MOTHER (LOVELY TO ME)

Verse One: 1
I got an immigrant mother, ain't no one like her
She struggle everyday so she's something like a fighter
See her on the streets carrying loads of groceries
See her on the streets carrying loads of broken dreams 5
It takes a whole lot to leave your homeland
And raise a few children with your own hands
She couldn't read well, but she could feed well
With a few hustles on the DL
Overworked, underpaid, so much my mother gave 10
It's through her, how I learned love is brave
Working to the evening, then cooking & cleaning,
But they straight ignored her at school meetings
Straight dissin' her, cuz she speak with an accent
But under the accent is a heart full of passion 15
You went through the fire to be a mother to me
Thank you for being so lovely to me

Chorus:
You've been lovely to me
A dear mother to me 20
Like no other to me
Lovely to me, lovely to me
I got an immigrant mother (Lovely to me)

Reprinted by permission of Taiyo Na.

Immigrant mother (A dear mother to me)
Immigrant mother (Like no other to me)   25
Lovely to me, lovely to me

Verse Two:
She on the subway trying to learn English
Wishing for her son to be distinguished
There lots of things she don't know how to say   30
So immigrant mothers they know how to pray
But they ain't perfect, and that's what hurt me
They need some damn help when they all by themselves
Cuz they'll break down, see my mom was single
Raised us alone since we was real little   35
She worked her ass off, Man, I saw it every night
Passed out on the couch, I tucked her in tight
But working all the time will make a woman crazy
And compromise her time with her dear babies
She got lonely, so she fell for stupid men   40
Like alcoholics, and I felt ruined then,
So I stepped up, said, Ma, you acting ugly
You deserve better cuz you so lovely

Chorus:
You've been lovely to me   45
A dear mother to me
Like no other to me
Lovely to me, lovely to me
I got an immigrant mother (Lovely to me)
Immigrant mother (A dear mother to me)   50
Immigrant mother (Like no other to me)
Lovely to me, lovely to me

Verse Three:
She smell like cumin, smell like garlic
Smell like adobo, smell like an artist   55
INS tests don't know nothing about this
About babies on your breasts and giving 'em happiness
About holding your own despite a broken home
She had no degree but she gave me poetry
Living through the struggle and giving cuz she loves you   60
I got an immigrant mother, I sing this cuz I'm humbled

Bridge:
She wakes up in the morning when the birds are loudest
Something about her feels like Mary
She needs strength just like anybody else   65
So when I see her in the kitchen I offer her my help

Chorus:
You've been lovely to me
A dear mother to me
Like no other to me   70
Lovely to me, lovely to me
I got an immigrant mother (Lovely to me)
Immigrant mother (A dear mother to me)
Immigrant mother (Like no other to me)
Lovely to me, lovely to me   75

The Place Where We Dwell

Gang Starr

Gang Starr is a hip hop duo that consisted of Guru and DJ Premier. They were an influential East Coast throughout the 1990s, and during this time, they were recognized as having pioneered the hardcore New York City rap sound. In 2006, Gang Starr split up, and Guru died of a heart attack in 2010. Readers probably have noticed that the lyrics in the song "The Place Where We Dwell," are also the title of this textbook. Gang Starr mentions many neighborhoods in New York City, as a way to announce their affiliation and connection to place and home.

THE PLACE WHERE WE DWELL

New York, New York is where we live and we're thorough   1
Never taking shorts cuz Brooklyn's the borough
Peace to Uptown, to queens and the Bronx
Long Island and Jersey get as fly as they want
Where we rest is no joke   5
So let me break it down to sections for you slowpokes
Fort Green, bedstuy, Flatbush, Brownsville
Crown Heights and East New York will be down till
Medina takes respect for the style's we bring
Cuz in Brooklyn, we be into our own thing   10
Alantic terminals, redhook bushwick
Come to Brooklyn frontin, and you'll get mushed quick
We ain't just know for flipping and turning out parties
But also for the take no bullshit hotties
On the subject of blackness, well let me share this   15
Brooklyn is the home for cultural awareness
So in all fairness, you can never compare this
Some good, some bad. Little hope for the weak
Dangerous streets and Coney Island Beach
All this included when you go for a tour   20
Some can get scandolous and outright raw
When you step, step correct and watch where you move
We pay dues so we ain't trying to lose
Here in Brooklyn
The home of the black and the beautiful   25
For a ruffrap sound, ain't a place more suitable
Other cities claim this, and others claim that

But let me give some props to the place where we be at
B-R-double O- K-L-Y-N
I came in for a visit and ever since then   30
I've been incorporated with select personel
Right here in Brooklyn, the place where we dwell

Way down in Brooklyn (3x)
Those who live in Brooklyn know just what I'm talking about

Peace to Boston, Philly, Conneticut, DC   35
All the east coast cities are fly to me
Peace to everybody down south and out west
But for me, Brooklyn, New York is the best
Don't be afraid to venture over the bridge
Although you may run in to some wild ass kids   40
Take the j train, the d or the a if you dare
And the 2,3,4,5 also comes here
There's so much to see cuz Brooklyn's historic
Fools act jealous but you have to ignore it
So I just lounge wit the fat clientele   45
Out here in Brooklyn, the place where we dwell

Way down in brooklyn
You know the place...

Central Park, Carousel

Meena Alexander

Meena Alexander was born in Allahabad, India. At eighteen she went to study in England. She is Distinguished Professor of English at the City University of New York and teaches in the MFA program at Hunter College and the Ph.D. Program at the Graduate Center. "Central Park, Carousel" is a post-9/11 poem that is inspired by the Hindu idea of *dukham,* which means sorrow experienced in the cycle of births and rebirths.

CENTRAL PARK, CAROUSEL

June already, it's your birth month,   1
nine months since the towers fell.
I set olive twigs in my hair
torn from a tree in Central Park,
I ride a painted horse, its mane a sullen wonder.   5
You are behind me on a lilting mare.
You whisper–What of happiness?
Dukham, Federico. Smoke fills my eyes.
Young, I was raised to a sorrow song
short fires and stubble on a monsoon coast.   10
The leaves in your cap are very green.
The eyes of your mare never close.
Somewhere you wrote: *Despedida.*
If I die leave the balcony open!

Life in the New World

George Guida

George Guida is the author of four books, including *The Pope Stories and Other Tales of Troubled Times* (forthcoming). His fiction, poetry, and criticism appear in many journals and anthologies. He is also a playwright and a popular and enthusiastic performer of his work. Guida is an Associate Professor of English at New York City College of Technology, the Poetry Editor of *2 Bridges Review*, and the President of the American Italian Historical Association.

LIFE IN THE NEW WORLD

I.

We are westbound, 1
a background of Brooklyn and Queens,
cell phones to ears for gleaning.
Rogue planes, jet fuel,
an absence of planted bombs 5
are rudely interrupting Manhattan.
The World Trade Center, like Godzilla,
absorbs suicide shrapnel,
as office managers' shrieks and roars
charge the autumn morning air. 10
Poets wait eternities for tragedies like this.
Aboard a bedroom community railroad,
I am only remotely connected.
An obese woman waving cell phone
invading my seat, claims 15
they want everyone out of the city.
I wonder where they all will go,
if they can risk suburban shelter.
At a time like this,
what becomes of Brooklyn 20
between those who see
Manhattan as symbol of America,
all triumphs and crimes laid bare to the world,
and those who see Manhattan as,
of all things, tourist Mecca? 25

A dusky, turbaned man across the aisle,
a regular commuter in intermittent dialogue
with a cherry-white office woman
dialing like mad for answers to her question,
"Will I get the day off?"   30
reads the gentle Arabic pen strokes
of a pocket-sized Koran.
At a time like this,
what becomes of him
aboard this middle-class car?   35
Sudden subject of suspicion,
he chats in unaccented American
with the conductor
who suddenly can't remember
the next train out.   40
Arrived in Brooklyn, I hear
the mayor has ordered us away.
Fleeing, watching the skyline die
in the distance, how now
can I wrestle shadows for this world?   45
How can I tolerate safety,
when a high school teammate,
fond, forgotten boy,
has known the sensation of eighty floors
trembling beneath him,   50
intimacy with smooth-skinned death?

II.

The twin towers have fallen,
and with them an empire of the senses,
the sense that this New York, new world,
is eternal, that we will always breath   55
the autumn air of poets' paeans,
that the subway will always take us home.
Everyone loses some beloved,
some past and future,
when a steel and glass dream falls.   60
On the Brooklyn streets, crowds gawk
at gray smoke,
at the spectacle of Manhattan,
as they always have, vigil now.
A miles-long cloud ribbons New York Harbor,   65
limiting vision to loss.
Two arrogant towers in death

suffocate our innocents,
some spared only by the north wind's mercy.
Businessmen klatsched to keep from shaking,   70
speak of death for all immigrants,
payback for crimes we have all committed.

III.
Escaped, beneath a trestle I am lost
in suburban sunlight and siren shadow,
half-witness to death,   75
to imagined wives and mothers
imploded like skyscrapers
that have collapsed our memory of peace,
in the million pieces that are each one lost
to plastic explosive anger,   80
poverty and dire religion.
I am staring at the suburban sun,
clinging to faith.
I pray for the 100th floor jumpers.
I pray for the acrid smoke inhalers,   85
for the sad generations
newly sworn to vengeance.
Safe in my family home, I opine,
the sins of the father,
cross-couch from my own,   90
retired law enforcer, warrior by taste,
watching as we watched ten years before
the smart-strafing of secular sons,
the hidden slaughter of daughters,
their misfortune to dream in Arabic,   95
under a different Sun,
lost to the blood-lusty cry,
"Bomb them back to the Stone Age."

IV.
We walk among rubble now,
as poisonous clouds drift out to sea,   100
where navy vessels steam
through red and black spume,
to rescue us from harm,
though all the harm to do is done,
every rumble in the distance   105
a declaration of war,
an assault on the ignorant peace of means.

Worst of all is absence:
of towers,
bankers,   110
secretaries,
firefighters,
Arab vendors,
cops like my father,
and still here   115
a callous leader chastened,
and we, eastbound, ocean-bound,
finally world-facing,
absent from our former selves.
White soot-covered zombies   120
of the new millennium,
we wash our hands like Pilate,
comprehend televised images
like special effects,
jumbo jets, American and United,   125
annihilating our national dream.

V.
We live now in a land
of detectors, cavity searches,
and snarling dogs.
We are the old world reborn.   130
The new has drifted beyond putrid clouds,
beyond serene blue skies.
We speak of death
as one with attack amnesia
might speak of Hawaii.   135
We live now with
King Kong, the primate,
beating his chest atop
the Empire State still upright
in the distance, a fantasy   140
of another American time.
We cling to that tower now,
through television screens,
as both heroes and beasts in agony,
conscious of our place, our dilemma,   145
and most of all our sense
that once we had a home.

The Dead of September 11

Toni Morrison

Toni Morrison was born Chloe Anthony Wofford on February 18, 1931 in Lorain, Ohio. She graduated from Howard University in 1953 with a B.A. in English. She then attended Cornell University and received a master's degree in 1955. She worked as an editor and taught writing before she became a writer. She is the author of *The Bluest Eyes* (1970), *Sula* (1973), *Song of Solomon* (1977), *Tar Baby* (1981), *Beloved* (1986), and *Jazz* (1992). In 1993, she became the first African-American woman to receive the Nobel Prize in Literature.

THE DEAD OF SEPTEMBER 11

Some have God's words; others have songs of comfort   1
for the bereaved. If I can pluck courage here, I would
like to speak directly to the dead—the September dead.
Those children of ancestors born in every continent
on the planet: Asia, Europe, Africa, the Americas...;   5
born of ancestors who wore kilts, obis, saris, gèlès,
wide straw hats, yamulkes, goatskin, wooden shoes
feathers and cloths to cover their hair. But I would not say
a word until I could set aside all I know or believe about
nations, war, leaders, the governed and ungovernable;   10
all I suspect about armor and entrails. First I would freshen
my tongue, abandon sentences crafted to know evil—wanton
or studied; explosive or quietly sinister; whether born of
a sated appetite or hunger; of vengeance or the simple
compulsion to stand up before falling down. I would purge   15
my language of hyperbole; of its eagerness to analyze
the levels of wickedness; ranking them; calculating their
higher or lower status among others of its kind.

Speaking to the broken and the dead is too difficult for
a mouth full of blood. Too holy an act for impure thoughts.   20
Because the dead are free, absolute; they cannot be
seduced by blitz.

To speak to you, the dead of September, I must not claim
false intimacy or summon an overheated heart glazed
just in time for a camera. I must be steady and I must be clear,   25
knowing all the time that I have nothing to say—no words
stronger than the steel that pressed you into itself; no scripture
older or more elegant than the ancient atoms you
have become.

And I have nothing to give either—except this gesture,   30
this thread thrown between your humanity and mine;
I want to hold you in my arms and as your soul got shot
of its box of flesh to understand, as you have done, the wit
of eternity: its gift of unhinged release tearing through
the darkness of its knell.   35

Researching New York

New York Museums:
Brooklyn Museum of Art
Ellis Island Immigration Museum
Guggenheim Museum
International Center for Photography
Lower East Side Tenement Museum
Metropolitan Museum of Art
Museum of Modern Art
Museum of the City of New York
Museum of the Moving Image (Queens)
Museo del Barrio
New York Transit Museum (Brooklyn)
Visual Arts Museum
Whitney Museum of American Art
Queens Historical Society
Staten Island Historical Society
Weeksville Society

For an overview of your topic, we recommend beginning with the following books:
The Encyclopedia of New York, edited by Kenneth T. Jackson (2nd ed.)
The Historical Atlas of New York, Eric Homberger
A Short and Remarkable History of New York City, Jane Mushabac
New York: An Illustrated History, Ric Burns and James Sanders

Recommended Websites
New York Public Library (nypl.org)
The New York Times (nytimes.com)
AM New York (amnewyork.com)
The Village Voice (villagevoice.com)
The New Yorker (newyorker.com)
Gotham Gazette (gothamgazette.com)
City Journal (cityjournal.org)
The Brooklyn Eagle (brooklyneagle.com)
The Brooklyn Rail (brooklynrail.org)
Mr. Beller's Neighborhood (mrbellersneighborhood.com)

New York Historical Societies and Centers:
Brooklyn Historical Society
Bronx Historical Society
Gotham Center for New York City History
New York Historical Society
Queens Historical Society
Schomburg Center for Research in Black Culture
Staten Island Historical Society
Weeksville Heritage Center

Selected Nineteenth-Century Literature about New York:
Horatio Alger, Jr. *Ragged Dick; or Street Life in New York* (1868)
Charles Frederick Briggs, *The Adventures of Harry Franco* (1839)
Abraham Cahan, *Yekl: A Tale of the New York Ghetto* (1896)
Alice Cary, *The Clovernook Children* (1855)
Stephen Crane, *Maggie* (1893)
Marion F. Crawford, *Katherine Lauderdale* (1894), *The Ralstons* (1895)
James Fenimore Cooper, *Home as Found* (1838)
Rebecca Harding Davis, *John Andross* (1874)
Evert and George Duyckinck, *Cyclopedia of American Literature* (1855)
Edgar Fawcett, *A Romance of Old New York* (1897)
Fanny Fern, *Ruth Hall* (1854)
George G. Foster, *New York in Slices, by an Experienced Carver* (1848)

William Dean Howells, *A Hazard of New Fortunes* (1890)

Washington Irving, *Knickerbocker's History of New York* (1809), "The Legend of Sleepy Hollow" (1820)

Henry James, *Washington Square* (1881), *The American Scene* (1907)

George Lippard, *The Empire City; or, New York by Night and Day* (1850)

Herman Melville, *Pierre; or the Ambiguities* (1852); "Bartleby the Scrivener" (1853)

Anna Cora Mowatt, *Fashion, or Life in New York* (1850)

Jacob Riis, *How the Other Half Lives* (1890)

Walt Whitman, *Leaves of Grass* (1855)

John Greenleaf Whittier, *Songs of Labor* (1850)

Selected Twentiety-Century Literature about New York:

Paul Auster, *The New York Trilogy* (1987)

Kevin Baker, *Dreamland* (1999)

James Baldwin, *Go Tell It on the Mountain* (1953)

Truman Capote, *Breakfast at Tiffany's* (1958)

Louis Chu, *Eat a Bowl of Tea* (1961)

Hart Crane, *The Bridge* (1930)

Countee Cullen, *One Way to Heaven* (1932)

Don DeLillo, *Underworld* (1997)

E.L. Doctorow, *Ragtime* (1975), *World's Fair* (1985), *The Waterworks* (1994)

John Dos Passos, *Manhattan Transfer* (1925)

Theodore Dreiser, *The Color of a Great City* (1923)

Brett Easton Ellis, *American Psycho* (1991)

Jessie Redmon Fauset, *Plum Bun: A Novel Without a Moral* (1928)

F. Scott Fitzgerald, *The Great Gatsby* (1925), *The Crack Up* (1931)

Allen Ginsberg, *Collected Poems 1947–1980* (1984)

Paul Goodman, *The Empire City: A Novel of New York City* (1942, 1946, 1959, 1977)

Michael Gold, *Jews Without Money* (1930)

Joseph Heller, *Good as Gold* (1979)

Oscar Hijuelos, *The Mambo Kings Play Songs of Love* (1989)

Chester Himes, *The Real Cool Killers* (1959)

Langston Hughes, *The Ways of White Folks* (1933)

Alfred Kazin, *A Walker in the City* (1951)

Jack Kerouac, *The Town and the City* (1950), *The Subterraneans* (1958)

Nella Larsen, *Passing* (1929)

Alain Locke, *The Negro in America* (1933)

Anita Loos, *Gentlemen Prefer Blonds* (1925)

Norman Mailer, *An American Dream* (1965)

Paule Marshall, *Brown Girl, Brownstones* (1951)

Jay McInerney, *Bright Lights, Big City* (1984)

Claude McKay, *Home to Harlem* (1928)

Arthur Miller, *Death of a Salesman* (1949), *A View from the Bridge* (1955)

Edna St. Vincent Millay, *Selected Poems/The Centenary Edition* (1992)

Steven Millhauser, *Martin Dressler: The Tale of an American Dreamer* (1996)

Marianne Moore, *Complete Poems* (1994)

Cynthia Ozick, *The Puttermesser Papers* (1997)

Grace Paley, *The Little Disturbances of Man* (1960)

Ann Petry, *The Street* (1947)

Earnest Poole, *The Harbor* (1915)

Dawn Powell, *The Golden Spur* (1962)

Mario Puzo, *The Godfather* (1969)

Henry Roth, *Call It Sleep* (1934)

Isaac Bashevis Singer, *Enemies, a Love Story* (1972)

Betty Smith, *A Tree Grows in Brooklyn* (1943)

Meredith Tax, *Union Square* (1988)

Gore Vidal, *Burr* (1973)

Edith Wharton, *The House of Mirth* (1905), *The Age of Innocence* (1920), *Old New York* (1924)

Thomas Wolfe, *You Can't Go Home Again* (1940)

Richard Wright, *Savage Holiday* (1954)

Anzia Yezierska, *Hungry Hearts* (1920)

Selected Twenty-First Century Literature about New York:

Candace Bushnell, *Sex and the City* (1997), *Trading Up* (2003), *Lipstick Jungle* (2005), *One Fifth Avenue* (2008)

Michael Chabon, *The Amazing Adventures of Cavalier and Clay* (2000)

Teju Cole, *Open City* (2012)

Don DeLillo, *Cosmopolis* (2003), *Falling Man* (2007)

Jonathan Safran Foer, *Extremely Loud and Incredibly Close* (2005)

Elizabeth Gaffney, *Metropolis* (2005)

Nelson George, *City Kid: A Memoir* (2009)

Pete Hamill, *Forever* (2003)

Peter Hedges, *The Heights* (2010)

Jonathan Lethem, *Motherless Brooklyn* (2000), *Fortress of Solitude* (2004), *Chronic City* (2010)

Collum McCann, *Let the Great World Spin* (2009)

Frank McCourt, *Angela's Ashes: A Memoir* (1999), *Tis: A Memoir* (2000), *Teacher Man: A Memoir* (2005)

Jay McInerney, *The Good Life* (2006)

Joseph O'Neill, *Netherland* (2008)

Salman Rushdie, *Fury* (2001)

Sapphire, *Push* (1996), *The Kid* (2011)

Elizabeth Schmidt, ed., *Poems of New York* (2002)

Colson Whitehead, *The Intuitionist* (1999), *Sag Harbor* (2009), *Zone One* (2011)

Non-Fiction Books about New York:

Sven Beckert, *The Monied Metropolis: New York City and the Consolidation of the Bourgeoisie, 1850–1900* (2001)

Thomas Bender, *The Unfinished City: New York and the Metropolitan Idea* (2002)

Marshall Berman, *All That Is Solid Melts Into Air: The Experience of Modernity* (1988), *On the Town: One Hundred Years of Spectacle in Times Square* (2006)

Elizabeth Blackmar, *Manhattan for Rent, 1785–1850* (1991)

M. Christine Boyer, *Manhattan Manners: Architecture and Style 1850–1900* (1985)

Ric Burns, James Sanders, and Lisa Ades, eds., *New York: An Illustrated History* (2003)

Edwin G. Burrows and Mike Wallace, *Gotham: A History of New York City to 1898* (1999)

Anne-Marie Cantwell and Diana Dizerega Wall, *Unearthing Gotham: The Archeology of New York City* (2001)

Robert A. Caro, *The Power Broker: Robert Moses and the Fall of New York* (1975)

Benjamin de Casseres, *Mirrors of New York* (1925)

Jeff Chang and DJ Kool Herc, *Can't Stop Won't Stop, A History of the Hip Hop Generation* (2005)

Patricia Cline Cohen, *The Murder of Helen Jewett: The Life an Death of a Prostitute in Nineteenth-Century New York* (1999)

Paul E. Cohen and Robert T. Augustyn, *Manhattan in Maps: 1527–1995* (1997)

Gloria Deák, *Picturing New York: The City from its Beginning to the Present* (2000)

Robert Ernst, *Immigrant Life in New York City: 1825–1863* (1949)

Nancy Foner, *From Ellis Island to JFK: New York's Two Great Waves of Immigration* (2000), *In a New Land: A Comparative View of Immigration* (2005)

Roger Gastman and Caleb Neelon, *The History of American Graffiti* (2010)

Paul Goldberger, *Up from Zero: Politics, Architecture, and the Rebuilding of New York (2005)*

Joyce D. Goodfriend, *Before the Melting Pot: Society and Culture in Colonial New York City, 1664–1730* (1992)

Richard Haw, *Brooklyn Bridge: A Cultural History* (2005)

Elizabeth Hawes, *New York New York: How the Apartment House Transformed Life in the City, 1869–1930* (1993)

Eric Homberger, *Scenes from the Life of a City: Corruption and Conscience in Old New York* (1994), *The Historical Atlas of New York City* (2005)

Clifton Hood, *722 miles: The Building of the Subways and How They Transformed New York* (1993)

Kenneth T. Jackson and David S. Dunbar, eds., *Empire City: New York Throughout the Centuries* (2002)

Johan Kugelberg, *Born in the Bronx: A Visual Record of the Early Days of Hip Hop* (2007)

Roger Kahn, *The Era: 1947–1957, When the Yankees, the Giants, and the Dodgers Ruled the World* (2002)

Jane Jacobs, *The Death and Life of Great American Cities* (1961)

Daniel Kane, *All Poets Welcome: The Lower East Side Poetry Scene* (2003)

Carole Klein, *Grammercy Park* (1999)

Gerard T. Koeppel, *Water for Gotham* (2000)

Rem Koolhaas, *Delirious New York: A Retroactive Manifesto* (1978)

Max Kozloff, *New York: Capital of Photography* (2002)

Charles Lockwood, *Manhattan Moves Uptown: An Illustrated History* (1976)

Phillip Lopate, *Waterfront: A Journey Around Manhattan* (2004), ed. *Writing New York: A Literary Anthology* (1998)

Mario Maffi, *Gateway to the Promised Land: Ethnic Cultures on New York's Lower East* Side (1994)

David G. McCullough, *The Great Bridge: The Epic Story of the Building of the Brooklyn Bridge* (2001)

Jan S. Ramirez, ed., *Painting the Town: Cityscapes of New York* (2000)

Tricia Rose, *Hip Hop Wars: What We Talk About When We Talk About Hip Hop—and Why It Matters* (2008)

Roy Rosenzweig and Elizabeth Blackmar, *The Park and The People: A History of Central Park* (1998)

Roger Sanjek, *The Future of Us All: Race and Neighborhood Politics in New York City* (2000)

Luc Sante, *Low Life, Lures and Snares of Old New York* (1991)

Kurt C. Schlichting, *Grand Central Terminal* (2001)

David M. Scobey, *Empire City: The Making and Meaning of the New York City Landscape* (2002)

Russell Shorto, *The Island at the Center of the World: The Untold Story of Dutch Manhattan and the Founding of New York* (2004)

Ellen M. Snyder-Grenier, *Brooklyn! An Illustrated History* (1996)

Leon Stein, *The Triangle Fire* (2002)

Robert Sullivan, *Rats: Observations on the History and Habitat of the City's Most Unwanted Inhabitants* (2004)

Alan Trachtenberg, *Brooklyn Bridge: Fact and Symbol* (1979)

David Von Drehle, *Triangle, The Fire that Changed America* (2004)

Selected Films about New York:

Literature and History:

New York: A Documentary (1999, 2003)

The House of Mirth (2000)

Washington Square (1997)

Age of Innocence (1993)

Malcolm X (1992)

Bonfire of the Vanities (1990)

Last Exit to Brooklyn (1989)

Ragtime (1981)

The Great Gatsby (1974, 2012)

Breakfast at Tiffany's (1961)

The Heiress (1949)

City Life:

Extremely Loud and Incredibly Close (2011)

The Boys of 2nd Street (2003)

Dark Days (2000)

Subway Stories (1997)

Blue on the Face (1995)

Smoke (1995)

Crooklyn (1994)

A Bronx Tale (1993)

Sidewalk Stories (1991)

Straight out of Brooklyn (1991)

Do the Right Thing (1989)

Wall Street (1987)

After Hours (1985)

Stranger than Paradise (1984)

Manhattan (1979)

Saturday Night Fever (1977)

Taxi Driver (1976)

Midnight Cowboy (1969)

The Producers (1968)

The Apartment (1960)

Shadows (1959)

Marty (1955)

Rear Window (1954)

On the Waterfront (1954)

On the Town (1949)

Naked City (194S)

A Tree Grows in Brooklyn (1945)

The Crowd (1928)

Speedy (1928)

Immigrant/ Ethnic Life:

The Visitor (2007)

32nd Street (2007)

The Namesake (2006)

Golden Venture (2006)

Man Push Cart (2006)

Washington Heights (2002)

In America (2004)

Raising Victor Vargas (2003)

Requiem for a Dream (2000)

La Ciudad (The City) (1999)

Household Saints (1993)

The Brothers McMullen (1995)

The Mambo Kings (1992)

Far and Away (1992)

Eat a Bowl of Tea (1989)

Moscow on the Hudson (1984)

The Chosen (1982)

Hester Street (1975)

Popi (1969)

West Side Story (1961)

My Girl Tisa (1948)

Music in My Heart (1940)

The Immigrant (1917)

Crime and Violence:

Gangs of New York (2002)

New Jack City (1991)

Once Upon a Time in America (1984)

Fort Apache, The Bronx (1981)

Taxi Driver (1976)

Dog Day Afternoon (1975)

Marathon Man (1976)

The Godfather 11(1974)

The Taking of Pelham One Two Three (1974, 1998)

Mean Streets (1973)

The French Connection (1971)

The Cross and the Switchblade (1970)

West Side Story (1961)

Sweet Smell of Success (1957)
Angels with Dirty Faces (1928)

Urban Art:
The Hip Hop Project (2006)
Style Wars (2004)
Tupac: Resurrection (2003)
Basquiat (1996)
Wild Style (1983)

Urban Education:
Precious (2009)
Freedom Writers (2007)
Blackboard Jungle (1955)

The City and Imagination:
Watchmen (2008)
Madagascar (2005)
Spider Man 2 (2004)
Blade Runner (1994)
Ghostbusters (1984)
The Muppets Take Manhattan (1984)
Superman (1978)
King Kong (1933)
Metropolis (1927)

INDEX

CPSIA information can be obtained
at www.ICGtesting.com
Printed in the USA
BVOW11s0109200717
489647BV00008B/61/P